REINCARNATION:

To kill an error is as good a service as, and sometimes better than, the establishing of a new truth or fact.

—Charles Darwin

Only that person is wise who finds everything in life but also finds nothing in death but death. To the intelligent person, life is its own end; for that very reason, it is a preparation for nothing.

—Ludwig Feuerbach

From time to time strange sects arise that endeavor to strike out extraordinary paths to eternal happiness. Religious insanity is very common in the United States.

—Alexis de Tocqueville

Do not feel envious of the happiness of those who live in a fool's paradise, for only a fool will think that it is happiness.

—Bertrand Russell

REINCARNATION:

A Critical Examination

PAUL EDWARDS

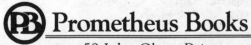 Prometheus Books

59 John Glenn Drive
Amherst, NewYork 14228-2197

Published 1996 by Prometheus Books

00 99 98 97 96   5 4 3 2 1

Library of Congress Cataloging-in-Publication Data

Edwards, Paul, 1923–
    Reincarnation : a critical examination / Paul Edwards.
        p.   cm.
    Includes bibliographical references.
    ISBN 1–57392–005–3 (hc : alk. paper)
    1. Reincarnation. I. Title.
BL515.E38   1996
133.9'01'3—dc20   95–47517
                                                    CIP

Printed in the United States of America on acid-free paper

To Dr. Morton Herskowitz

Contents

Introduction

It is well-known that the main philosophical tenets of Christianity and Judaism—belief in God, life after death, and miracles—have been subjected to a devastating critical examination by a number of the greatest Western philosophers. Hume, Diderot, Kant, Mill, and Bertrand Russell are just some of the names that occur to one at once in this connection. No Western philosopher has offered a similarly detailed critique of reincarnation and the related doctrine of Karma probably because very few people in the West had taken these theories seriously. Unfortunately this is no longer true. The belief in reincarnation and Karma has been steadily gaining support in recent decades. This is no doubt due to the decline of Christianity, but it is also, very regrettably, one aspect of the tide of irrationalism that has been flooding the Western World, especially the United States. There is an urgent need for a comprehensive and systematic evaluation of reincarnation and Karma and the present volume is designed to fill this gap.

I have attempted to state, fairly and fully, all the main arguments offered in support of reincarnation and Karma. I have tried to show that this evidence is worthless. It has been claimed that such facts as child prodigies, déjà vu experiences, hypnotic regressions, and the reincarnation memories of a number of children, mainly in India and in other countries where belief in reincarnation is widespread, can only be explained by reincarnation. None of these claims stands up under critical examination.

I also try to show that there are grave conceptual problems connected with these doctrines. I try to show that the law of Karma is no law at all, offering only *post hoc* explanations. Reincarnationism is not an empty theory in the same way, but many facts are clearly inconsistent with it. These facts include, but are not limited to, population increases, the fact that life in the universe is relatively recent, and various fea-

7

tures of evolutionary history. There are other more basic reasons for rejecting reincarnation. One of these concerns personal identity. Neither of the two criteria for personal identity—bodily continuity and memory—are satisfied in alleged cases of reincarnation. There is also the altogether fatal problem of specifying a credible way in
which a person can come to inhabit another body after its original body has died.
Reincarnationists are committed to the absurd notion of an astral or "spiritual" body
and the even more absurd view that such a body invades the prospective mother's
womb at conception or at some stage during gestation. Finally, we have enormous evidence that the mind or consciousness cannot exist without the brain. Reincarnationists and other friends of the occult get extremely irritated and defensive when the
brain-mind dependence facts are mentioned, but their irritation will not make these
disturbing facts go away.

I refer to the problems of finding a way in which the mind of a human being
could make its transition from one body to another as the "*modus operandi* problem."
This problem also arises in connection with the belief in a God who is supposed to
interfere in the world. I have added to the main body of the book an "Irreverent Postscript" on the difficulties that believers face in this connection. This postscript is "irreverent" but entirely serious. I don't think that believers have an answer.

The description just offered does not cover the entire scope of the book. I have
also dealt in considerable detail with the claims of leading figures of the new immortality movement which arose in the United States in the mid-1970s. The writers
targeted in this connection are Elisabeth Kübler-Ross; Raymond Moody, the author
of the bestselling *Life After Life*; Karlis Osis and Erlandur Haraldsson, who special-
ize in deathbed visions; and Stanislav Grof and Joan Halifax, who have argued that
certain experiences during LSD sessions support reincarnation as well as other su-
pernaturalistic theories.

I have not discussed one phenomenon on which some reincarnationists base
their views. This is Xenoglossy, the alleged capacity of some individuals to understand and speak a language they did not learn in their present life. This topic has been
treated in two splendid articles by Professor Sarah G. Thomason, a professional lin-
guist, and in Ian Wilson's *Mind Out of Time*. I could not add anything of significance
to their discussions and I refer the interested reader to their publications*

The writer most frequently criticized in this book is Professor Ian Stevenson of
the University of Virginia. I should like to make it clear that there is nothing the least
bit personal in these comments. I have never met Professor Stevenson. I have occasionally corresponded with him and he has always courteously responded to requests
for reprints of his publications. He has written more fully and more intelligibly in de-

---

*S. G. Thomason, "Do You Remember Your Previous Life's Language in Your Present Incarnation?"
American Speech (1984), and "Past Tongues Remembered?" *Skeptical Inquirer* (Summer 1987). Wilson's
book was published in London and New York in 1982. The discussions of Xenoglossy occur in Chapters
5 and 6. There is a reply to Thomason by R. Almeder in *Skeptical Inquirer* (Spring 1988). The same issue
contains a rejoinder by Thomason.

fense of reincarnation than anybody else and this is the only reason why he features so prominently in my discussions.

In 1986–1987, I published a four-part series of articles, "The Case Against Reincarnation," in *Free Inquiry,* and something should be said about the relation between that series and the present book. Space limitations prevented me from discussing several significant aspects of the subject in the articles and they are now covered in considerable detail. The discussion of the other topics that were covered in the *Free Inquiry* series has been greatly expanded. The articles generated a great deal of correspondence, a selection of which was published in the Fall 1987 issue of *Free Inquiry.* Most of the correspondents expressed their relief and pleasure that the case against reincarnation had at last been presented to a wide public. A letter I particularly cherish referred to my "irrepressible Voltairean sense of humor." The pronouncements of many religious apologists lend themselves to such treatment, but reincarnationists are perhaps better at offering wild absurdities than the apologists for Christianity and Judaism. I don't think I have missed too many Voltairean opportunities.

I am indebted to my good friend Professor Michael Wreen, who read the whole manuscript and made innumerable helpful suggestions. I also wish to thank Tim Madigan and Champe Ransom for reading several chapters and offering valuable advice. Two good friends and former students, Pattie Eaton and Chris Padgett, helped me with the research for the original *Free Inquiry* articles. There was no way of expressing my gratitude at the time and I am happy to do so now. I am greatly obliged to Professor Bruce Reichenbach for sending me his publications on Karma and the work of other writers which I could not have easily obtained. I also want to thank my friend John Belloff, the editor of the *Journal of the Society for Psychical Research,* for repeatedly supplying me with bibliographical material. Joe Nickell kindly helped me to track down material about Sathya Sai Baba, a holy miracle worker who has a huge following in India and who has also impressed some Western writers. Finally, I wish to thank Susan Tiller, who has been typing all my manuscripts for close to twenty years. She is not only a superb typist, but she has also been a wonderfully supportive friend.

1

Reincarnation, Karma, and Competing Doctrines of Survival

※

Reincarnation and Karma

The beliefs in reincarnation or rebirth and in the Law of Karma are generally held together, but they are logically distinct theories. There are numerous arguments that, if valid, would prove reincarnation without proving Karma, and conversely there are objections to the doctrine of Karma that do not automatically refute reincarnation. The main purpose of this book is to examine the arguments that support both theories, showing their fatal flaws, and to offer a number of reasons for rejecting both of them.

Reincarnation may be defined as the belief that human beings do not, as most of us assume, live only once, but on the contrary live many, perhaps an infinite number of lives, acquiring a new body for each incarnation. An important difference between reincarnation and Western beliefs in survival is the view that human beings, or rather the souls that inhabit their bodies, do not have a beginning. Incarnations stretch infinitely into the past. In the Hindu Bhagavad Gita, which dates back to about 500 B.C.E., and thus precedes the rise of Buddhism, Krishna, the god of love, assures his as-yet-unenlightened companion Arjuna that grief and sorrow are quite inappropriate emotions in relation to the death of somebody we loved. The reason is that a human being will live forever and that "the eternal in man cannot die." A person's birth is not the beginning of his existence, nor is his death the end:

> We have all been for all time: I, and thou, and those kings of men. And we all shall
> be for all time, we all for ever and ever.[1]

---

1. Bhagavad Gita, Chapter II, pp. 12–13.

11

The last sentence of this passage must not be misunderstood as meaning that the series of incarnations will also stretch into the future without limit. Eventually those who have lived sufficiently good lives will attain a state of enlightenment and reach Nirvana, which is not, as is frequently supposed, the absence of all consciousness, but a kind of Absolute or Cosmic Consciousness. Recent Western converts to reincarnation who have been brought up in a Judeo-Christian background have great difficulty with the notion of an infinite past, and in most cases they simply ignore this question. They also do not seem to concern themselves with the question of the "ultimate" fate of the soul. Their main concern seems to be that death, i.e., the death after the present life, should not be the end, and a few additional lives would probably be quite sufficient to appease their longings.

Belief in reincarnation comes in many forms. Reincarnationists in the West and also the more sophisticated Eastern believers teach that human beings always inhabit human bodies; all their previous incarnations were in human bodies and the same is true of their later lives. However, it has also been a widely held belief that the body into which a person migrates is not necessarily another human body, it can be that of an animal, a plant, or even an inanimate object. According to a well-known story, Pythagoras stopped someone from beating a dog, because he had recognized the voice of a friend in the yelping of the dog. The late Austrian conductor Herbert von Karajan did not claim to have been an animal in a previous life, but he was sure that he would return as an eagle. In the Brihadaranyaka Upanishad it is taught that some wicked human beings are reborn as insects—wasps, gnats, and mosquitoes. The Harvard anthropologist Oscar Lewis, who studied the behavior and beliefs of peasants in an Indian village, was told that people guilty of serious crimes may in a future life sink so low as to become jars.[2] Presumably it is believed that such jars have an inner life; they cannot communicate with anybody but they realize their fate as a dreadful deprivation. According to *The Tomorrow of Death,* a book published in Boston in 1888, "the soul of a musically inclined child" may not have come from a human being at all but from "the nightingale, the sweet singer of our woods." As for children with a talent for architecture, it only stands to reason that they should have inherited "the soul of a beaver, the architect of the woods and waters."[3] The author of this charming work does not express any opinion about how some New York City landlords acquired their blackmailing proclivities. My own opinion is that they once were sharks. It is widely believed that the poet Edith Sitwell was a flamingo in an earlier life and there cannot be a serious doubt that Winston Churchill had once been a bulldog. Bull terriers, the lovable little dogs whose noses look as though they had been bashed in, were probably prize fighters in a previous life. As for Marlene Dietrich, the general consensus now is that she once was an emu. There seems to be no other way of ex-

---

2. *Village Life in Northern India* (New York: n.p., 1968), p. 25.
3. *The Tomorrow of Death* (1888), p. 247.

plaining her treatment of her daughter, Maria Riva.[4] J. Edgar Hoover was almost certainly a praying mantis[5] and the same is probably true of Richard Nixon and his criminal associates who brought us Watergate. I will mostly confine myself to the less colorful version of reincarnationism, which maintains that human beings can incarnate only in human bodies. I will do this both because it is the view of most Western believers and also because I have to admit, rather reluctantly, that it is slightly less vulnerable to criticism.

It is not easy to find a clear and unambiguous statement of the Law of Karma. However, insofar as it concerns the immediate human scene, the basic idea is quite straightforward. The doctrine maintains that the world is just, and justice is equated with retribution. Everything good that happens to a human being is a reward for some previous good deed, and everything bad that happens is punishment for an evil deed. As we shall see later, far larger claims are also made, but for the time being it will be convenient to ignore them. It should also be mentioned that, although many supporters of Karma, especially Hindus, believe in gods or in a supreme God, many others do not. In the West, reincarnation and Karma are frequently offered as an alternative philosophy to those of theism and deism.

Believers in Karma have a very simple-minded conception of moral problems. It is tacitly assumed that for every moral question there is a clear-cut, objectively valid answer. A person is punished for his wrong acts and rewarded for those which are right, and there can be no question about the wrongness or rightness of the acts. There are two objections to such a view. In the first place, many philosophers deny that moral judgments can ever be objectively valid; but, perhaps equally important, even if the objectivity is not questioned, very often the issues are so complex that intelligent and decent people will disagree about the correct answer. I do not propose to press these objections and to assume, for the sake of argument, that moral judgments are in some significant sense objective and that there are definite answers to all or most moral issues.

Believers in Karma are fond of quoting St. Paul's statement in his letter to the Galatian churches that "whatever a man sows, that he shall also reap," and they regard this statement as a law as descriptive of the world as the laws of the natural sciences. Thus the late Dr. Raynor Johnson, a Christian reincarnationist who was for many years Master of Queens College of the University of Melbourne, asserted that "whether in the field of action or thought, some time and somewhere a man will reap the fruits of whatever he has sown," adding that we have here a "reasonable law of justice which runs through the world on all levels" and applies "equally to good and evil things."[6] Professor Joseph Prabhu, an Indian Buddhist currently teaching in the

---

4. See Maria Riva, *Marlene Dietrich* (New York, 1993). An emu is a flightless Australian bird resembling an ostrich. A female emu willingly abandons her offspring at the slightest sign of danger.

5. An insect that captures its prey by deception. The female is known to devour her mate.

6. *The Imprisoned Splendor* (1954), p. 337.

United States, explains that the "reaping" may but need not occur in the present life. If the reaping does not come in the present life, it will surely happen "in some later one." Not infrequently disasters occur in a person's life that cannot reasonably be regarded as the appropriate punishment for anything he has done. This is particularly obvious in the case of "children and infants stricken with illnesses or handicaps." It must not for a moment be thought that these children and infants are innocent of wrongdoing. Quite the opposite is true: their illnesses and handicaps are the fully deserved punishment of "some crime committed in a previous life."[7] The same line of reasoning is found in the writings of Christmas Humphreys, a distinguished English prosecutor who founded the British Buddhist Society in 1924 and who until his recent death was one of the-leading figures in Anglo-Saxon Buddhism. Humphreys illustrates the Karmic teaching by considering the "biblical inquiry" into the responsibility for the blindness of men born blind. To the question "Who did sin, this man or his parents, that he was born blind?" the believer in Karma answers that it must have been the blind man himself who had sinned. In a previous life he had behaved so "as to cause . . . the effect of his blindness."[8] This passage is quoted from *Buddhism,* a Penguin Book that was published in 1951 and must have had very wide circulation. In 1983, when he published a new edition of *Karma and Rebirth,* Humphreys had not softened his attitude in any way. "He who suffers," he writes, "suffers from his deliberate use of his own free will." We must not show any sympathy for "cripples, dwarfs, and those born deaf or blind," because their afflictions "are the products of their own past actions."[9] Instead of bewailing these afflictions, we should assist "the newborn brain to appreciate its own responsibility and to produce new causes whose result will be the undoing of the evil whose results are manifest.[10] I frankly find these sentiments unbearably cruel and I wonder if Humphreys really practiced what he preached. It never seems to have occurred to him that he just might be mistaken. As we shall see later in this book, it is quite certain that he was.

Reincarnation and Dualism

It is evident that reincarnationism makes several huge assumptions that have been the target of severe criticisms by Western philosophers in recent decades and, in some instances, for many centuries. To begin with, reincarnation logically presupposes an extreme form of dualism. If we include as dualists all those who agree that mental events and processes cannot be identified either with actual and possible behavior or with any bodily states or processes, then we may distinguish the more moderate variety,

---

7. "The Idea of Reincarnation," in S. T. Davis (Ed.), *Death and Afterlife* (London: Macmillan, 1989), p. 73.

8. *Buddhism* (London: Penguin Books, 1951), pp. 100–101.

9. Christmas Humphreys, *Karma and Rebirth* (London, 1983, originally published in 1943), p. 55.

10. Ibid.

which holds that a person is *both* a mind and a body, from the extreme form, which maintains that a person *is* his mind and that the body is simply one of his possessions. Classic statements of the more extreme form of dualism are found in Plato and Descartes. "Soul is utterly superior to body," Plato wrote and

> what gives each one of us his being is nothing else but his soul; whereas the body is no more than a shadow that keeps us company. So it is well said of the deceased that the corpse is only a ghost.[11]

"I am a substance," according to Descartes

> whose whole essence or nature is to be conscious and whose being requires no place and depends on no material thing. Thus this self, that is to say the soul, by which I am what I am, is entirely distinct from the body, and is even more easily known; and even if the body were not there at all, the soul would be just what it is.[12]

It is clear that reincarnationists are committed to the more extreme form of dualism. A person's body is different in every incarnation, but he is the same since it is the same mind or soul that animates all the different bodies. In the words of the Bhagavad Gita:

> As a man leaves an old garment and puts on one that is new, the Spirit leaves his mortal body and then puts on one that is new.[13]

To refute reincarnationism it is quite sufficient to show that the extreme form of dualism is untenable; and I think that the great majority of contemporary philosophers—reductive materialists, identity-theorists, and moderate dualists (including epiphenomenalists among the last group)—would unhesitatingly agree that the extreme form of dualism *is* quite indefensible.

Not only is reincarnation opposed to all of the most widely held views on the mind-body problem, it also follows from what has been said that it is opposed to one of the major current theories about personal identity. This view holds that however much more than a body a human being may be, personal identity involves bodily continuity. If we refer to this view as "corporealism" it should be emphasized that it is not the same as either reductive materialism or the identity theory. These do indeed presuppose corporealism, but the reverse is not true. What concerns us here is that, unless corporealism can be shown to be false, reincarnation is ruled out from the start.

Finally, although a reincarnationist need not hold the view that the mind can or ever does exist without a bodily foundation or concomitant, he *is* committed to the

---

11. *Laws* 969a–b.
12. *Discourse on Method*, Section 4.
13. III/22, Chapter 2.

assumption that a person's mind does not require the *particular* body or brain with which it is connected in the present life. This follows from the claim that in other lives the mind will be tied to different bodies and brains. I shall try to show in the last chapter that this assumption of the causal independence of the mind from the person's body and brain is almost certainly false.

I should add that a number of contemporary philosophers who are not materialists would even object to what I have called the moderate version of dualism on the ground that although there is indeed such a thing as the body, there is no such "thing" as the mind. The body and the mind, in technical language, do not have the same ontological status. There are mental events and processes—feelings, thoughts, dreams, and sensations—but there is no "mind" over and above them. The word "mind" is a noun just like the word "body" and we automatically assume that both stand for things. Only the "snare of language," wrote Nietzsche in the *Genealogy of Morals,* "blinds us" to the fact that there is no mind. The view that a human being is a body "and" a mind is also objectionable because the relation between physical and mental facts is much closer than this formulation suggests. It would be better to call a person an "animated body." I will return to some of these questions in later chapters. For the time being, so as not to foreclose discussion, I will assume that some form of fairly conventional dualism is acceptable.

The Logical Advantages of Reincarnation
Over Other Forms of Survival

Several writers, including some famous philosophers, have insisted that reincarnation has certain logical advantages over other forms of survival and as a result is less inherently incredible. We shall find that some of these advantages are illusory, but others are quite real.

In the first place, although many Eastern reincarnationists do believe in a "higher region," this is not an essential part of the theory and it is quite consistent for a reincarnationist to rule out any kind of "beyond." This means that reincarnationists can dispense with anything like heaven and hell. Survival is said to take place right here on earth, not in a mysterious realm whose location cannot be specified and which has never been seen or otherwise observed by anybody. Next, reincarnationism seems to be able to dispense with the notion of the disembodied mind as the vehicle of survival. Many liberal Protestants are stuck with this view and, although believers who follow Aquinas take the position that the soul will eventually be united with a resurrected body, they are committed to a disembodied mind at least for the period between death and the availability of the resurrected body. Now, the notion of a disembodied mind seems to many philosophers quite incoherent; but even if it is not incoherent, it appears incompatible with the evidence from neurology concerning the dependence of consciousness on the brain. The other main form of survival believed in the West involves the notion that after we die our bodies will be resurrected. Except for a small number of professional theologians, this view seems nowadays as incredible to educated believers as to nonbelievers. Reincarnationists have not been slow to heap scorn on it. Thus Professor C. J. Ducasse, the leading philosophical supporter of reincarnation in recent decades, protests that nothing in the position of reincarnationists is remotely as paradoxical as the belief in the "resurrection of the flesh," which is or was accepted by many Christians "notwithstanding the dispersion of the dead body's material by cremation or by incorporation of its particles into the living bodies of worms, sharks, or vultures."[14] Ducasse does not address himself to the more sophisticated version of resurrectionism, which teaches that somehow, somewhere replicas of our original bodies will be created to serve as the physical underpinning of our conscious lives. Aside from presenting serious problems concerning personal identity, such a claim strikes most people as utterly fantastic, no less fantastic than the literal resurrection of the flesh. Both forms of resurrectionism also require the assumption of a Resurrector. This amounts to the assumption that there is a God and that God resurrects all or at least many human beings. Reincarnationists are not burdened with these purely *ad hoc* assumptions. Many Christian theologians proceed as if there is no difficulty about resurrection. I must therefore emphasize that we are not informed where and how these resurrections take place; and of course nobody has ever observed them.

Another advantage or apparent advantage of reincarnation may be described as its "symmetry" as opposed to the "asymmetry" of Western beliefs in survival. In a well-known passage Santayana observed that "the fact of having been born is a bad augury for immortality."[15] Santayana was only concerned to point out the antecedent implausibility of Western beliefs in survival. Schopenhauer and Hume made similar remarks with the explicit purpose of showing the logical superiority of reincarnation or, as Hume preferred to call it, "metempsychosis." "Judaism," Schopenhauer wrote, "together with the two religions which sprang from it, teach the creation of man out of nothing." It then becomes a "hard task" to "link on" to beings with a finite past, "an endless existence *a parte post*."[16] Unlike Schopenhauer, Hume did not believe in reincarnation, but he also regarded it as logically superior to the Christian view. "Reasoning from the common course of nature," he observes in a passage that has frequently been quoted by reincarnationists, we must hold that "what is incorruptible must also be ingenerable," and hence that "the soul, if immortal, existed before our birth."[17] A little later he adds that "the metempsychosis is the only system of this kind that philosophers can harken to."[18]

Emphasis on the superiority of reincarnation because of its avoidance of the asym-

---

14. "Life After Death Conceived As Reincarnation," in A. N. Newman, et al., *In Search of God and Immortality* (Boston, 1961), p. 144.

15. *Reason in Religion* (New York, 1962), p. 165.

16. *The World As Will and Idea* (London, 1883), Vol. 3, p. 305.

17. "On the Immortality of the Soul," in P. Edwards (Ed.), *Immortality*, p. 139. Hume's italics.

18. Ibid.

metry of the Western view is usually accompanied in the writings of reincarnationists by scornful comments about the absurdity and incredibility of the Christian doctrine of "special creation," which holds that at conception God infuses a soul into a newly formed embryo. "If we claim that some divine power creates the soul," writes Irving S. Cooper, one of my favorite theosophists, "it is rather difficult to explain why the exercise of that power is dependent upon the sexual passion of man."[19] Similarly, Professor Ducasse speaks of "the shocking supposition," among Christians that when two human beings mate, "be it in wedlock or in wanton debauchery" an infinitely loving God creates "outright from nothing," an immortal human soul and that "arbitrarily with a particular one out of many possible sets of latent capacities and incapacities."[20]

I unreservedly endorse these criticisms of the Christian position. It seems ludicrous that something as important as the creation of a soul that is going to exist forever should be tied to such accidents as the failure of a birth-control appliance. It is safe to say that educated Christians and Jews do not believe in the special creation of the soul any more than atheists and agnostics and that they adopt a completely naturalistic view about the origin of human beings—their psychological no less than their physical attributes.

The Body Snatchers

Like other minority groups, especially those advocating positions that are widely regarded as preposterous, Western reincarnationists frequently present lists of famous men and women who shared their views. The suggestion is of course that the theory cannot be absurd if it has such distinguished backers. Pythagoras, Plato, Empedocles, Plotinus, the Cambridge Platonists, Goethe, Shelley, Schopenhauer, and Victor Hugo are usually included among the philosophers and creative writers who were reincarnationists. These names appear quite properly on the lists although it should be pointed out that while Goethe and Shelley did say things that implied they were reincarnationists, they also frequently made statements implying quite a different outlook. Goethe on several occasions called himself a disciple of Lucretius and in his earlier years Shelley was an ardent exponent of the atheistic materialism of Holbach and other Encyclopedists. Most reincarnationists are not aware that the admirable G. E. Lessing, the German playwright, philosopher, and champion of religious toleration, sympathized with reincarnation, but they do almost invariably mention the less admirable Henry Ford and the still less admirable George Patton, Jr.

I do not begrudge the reincarnationists their big names, but for the historical record I must protest their appropriation of numerous distinguished persons who most emphatically did not believe in reincarnation. Mory Bernstein, the author of *The Search for Bridey Murphy,* includes Julius Caesar, Spinoza, and T. H. Huxley in his

19. *Reincarnation: A Hope of the World,* p. 58.
20. *A Critical Examination of the Belief in Life After Death,* p. 210.

list. There is not the slightest evidence that either Caesar[21] or Spinoza believed in reincarnation or in any doctrine bearing even a remote likeness to it. I am not an expert on Spinoza, but I could not remember reading anything that seemed an endorsement of reincarnation. To make sure, I consulted Professor Lee Rice of Marquette University, a specialist in the period, and he fully confirmed my impression.[22] The inclusion of T. H. Huxley is more excusable. In "Evolution and Ethics," the Romanes Lecture of 1893, Huxley compared the idea of "heredity of character" with "what the Indian philosophers call 'Karma.' " Here he does sound like a reincarnationist, but he was in fact nothing of the kind. Huxley was a proponent and in fact a pioneer of epiphenomenalism,[23] a theory about the body-mind problem which implies that human beings do not survive the death of their bodies in any form whatsoever.

David Hume appears on Bernstein's list and on practically every other one with which I am familiar. To the best of my knowledge the only statement about reincarnation (or "metempsychosis") found in Hume's work is the one quoted above—"the soul, *if* immortal, existed before our life"—and it does not of course assert or imply the truth of metempsychosis. In the same essay ("Of the Immortality of the Soul") Hume supports in no uncertain terms the body-mind dependence argument that is presented in chapter 17 of this book. Numerous statements in his correspondence and conversation make it abundantly clear that for him death meant annihilation. On July 7, 1776, James Boswell, a fellow Scot, took it upon himself to visit the dying Hume to discover whether he persisted in his "infidelity" even when "he had death before his eyes." Much to his astonishment he found Hume entirely serene. To Boswell's question if "it was not possible that there might be a future state" Hume answered that it was possible that a piece of coal put on the fire would not burn, calling belief in an afterlife a foolish and absurd notion. To Boswell's question if the thought of death ever gave him any "uneasiness" he answered "not the least," quoting the remark by Lucretius that nonexistence after death is no more painful than nonexistence before birth. Boswell, who considered himself a pious Christian, was temporarily shaken in his own faith. "I was like a man in sudden danger eagerly seeking his defensive arms," he later wrote, "and I could not but be assailed by momentary doubt while I had actually before me a man of such strong abilities and extensive inquiry dying in the persuasion of being annihilated."[24]

---

21. The listing of Julius Caesar is particularly wild. Bernstein's source may be, directly or indirectly, the following passage in the article "Transmigration" in the *Hastings Encyclopedia of Ethics and Religion* (Vol. 12, p. 430). "There are two passages which clearly assert the belief in metempsychosis among the ancient Celts. Caesar (de Bell Gall vi, 14) tells us that the principle point in the teaching of the Druids is that the soul does not perish, but, after death, passes from one body into another." This would be quite enough for somebody like Bernstein to claim Caesar as a believer.

22. See Rice, "Mind Eternity and Spinoza," *The Jerusalem Philosophical Quarterly,* 1992, 319–34.

23. See pp. 291–92 below.

24. This and all other quotations in this paragraph are from "An Account of My Last Interview with David Hume, Esq." first published in *The Private Papers of James Boswell,* Vol. XII, reprinted in the N. Kemp Smith edition of Hume's *Dialogues Concerning Natural Religion.*

More recently Voltaire and Nietzsche made their appearance as reincarnationists. Practically every apologist writing during the last twenty years quotes Voltaire's remark that "it is no more surprising to be born twice than it is to be born once." It is usually suggested that this makes Voltaire a fellow-believer. Nietzsche has been appropriated by Robert Almeder, who lists him as one of the "serious" thinkers who "have argued for reincarnation on purely philosophical grounds."[25]

Voltaire's remark that it is no more surprising to be born twice than once is somewhat enigmatic and cannot be evaluated without a detailed discussion of the different contexts in which we speak of an event as surprising. It most emphatically does not imply that he believed in any kind of survival and we have ample evidence that he was a total unbeliever on this topic. "Is this system [meaning reincarnation]," he asks in his *Treatise on Metaphysics,* the most systematic of his philosophical writings, "any more probable than the *Thousand and One Nights?*" He answers that it is "Just the fruit of the lively and absurd imagination of the majority of Oriental philosophers."[26] Just like Hume, Voltaire fully endorsed the body-mind dependence argument. "Reason has taught me," he writes, that "all the ideas of men and animals come to them through the senses" and it is surely preposterous that men will still have ideas after they have lost their senses. Thinking and feeling are caused by the senses and the brain and it is "a little strange" to suggest that "the results of the organs" continue after the organs themselves have perished. One might as well say that a man will go on eating and drinking without a mouth and stomach. God has connected our capacity for thinking to a certain area of the brain, and it is no more possible for thinking to continue without this organ than it is for the song of a bird to continue after its throat has been destroyed in death. God *could* indeed have supplied both animals and men with an immortal soul, and he *could* have arranged matters in such a way that this immortal soul could exist independent of the body, just as he could have made human beings with two noses and four hands, and with wings and claws. God *could* have given us an immortal soul, but all indications are that he did not. The *Treatise* was published posthumously. In the works published during his lifetime Voltaire expressed himself with more caution, usually attributing his views to a character in a dialogue.

During the last decade of his active life, Nietzsche embraced the doctrine of eternal recurrence or the Eternal Return, which he had found in some of the ancient philosophers and which he believed to be supported by the physics of his day. The doctrine of the Eternal Return is something quite different from reincarnation. Reincarnation means the transmigration of souls, i.e., incarnations in different bodies. Eternal recurrence means a return in the *same* body. A believer in the Eternal Return believes in a cyclical universe. Let us suppose that each cycle lasts twenty billion years and let us call the first event A and the last one Z. The Eternal Return asserts that Z will be followed by a repetition of A and then the whole cycle will be repeated

---

25. *Death and Personal Survival,* p. 1.
26. Paul Edwards (Ed.), *Voltaire* (1989), p. 85.

ad infinitum. After Richard Nixon resigned a student asked me if I thought that there was any chance of his returning to the presidency since he had not served out the eight-year limit. I thought for a moment and then said, "Only if Nietzsche's Eternal Return is true, but then of course he will once again be forced to resign and you will once again ask this question. What is more, all of this has already happened an infinite number of times." It is scarcely credible that Almeder actually read Nietzsche and misconstrued him to be a believer in reincarnation. What seems to me more likely is that he looked at *Reincarnation in World Thought,* a huge propaganda anthology edited by J. Head and S. L. Cranston, which is sometimes regarded as a standard work on the subject. Head and Cranston do include numerous selections defending reincarnation, but they also include a great deal that is not really relevant to their subject, e.g., the inability of Bertrand Russell's son to conceive anything in the past without his being present or Winston Churchill's statement that he does not believe in life after death. There is a section on Nietzsche that reprints some of his discussions of the Eternal Return but nothing is said either in the title or in the table of contents indicating that the extracts are *not* about reincarnation. A casual browser is liable to infer that Nietzsche is another famous philosopher who supported reincarnation. The alternative to this explanation of Almeder's misclassification is deliberate deceit. I prefer my more charitable assumption.

Choosing Our Parents or McTaggart's Hats

According to reincarnationism the biological parents are not the cause of their child considered as a total human being. A human being is much more than a body, and what the biological parents contribute is "the body alone." I am quoting the phrase "the body alone" from a book by Christmas Humphreys, the English prosecutor whose harsh views about the guilt of children with hereditary diseases and handicaps I mentioned earlier. Humphreys likens the body to a house built by a landlord and emphasizes that the tenant need not take the house against his will. In the same way, although the "self" or "consciousness" cannot be said to be the creator of its new body, it nevertheless, like a tenant looking for the right house, chooses it as "the instrument most suited to its needs."[27] To illustrate his view Humphreys discusses the inheritance of musical gifts. "In the West," he writes, "we say that the child of a musical father is musical because of heredity." Among Buddhists, on the other hand, it would be explained that "the child was born into a musical family because it had developed musical propensity in previous lives" and was therefore "attracted to an environment suitable for the expression of those gifts."[28]

A more systematic and sophisticated statement of this view is found in the writ-

---

27. *Buddhism,* p. 104.
28. Ibid.

ings of C. J. Ducasse and J. M. E. McTaggart who were probably the most prominent twentieth-century philosophers to support reincarnation. McTaggart illustrates the way in which reincarnation and inheritance may cooperate to produce a human being by an analogy with the selection of hats, which has frequently been quoted in discussions of reincarnation. McTaggart invites us to consider the fact that if we observe people walking through the streets of a big city like London, "it is extremely rare to meet a man whose hat shows no sort of adaptation to his head."[29] There is no mystery about the cause of this adaptation. A man's head is never, of course, made to fit his hat and, except in special cases, the hat a man wears was not made to fit *his* head. The adaptation is the result of his selection "from hats made without any special reference to his particular head" of the hat that will suit his head best. McTaggart is convinced that something similar happens in the choice of parents. A person about to be reborn will choose the parents of his next incarnation according to the similarity of their character to his own, but he would not directly cause the birth of the body in which he will spend his next life.

Ducasse, who is in complete agreement with McTaggart, elaborates their common position by distinguishing between what he calls skills and aptitudes. Swimming, playing the violin, operating a computer, or speaking a language would be instances of skills. These are acquired during our lives, but skills presuppose aptitudes. An aptitude is a latent ability "to acquire more or less easily or well various more particular abilities in response to training and circumstances."[30] Gifts for music, sports, or intellectual pursuits would be examples of aptitudes. To the assertion that biological heredity is what determines one's native aptitudes, the reply would be that "this is not known to be true of *every* aptitude an individual is born with."[31] Some of these at least may be "products of his strivings or experiences in earlier lives." What is more—and here Ducasse refers with approval to McTaggart and his hats—it "might well be" that the nature of the psychological aptitudes of a reincarnating individual determines "his being drawn to birth in a certain body."[32]

How do human beings go about choosing their parents, if they really do so? It should be emphasized that the selection here cannot be exactly like the selection of hats or anything else during our earthly lives. For the agents are now "interim" entities. They no longer have their old bodies and they do not as yet have the new ones. As we shall see in chapter 15, the question of just what they are at this stage and where they live is one of the most difficult issues reincarnationists have to face. On one view they are pure minds, on another they are some kind of "spiritual" or astral body. How can such beings choose and, more basically, how can they obtain the information to make a meaningful choice? Several different answers have been put for-

29. *Some Dogmas of Religion* (London, 1906), p. 125.
30. "Life After Death Conceived as Reincarnation," *In Search of God and Immortality,* op. cit., p. 150.
31. Ibid., Ducasse's italics.
32. Ibid., pp. 150–51.

ward. Roshi Yasutani, a Japanese zen master, teaches that "the intermediate being" has the "mysterious power of seeing, feeling, and finding its parents-to-be" and even "to be aware of the sexual intercourse by which it may be conceived."[33] For Francis Story, a leading British Buddhist about whom I shall say more in later chapters, it is a matter of "attraction" perhaps not unlike that exhibited by gravitational and magnetic phenomena. The "thought force" that exists in the interim state:

> is attracted to the physical conditions of human procreation which will enable it to remanifest and thus give expression to its craving-potential. The released energy in some way operates on and through the combination of male and female generative cells on much the same principle as that of the electric current working on the filaments in the lamp to produce light.[34]

The "craving-potential" possesses a "blind creative power" that "adopts and develops" the male and female generative cells, "molding the structure of their growth in such a way as to make it serve its purpose."[35] McTaggart does not quite use Story's language, but his basic position is the same. To the question of how a person is "brought into connection" with his new body or rather with the parents of his new body, the answer is that it is something like a "chemical affinity."[36] We know that various substances have chemical affinities for one another. They "meet and combine," separating themselves to do so, from other substances with which they had previously been in connection. There is nothing stranger or more paradoxical in the notion that "each person enters into connections with the body that is most fitted to be connected with him."[37]

A critical reader of these pronouncements will want to ask two questions. First, is there any reason to suppose that *any* human aptitudes, to use Ducasse's terminology, require an explanation in terms of reincarnation and cannot be adequately explained by natural causes? I deliberately use the word "natural" rather than "genetic" because it is not at all clear that aptitudes may not be partly caused by environmental influences. Evidently, if they can be explained by a conjunction of genetic and environmental factors, reincarnation becomes just as redundant here as in the case of an explanation in purely genetic terms. It should be noted that Ducasse does not specify a single aptitude that he regards as incapable of a naturalistic explanation. McTaggart talks of the character of people rather than their aptitudes but he too does not point to any character trait that requires a reincarnationist account.

The second critical question concerns the descriptions offered by Yasutani, Story,

---

33. *Eight Bases of Belief in Buddhism,* reprinted in T. Kapleau (Ed.), *The Wheel of Death* (London, 1972), p. 44.

34. "Rebirth and the Western Thinker," reprinted in Kapleau, op. cit.; see also Story's *Rebirth As Doctrine and Experience* (Kandey, Sri Lanka, 1975), pp. 37ff.

35. Ibid.

36. *Some Dogmas of Religion,* op. cit., p. 126.

37. Ibid.

and McTaggart of the process of selecting prospective parents. It is worth reminding ourselves that in spite of the show of confidence of these writers, none of them has or could have observed the "thought forces" or the quasi-chemical affinity that supposedly leads human beings to appropriate parents. Not only that, but their descriptions are tremendously vague and really border on unintelligibility. I will return to this topic in Chapter 15.

The Alleged Benefits of Belief in Reincarnation

I recently came across the following statement by Henry Ford:

> I adopted the theory of reincarnation when I was twenty-six. Religion offered nothing to the point. Even work could not give me complete satisfaction. Work is futile if we cannot utilize the experience we collect in one life in the next. When I discovered reincarnation . . . time was no longer limited. I was no longer a slave to the hands of the clock. . . . I would like to communicate to others the calmness that the long view of life gives to us.[38]

Ford did not claim that belief in reincarnation would improve our character or that it was a deterrent to harmful behavior. This is precisely the kind of thing asserted by C. D. Broad, a very able and influential philosopher of an earlier generation, and by Ian Stevenson, the psychiatrist and parapsychologist whom I already mentioned in the Introduction and to whom I shall be referring repeatedly in this book. It should be explained that Broad was an agnostic on the question of survival, but he did regard reincarnation "on general grounds to be the most plausible form of the doctrine of survival."[39] This sentence is quoted from an article published in 1958. Twenty years earlier Broad had addressed himself to the moral benefits of belief in reincarnation. This belief, he wrote,

> furnishes a reasonable motive for right action. We have to conduct our present lives on *some* postulate or other, positive or negative, about what happens to our minds at the death of our bodies. We shall behave all the better if we act on the assumption that we may survive; that actions which tend to strengthen and enrich our characters in this life will probably have a favorable influence on the dispositions with which we begin our next lives; and that actions which tend to disintegrate our characters in this life will probably cause us to enter on our next life "halt and maimed." If we suppose that our future lives will be of the same general nature as our present lives,

---

38. Hans Tendam, *Exploring Reincarnation* (London, 1990), p. 377.

39. "Personal Identity and Survival," *Newsletter of the Parapsychology Foundation,* 1958, reprinted in A. Flew (Ed.), *Readings in the Philosophical Problems of Parapsychology* (Amherst, N.Y.: Prometheus Books, 1987), p. 315.

this postulate, which is in itself intelligible and not unreasonable, gains enormously in concreteness and therefore in practical effect on our conduct.[40]

I will discuss at some length in chapter 7 the case of Edward Ryall, an elderly Englishman who in the 1970s claimed "total recall" of a life in the seventeenth century. Among those who took Ryall seriously and believed it likely that his recollections were veridical was Ian Stevenson, who supplied a highly complimentary introduction to Ryall's *Second Time Around* (1974). Stevenson concluded his introduction with remarks about the benefits to the human race resulting from acquaintance with Ryall's case and "others of its type," which Stevenson considers "genuine." Here is the full text of his statement:

> I happen to be a person who does not think the times we live in worse than any other. But if they are, then I would attribute the fact not to our widespread materialism as regards physical objects, but to the equally widespread and much more doleful materialism concerning our own natures. I do not think that such materialism creates selfishness and despair, but it certainly encourages them. The idea of a second time around suggests both hope and an incentive to better conduct.[41]

I hope that Henry Ford really derived some "calmness" from his belief in reincarnation. If he became calmer with age, other causes may well have been responsible. What amazes me is that he did not seem to show the slightest interest in the question of whether the belief in reincarnation was really true, whether there was good evidence for it or perhaps on the contrary strong reasons for rejecting it. I find such an attitude, especially in a reasonably intelligent person, thoroughly immoral because it offends against what Bertrand Russell called the "precept of veracity."[42] It is not only immoral but in the long run exceedingly harmful since it encourages people to believe whatever they like to believe simply because they like it, with the occasional corollary that those who believe otherwise are to be suppressed. As for Broad and Stevenson, who sound here like old-fashioned Christian preachers, not to speak of right-wing Republican orators, their assertions that belief in reincarnation is likely to be "an incentive to better conduct" betrays a totally unrealistic view about human motivation. Confining myself to destructive and antisocial acts, disapproval by other human beings, and the threat of *earthly* punishments, especially if they are prompt and very probable, frequently do have a deterrent effect. Threats about punishment in the hereafter are too vague and too far in the future to overcome selfish or sadistic impulses. What is more, most "believers" in an afterlife, whether in the familiar Western or the reincarnationist form, do not fully believe in it, if they believe in it at all. Bertrand Russell tells a story about F. W. H. Myers, the classical scholar and pi-

---

40. *An Examination of McTaggart's Philosophy* (Cambridge, 1938), p. 639.

41. Introduction, Edward Ryall, *Second Time Around* (Jersey, Channel Islands, 1974), p. 29.

42. *A History of Western Philosophy* (London, 1946), p. 843.

oneer parapsychologist, who asked a man at a dinner table what he thought would happen to him when he died. The man tried to ignore the question, but on being pressed he replied, "Oh well, I suppose I shall inherit eternal bliss, but I wish you wouldn't talk about such unpleasant subjects."[43] In most people, Russell adds, belief in a hereafter "exists only in the region of conscious thought, and has not succeeded in modifying unconscious mechanisms."[44] Some years ago when this topic came up in a class, a student told the following story. His father, a religious man, was to undergo a serious operation and was understandably very worried. The son tried to reassure him by talking about the high reputation of the surgeon and by quoting statistics about the frequent success of this kind of surgery. The father was not reassured. "Since you believe in life after death," the son finally said, "you will go on even if the operation is a failure." "Stop joking, this is serious," was the father's reply.

The Plan of This Book

A few words about the supposed benefits of belief in reincarnation were not, I think, out of place here. However, this is not the question with which I am primarily concerned in this book. I am concerned with what may be called the logical standing of reincarnation: Is it true or false or neither? How are we to evaluate the evidence for and against it; and I am also interested in similar questions about the doctrine of Karma. It should be explained here that both Western and Eastern defenders of reincarnation have claimed that their theory is entirely rational. It is alleged to be backed by solid evidence and need not be accepted on faith.

One kind of evidence is the injustice of the world. This fact, together with certain assumptions, is claimed to lead to the conclusion that we must live again. This is the so-called moral argument which I discuss in Chapter 2. Chapter 3 is about Karma. I have tried to show that the so-called Law of Karma is no law at all but a pronouncement without content. Several of the subsequent chapters are devoted to empirical arguments. Chapter 4 deals with child prodigies, déjà vu experiences and various other facts which, it is maintained, are best explained by reincarnation.

Some human beings have claimed to have memories of earlier lives, either spontaneously or under hypnosis. Spontaneous memories are discussed in Chapters 7 and 16; hypnotic regressions in Chapters 5 and 6. Chapter 5 is devoted to the famous case of Bridey Murphy, Chapter 6 to later less well-known cases and also to hypnotic "progressions" in the course of which the subjects are "progressed" into the future.

In Chapter 8 I discuss the view that, corresponding to the principle of conservation of mass and energy accepted by most physicists, there is a conservation principle of "spiritual" energy and that this principle logically leads to a reincarnationist conclusion.

---

43. "Stoicism and Mental Health," reprinted in *In Praise of Idleness* (London, 1935), p. 133.
44. Pp. 133–34.

Chapter 11 deals with the claim that certain birthmarks and birth defects are evidence for earlier lives. The main, though not the only, objection to such a claim is that there is no credible "modus operandi" for the transmission of the wounds in the previous body to the new embryo. Later in the book I elaborate on how all forms of reincarnation are beset by unanswerable *modus operandi* problems.

I discuss in Chapter 13 the view of Dr. Grof, a Czech psychiatrist now living in the United States, and his ex-wife Joan Halifax. They maintain that certain experiences of dying people who had been given LSD are evidence for reincarnation. On his own Dr. Grof reported LSD experiences of psychotic patients which can best be explained on the assumption that they have had previous lives.

In Chapter 15 I discuss what I call the "interregnum"—the realm in which human beings are said to reside between incarnations. It is difficult to give an account of the interregnum existence without introducing the astral body or something of the same general nature. The astral body, as I shall explain in detail, is the immaterial double possessed by every human being. This notion is evaluated in Chapter 9. In this chapter, I show in detail why the notion of the astral body is absurd and why any theory that presupposes its existence must also be absurd.

Chapters 10 and 11 deal with the ideas of Dr. Kübler-Ross. In Chapter 10, after describing her valuable work with dying patients, I discuss her claim that "near death experiences" prove immortality "beyond the shadow of a doubt." I also discuss the work of other leading figures in the new immortality movement who have received Kübler-Ross's blessings: Raymond Moody and Karlis Osis and Erlandur Haraldsson. I try to show that their "facts" are for the most part not facts at all and that if we give them every benefit of the doubt, these facts will prove nothing at all. In Moody's case I also show his utter disingenuousness. In Chapter 11, I discuss Kübler-Ross's astral adventures and various of her other strange experiences, including a visit from a dead patient.

The objections to reincarnation, other than that it presupposes the existence of an astral body, are discussed in Chapters 14 and 17. In Chapter 14 I cover Tertullian's argument that in a new incarnation the individual invariably starts as a baby and not at the age at which he died in his previous life, the incompatibility of reincarnation with Darwinian evolution and with the "recency" of life on the earth, and the enormous population increases throughout human history. I have tried to show that this increase is incompatible with most, though not with all, forms of reincarnation. In the same chapter, I explain why the absence of genuine memories of previous lives constitutes powerful evidence *against* reincarnation.

Chapter 17 deals with the dependence of consciousness on the brain. I try to show that this dependence rules out reincarnation and also almost all other forms of survival after death. As I mentioned in the Introduction, because of its vast implications, this seems to me the most important chapter of the book. Numerous attempts have been made—by reincarnationists as well as by Western believers in survival—to show that the brain-consciousness-dependence argument does not prove or make plausible the view that human beings do not survive death. I examine all major efforts in this direction and find them to be without merit. Regrettable as this conclusion may seem, when we die, we are *really* dead.

A few words are in order about whether the belief in reincarnation should be regarded as false or as conceptually incoherent. I strongly incline to the latter view because of the nonsensicality of such notions as the invasions of the womb of the prospective mother by the soul or the astral body. If an assertion is conceptually incoherent or meaningless it can be rejected without examining the supposed evidence in its favor. There are, however, a number of reasons for not adopting such a course in the case of reincarnation. For one thing, in the course of presenting their views, reincarnationists make or imply a number of claims that are definitely not meaningless—that apparently accurate memories obtained under hypnosis cannot be explained except by reincarnation, that there cannot be naturalistic explanations for child geniuses, déjà vu experiences and much more, and above all that a person's consciousness can exist without his brain. All these statements are false and not meaningless. Furthermore, many people, including the present writer, are not emotionally satisfied unless the evidence has been examined just in case the main reincarnationist assertion is after all not incoherent.

2

The Moral Argument

In this chapter I will discuss the so-called moral argument. It is also commonly referred to as the argument from justice, although it could just as appropriately be called "the argument from *in*justice." It is used by the great majority of the defenders of reincarnation, the more articulate and educated writers as well as the more primitive believers. It closely resembles the "moral" arguments for the existence of God and life after death found in Kant and numerous Christian and Jewish apologists. To many of its supporters the argument seems so overwhelmingly plausible that they find it difficult to conceive how anybody could fail to see its cogency. Unlike most of the other arguments to be considered, the moral argument would, if valid, prove Karma as well as reincarnation.

The first step in the argument is a declaration that the world as we know it contains a vast amount of injustice. It will be helpful to distinguish three kinds of injustice. To begin with, there is the undeniable fact that human beings are born with very unequal endowments and into environments offering very unequal opportunities. Some are born intelligent, with healthy and handsome bodies; others are born with less intelligence and are sickly or even crippled. Some are born to parents who are affectionate and well-to-do; others into families that are unloving, uneducated, poor, and into a society in which the prospects for happiness are exceedingly slim. Next, there is the suffering later in life resulting from illnesses, accidents, and natural disasters like floods, fires, and earthquakes, which are not in any obvious way due to voluntary human actions. Finally, there is the injustice inflicted by other human beings.

To make the issues involved in this argument come to life I will give two illustrations, the first fictional, the second real. Nathaniel West's *Miss Lonelyhearts* is a short novel about how a reporter who has been assigned to cover the "agony column" of his newspaper is caught up in the suffering described in the letters from his readers. The following is a letter signed, "Desperate":

Dear Miss Lonelyhearts–

I am sixteen years old now and I dont know what to do and would appreciate it if you could tell me what to do. When I was a little girl it was not so bad because I got used to the kids on the block making fun of me, but now I would like to have boy friends like the other girls and go out on Saturday nites, but no boy will take me because I was born without a nose—although I am a good dancer and have a nice-shape and my father buys me pretty clothes.

I sit and look at myself all day and cry. I have a big hole in the middle of my face that scares people even myself so I can't blame the boys for not wanting to take me out. My mother loves me, but she crys terrible when she looks at me.

What did I do to deserve such a terrible bad fate? Even if I did do some bad things I didnt do any before I was a year old and I was born this way. I asked Papa and he says he doesnt know, but that maybe I did something in the other world before I was born or that maybe I was being punished for his sins. I don't believe that because he is a very nice man. Ought I commit suicide?[1]

My second illustration of apparently totally undeserved suffering concerns Sunya Margulies, a six-year-old girl who was critically injured in an accident on May 18, 1993. The accident occurred on Broadway and 78th Street in New York City, half a block from where I live. Sunya was injured when a van forced a car up onto a sidewalk where it hit her and threw her up on the car's hood. The car slammed into the steel security gate of a restaurant with such force that the crumpled metal smashed a plate-glass window. Sunya had been walking to school with her mother on a beautiful spring morning. Everybody who knew the girl described her as lovely, friendly, and intelligent. The *New York Times* had a report about the accident but there has been no follow-up and I do not know anything about later developments. Like a religious person I could not help asking myself "Why—why does this sort of thing happen? Why does it happen to anybody, but especially to a lovely girl who is just beginning her life?"

Let me now return to the moral argument for reincarnation. In the remainder of my exposition I will follow Dr. Raynor Johnson and two other Christian reincarnationists, Leslie Weatherhead and Quincey Howe, Jr. After listing numerous instances of injustice, Dr. Johnson mentions "mere chance" and God's plan as two ways of explaining the facts. Chance is no explanation of anything, and it would be highly paradoxical to saddle a good God with the responsibility for the world's injustice. He then asks this question:

---

1. *Miss Lonelyhearts* and *The Day of the Locust*, pp. 2–3.

If neither of these alternatives is acceptable, what explanations have we to offer which carries with it [sic] the reasonable assurance that we live in a just world?[2]

Fortunately there is a third alternative. We can discover it if we have the courage to extend the "Law of Cause and Effect" from the physical domain to the "levels of desire and thought" and to human behavior and consciousness generally, even if in doing so we endanger the freedom of the will. Surely it is "most improbable" that mental phenomena are any less subject to cause and effect than those that are purely material. Now, if we extend the Law of Cause and Effect to the mental domain we have to maintain that "the grossly unequal conditions of birth and childhood," to confine ourselves to one form of injustice, "are the results of prior causes." However, since such causes are "not by any means apparent in the present life," we must "as a logical necessity" affirm "the pre-existence of souls." We must affirm that "we are the product of self-generated forces in states of prior existence."[3] In this way we arrive at "the great law of Karma," which teaches that

> Whatsoever a man sows, whether in the field of action or thought, sometime and somewhere the fruits of it will be reaped by him.[4]

To quote Quincey Howe:

> Karma introduces an element of reason and logic into a problem that has vexed many a devout Christian. How are we to believe in a perfect and loving God if He persistently seems to place man in tragic and painful situations?[5]

Leslie Weatherhead, a liberal Protestant theologian and the author of a well-known book *The Agnostic Christian* was attracted by reincarnation and Karma because they seem to "make sense of some situations which otherwise seem terribly unjust and beyond understanding."[6]

It is amazing that an argument that is so transparently fallacious should have gained such widespread support. First of all, Johnson and all the other reincarnationist writers who argue along the same lines are grossly confused about what extending the "Law of Cause and Effect" to mental phenomena involves. It involves the search for and, where one succeeds, the discovery of causal explanations. It most emphatically does not involve the demonstration that justice in the karmic or any other familiar sense prevails. If we show that a given mental phenomenon is the result of certain conditions or factors, we *have* causally explained it, regardless of whether it has

---

2. *The Imprisoned Splendour*, p. 376.
3. Ibid.
4. p. 377.
5. *Reincarnation for the Christian*, p. 32.
6. *Life Begins at Death*, p. 71.

thereby been shown to be a just reward or punishment. Sometimes indeed, finding the causal explanation of an act may at the same time show it to be just. Thus a child who for the first time reads about the Nuremberg War Crimes Trial will discover why the Nazi leaders were tried and executed. In this case she will simultaneously discover the cause and the justice of the punishment. At other times finding the cause may at the same time reveal the injustice of the deed. In reading various works about the Soviet Union during the Stalinist dictatorship one will find out something about the paranoia and the colossal sadism of the dictator that made him destroy people who were totally innocent of any of the crimes with which they were charged. In learning the cause one will at the same time realize the injustice of the proceedings. Most of the time, however, causal explanations of human actions have nothing to do with justice or injustice. Explaining why a person prefers one restaurant to another or why he has decided to go to a concert rather than to a movie are cases in point; and they could be multiplied indefinitely. Reincarnationists habitually conflate the following two propositions:

(1) Everything has a cause—the principle of universal causation
(2) Happiness and unhappiness are always rewards or punishments for past deeds— what we may call the principle of universal retribution.

These are quite distinct claims and neither implies the other. Subject to certain qualifications, (1) is plausible but (2) is not, and it is the latter which reincarnationists need for their argument.

Reincarnationists habitually state the available alternatives inadequately. We saw that Johnson presents us with the three alternatives of "mere chance," God's plan, and reincarnation. This simply ignores the theory known as "naturalism," which holds that all phenomena, if they are caused at all, are the result of natural causes. Needless to say, a naturalist regards the hereditary inequalities of individuals as resulting from purely biological factors. Since he does not go beyond natural phenomena, a naturalist cannot escape the conclusion that the world is not just. Reincarnationists are so wedded to their position that they seem quite incapable of stating naturalism fairly and they also have a tendency to beg crucial issues by the very way in which they formulate their questions. One of the few American philosophers during the period between the two world wars who championed reincarnation was A. G. Widgery, who taught at Duke University for many years. In an article on "Reincarnation and Karma" in *The Aryan Path* of October 1936 he poses the apparently innocuous question: "Why is an individual born with this or that kind of body?" He complains that "occidental thought" ignores this "problem," but that the "doctrine of reincarnation" gives an answer to it. It is evident that Widgery will not accept the usual occidental answer in terms of biological causes. He thereby assumes at once, in the very act of raising the question, that there must be a "moral" justification for hereditary endowments and this, by the usual route, leads to good and bad deeds in previous lives. Widgery is not of course alone in begging the question. Johnson assumes that there is an explanation that carries with it "the reasonable assurance that we live in a just world"; Weather-head accepts reincarnation and Karma because they "make sense" of otherwise morally incomprehensible situations, and Quincey Howe maintains that without bringing in Karma we cannot "account for life's apparent injustice."[7] That the world is just, that it makes moral sense, that we can "account" for the injustice of life is what has to be proved. This is what the unbeliever does not grant.

I cannot resist observing that Johnson and the other supporters of the moral argument leave out a fourth alternative, that of an evil God. I do not myself believe in any God, good or evil, and for reasons I will briefly explain in the "Irreverent Postscript," I could never believe in a God conceived as a pure mind who interferes in the world. However, if the objections to believing in any God are waived, the theory of an evil God seems to make much more sense than the familiar one of a good God. Only an evil God could have set up the world in such a way that most animals can survive only by killing other animals and that all organisms must age (with all that aging involves) and eventually die. "If the world in which we live," to quote Bertrand Russell, "has been produced in accordance with a Plan, we shall have to reckon Nero a saint in comparison with the Author of that Plan."[8] However, even without bringing in this fourth alternative, the moral argument obviously fails.

It should be added that the moral argument proceeds in a counterinductive fashion, which in any everyday situation would be dismissed as totally perverse. Let us suppose that in a course of weekly lectures the instructor has been excruciatingly boring the first ten times. It is not impossible that on the eleventh occasion he will have an off day and surprise everybody by being lively and interesting. This is not impossible, but we have no right whatever to infer it from the ten preceding performances. If anything, we have reason to believe that on the eleventh occasion he will be just as tedious. To argue that *since* the lecturer was boring in all the ten previous classes he will be interesting during the eleventh class is utterly perverse. In the absence of proof that the universe *is* just, the reasoning of reincarnationists is just as perverse. From the undisputed fact that we have observed vast amounts of injustice in the past, it most certainly *cannot* be inferred that in the future, here or anywhere else, everything will be perfectly just.

Many years ago, when I was a high school student in Australia, I saw a movie entitled "We Are Not Alone," which starred the great Paul Muni. It was based on novel by James Hilton, a popular British novelist at that time. The story concerned an English country doctor with a wife who was a hypochondriac and who made his life miserable. He also had a pretty young nurse with whom he was in love. One day the wife took an overdose of one of her medications and died. Local busybodies spread the story that she was murdered by the doctor and his nurse. The two were tried and convicted. In the scene that I remember most clearly they are allowed to meet for

---

7. *Reincarnation for the Christian*, p. 31.
8. *The Scientific Outlook*, p. 131.

the last time the night before the execution. "This cannot be the end," the nurse tells the doctor, "It just isn't right." I forget what the doctor replied.

Ultimately the only reason why naturalism and its consequences that the world is not just are rejected is that they are emotionally unsatisfying. Reincarnationists and also many of the defenders of Western religions cannot bear the thought that good people should suffer and that death should be the end for them. Some of the Eastern defenders of reincarnation are quite frank about this. Thus Swami Nikhilananda, the very able editor of an abridged edition of *The Upanishads*, maintains that "the theory of total annihilation is not satisfactory," and prominent among the reasons is the fact that "it is inconsistent with the self-love we all possess." Such an outlook is understandable, but it is logically indefensible. It does not follow from the fact that something is "inconsistent with our self-love" that it therefore cannot be real. "However ardently I, or all mankind, may desire something, however necessary it may be to human happiness," to quote Bertrand Russell, "that is no ground for supposing this something to exist. There is no law of nature guaranteeing that mankind should be happy."[9]

---

9. *A History of Western Philosophy*, p. 720.

3

The Law of Karma

The Law of Karma appears to be an empirical claim, asserting that everything good happening to a human being is a reward for some previous good deed, and everything bad happening to him is punishment for an evil deed. It asserts a causal connection in both directions between two classes of observable phenomena—suffering and happiness are, at least in a broad sense, observable, and so are sinful and meritorious actions. There is admittedly some difficulty about getting a consensus as to what counts as sinful and meritorious behavior, but we may here ignore all problems of this kind. Except for its vastly greater significance, the Law of Karma is regarded by its proponents as entirely comparable to "natural" or scientific laws. Karma, writes Annie Besant, is a "natural law" and as such it "is no more sacred than any other natural law."[1] "The sins of the previous life of the Ego," to quote Madame Blavatsky, are punished by "this mysterious, inexorable, but in the equity and wisdom of its decrees infallible law."[2]

The Pseudo-Empirical Nature of this Law

Now a little reflection shows that the Law of Karma is not an empirical statement and that it is wholly unlike "natural" laws. To begin with, the Law of Karma has no predictive value whatsoever. A simple example will make this clear. Let us suppose that a plane takes off in which all the crew and passengers are, as far as we can tell, thoroughly decent people. The believer in Karma cannot predict any more or less confidently than

1. *A Study in Karma* (Krotona, 1918), pp. 5–6.
2. Quoted in R. W. Neufeldt, *Karma and Rebirth* (Albany: State University of New York Press, 1986), p. 243.

the unbeliever that the plane will not crash. The best he can do is offer a statistical prediction based not on Karma but on data concerning the safety of airplanes or, perhaps more specifically, of the kind of plane in which these people are flying. Let us now suppose that a madman or a terrorist planted a time bomb on the plane and, furthermore, that it is a very efficiently constructed time bomb. The lunatic, because of his empirical information, can predict with high probability that the plane is going to crash.

It may be argued that the lack of predictive content of Karma is not a serious matter since some scientific laws, notably Darwin's theory of natural selection, also lack predictive content. I do not think that this comparison is sound, but I will not press the point and will concentrate on a more basic consideration that incorporates whatever is significant in the observation that the Karmic Law is devoid of predictive value.

Scientific laws and indeed all statements that are not empty are not compatible with anything that may happen. All of them exclude some conceivable state of affairs: if such an excluded state of affairs were to obtain, the statement would be false. Just like Boyle's law or the second law of thermodynamics, Darwin's theory of natural selection is not compatible with anything.

The Law of Karma on the other hand *is* compatible with anything. The emptiness of the karmic theory can be seen most clearly if we compare it to another pseudoscientific theory that on analysis turns out to be completely empty. I am thinking of social Darwinism as advocated, for example, by the American sociologist William Graham Sumner. Sumner was a militant opponent of any kind of social legislation that might help the poor, the sick, or even the unemployed, and he justified his stand by reference to the principle that those who are successful have thereby proven their fitness while those who are downtrodden have thereby proven their unfitness and inferiority. The following is a report, provided by one of Sumner's admirers, of a conversation between Sumner and a student dissenter:

"Professor, don't you believe in any government aid to industries?"
"No! it's root, hog, or die."
"Yes, but hasn't the hog got a right to root?"
"There are no rights. The world owes nobody a living."
"You believe then, Professor, in only one system, the contract-competitive system?"
"That's the only sound economic system. All others are fallacies."
"Well, suppose some professor of political economy came along and took your job away from you. Wouldn't you be sore?"
"Any other professor is welcome to try. If he gets my job, it is my fault. My business is to teach the subject so well that no one can take the job away from me.[3]

There is some evasion in the last statement, in which Sumner talks about his teach-

3. Quoted in R. Hofstadter, *Social Darwinism in American Thought* (Boston: Beacon Press, 1955), p. 54.

ing the subject so well that no one else can take the job away from him. Many people who, by all usual standards, are inferior teachers might take his job away from him—by intrigues, by spreading rumors about his private life, or perhaps by such drastic measures as poisoning him. However, what is relevant for our purposes is that Sumner does not know who is fittest until the outcome, until the competition has been resolved. He, Sumner, is the fittest if he keeps his job. If somebody else, X, gets the job in his place, then X has turned out to be the fittest in virtue of his success. It should be remarked parenthetically that in Darwinism or neo-Darwinian theory, as contrasted with Social Darwinism, "fit" can be defined in such a way that it is *not* synonymous with "surviving" or "winning out," so that the statement "the fittest tend to win out in the competition for the means of survival" is a synthetic statement and not a tautology. In Social Darwinism, at least in Sumner's version, the statement that the fittest succeed *is* a tautology. Sumner does not define "fittest" or "fit" independently of succeeding. We do *not* have a statement about the connection between two characteristics but two words for the same characteristic. The theory is empty and totally *post hoc*. We know who is fittest only after the issue has been resolved. Sumner's claim is consistent with anything whatever. Sumner himself had no doubt that socialist revolutionaries would never win out; but, if they had, they would automatically have shown themselves to be the fittest.

It is easy to see that the Law of Karma is also compatible with anything and hence totally empty. Let us suppose that a horrible criminal like Hitler is finally brought to justice. This of course confirms the principle since the criminal's suffering was the result of his evil deeds. Suppose, however, that a person who, according to all the best available information, is decent and kind comes to a bad end, as the result of being run over by a drunken driver, a judicial frameup, or perhaps because of some dreadful illness. Would this disconfirm the principle? Not at all. It only shows that in a previous life he committed evil deeds of which his present suffering is the just punishment. Let us suppose that we know that the next incarnation of this individual is going to be one long horrendous nightmare of torture and persecution. Would this show that the Law of Karma is not true? Not at all: It would only show that his sins in past lives were so enormous that the disasters of his present life were insufficient punishment.

In 1965 there was an instructive exchange in the *Philosophical Quarterly*, an Indian publication not to be confused with the Scottish journal of the same name, between Professor Warren E. Steinkraus, a liberal Christian with an interest in Oriental philosophy, and Professor G. R. Malkani, a Hindu believer in Karma. Professor Steinkraus expressed his consternation as to how the Law of Karma can be reconciled with the staggering sufferings experienced by a great many people:

> The punishments do not fit the crime. Some of the miseries of disease and the excruciating pains of injuries suffered by human beings would not be inflicted by the

---

4. *Philosophical Quarterly*, 1965, p. 151.

most vindictive of human judges for the most heinous crimes.[4]

Steinkraus concludes by raising the question:

> Can the defender of Karma admit that some suffering is outrageously severe or must he say that all suffering is *a priori* just and necessarily deserved merely because it occurs?[5]

Steinkraus was firmly put in his place by Malkani, who, as editor of the *Philosophical Quarterly*, saw to it that he had the last word. After remarking, quite irrelevantly, that any explanation of evil and injustice in the world must leave God "blameless," Malkani insisted that there are certain ultimate mysteries that we must "not seek to probe any further." One of these is the question of "what punishment is appropriate for what sin or accumulation of sins." We are not gods and cannot know the answer to the question of why there is "so much punishment and for what." This unavoidable human ignorance is not, it appears, incompatible with total assurance that the world is just and that what may appear to be excessive punishment is not in fact excessive at all:

> It should suffice to console us that there is no limit to the enormity of the errors of omission and commission which an individual might have committed in his countless past lives.[6]

It should be emphasized that, when the partisans of Karma "explain" the misfortunes that befall apparently decent human beings by telling us that they sinned in a previous life, their pronouncements are just like Sumner's claims about who is fittest, *totally post hoc*. Sumner could not identify an individual as "the fittest" until he was sure that he had won out, and the karmic theorists cannot say anything about past misdeeds until suffering and misfortune have befallen a human being. To this it must be added that the "wisdom after the event" possessed by Sumner and by the Karmic believer is radically different from the real wisdom after the event that we often possess as the result of causal investigations. All of us are often wise only after the event, but we are *really* wise if we can offer a retrodictive explanation that is supported by adequate evidence. A plane crashes on takeoff at the Miami airport. It was not predicted, but we find evidence that a certain defect in the engine caused the crash. The karmic procedure is also *post hoc* but it does not provide any genuine wisdom after the event. After a person who was a fine human being is run over by a drunken driver the karmic theorist tells us that this happened because of his sins in a previous life. Unlike the investigators of the plane crash, he is *not* wise after the event. For he cannot tell us how and where the person had sinned. He does not have any informa-

---

5. Ibid.
6. *Philosophical Quarterly*, 1966, p. 45.

tion corresponding to the information obtained by the crash investigators about the engine defect. He makes a retrodictive claim, but, unlike the retrodictive statement about the cause of the crash, his claim is pure dogmatism. To avoid unfairness to certain reincarnationists, the above remarks require one qualification. Some karmic theorists who also believe in Nirvana or a superhuman Absolute Mind maintain that after his last incarnation the individual will be able to review in one glance the infinite number of lives he has lived. Reincarnationists holding this view could consistently allow that *their* karmic theory is falsifiable by a review that showed the absence of any dependable moral pattern. Their position is thus not compatible with any conceivable state of affairs and hence it is not open to the charge that it is empty. However, one cannot help wondering how a human being could "in one glance" or for that matter in more than one glance survey an infinite number of past lives; and, furthermore, all the pronouncements about misdeeds in past lives are just as *post hoc* and just as much pure *ipse dixits* as those of karmic believers who do not allow a final review.

Karmic Administration Problems

Anybody not intimidated by the virulence with which the champions of Karma brush off objections to their theory will want to raise a very simple and, as it seems to me, utterly devastating question about the execution and more generally the "administration" of Karmic ordinances. It should here be emphasized that many of the believers in Karma do not believe in a god and that those who do nevertheless maintain that the Law of Karma operates autonomously. Professor Malkani combines belief in the karmic law with "the best form of theism," but he does not maintain that God is in any way involved in the administration of Karma. On the inexorable and autonomous operation of Karma, Malkani, who here fairly represents the Hindu position, is in complete agreement with the atheist and agnostic supporters of Karma. Karma, he writes, "automatically produces the appropriate results like any other law in the natural domain. Nobody can cheat the law. It is as inexorable as any natural law."[7]

    The claim that Karma operates autonomously invites the following questions: How, to begin with, are good and bad deeds registered? Is there some cosmic repository like a huge central social security office in which the relevant information is recorded and translated into some kind of "balance"? Next, how and where is it decided what will happen to a person in his next incarnation as a result of the balance of his acts in a given life? How and where, for example, is it decided that in the next life he will become a human being rather than a roach, a man rather than a woman, an American rather than an Indian, black rather than white, physically well-formed rather than crippled, intelligent rather than retarded, sane rather than insane? Finally, there is still the problem of how such decisions are translated into reality. As an il-

---

7. Op. cit., p. 43.

lustration I will use a natural disaster, the famous Lisbon earthquake of 1755. A large number of people perished as a result of it. An even larger number were injured and also lost their possessions; and a number of people indirectly benefited because of the death and injury of others. Somebody who does not believe in Karma and who also does not believe that the earthquake was a special intervention on the part of the deity would of course regard it as a purely natural phenomenon that is entirely explicable in terms of natural, in this instance, geological, causes. The believer in Karma, by contrast, must be prepared to claim that the earthquake was brought about in order to punish or reward the various people who suffered or benefited from the earthquake. How and where were the bad deeds of those killed and injured and the good deeds of those spared registered? How and where were the penalties and rewards decided? And just how did Karma determine the geological conditions whose existence is not disputed as the "natural" or at least the "immediate" cause of the disaster? Surely, if ever intelligent planning was needed, this is a case in point. Let us assume that the chief of a terrorist organization is about to send his forces into a town in which there are 5,000 houses. His instructions are to burn down all but the hundred that belong to secret supporters of his cause. Let us also suppose that these hundred houses are spread all over the town. Such an operation obviously requires a great deal of careful planning and a high level of intelligence on the part of the planners. Even then it is entirely possible that mistakes will be made so that some houses of the sympathizers will be destroyed while some belonging to the enemy will be spared. The Law of Karma by contrast is infallible. It never punishes the innocent and never spares the guilty; and it does so although it is not an intelligent person or principle. To rephrase our earlier question: just how did this nonintelligent principle set up the geological forces so as to achieve the desired results with complete precision?

In this connection even the otherwise so confident Professor Malkani is almost reduced to silence. All he can offer is the following lame response:

> Does the Law of Karma act upon the forces of nature and bring about cyclones, earthquakes, floods, etc., which in their turn cause widespread havoc and destruction of both life and property affecting millions? But if a metaphysical law, like the Law of Karma, cannot do that, can it do anything whatsoever? Is it a law only in name? A powerless law is as good as no law.[8]

This bluff and bluster answers nothing. If defenders of Karma cannot do better they should surely adopt the alternative mentioned in a tone of horror at the end of Malkani's outburst and admit that Karma "is as good as no law." One has to emphasize that Malkani has not shown how Karma can have an impact on geological conditions. For that matter, I do not know of any sane person, reincarnationist or otherwise, who maintains that geologists would be better able to predict earthquakes (or anything else) if they believed in Karma.

---

8. Op. cit., p. 43.

Unlike the more sophisticated champions of Karma, Mrs. Besant saw the need for introducing divine karmic administrators. In *The Ancient Wisdom*, her best-known work, she first insists that "in no case can a man suffer that which he has not deserved."[9] She then speaks of the "Lords of Karma" who are "great spiritual intelligences" keeping "the karmic records" and adjusting "the complicated workings of karmic law." They know the karmic record of every man and with their "omniscient wisdom" they "select and combine portions of that record to form a plan of a single life."[10] This means primarily that they select the race, the country, and the parents of the soul or Ego in its next incarnation. Thus an Ego with highly developed musical faculties will be "guided to take its physical body in a musical family"; an Ego of a "very evil type" will be guided "to a coarse and vicious family, whose bodies were built of the coarsest combination"; while an Ego who yields to drunkenness will be led to a "family whose nervous systems were weakened by excess," and he will be born from "drunken parents who would supply diseased materials for his physical envelope."[11] It is in this way that the Lords of Karma "adjust means to ends," ensure the doing of justice, and see to it that the Ego can carry his "karmic possessions and faculties" into his next life.

This solution of the "administration" problem calls for two comments. In the first place, the lords of Karma have not been seen by anybody recently and, even during the decades when Mrs. Besant flourished, they were, as far as I know, not perceived by anybody other than Mrs. Besant, not even by Madame Blavatsky. Second, Mrs. Besant did not have an adequate grasp of the scope of the problem. To solve it we not only need an explanation of how the Lords of Karma secure appropriate bodies for Egos in subsequent incarnations. We also need to be told how they affect natural objects and forces to bring about events like the Lisbon earthquake of 1755 that in one swoop punish thousands of the wicked and reward large numbers of the good. To this question Mrs. Besant totally failed to address herself. We are touching a problem that equally affects all believers in Karma, whether they bring in gods or not; and it also affects Western believers in God: How can a nonphysical force or person have any effects on physical objects like geological formations? This is what I call the *modus operandi* problem. I will discuss it in some detail in Chapter 10 as it relates to reincarnation and in the "Irreverent Postscript" as it relates to God. It is a very basic difficulty for believers and one they hardly ever face.

Events involving massive deaths in a fairly small area such as earthquakes or genocide are particularly difficult to explain in terms of just punishments and rewards. It is farfetched, to put it very mildly, to suppose that all the people who perished in Lisbon or all the Jews murdered by the Nazis deserved exactly the same treatment. Common sense rebels against this notion especially if we have concrete knowledge of the enormous differences between different members of these groups. Needless to say,

---

9. *The Ancient Wisdom* (London: Theosophical Publishing Society, 1897), p. 293.
10. Op. cit., pp. 293–294.
11. Op. cit., p. 295.

apologists for Karma will not be impressed by this consideration. They will tell us that the victims of the Lisbon earthquake, to stay with this illustration, may have been no worse in *this* life than those who were spared, but the same is not necessarily true of earlier lives. We may rest assured that the victims were punished for misdeeds committed before they were born. Since their theory is compatible with anything, the karmic believers need never give up, but we have already seen that the price paid for this immunity from refutation is very steep: it deprives the theory of any real content.

The Emptiness of Karmic Directives

So, far from providing moral guidance, the doctrine of Karma is bound to lead to perplexity, and it is hence apt to paralyze action. The ordinary person who does not believe in Karma usually has no difficulty in deciding whether it is right to help people who are ill, who have become the victims of accidents, or who are in various other kinds of difficulties. Things are not so easy for the believer in Karma. The suffering individual in his view *deserves* to suffer because he committed evil acts in this or else in a previous life. It is not only not our duty to help him but it would seem on karmic principles that it is our duty *not* to help him. "It would be impossible," wrote Madame Blavatsky, "either to delay or to hasten the Karma in the fulfillment of justice," and in order to expiate one's sins fully it is necessary "to suffer all the consequences to the bitter end to exhaust all the defects until they have reached their plenitude."[12] Mrs. Besant, who started her career as a radical, apparently had not lost all her humanity after she succeeded Madame Blavatsky as leader of the theosophists. She reports some members saying "I cannot help this man since what he is suffering is his karma." She thought them cruel and wrongheaded and compared them to somebody who says, "I cannot pick up this child who just fell, since the Law of gravitation is opposed to it."[13]

I do not think that this is a fair analogy and it does not answer the members who refuse to help people in need. The law of gravitation is not a moral law and the fact that the child fell down does not, without bringing in karmic morality, imply that it is now being punished for an earlier sin. As far as I can see, no prescription of any kind can be derived from the Law of Karma for this situation or for any other; and, if this is so, Karma is completely vacuous as a principle of moral guidance. No matter what we do, whether we help the individual or refuse to help him, we will be doing the right thing. If we help him and cut short his suffering, this means that his earlier deed did not require more severe punishment than what he suffered until we brought relief. If, on the other hand, we ignore him and let him continue in his misery, this shows that his sin was so great as to deserve the total amount of his suffering—what

---

12. Quoted in P. Siwek, *The Enigma of the Hereafter* (New York, 1952), p. 122.
13. *Popular Lectures on Theosophy* (Chicago, 1910).

he suffered before we could have intervened as well as what he suffered afterward when we failed to come to his assistance. Believers in Karma constantly and emphatically insist that their theory does not imply fatalism, that, quite the contrary, it is entirely compatible with belief in human freedom, understood as the ability to shape our lives, within limits, in accordance with our desires and choices, and that our efforts frequently do make a great deal of difference to what happens. I see no reason to dispute this claim, but it in no way answers the challenge of vacuousness. The vacuousness, as far as moral prescriptions are concerned, follows from the karmic doctrine that the world is just. A karmic believer's commitment to this proposition is unqualified—it is categorical and not merely hypothetical. He does not maintain that the world *would* be just if we did certain things: he maintains that the world *is* just regardless of what in fact we do. No matter what happens, whether we help the underdog or not, whether our efforts at making lives less full of suffering and sorrow succeed or not, the ultimate outcome will be just, in the sense that every human being will be getting exactly—no more and no less—what he deserves.

Some Startling Implications

Karma provides no guidance on how to act but it does have implications concerning the appropriate attitude toward successful and unsuccessful people, towards those who are happy and those who are suffering: we should applaud and admire the former and despise or even hate the latter. Some of these implications are truly horrifying and believers in Karma, especially those in the West, are careful not to spell them out, if they are aware of them. It follows from their principle that Abraham Lincoln, Jean Jaurès, the two Kennedy brothers, and Martin Luther King, Jr. got no more than they deserved when they were assassinated. It equally follows that the six million Jews exterminated by the Nazis deserved their fate. It follows that all who were ever persecuted for their beliefs or for belonging to a certain group or nation were justly treated—the heretics burnt by the Inquisition, the African blacks captured by slave traders and shipped to America, the Armenians killed by the Turks, the millions murdered or imprisoned by Stalin and his henchmen, and most recently the Bosnian Muslims, to mention but a small selection. The inhabitants of London and Coventry, who were killed or maimed during the Blitz had it coming to them and of course the same is true of the Germans who perished as the result of the British air raids; not only the pro-Nazis among them, but also those who courageously opposed the Nazi regime. In December 1993 a crazed gunman opened fire on the passengers of a Long Island Railroad train, killing five and seriously injuring many others, some of whom are permanently paralyzed. All these victims deserved their fates. I will add one more of the morally outrageous consequences of Karma. Contrary to what almost everybody believed and believes, the seven astronauts who perished in the *Challenger* space shuttle in 1986 were entirely responsible for their deaths, and the grief felt by millions of people all over the world was quite out of place. The reckless NASA officials whom the Rogers Commission found to be responsible for the *Challenger* explosion were in fact (not consciously, of course) only executing the ordinances of Karma. The case of the astronauts illustrates particularly well the completely *post hoc* procedure of the Karmic theorists. Is there the slightest empirical evidence that the seven astronauts who died were morally any worse than the astronauts who did not participate in the mission and were thus spared? Of course there is no such evidence. The only reason a Karmic theorist would or could give is that they in fact died while the others are alive. Returning to the Jews and their Nazi exterminators, it would seem that, since the Jews deserved extinction, the Nazis were not really criminals and should not have been prosecuted. I assume that Eichmann deserved to be hanged since he *was* hanged, but the many Nazis who escaped deserved to escape. Speaking of executions, the main argument against the death penalty evidently collapses if the Law of Karma is true. For in that case no innocent man can ever be executed. People may indeed be innocent of the crime with which they are charged, but if they are executed this is what they deserved. It makes one dizzy.

Karma and a Fair Starting Point

It has been argued that unless we believe in Karma we cannot really blame anybody for his crimes and more generally for his evil deeds. *Early Western Buddhists,* a collection of extracts from articles published in *The Buddhist Review* between 1909 and 1914, reprints a piece by Ernest R. Carlos who is described as a "scientific writer" and who held M.A. and B.S. degrees. In discussing the Christian belief in "original sin and future punishment" Carlos remarks that "it is difficult to conceive how a man can be responsible for a sin in which he had no share."[13] He then very plausibly explains why Christians and Jews have no convincing answer to the criminal who disclaims responsibility for his acts:

> What answer can be given to the criminal, who, in reply to our exhortation to love justice and kindness says, "How can I help being so? Blame him who has put me in bad surroundings. I was born in a slum, brought up by drunkards, heard little more than curses and filthy language in my youth, and was taught nothing that was noble. Can you wonder that I am wicked? I was not so fortunate as you, who, through no merit of your own, were placed among refined people full of tenderness, giving you everything you wanted, and offering you no daily temptations to steal. I had not your education, why blame me? Blame my environment."[14]

There is some merit in this challenge, but it would be more appropriate to speak

---

13. Francis Story (Ed.), *Early Western Buddhists* (Kandy, Ceylon, 1962), p. 14.
14. Ibid., p. 13.

of fairness than of justice. The complaint is that the universe as conceived by "material science" is not fair while the karmic universe is fair. I think that the first part of this claim is correct, but the second is not. In a hundred-meter race all runners start from the same line and in a tennis match there is no opening score, i.e., both players start at zero. This is fair and those of us who believe that our present life is the only one we have are indeed stuck with an unfair universe in which the "contestants" do not start at the same line or in which not all players start at zero.

It is easy to see that the karmic believer is in no better position. In each incarnation, on his view, people are rewarded and punished for what they did in their current life or in previous lives, but there is no suggestion that they ever began in equally favorable or unfavorable environments or for that matter with equally advantageous or disadvantageous heredity. He is replacing one unfair universe with an infinite number of unfair universes.

How Karma Consoles a Grieving Mother

Quincy Howe, the Christian reincarnationist whom we met in Chapter 2, is convinced that the believer in Karma is able to provide consolation where the Christian and also, needless to say, the unbeliever must fail: "What can the Christian pastor say to the mother of a defective child?"[15] What—here I am no longer quoting Howe—could he say to the mother of the six-year-old girl mentioned in the previous chapter who was smashed up by a van as she and her mother were walking to school? All the Christian pastor can say is that "the counsels of God are hidden from man, so that he may learn to grow in faith."[16]

Howe is surely right: The Christian pastor, the Jewish pastor, and the unbeliever can speak nothing but platitudes which are totally devoid of consoling power. The implication is that the believer in Karma can do better, since his doctrine introduces "an element of reason and logic" into *all* situations, including those of the deformed and the maimed child and, of course, all the other victims of apparently senseless suffering. Howe does not spell out what the karmic pastor can say to the mother but I will do it on his behalf: "It all makes sense—your child deserved her fate; she sinned in a previous life, and in view of the severity of her suffering we may assume that her sins were enormous. What is more, you yourself are acutely suffering and there is no doubt that you are being punished for some serious transgressions either in this or an earlier life or both. You can see that, as always, justice prevails." It may be questioned whether the mother would be consoled by this speech. If I were the mother and a baseball bat were handy, I would hit the karmic pastor over the head and, as he screams in pain, I would say: "You deserve your pain not because of a sin in a previous life but because you are a monster right now. You see that justice has prevailed."

---

15. *Reincarnation for the Christian,* op. cit., p. 32.
16. Ibid.

I do not know any Buddhist pastors but my guess is that most of them would not have the heart to make such a revolting speech to the grieving mother. It is one thing to state a cruel doctrine in general terms and quite another to apply it to particular cases. Religious believers are often much kinder than the teachings of their religion. Most Christian sects condemn suicide as a terrible sin, but, except for a few deranged preachers, even very religious Christians do not in practice blame or denounce people who committed suicide but on the contrary react with sympathy and compassion. For all I know there may be karmic fanatics who would really tell a grieving mother that it is all her fault and the fault of the child. The tough statements by Professor Prabhu and Christmas Humphreys, quoted earlier suggest that they were quite capable of such an outrage. What amazes me about such people is their smug dogmatism and their colossal arrogance. They "know," and are completely certain of things that *cannot* be known, and their "knowledge" is not harmless because it is made the basis for vicious conduct. To such fanatics one can only quote the words (suitably adjusted) of Oliver Cromwell in a letter he wrote to the General Assembly of the Church of Scotland: "I beseech you, in the bowels of Gautama, think it possible you may be mistaken."

I have been told that even if reincarnation is nonsense and if there is not the slightest reason for supposing that the child's handicaps are punishment for her or the mother's misdeeds, the pastor would still be doing something valuable. It is said that nothing is more difficult to bear than a disaster that has no moral meaning and that the mother would be less distraught if she could attribute the child's misfortune to misdeeds in a previous life. I doubt that this would be true of most human beings, but even if it were, it would not justify one blaming her or the child in the absence of concrete evidence. It may be that there are people in the world whose guilt feelings would be appeased by being sentenced to death or at least incarcerated when in fact they committed no crimes. It would be quite wrong to execute or incarcerate them even then, simply because they are innocent. Simone Weil, the French mystic, felt a tremendous need to undergo intense suffering. "Every time I pass a picture of Jesus on the cross," she once remarked, "I get green with envy." She eventually starved herself to death which was her good right, but it would have been quite wrong for others to torture or crucify her.

Returning to the main topic of this section, the bottom line is that the world *is* cruel and unjust, a fact which is very difficult to accept. We do not make the world better but we make it worse by blaming the victims.

"Cosmic" Claims

My discussion of Karma would be incomplete without saying a few words about certain "cosmic" claims found in the writings of reincarnationists. It is commonly asserted that all lawful connections in the universe are really "nothing more" than instances of Karma. Dr. Raynor Johnson, the Christian reincarnationist mentioned

17. *The Imprisoned Splendor*, p. 388.

earlier, writes that "the law of cause and effect, as we know it in the material world," is really "nothing more than a special case" of the Law of Karma.[17] Again, it has been claimed—and perhaps this is what Dr. Johnson had in mind—that the same tendency to restore balance or equilibrium that appropriate punishments and rewards exemplify is found throughout the universe. In a rather haughty note in the *Aryan Review* of October 1936, in which the editor offers advice to the author of the preceding article, the author being none other than A. J. Ayer, we are assured that "Karma is an undeviating and unerring tendency in the universe to restore equilibrium." It "operates incessantly" and, what is more, "it operates on all things and beings from the minutest conceivable atom to the highest of human souls."[18] According to Quincy Howe, Karma "is the inevitable succession of cause and effect that governs existence at all levels."[19] L. H. Leslie-Smith, a former member of the editorial staff of the *London Times* and a disciple of Madame Blavatsky, is emphatic that Karma does not only "adjust all our relationships," but also "keeps the stars on their courses and every atom in being."[20] All such claims are open to the criticism that, if they are interpreted in a straightforward way, they are simply absurd and, if they are interpreted in such a way as to avoid absurdity, they say absolutely nothing. If it is maintained that the lawful behavior of molecules, mountains, or planets are instances of rewards and punishments, this is plainly absurd, since molecules, planets, and mountains cannot perform good or evil deeds. If, to avoid this absurdity, "Karma" is taken in a broader sense in which it is simply a synonym for "lawfulness" or "regularity," then calling the various laws of nature instances of Karma is saying nothing at all. It is plain that we do not understand the regularities of the world any better and nothing whatever has been added to the content of any known law. Calling natural regularities instances of Karma is about as enlightening as describing them as manifestations of the Absolute Mind or as instances of the dialectical interplay of Being and Non-Being.

---

18. *The Aryan Review*, 1936, p. 450.
19. Op. cit., p. 30.
20. "Karma and Reincarnation," in V. Hanson and R. Stewart (Eds.), *Karma—The Universal Law of Harmony*, p. 52.

4

Child Prodigies, Déjà Vu Experiences, and Group Reincarnations

Child Prodigies, Homosexuality and Other "Unexplained" Facts

The arguments discussed in this chapter are of a quasi-scientific nature. Various empirical facts are enumerated, and it is claimed that they cannot be adequately explained in terms of natural or, more specifically, biological causes. Only an explanation along reincarnationist lines is plausible. Existence in one or more previous lives is here advanced as an explanatory hypothesis. Since the structure of these arguments resembles that of many arguments in the sciences, it is tempting to call them "scientific," but since reincarnation is most emphatically not a testable or falsifiable theory I will refer to them as "quasi-scientific." Among the facts frequently mentioned in this connection, both by Western and Eastern believers, are "infant geniuses" and remarkably precocious performances generally, the so-called déjà vu experiences, love at first sight and striking differences between children of the same parents.

The prize case of Western reincarnationists is that of the Irish mathematician Sir William Hamilton (1805–1865) who, in addition to stupendous mathematical feats at a very young age, had mastered no less than thirteen languages by the time he reached adolescence. These included not only modern languages like French, German, Italian, and Spanish but also Persian, Arabic, Sanskrit, Hindustani, and Malay. There are also of course the cases of musical geniuses like Mozart, Schubert, and Mendelssohn who composed some of the world's greatest music at a very early age. Referring to a girl who, although coming from a quite unremarkable family, conducted the London Philharmonic Orchestra in a difficult program at the age of eight, Leslie Weatherhead asks the question:

48

Is it an accidental group of genes that makes a little girl of eight a musician far in advance of grown men and women, who have slaved for many years in that field?[1]

Returning to Sir William Hamilton, he asks if it is nothing more than "a piece of luck that a boy of fourteen can write perfect Persian?" If the answer is in the affirmative then life is "unjust as well as chancy." Fortunately the answer is not in the affirmative. It seems evident to Weatherhead that these child prodigies acquired their skills and knowledge in a previous life, and he quotes Plato's *Meno* as supporting this conclusion.

Homosexuality is not usually regarded as requiring an explanation in reincarnationist terms, but at least one writer, a very famous one, was convinced that no other explanation is adequate. In E. D. Walker's *Reincarnation: A Study of Forgotten Truth*, which was published in 1888 and has frequently been reprinted, Louisa M. Alcott, the author of *Little Women*, is quoted as saying, "I must have been masculine [in my previous life] because my love is all for girls." I am not aware that any male homosexual has offered this kind of explanation for his sexual orientation, but if it is true for lesbians there seems to be no reason why it should not equally hold for their male counterparts.

Many other puzzling facts seem to lend themselves to the same treatment. How are we to explain the characteristic differences between the English and the French? According to one of my favorite theosophists, Irving S. Cooper, the English display a "tendency toward colonization," a "lawmaking instinct," a thoroughness in every undertaking, and a "massive style of architecture." These admirable characteristics, it must be noted with regret, are accompanied by a "sacrificing of beauty to utility and strength" and a "lack of imagination in art, religion, and philosophy." In France it is just the opposite. There is very little interest in colonization and no lawmaking instinct worth mentioning. However, the French have an "imaginative touch," a love of beauty, a "worship of form and expression," and a special "intellectual keenness." There is only one way of accounting for these differences in "racial" characteristics. May it not be, writes Cooper, in what is a purely rhetorical question, "that in a mass the egos of Greece have taken incarnation in France, the egos of Rome in England?"[2]

There are many other pearls in Cooper's remarkable book. He calls attention to the fact that great painters, composers, and writers frequently come in clusters. It is surely significant that "the founders of music" lived around the same time, an idea that Cooper obscurely expresses by telling us that all of them were "born in a singular way." He then enumerates the founders of modern music:

First came Handel and Bach, then Mendelssohn, Mozart and Beethoven, and lastly, in quick succession, a large group composed of Schubert, Chopin, Schumann, Liszt, Wagner, Rubinstein, Brahms, and Grieg.[3]

---

1. *The Christian Agnostic*, p. 300.
2. *Reincarnation—A Hope of the World*, p. 67.
3. Op. cit., p. 68.

Cooper's chronology is slightly off in the case of Mendelssohn, and there is much else about his list that is defective. Be this as it may, another "suggestive phenomenon" that cries out for explanation is the "appearance of an isolated group of American writers" all of whom were "born together in one section of the United States, and many of them, later on, became intimate friends."[4] The most important members of this group were Bryant, Emerson, Longfellow, Whittier, Poe, Thoreau, Whitman, and Lowell. These remarkable clusters suggest the thought that "life after life, groups of intimate friends and co-workers incarnate together to continue their activities." For all we can tell such group incarnations of composers and writers are going on right now. How can we be sure, for example, that Norman Mailer is not Charles Dickens, Saul Bellow William Thackeray, Phillip Roth Henry James, and Susan Sontag George Eliot?

I do not doubt that the same applies to philosophers and that there is reason to believe that Russell, Moore, and Whitehead were the reincarnations of Socrates, Plato, and Aristotle. A sojourn of over two thousand years in the astral world, although considerably longer than the average, is not by any means unique and would seem to be appropriate in the circumstances, given the extensive preparation that was required for their work in the new incarnation. I personally cannot see how *Principia Mathematica* could ever have been completed if Russell and Whitehead had not started on it long before they were born.

Some of the writers just quoted are a delight, but their arguments are incredibly flimsy. Most reincarnationists know absolutely nothing about science and they do not show the slightest interest in remedying their ignorance. The authors of the quasi-scientific arguments evidently work with a pre-Mendelian, "common sense" theory of genetics holding that all features in an offspring must have been exhibited in one or both parents. It appears that they have heard neither of recessive genes nor of mutations. The differences between siblings are in part due to environmental influences (no two children are treated exactly alike by their parents or by other people), but they are undoubtedly in large measure genetic. There is nothing here in the least inconsistent with contemporary genetic theory.

Love at first sight and instant or almost instant likes and dislikes have not been studied in any systematic way by psychologists, but I think few people cannot give at least a partial account of what draws them to or repels them from certain individuals. Those familiar with Reichian psychiatry know that deeply rooted emotional attitudes like contempt, disgust, sadism, and many more are revealed by various chronic muscle-tensions, some of them in the face, especially in the eyes, the chin, and the mouth. People who know nothing about psychiatry nevertheless perceive these chronic expressions and this at least in part accounts for their instantaneous reactions.

The case for reincarnation seems to be strongest when we come to child prodigies. For here it must be admitted that so far genetics and psychology have told us very little that is specific. Nevertheless the reincarnationist argument is also quite

---

4. Ibid.

worthless in this case. There is not the slightest reason to suppose that to explain the extraordinary gifts of men like Mozart or William Hamilton we have to go outside a study of the human brain. It should be remembered that in spite of the impressive progress of recent years, brain research is still in its infancy. I think very few brain researchers have any serious doubts that with further improvements in our instrumentation we will be able to shed much light on these problems. It seems entirely plausible, for example, that Mozart's auditory cortex was in certain ways significantly different from that of people lacking his gifts. To foreclose further research in this area would be utterly defeatist. To substitute an explanation in terms of the acquisition of musical skill in an earlier life—for which there is not the slightest positive evidence—would be like abandoning medical research into the causes of cancer and substituting theological speculation on the ground that medical science has so far provided us with only a very limited understanding of cancer. Even if a thousand or ten thousand years from now researchers have not come up with a satisfactory theory, this would in no way support a reincarnationist explanation. It would only show that up to then no naturalistic explanation had been discovered. It would not and could not show that none is possible.

Déjà Vu Experiences

The term "déjà vu experience" was introduced into psychological literature by F. L. Arnauld in 1896,[5] but the phenomenon itself has of course been familiar for many centuries. We meet somebody for the first time and are positive that we have met this person before, or we visit a new city and the scenes seem quite familiar. Several novelists have offered vivid descriptions of déjà vu experiences. The following is a diary entry by Sir Walter Scott dated February 17, 1828:

> I cannot, I am sure, tell if it is worth marking down, that yesterday, at dinner time, I was strangely haunted by what I would call the sense of preexistence, viz., a confused idea that nothing that passed was said for the first time; that the same topics had been discussed and the same persons had stated the same opinions on them."[6]

A similar passage occurs in Chapter 39 of Dickens's *David Copperfield*:

> We have all some experience of a feeling that comes over us occasionally of what we are saying and doing having been said and done before, in a remote time—of our having been surrounded, dim ages ago, by the same faces, objects, and circumstances—of our knowing perfectly what will be said next as if we suddenly remembered it.

---

5. R. E. Guley, *Harper's Encyclopedia of Mystical and Paranormal Experiences*, p. 144.
6. Quoted in E. D. Walker, *Reincarnation: A Study of Forgotten Truths*, p. 37.

The reality and the frequency of déjà vu experiences can hardly be questioned. What can be questioned is whether they support reincarnationism. By no means all reincarnationists have regarded them as evidence. Professor Ducasse rejected the appeal to déjà vu experiences outright. Ian Stevenson, too, does not accept this argument but, as is usual with him in the case of arguments he finds inadequate, he sees some significant merits in it.[7] The tabloid philosophers, however, have pounced upon these experiences as impressive evidence and so has Dr. Elisabeth Kübler-Ross who never hears of an argument for any kind of life after death that she does not wholeheartedly endorse. I should mention in passing that Dr. Kübler-Ross is probably the most uncritical person in the history of the world compared with whom the most dogmatic Christian and Jewish theologians of the Middle Ages are veritable doubting Thomases. She has said that she once was a skeptic. Perhaps, but this must have been in another life. Anyhow, here is what she says about déjà vu experiences:

> Many people have had encounters with a fellow-man who seemed to them so familiar, as if they had known each other for decades and not just for a brief moment. And they often say jokingly, "Maybe we have been together in another lifetime." If they only knew how true this is in many cases. Many of us have gone to faraway places on this planet earth and had a feeling of déjà vu, a sense of recognizing a place and being totally aware of details in a way that no one could explain scientifically. Yet, it is often a re-recognition of a place where we have spent time in a previous physical existence.[8]

Aside from the tabloid philosophers and Kübler-Ross, several midbrow reincarnationists like Raynor Johnson and Leslie Weatherhead have supported the déjà vu argument. Johnson has reported a rather elaborate case that has frequently been quoted. It concerns the "amazing experience" of a married couple he met in Australia:

> The lady had many psychic experiences by which she felt certain that none of her girlhood's boy friends would have any special significance for her, but that if she waited, her true mate would turn up. When she was in her middle thirties, she met her present husband at a public function, and both had an overwhelming and simultaneous conviction that, in an earlier life, they had been man and wife. They have now been happily married for over twenty-five years and both are convinced that this is their second incarnation. A year or two before meeting her husband, the lady had a vivid waking-dream of being in bed after the birth of a child whom she never saw. In the dream, her husband had to leave her in this distress to go on a forlorn and dangerous expedition on behalf of his king. The poignancy of parting was terrible, and in the waking-dream—experienced, let me repeat, a year or so before she met her husband—the lady wept bitterly. When she met her husband, she knew that he was the father of this child and the hero of this dream.[9]

---

7. *Children Who Remember Previous Lives,* pp 47–48.
8. Foreword to J. Head and S. L. Cranston (Eds.), *Reincarnation: The Phoenix Fire Mystery*, p. ix.
9. *The Imprisoned Splendor*. Johnson also offers a less enthusiastic version of this case in *A Religious Outlook for Modern Man*, p. 181.

Leslie Weatherhead vouches for the existence of this married couple to whom Raynor Johnson introduced him in Melbourne. Unfortunately all the participants are dead and can no longer be interviewed.

It is of some interest to note that C. J. Jung had a déjà vu experience which moved him profoundly. It occurred while he was traveling in Africa in the 1920s:

> The train, swathed in a red cloud of dust, was just making a turn around a steep red cliff. On a jagged rock above us a slim, brownish-black figure stood motionless, leaning on a long spear, looking down at the train. Beside him towered a gigantic candelabrum cactus.

Jung tells us that he was enchanted by the sight and he spoke of it as a "most intense *sentiment du déjà vu*":

> I had the feeling that I had already experienced this moment and had always known this world which was separated from me only by distance in time. It was as if I were at this moment returning to the land of my youth, and as if I knew that dark-skinned man who had been waiting for me for five thousand years.[10]

A little later he refers to the experience as a "recognition of the immemorially known" and he concludes his account with what seems to be an endorsement of reincarnation:

> I could not guess what string within myself was plucked at the sight of that solitary dark hunter. I knew only that his world had been mine for countless millennia.[11]

Jung was certainly a friend of the occult, but it is not at all clear that he believed in reincarnation. Some commentators have interpreted him as referring to the collective unconscious in which memories are stored and to whose content we occasionally have access. All of this is exceedingly vague and there seems to be no reason to bring in the collective unconscious, a dubious concept at best, to account for Jung's experience.

A famous American who had powerful déjà vu experiences was General George S. Patton, Jr., who is now remembered primarily for his brilliance as a military strategist and for two unfortunate episodes in North Africa when he slapped shell-shocked soldiers. It is not so well known that Patton possessed a variety of supernatural gifts which, he was certain had been passed on to him by his paternal grandmother, a lady with stunning precognitive powers. Apparitions were one of Patton's specialties. During a battle in France in the First World War Patton was lying on his belly, scared to death, hardly daring to lift his head. At this stage the faces of his late grandfather and several granduncles appeared urging "Georgie" to stop being a coward. Georgie thereupon got up, drew his gun, and started giving commands. Needless to say, the battle was won. It is

---

10. *Memories, Dreams, Reflections*, p. 254.
11. Op. cit., p. 255.

not generally known that Patton's intercession with the deity caused the Allied victory in the Battle of the Bulge in January of 1945. Severe rainfalls were making a counteroffensive by the American and British troops impossible. To change the weather, Patton ordered a prayer to be recited in which the "Almighty and most merciful Father" was beseeched to "restrain these immoderate rains" so that the American army could "crush the oppression and wickedness of our enemies." Moved by the fervor of this plea, the Almighty caused the rains to stop and the fogs to lift. The sun shone clearly the next day, and the Allied forces went on to score a decisive victory. It is rather astonishing that Patton's fateful prayer is not mentioned in a single history of World War II.

All this is by way of preface to Patton's déjà vu experiences. Patton was a lifelong believer in reincarnation, occasionally expressing his views in memorable verse. Fred Ayer, Jr., Patton's nephew and biographer, once asked him if he really believed in reincarnation. Patton answered that he could not speak for other people but that he "damn well knew" that he had lived before. During World War I, when he took over his first command at Langres in France, a young French liaison officer offered to show him around since Patton had never been in Langres. It turned out that there was no need for this. Without any assistance from the French officer, Patton told the driver how to get to the Roman Amphitheater, the drill ground, the Forum, and the Temples of Mars and Apollo. He even showed the officer the spot where Caesar had pitched his tent. It was evident that Patton had been in this place in a previous life. In addition to living a previous life as a Roman legionnaire, Patton had also been a Greek hoplite, a cavalryman with Bellisarius, a highlander with the House of Stuart, and a trooper with Napoleon.[12]

We found Dr. Kübler-Ross declaring with total assurance that "no one can explain déjà vu experiences scientifically." She obviously knows absolutely nothing about the extensive scientific literature on the subject. In the chapter on memory in his great *Principles of Psychology* (1890) William James discusses déjà vu experiences in some detail although without using the words "déjà vu." He notes that the "sense of preexistence" which attaches to such experiences "has been treated as a great mystery and occasioned much speculation."[13] James offers two nonmystical explanations. The first is a commonsense explanation that unquestionably covers a great many cases. The "recognized" scene or person closely resembles one he have seen before but in our memory we fail to distinguish the two. As soon as the mem-

---

12. This account is based on Fred Ayer, Jr., *Before the Colors Fade—Portrait of a Soldier, George S. Patton, Jr.* (Dunwoody, Georgia, 1971), M. Blumenson, *Patton: The Man Behind the Legend* (New York, 1985) and on Carlo d'Este, *A Genius for War: A Life of General Patton* (New York, 1955). The last of these, which is the most comprehensive and carefully researched biography, mentions several other exciting incarnations. I gather that Ayer did not take Patton's tale about his déjà vu experience in Langres very seriously. The following is a sample of Patton's poetry as reprinted by Ayer:

> And now again I am here for war
> Where as Roman and knight I have been.
> Again I practice to fight the Hun
> And attack him by machine.

13. William James, *Principles of Psychology*, Vol. 2, p. 675.

ory of the past experience becomes more distinct "the emotion of weirdness fades from the experience." The other is a physiological explanation published as early as 1844 by the English physician Wijan in his book *The Duality of Mind*. According to Wijan, déjà vu experiences are due to a "disassociation of the action of the brain's two hemispheres, one of them becoming conscious a little later than the other, but both of the same fact."[14] More recent investigators have come up with explanations very similar to Wijan's. One theory reported by Arthur Reber in the Penguin *Dictionary of Psychology* (1985) maintains that these experiences are "due to a kind of momentary neural 'short circuit' so that the impression of the scene arrives at the memory store [metaphorically speaking] before it registers in the sensorium."[15] Reber adds that although this theory is not proved there is some evidence for it since déjà vu experiences are known to be symptomatic of certain kinds of brain damage. I do not feel competent to evaluate the soundness of this theory or of other physiological theories that have been proposed since the subject began to be seriously studied. Suffice it to say that none of the investigators regards reincarnation as a candidate in the running.[16]

It must be conceded that neither the physiological theories nor James's commonsense explanation could account for an elaborate scenario like that of the Australian lady and her husband. Unfortunately we only possess the report by Johnson and Weatherhead's confirmation that he met the couple. The case has not been investigated by skeptics like Susan Blackmore, Melvin Harris or Ian Wilson. My guess is that such an investigation would have revealed it to be an instance of the Ritchie-Wilmot syndrome.[17] It would have turned out that the "facts" are not quite what Raynor Johnson reported them to be. Unlike the tabloid philosophers, Raynor Johnson and Leslie Weatherhead appear to have been thoroughly honest men, but there is reason to believe that neither was sufficiently critical when it came to judging psychic claims. I do not doubt that several of the cases exposed by Blackmore, Harris, Wilson, and other skeptical investigators as fraudulent or otherwise worthless would have been passed by Johnson and Weatherhead. On the flimsiest evidence Johnson accepted the astral body and Weatherhead, just two pages before his endorsement of the case of the Australian lady, referred to Joan Grant, a well-known British psychic, who, among many other things, was an Egyptian princess in an earlier life. Weatherhead tells us that he had "discussed the matter with her" and found the story entirely convincing. I should add that I was relieved to hear that the marriage of the Australian

14. *Duality of the Mind*, p. 84, quoted by James, op. cit., p. 675.

15. *Dictionary of Psychology*, p. 183.

16. Freud discusses déjà vu experiences in several places, most fully in the last chapter of *The Psychopathology of Everyday Life*. He asserts that these experience "correspond to the recollections of unconscious fantasies." Very possibly there is something to this claim, but the notion of an unconscious fantasy would need to be clarified—something Freud does not do—before it can be evaluated.

17. The cases of Mr. and Mrs. Wilmot and Dr. George Ritchie are discussed in detail in Chapter 9. Susan Blackmore deserves the credit for unearthing the real facts of the former case. My discussion of Dr. Ritchie shows, among other things, the bogus nature of his "corroborations." Ian Wilson and Melvin Harris are among the writers showing the worthlessness of various hypnotic regressions (see Chapters 5 and 6).

lady and her dream-hero turned out to be happy. My experience with ladies who receive "psychic" messages would have made me expect the opposite.

Reincarnation and the God-of-the-Gaps

Reincarnationists, at least those who know a little science, constantly look for gaps in existing scientific explanations, which reincarnation is then supposed to fill. Thus, in a section entitled "The Limits of Genetic and Environmental Explanations," of *Children Who Remember Previous Lives,* Stevenson, who is one of the worst offenders on this score, discusses the causes of schizophrenia and of differences in personality. He expresses his dissatisfaction with existing theories:

> The advocates of genetics and of environmental influences have in common that each thinks of the other party as the only adversary; claims are made and faults are found by members of both groups without any awareness that a third explanation for the gaps in knowledge awaits further examination.[18]

Not only schizophrenia and personality differences but also the choice of career by certain famous men and women cannot be adequately accounted for in terms of either heredity or environment. George Frederick Handel, for example, had parents who were strongly opposed to his becoming a musician. He did have a maternal aunt who encouraged him but it "taxes credulity to suggest that her covert support was sufficient to counteract his parents' wishes in the matter unless some other influence had been in play."[19] Something similar was true of Elizabeth Fry, the prison reformer, and Florence Nightingale, the founder of modern nursing. In the case of Heinrich Schliemann, the great archeologist who excavated Troy, and Jean François Champollion, the founder of Egyptology, the problem is not opposition on the part of parents but the extremely early age at which the profession was chosen. Schliemann, Stevenson tells us, was less than eight years old when he announced his choice,[20] Champollion not yet twelve. In these two cases it is "the extremely early manifestation of an intense interest in a subject" that seems to call for "some factor in addition to heredity and an environmental support." Stevenson observes that so far as he knows none of these persons had memories of a previous life. However, if reincarnation occurs, behavior may be "carried over from one life to another without corresponding imaged memories." And since no other explanation is at hand for the unusual interest shown

---

18. P. 205.

19. "The Explanatory Value of the Idea of Reincarnation" *Journal of Nervous and Mental Diseases,* 1977, p. 313.

20. Stevenson evidently accepted Schliemann's account in his autobiography. This has been questioned by recent biographers. David A. Traill in his meticulously researched *Schliemann of Troy* (1995) dismissed Schliemann's statement about his interest in excavation at the age of eight as pure fiction.

in childhood, "reincarnation is at least worthy of consideration as a possible explanation."[21]

All of this is preposterous. Human beings are extremely complex and the influences on them, both obvious and subtle, are huge in number and of the most various kinds. If we could have watched Handel from minute to minute, which no biographer did, we would be much nearer to an explanation of why he became a composer. However, without access to his inner thoughts and feelings and, more important, to what was going on in his brain, our explanation would still be incomplete. If we had this access and, on the assumption that brain physiology had reached a very advanced level, most of our puzzlement would surely disappear. Even then there might be some gap in our account simply because our knowledge of the relevant psychological and physiological factors would be very extensive but not total. All this equally applies to the other celebrities on Stevenson's list. These reflections are sufficient to show that there is no need to bring in reincarnation or any other occult causes.

Stevenson is clearly guilty of what has been called the God-of-the-gap fallacy. It used to be the practice of believers to bring in God as an explanation of facts that science had not yet explained—the origin of consciousness, of the human race, and especially of life. Such a practice is both illogical and self-defeating. It is illogical because from ignorance one cannot infer any positive conclusion and it is self-defeating because sooner or later scientists are liable to come up with the answer and then the believer who adopted this stance will look foolish. [22]

This brings me to the most basic objection to reincarnationist attempts to offer explanations of *any* phenomena. Reincarnation is put forward in this context as a scientific hypothesis, but it can be shown—and I shall try to show this in detail in chapter 15—that it is nothing of the kind. If this is so and if reincarnation is not an empirical or scientific hypothesis but a metaphysical theory, then, whatever value it may have, it *cannot* be a competitor to genuine scientific hypotheses and it cannot explain empirical facts in the sense that is relevant here. A simple illustration will make this clear. Mr. X, a notoriously vicious person, suddenly collapses and dies. We want to find out why he died. Somebody answers that he was a sinner, that God was fed up with him and therefore eliminated him from the world. Let us grant that this is true. It still does not explain X's death in a scientific way. We were inquiring into the medical cause of his death. Did he die of a cerebral hemorrhage, a sudden heart attack, or perhaps an overdose of cocaine? Did he take Tylenol capsules laced with cyanide? To our *empirical* question concerning X's death, the statement about God's decision to eliminate the malefactor is no answer at all. A coroner who happens to be a religious man and who in fact believes in this theological claim would not enter such a nonempirical explanation into his report. It is exactly the same with questions about the cause of ge-

---

21. Ibid., op cit pp. 313–314.

22. I am not sure who first used the phrase "God-of-the-gaps." I first came across it in Bishop John A. T. Robinson's *Honest to God* (London, 1963), who seems to have derived it from writings of Rudolf Bultmann and Dietrich Bonhoeffer.

nius, déjà vu experiences, love at first sight, and all of the other phenomena for which reincarnation is supposed to be the best explanation. Reincarnation may or may not have value as a metaphysical theory, but it cannot compete with physiological, genetic, and psychological theories as a scientific explanation of *any* facts.

Perhaps one further observation on the origin of the special skills and aptitudes of a child genius like Mozart may help to clarify this issue. Reincarnationists are in the habit of talking very vaguely about the soul's acquiring skills and knowledge in a previous life and taking these along into the next incarnation. One must pin them down and inquire about the "mechanics" of this transmission. Let us assume that, before it came to inhabit the body of Wolfgang Amadeus, the soul of Mozart lived in the body of Heinrich Hanauer and that it was during that incarnation that it acquired the knowledge passed on to the Mozart body. I think that reincarnationists who are not altogether lost to some fantastic form of occultism will admit that the transmission from the Hanauer to the Mozart body occurred via the brain and nervous system of the new embryo. If they admit this they have tacitly admitted that Mozart's special ability is due to certain features of his brain that are not present in the brains of other human beings. Reincarnation has in a sense become redundant. It will no doubt be replied that reincarnation is still necessary to account for the special features of Mozart's brain. However, if we have reason to believe in what I call the "sufficiency" of genetics and embryology, this will take care of the last reincarnationist stand. I will discuss this issue in Chapter 15.

5

The Rise and Fall of Bridey Murphy

What I have called "spontaneous" memories of past lives are relatively rare. Even in countries like India, where large segments of the population believe in reincarnation, only a handful of people claim to remember an earlier existence. Recollections of earlier lives under hypnosis on the other hand are quite common. Hypnotic regressions can be very impressive when the subject displays knowledge of historical details which—so it would seem—she could not have learned through normal channels. In this and the succeeding chapter, both of which are devoted to hypnotic regressions, I will first discuss the Bridey Murphy case whose subject has been described in the Time-Life book *Psychic Voyages* as the "all-time superstar"[1] among people who have been regressed. The Bridey Murphy case still has some champions but I will show that it is utterly worthless as evidence for reincarnation. It did, however, possess the merit of stimulating research into the sources of the "remarkable" knowledge displayed by some hypnotic subjects and I will briefly summarize the results of this research. In chapter 6 I will deal with the interplanetary past-life regressions and other occult performances by Sir Alexander Cannon, a pioneer to whom Morey Bernstein, the author of *The Search for Bridey Murphy*, called our attention. Sir Alexander was one of Bernstein's predecessors and in the following section I will discuss various later Brideys, many of them the work of H. N. Banerjee, a holy man from India who for a number of years was the leading regressionist in this country. Shirley MacLaine did not regress by means of hypnosis, but the present book would be incomplete without an account of her beheading by Louis XV in the eighteenth century. This is followed by an exhilarating British case reported in *Reincarnation International*. In this case Jenny Cockell, an English housewife, discovered the children

---

1. *Psychic Voyages,* p. 114.

of her previous life, all of whom are considerably older than she, thus disproving the widely held view that a mother must be older than her children. In the section entitled "Futurology" I report on the exploration of the future by means of hypnosis. The pioneers of this line of research are the late Helen Wambach, an American psychologist; Chet Snow, Wambach's spiritual heir, who in 1983 "witnessed" the invasion of West Germany by Soviet troops in 1997; and Bruce Goldberg, an ex-dentist from Baltimore, who has hypnotically explored the world as it will be in the year 2542 and who has cured present disturbances by tracing their root to future traumas. In the last section of Chapter 6 I discuss "past life therapy," a largely fraudulent form of psychotherapy, which does, however, occasionally appear to achieve some results.

Virginia Tighe and Bridey Murphy

This case goes back to the early 1950s and nobody who was alive when the book about it came out in early 1956 is likely to forget the mania that swept both the United States and several other countries at that time. Between November 1952 and October 1953 a Colorado businessman by the name of Morey Bernstein, an amateur hypnotist and a believer in reincarnation, conducted six hypnotic sessions with Virginia Tighe, a twenty-nine-year-old housewife. The sessions were taped and several witnesses, including Virginia's husband, Hugh Tighe, attended them. Virginia proved an excellent hypnotic subject and Bernstein had no difficulty putting her into a deep trance. After no more than minimal suggestions to go back to the period before her birth and describe "scenes from faraway lands and distant places" Virginia began to speak in a soft Irish brogue. During this and the succeeding sessions she identified herself as Bridey Murphy, born in 1798 in the Irish town of Cork to a Protestant barrister, Duncan Murphy, and his wife, Kathleen. She describes her conventional schooling and her marriage at the age of twenty to Sean Brian Joseph MacCarthy, the son of another Cork barrister. After a Protestant ceremony in Cork, the couple went through a second Catholic wedding in Belfast conducted by Father John Joseph Gorman at St. Theresa's Church. Bridey agreed to the Catholic ceremony to please Brian and his family and she also agreed that any children they might have would be raised as Catholics. She herself did not convert. The couple had no children and Bridey's life appears to have been singularly drab and uneventful. Brian became a barrister and after 1847 he also taught at Queens University in Belfast. Throughout their marriage Bridey and Brian resided on Dooley Road in Belfast. In her early sixties Bridey had a bad fall breaking some bones in her hip. From then on she became a "burden" and had to be "carried about." Brian took good care of her, but she remembered him as being extremely tired all the time. Eventually she just "withered away," dying on a Sunday in 1864 when she was sixty-six.

Bernstein as well as the others attending the sessions found several of the features of Bridey's responses overwhelmingly convincing. Her Irish brogue seemed entirely genuine. She constantly used strange Irish words and she seemed to possess a wealth of information about nineteenth-century Ireland. One episode which was particularly impressive to them concerned the "Morning Jig," an Irish dance mentioned by Virginia during one of the sessions. Bernstein gave her a posthypnotic suggestion to dance the jig after coming out of her trance. When Virginia came back, after some urging on Bernstein's part, she suddenly "became vibrantly alive" and "her feet were flying in a cute little dance." Then she looked dazed and unaware of what she had done. The episode was doubly impressive because Virginia was known to be a poor dancer. She was also not given to reading books and, according to Bernstein's account, there is no evidence that she had ever engaged in the study of Irish history and customs. When the tapes were played back to Virginia and her husband, they became convinced that her recollections were authentic. Neither had believed in reincarnation prior to the hypnotic sessions, but they could not conceive of any other explanation of the material on the tapes. "My wife and I," Hugh observed, "know all that information could not be pouring out of Virginia." He explained that they did not own an encyclopedia or any reference books and that they did not even have a library card.

The first published account of the Bridey Murphy case appeared in three installments in the *Denver Post*'s *Sunday Supplement, Empire,* in September 1954. The author was William J. Barker, the assistant editor of *Empire* who had been greatly impressed by the tapes and who in several subsequent publications defended the reincarnation explanation of Virginia Tighe's recollections. The reader response to Barker's articles suggested that they contained material for a national best seller and Doubleday contracted Bernstein to write a book on the case. *The Search for Bridey Murphy* appeared on January 5, 1956. The Tighes insisted on anonymity and were referred to as Ruth and Rex Simmons.

While Bernstein was writing his book, Doubleday approached a legal firm in Ireland in the hope of providing documentary support for the accuracy of Virginia's hypnotic memories. The Irish lawyers did not come up with any significant information, but this did not prevent Doubleday from going ahead with publication. The book instantly became a best seller. For many weeks it headed the nation's best seller lists. It was translated into five languages and had enormous sales throughout the world. By the middle of March 1956, 170,500 copies of the original hard cover edition were in print and eventually, after being reprinted as a paperback, it sold well over a million copies. *True* magazine, which has not existed for a long time, but which had a huge circulation in the 1950s, condensed the book and more than forty newspapers syndicated it. Movie rights were sold although no movie was ever produced. A twelve-inch LP with a transcription of the tape of the first Bridey Murphy session also had vast sales.

Books on reincarnation and hypnosis mentioned by Bernstein were selling briskly. Melvin Powers, the major distributor of books on hypnosis, found that his business had multiplied fifteen times over. The mania for hypnotic regression sweeping the country was described in detail in the March 15 issue of *Life* which featured a lengthy illustrated article entitled "Bridey Murphy Puts Nation in a Hypnotizzy." The article referred to Bridey Murphy costume parties ("Come As You Were") and to many new Bridey Murphy-like regressions. In California a "Mr. Hypnosis" advertised regressions for a fee of $25 per previous life. He claimed to have regressed a woman as far back as 1800 when she recalled being a horse. In Shreveport, Louisiana, a high school senior hypnotized a young woman and took her back no less than 10,000 years. The Bridey Murphy mania reached a tragic climax when a nineteen-year-old newsboy in Shawnee, Oklahoma, shot himself with a rifle leaving a note that said "I am curious about the Bridey Murphy story—so I am going to investigate the theory in person."

"A Parapsychological Classic"

The back jacket of the Pocket Book reprint of *The Search for Bridey Murphy* quotes a *New York Times* description of the book as "a parapsychological classic . . . a charming book." It also quotes the *Pittsburgh Press* whose reviewer wrote that "there is one thing you cannot do: put the book down after you have started." Such comments are quite inexplicable because *The Search for Bridey Murphy* is almost by any standards a very poor production. Far better books in defense of reincarnation—containing more substantial documentation and less flimsy arguments—have been totally ignored by the press. Reviewers who did not lose their heads correctly pointed to the extreme dreariness of Bridey's answers to Bernstein's questions. W. B. Ready, an Irish scholar who was a librarian at Leland Stanford University, wrote an amusing review in *Fantasy and Science Fiction* of August 1956. Bernstein's book, Ready wrote, pictures "an Ireland that never was, save in the minds of the uninformed and the vulgar." I quote these statements from *Fads and Fallacies* by Martin Gardner, the redoubtable foe of fraud and humbug. Gardner offered a devastating verdict on Bernstein's book. "One would be hard put," he wrote, "to find a choicer sample of an utterly worthless book designed to exploit a mass hunger for scientific evidence of life after death, or a better example of the power of modern huckstering to swindle the gullible, simple folk who take such books seriously." He also observed that the book did not sell on its literary merits, but "because readers of little faith thought that here at last was some sort of tangible 'proof' of life after death."[2] The following remarks will show that Gardner's verdict is entirely justified.

The first half of *The Search for Bridey Murphy* consists of an autobiographical account of Bernstein's journey from his early acceptance of a materialistic philosophy to his discovery of ESP, Edgar Cayce,[3] and his eventual conversion to reincar-

---

2. *Fads and Fallacies*, p. 316.

3. The following is a summary quoted from Richard Cavendish (Ed.), *Encyclopedia of the Unexplained* (London, 1976), pp. 63–64: "Edgar Cayce (1877–1945). In trance he appeared to have the ability to diagnose his own and other people's illnesses even when a patient was far distant from him—and to prescribe what were often effective, if sometimes distinctly odd, treatments. He also described people's previous lives in trance and predicted the future. He was interested in Atlantis and believed that the Atlantean

nation. At the age of fifteen, Bernstein tells us, he read Somerset Maugham's *Of Human Bondage* and for several years he subscribed to the gloomy materialism espoused by its principal character who held that life had no meaning, observing that "the rain falls alike upon the just and the unjust," and that "for nothing is there a why and a wherefore." From then on Bernstein could not believe in "any sort of divine justice." He was confirmed in his rejection of "religion and immortality as fables" when he found that most of his teachers in college shared the same outlook. His discovery of ESP and his contacts with J. B. Rhine showed him what he very much wanted to believe—that "men are something more than bodies, that they have minds with freedom from physical law, that these minds have unique creative forces which transcend the space-time-mass relations of matter," and that the mind is "a factor in its own right and not something which is centered completely in the gray matter of the organic brain."[4] Reincarnation finally satisfied his spiritual cravings by showing that, although there may not be any divine justice, the world is not morally meaningless. As I pointed out in Chapter 1, it is Karma and not reincarnation by itself which would make the universe morally meaningful. Bernstein does not distinguish between Karma and reincarnation, but he evidently came to believe in both. It is worth pointing out that even if the Bridey Murphy regressions *proved* reincarnation, they would not by themselves constitute the slightest evidence for Karma.

In addition to the account of his intellectual development and the text of the tapes, the latter interspersed with frequent explanations, Bernstein's book contains three theoretical chapters in which he argues that reincarnation theory is by far the best explanation of the material contained on the tapes. At the opening of Chapter 16 he remarks that he made a special effort to seek out "keen thinkers" to listen to the tapes. The "incisive analyses" of these keen thinkers would "probe all possible explanations of the Bridey Murphy phenomenon."[5] He was specially concerned to get the response of one listener "whose brilliance and penetrating logic had won him national prominence." Unfortunately the name of this "nationally prominent" individual is not disclosed. He is said to have supplied a rather elaborate analysis that won Bernstein's wholehearted endorsement. The unnamed brilliant thinker enumerated three possible explanations. One was fraud on Virginia's part. This was ruled out as totally untenable. If Virginia's responses were simply a "histrionic performance," then she is "a greater actress than Sarah Bernhardt." This leaves reincarnation and the theory that Virginia had read or heard a story containing the Bridey Murphy material and

---

civilization was founded on the use of 'Terrible Crystals' which 'could draw forth from stars when triggered by psychic concentration." For more critical accounts the reader is referred to pp. 216–19 of Martin Gardner's *Fads and Fallacies,* op. cit., James Randi, *Flim-Flam!* (Amherst, N.Y.: Prometheus Books, 1987), and Dale Beyerstein, "Edgar Cayce: 'The Prophet' Who 'Slept' His Way to the Top," *Skeptical Inquirer,* Jan.-Feb. 1996. It appears that Bernstein fully accepted the claims about Cayce's diagnoses, prescriptions, and discoveries of earlier lives.

4. *The Search for Bridey Murphy*, pp. 77–78. All quotations unless otherwise indicated are from the Pocketbook paperback reprint of 1978.

5. Op. cit., p. 250.

had under hypnosis transformed the elements of the story into events that had happened to herself. This theory, however, had "too many shortcomings" to be acceptable. It would not account for Virginia's "subtle Irish brogue under hypnosis" and it equally would not account for her ability to dance the Morning Jig. Furthermore, Bridey's life was much too drab and unromantic to have been the theme of any story. Moreover, there is no evidence that such a story has ever been written. As we shall see more fully in a later section, Virginia not only spoke about events in the life of Bridey Murphy, but also about the nature of her existence after her death as Bridey Murphy and before her birth many years later as Virginia Tighe. The prominent man is said to have observed that even if there were a story containing episodes similar to those occurring in Bridey Murphy's life, it is extremely unlikely that it would contain any of the postmortem material mentioned by Virginia. Finally, the "spontaneity and character" of Virginia's responses indicate that "this is a person who is actually relating her own experiences and not merely repeating a tale."[6] The reincarnation hypothesis was the only one that seemed to fit all the "facts." It is hardly surprising that, as an ardent believer in reincarnation, Bernstein accepted this conclusion. What is more, I cannot rid myself of the suspicion that the brilliant thinker quoted here is none other than Bernstein himself.

In the last two chapters of *The Search for Bridey Murphy* Bernstein attempts to answer the major objections to reincarnation or at least those with which he was familiar. He also discusses the future prospects of "experimental" reincarnationism. Bernstein regarded these prospects as very exciting. Now that "many investigators are beginning to delve into this field," there will "undoubtedly be forthcoming, from time to time, experiments" by comparison with which his own efforts will seem quite amateurish. He concludes the book with the hint that, stimulated by suggestions made to him by an unnamed physician, he himself will conduct one of these new experiments. The idea of such an experiment is so "fascinating" that Bernstein could "hardly wait" to go ahead with it. "It looks," he concludes the book, "as though I am about to take another step on the long bridge."[7]

The Hearst Exposé

The words just quoted were written in 1955. To this day nothing has been heard about the even more fascinating reincarnation experiments Bernstein could "hardly wait" to carry out. Whatever the reason for Bernstein's subsequent silence, most people concluded not long after the Bridey Murphy mania was at its peak that the contents of Virginia Tighe's recollections had been explained in a simple and unmysterious fashion and that the reincarnation explanation adopted by Bernstein and his supporters was totally unfounded. In a series of articles that first appeared in the *Chicago Amer-*

6. Op. cit., p. 251.
7. Op. cit., p. 271.

ican in May and June 1956, and which were subsequently syndicated in all the papers of the Hearst chain, the truth—or rather what the Hearst papers claimed to be the truth—about Bridey Murphy was revealed in minute detail. The articles were written by a team of reporters from the *Chicago American* whose owners resented the fact that its archrival, the *Chicago Daily News,* had obtained the local syndication rights to the original Bridey Murphy story. The reporters experienced no difficulty in penetrating the pseudonyms used in Bernstein's book and in identifying Virginia Tighe as the subject of the regressions. They soon discovered that Virginia had spent most of her childhood and adolescence in Chicago. After extensive interviews with just about everybody who knew or claimed to have known Virginia during her Chicago years, the Hearst reporters offered an account containing the following highlights. First, they located "the real Bridey Murphy," Mrs. Bridie Murphy Corkell, who had come to America from County Mayo in Ireland and who had lived across the street from the apartment in which Virginia had spent her Chicago years. It was claimed that Virginia not only knew Mrs. Corkell but that she had frequently been to her home. One of Virginia's old friends was quoted as saying that Virginia had had a "mad crush" on Mrs. Corkell's son, John. Next, it was revealed that Virginia had an Irish aunt, no longer living in 1956, of whom she had been extremely fond and who used to tell her tales about Ireland. Her teacher in the high school she attended on Chicago's north side recalled that Virginia had been active in school dramatics. More specifically, she remembered that Virginia had memorized Irish monologues in a heavy brogue. One of these was entitled "Mr. Dooley on Archey Road." One of the characters appearing in Virginia's recollections was "Uncle Plazz," whom she had described as her husband's uncle. Uncle Plazz had married a Protestant and Bridey mentioned that Brian's father had been very upset about this. The Hearst reporters claimed to have located a friend of Virginia's foster parents whose first name was Plezz and who told them that he could clearly remember Virginia. Bridey Murphy spoke of a brother who had died of "the black something" when she was four. The Hearst reporters claimed to have discovered that Virginia herself had a brother who died stillborn; and so the articles continued to trace parallel after parallel between the events in Bridey Murphy's supposed life and Virginia's real life in Chicago.

The exposé in the Hearst papers effectively destroyed whatever credibility the Bridey Murphy story had possessed. It was reported all over the world and treated as authentic by the very newspapers that had just a few months earlier written with awe about Bernstein's remarkable feat. The discovery of the "real Bridey Murphy" was reported in *Time* of June 18, 1956 under the heading "Yes Virginia, there is a Bridey" and in *Life* of June 25 with the caption "Bridey Search Ends at Last." The article in *Life* was accompanied by a photo of the "real" Bridey Murphy, Mrs. Corkell, surrounded by her grandchildren.

At this late date it is impossible to determine how much truth the Hearst articles contained. What is certain is that they were an extremely shoddy piece of journalism. They contained numerous demonstrable inaccuracies and in view of the refusal of key figures to allow themselves to be interviewed, there must be a strong suspicion that the most damaging "facts" were simply invented. The *Denver Post* sent one of its most trusted reporters, Bob Byers, to Chicago to check out the various claims published in the Hearst articles. Unlike Barker, Byers was not a believer in reincarnation and had not been involved in the publication of the original Bridey Murphy articles. Byers located Mrs. Saulnier, the teacher who had been quoted about Virginia's dramatic talents and her recitation of Irish monologues. Mrs. Saulnier told Byers that Virginia must have been a very mediocre student because she could barely remember her. She had no recollection that Virginia ever memorized Irish monologues and she specifically denied that she had heard Virginia recite "Mr. Dooley on Archey Road." Before going to Chicago, Byers had spoken to Virginia who flatly denied that she had ever known a man whom she called "Uncle Plezz." Byers tried to interview the "sixty-one-year old retired city employee" whom the Hearst articles had identified as "Uncle Plezz." The Hearst papers would not supply his last name "in order to protect his privacy." Virginia admitted that she had lived opposite Mrs. Corkell and had known her son "Buddy," as John was called by the neighborhood children. However, there had been no "mad crush." Virginia told Byers that Buddy was seven or eight years older than she and that he was married by the time she was old enough to have any romantic interest in boys. More significantly, she denied ever having spoken to Mrs. Corkell and she also denied any knowledge that her name was Bridie. Byers was naturally eager to speak to Mrs. Corkell to get her side of the story. Mrs. Corkell would not answer any of his calls and it turned out that her son Buddy, on whom Virginia was supposed to have a mad crush, was now—of all things—the editor of the Sunday *Chicago American* in which the Hearst exposé first appeared. Inquiries with Mrs. Corkell's parish priest revealed that her Christian name was indeed Bridie, but nobody could confirm that her maiden name had been Murphy. As for Virginia's favorite Irish aunt who was supposed to have "regaled" her with stories about Ireland, Virginia admitted that such a person, a Mrs. Marie Burns, had indeed existed. Although of Scottish-Irish descent, she had been born in New York and not in Ireland and became well-known to Virginia only when she was already eighteen. Virginia denied that this aunt had ever told her stories about Ireland. Perhaps nothing illustrates the recklessness of the Hearst reporters more than the parallel between Bridey Murphy's baby brother who had died at the age of four and Virginia's brother who was said to have died stillborn. The fact is that Virginia never had a brother.

The Real Case Against Bernstein

To show that the Bridey Murphy tapes were utterly worthless as evidence for reincarnation it was not at all necessary to resort to the tactics employed by the Hearst reporters. In the first place, checking Bridey's memories against Irish records produced almost uniformly negative results on all points of importance. Bridey said that she was born on December 20, 1798, in Cork and that she had died on a Sunday in 1864 in Belfast. Irish records of births and deaths do not go back beyond 1864, but they do cover 1864 and some church records go further back. None list Bridey's birth or death. Cork city directories are almost complete from 1820 on and they do not mention her family. As a lawyer's wife she might be expected to have left a will, but none has been found. Belfast newspapers carried no obituary for a Mrs. Bridget MacCarthy at any time in 1864. Church records do not mention the existence of a Father John Joseph Gorman. They do mention a Father William Gorman as living in the early nineteenth century, but he was at Kilmore, Meath, and not in Belfast. Bridey recalled a Catholic wedding ceremony at St. Theresa's Church, but no such church existed in Belfast before 1910. Bridey recalled that throughout their married lives, she and Brian resided at Dooley Road, but no such road has ever existed in Belfast. While living in Cork Bridey supposedly attended Mrs. Strayne's Day School. There are early directories listing the schools then in existence but no school bearing this name or any name that sounds similar has been found. Bridey asserted that her husband taught law at Queens University. Asked to mention other teachers at Queens University she named William McGlone, Fitzhugh, and Fitzmaurice. Neither her husband's name nor those of McGlone, Fitzhugh, or Fitzmaurice appear on the faculty records, although the records for 1859 do contain a Patrick Fitzmaurice and a Patrick McCloin as members of the University, but apparently not as teachers. Bridey asserted that she had bought a camisole at a store selling "ladies' things" to which she referred as "Cadenns House." Such stores frequently advertised in papers like the Belfast *News-Letter* (a paper correctly named by Bridey), but there is no trace of a Cadenns House. There was, however, a department store by this name in the Chicago neighborhood in which Virginia spent her childhood. Again, Bridey's answers contain numerous typically American expressions such as "candy," "downtown" and "just mad" which are quite out of character with the speech of nineteenth-century Irishmen. William Barker, who had written the original Bridey Murphy articles and who became Bernstein's foremost champion, replied to this criticism by arguing that since Bridey's memories were conveyed through the body of a twentieth-century American, such "Americanisms" are to be expected and do not detract from the evidential value of the recollections. A defense along these lines may be appropriate in the case of "spontaneous" memories of past lives when an individual in his present conscious state is trying to describe events he remembers. It is hardly appropriate for cases in which hypnosis is supposed to bring us in contact with the earlier personality itself *as it then was*.

There is a second and more basic reason for regarding the Bridey Murphy recollections as having no evidential value. Even if they had been in complete agreement with the historical records, this would not at all mean that Virginia was recalling the events of a previous life. As we shall see shortly, numerous cases are on record in which subjects recalled under hypnosis events in the distant past which were fully authenticated by independent checks; and yet their knowledge of these events could be easily explained without assuming an earlier life.

The summer 1956 issue of *Tomorrow,* a popular quarterly review of psychic research that often allowed space to complete skeptics, was entirely devoted to the Bridey Murphy case. Dr. Eric Dingwall, a British investigator who started his professional life as an assistant to Harry Houdini and who had spent many years exposing fraud and unscientific practices among psychical researchers, contributed a devastating analysis entitled "The Woman Who Never Was." Dingwall, who had made an extensive study of hypnotic regressions, pointed out that it is not unusual for hypnotized subjects to know a great many things which they do not know in their conscious state and also to exhibit marked dramatic ability. When questioned under hypnosis they themselves frequently supply the source of the knowledge and the skills they display in the hypnotic state. The source of their knowledge is usually something they had read or been told about while very young. Dr. Dingwall could see nothing in Virginia Tighe's responses to Bernstein's questions that would "warrant an assumption that this case differs in any striking degree from the many cases where normal sources of knowledge and a moderate power of dramatization are all that are required to supply a reasonable explanation of the phenomena."[8]

It should be added that in the first of its two articles on the case which, unlike the later one, was carefully researched, *Life* consulted two of the leading psychiatric experts on hypnosis at the time, Professors Jerome M. Schneck and Lewis R. Wolberg. They fully concurred with Dingwall's judgment. They pointed out that hypnotized subjects can display uncanny inventiveness especially if a deep trance has been induced. The subjects also tend to give the hypnotist what he wants to hear and it is clear from the text that, far from adhering to the reserve of a detached scientist, Bernstein suggested to Virginia what he was hoping to find. She was allowed to hear the earlier tapes and this, together with Bernstein's known views and bias, was most likely to confirm her in her original story and lead to all kinds of embellishments. In the book Bernstein supplied only the scantiest information about Virginia's early life, reporting that she "had been raised . . . by a Norwegian uncle and a German-Scotch-Irish aunt." The author of the article in *Life* revealed that both real parents with whom she lived for the first three and a half years were part Irish. This statement was never challenged. Both Dr. Schneck and Dr. Wolberg were sure that questioning Virginia under hypnosis about her early life would have revealed the source of her Irish recollections. There was nothing in Bridey's story that could not be explained "either on the basis of occasional coincidence or on subconscious memory of overheard conversation from someone well familiar with Ireland circa 1910."[9] What about the Morning Jig that Virginia per-

---

8. "The Woman Who Never Was," *Tomorrow,* Summer 1956, p. 10. It was Dingwall who discovered that a Patrick Fitzmaurice and a Patrick McCloin had been members of Queens University. Barker mentions this among his list of the accurate recollections on Bridey's part. He omits to mention that, according to Dingwall, they were "members of the University" but apparently not teachers. He also fails to inform his readers that Dingwall mentions this fact in an article which is extremely critical of Bernstein's book and totally rejects any explanation in terms of reincarnation.

9. *Life,* March 15, 1956, p. 33.

formed after coming out of one of her trances? Dr. Wolberg was not impressed. He once had a patient who under hypnosis displayed three other personalities—those of an Englishman, a black man, and an army colonel, "with the appropriate accents, mannerisms, and voice reproductions." A mere jig, he added, would not be hard to reproduce for someone who had seen one in a theater or movie. It is of some interest to note that at the time of writing his book Bernstein was entirely familiar with the work of Dr. Wolberg. In one of the editorial comments that he inserted into the text of the first tape, he quotes Wolberg and describes him as a "famous medical hypnotist and psychiatrist." It is perhaps unnecessary to add that later editions of *The Search for Bridey Murphy* do not inform the reader that the "famous medical hypnotist" totally rejected the reincarnation explanation of Virginia's trance behavior.

Dr. Dingwall concluded his article with the remark that if Virginia Tighe were asked under hypnosis where she had obtained the story of Bridey Murphy, the source might be given. "It is curious," he adds, "that this was not tried at the time." In one place Bernstein briefly adverts to the fact that Virginia did not reveal any experience in her present twentieth-century life as source of the Bridey Murphy personality. The unnamed "keen thinker" of "national prominence" whom Bernstein claims to have consulted and who persuaded him that reincarnation was the only plausible explanation is quoted as saying that "if she had read or heard all of this, your subject could easily explain that fact under hypnosis." Very possibly Virginia could have done so if Bernstein had asked a few questions about the source of her recollections. To bring up the fact that Virginia did not reveal the source of "recollections" as evidence favoring reincarnation is surely a brazen coverup of Bernstein's failure to ask her about it. It is impossible to find an excuse for this failure on his part. When he set out on his past-life regressions he was an experienced hypnotist and he gives every evidence of having extensively studied the literature on the subject. If, nevertheless, he did not know that such questions frequently reveal the source of the subject's information, his ignorance was culpable. If, what is far more likely, he did know about the need for such questioning and nevertheless failed to do it, one can only wonder about his motives. Was it the fear on the part of an ardent reincarnationist of losing a good case or were perhaps visions of a potential best seller already crossing his mind during the sessions?

The guesses offered by Drs. Schneck and Wolberg were fully confirmed by the research of Melvin Harris, an English radio and television script writer.[10] Bernstein, Barker, and their supporters expressed amazement at Virginia's familiarity with the custom of kissing the Blarney Stone, the Uillean pipes, the Irish jigs, and various Irish customs. However, as Harris observes, Americans had the opportunity of becoming intimately acquainted with Irish life and customs in the late nineteenth century without having to visit Ireland. In 1893 Chicago was the home for the World's Colombian Exposition, where one of the prize exhibits was a huge Irish village consisting of fifteen

---

10. See M. Harris, "Are Past Life Regressions Evidence of Reincarnation?" *Free Inquiry,* Fall 1986 and Chapters 16–18 of *Investigating the Unexplained* (Amherst, N.Y.: Prometheus Books, 1986).

cottages. The village was the idea of Lady Aberdeen who traveled all over Ireland to find girls who could spin, sing, and dance jigs. Every day for the six months of the fair, to quote Harris, "visitors could hear the burbling Uillean pipes, listen to the songs of old Ireland, and see traditional jigs danced on the green."[11] The exhibit contained a full size replica of the Tower of Blarney Castle and a replica of the Blarney Stone at the top of the tower that could be kissed in the traditional manner by visitors.

Huge crowds visited the Exposition and the Irish village turned out to be one of its main attractions. When the fair ended after six months the number of visitors amounted to three and a half million. It should be remembered that this was an age when there were no movies, no radios and no television so that expositions were one of the relatively few amusements available. The success of the Irish village was so enormous that another one, complete with the Tower of Blarney Castle, was erected for the St. Louis Fair of 1904. Harris concludes that during her formative years Virginia probably met "a veritable army of people" who had visited these Irish villages. Thus she could easily have acquired all her information about nineteenth-century Ireland without ever reading a book on the subject. Whether she actually did acquire her knowledge in this way is something we shall never know because of Bernstein's willful refusal to ask the necessary questions.

Before proceeding it may be of interest to illustrate Bernstein's unscrupulous handling of facts by an item that I discovered almost accidentally. The following paragraph occurs on pages eleven and twelve of Dingwall's article:

> Similarly, she [Virginia in one of her sessions] mentioned a book called *The Green Bay*. Here again, Mr. Bernstein stated in his book that information from Ireland affirmed that more than one book with that title was published there in the nineteenth century, but no details were given. Every effort made in Ireland and in England has failed to trace even one book with that title.

I read Dingwall's article shortly after I had read *The Search for Bridey Murphy* in its paperback edition which, aside from the new material contributed by Barker, is advertised as containing "Morey Bernstein's original text." I did not recall that Bernstein claimed to have information from Ireland that more than one book entitled "The Green Bay" had been published there in the nineteenth century. I became suspicious and guessed that such a claim had indeed been present in the original edition which was criticized by Dingwall, but that after Dingwall had exposed the falseness of this claim, it was then omitted in the revised paperback edition. This is exactly what a comparison of the two editions confirmed. In the original edition the following paragraph appears:

> Bridey provided several bits of evidence which did not seem particularly significant at the time but which later, owing to various peculiar twists, took on added weight.

---

11. *Free Inquiry,* Fall 1986, p. 21.

She had told us, for instance, that she had read a book entitled *The Green Bay*. I thought this of little consequence, because I presumed there would be several books similarly titled in twentieth-century America. To my surprise, however, I have been unable to find even one such title. (The New York Public Library listed *The Green Bay Tree* but not a single *The Green Bay*.) Yet the Irish investigators report that there was such a book—more than one—in nineteenth-century Ireland.[12]

In the later edition, which is evidently not quite the "original text," Bernstein reproduces the same paragraph on page 266, but simply omits the last sentence: "Yet the Irish investigators report that there was such a book—more than one—in nineteenth-century Ireland." This is not only thoroughly dishonest, but it also deprives the paragraph of any point. The fact that Bernstein did not find "The Green Bay" listed in the New York Public Library by itself in no way supports Bridey's assertion. It would do so only if the Irish investigators had come up with such a title in nineteenth-century Ireland. The conclusion is irresistible that the omitted claim was simply invented by Bernstein in the hope that nobody would bother to check it.

Cryptomnesia

Bridey Murphy's knowledge of Irish history and customs was almost certainly an instance of "cryptomnesia" or source amnesia in which the subjects obtain their knowledge through normal channels but are unable to recall them. Harold Rosen, a Canadian psychiatrist, describes the case of a patient who, under hypnosis, started writing in Oscan, a language spoken in Western Italy up to the first century B.C.E. The patient denied having ever seen the words he had written and also insisted that he had never so much as heard of Oscan. When rehypnotized, however, he recalled sitting in the library while somebody next to him opened a book on a page that contained the Oscan "Curse of Vibia." It was this Oscan curse that he had reproduced.[13] Numerous similar cases are on record. One of them concerns a woman referred to as Miss C., going back to 1906. It was investigated for the British Society for Psychical Research by the well-known classical scholar G. Lowes Dickinson who, after considerable effort, traced his subject's remarkably detailed knowledge of the personalities at the court of Richard II to her reading of a historical novel as a child. As a result of the work of Dickinson[14] and the more recent research of Edwin S. Zolik of Marquette University,[15]

12. *The Search for Bridey Murphy*, op. cit., pp. 220–21.
13. For Rosen's discussion see his Introduction to M. V. Kline (Ed.), *A Scientific Report on "The Search for Bridey Murphy"* (New York: Julian Press, 1956).
14. G. Lowes Dickinson, "A Case of Emergence of a Latent Memory under Hypnosis," *Proceedings of the Society for Psychical Research*, Vol. 25, 1911.
15. E. S. Zolik, "An Experimental Investigation of the Psychodynamic Implications of the Hypnotic 'Previous Existence,' " *Journal of Clinical Psychology*, 1958; and "Reincarnation Phenomena in Hypnotic States," *International Journal of Parapsychology*, 1962.

the Finnish psychiatrist Reima Kampman,[16] Melvin Harris, and the psychologists N. P. Spanos,[17] Robert Baker,[18] and J. Venn,[19] this phenomenon has been completely demystified.

Bridey Murphy in the Astral World

On November 22, 1970, nearly twenty years after the Bridey Murphy tapes were recorded, *Newsweek* featured an interview with Virginia Tighe. She had divorced her husband in 1968 and was living quietly in Denver with the youngest of her three daughters. In the fifties she and her husband had vigorously supported Bernstein's reincarnation interpretation of her memories. Now she took a more skeptical view. Her association with Bernstein, the article concludes, "has not even made her a firm believer in reincarnation. 'Still,' she says with a smile, 'I consider it a delightful possibility the older I get.' "*

Virginia sounds like a basically sensible, down-to-earth middle American, quite different from most of the insane or semi-insane persons who are attracted to the occult. I doubt that she would ever take any talk about astral bodies seriously. Bernstein on the other hand had no doubts whatever on the subject and he managed to elicit several descriptions of the astral world from Virginia in her role as Bridey Murphy. He seemed quite convinced that during the interregnum, which in Virginia's case lasted from the time of her death in Belfast in 1864 until her rebirth in Wisconsin in 1923, she had lived in the astral world. The subject came up already during the first session. In the course of describing her last days as Bridey Murphy, Virginia mentioned that she died while her husband, Brian, was in church. He had not realized that Bridey was "going so fast" and had asked a lady to stay with her. Later, Virginia said, Brian had been "terribly upset" because he was not with Bridey when she expired. Bernstein reasoned that her comment would be understandable only on the assumption that she had been conscious of what took place after her death. He therefore began to question her about these events and at once received a reply that deeply impressed both him and the other listeners. Bridey flatly denied that she had gone to purgatory: "I

16. R. Kampman and R. Hirvonoja, "Dynamic Relation to the Secondary Personality Induced by Hypnosis to the Present Personality," in F. H. Frankel and H. S. Zamansky (Eds.), *Hypnosis at Its Bicentennial* (New York: Plenum, 1976), There is a lucid summary of Kampman's work on pp. 127–34 of Ian Wilson, *Mind Out of Time* (London: Gollancz, 1981).

17. N. P. Spanos, "Past-Life Hypnotic Regression: A Critical View," *Skeptical Inquirer,* Winter 1987–88.

18. R. A. Baker, "The Effect of Suggestion on Past-Life Regression," *American Journal of Clinical Hypnosis,* 1982; and *Hidden Memories* (Amherst, N.Y.: Prometheus Books, 1992).

19. J. Venn, "Hypnosis and the Reincarnation Hypothesis," *Journal of the American Society for Psychical Research,* 1986.

*I was sorry to learn from an obituary in the *New York Times* that Virginia died of cancer in a hospice outside Denver on July 12, 1995.

didn't do . . . like Father John said. I didn't go to purgatory!"[20] This "particularly meaningful" and "emotional" outburst could best be explained by supposing that, as a result of listening to Father John's sermons about the next world, Bridey had become greatly concerned about "this purgatory problem" and was much relieved when she did not find herself in such a menacing environment. Contrary to Catholic teaching Bridey remained earthbound. During the second session, when Bernstein again asked her about her recollections of the period immediately following her death, she recalled watching "them ditch my body."[21] There has been some dispute as to whether the word "ditch" was used by nineteenth-century Irish speakers to mean the same as "bury," but it is evident that Virginia was here referring to her own funeral. After she had been "ditched," she returned to her house to be with Brian, but Brian did not notice her presence. She tried to talk to him without obtaining any response. Father John frequently visited Brian. However, before long, he too died. Bridey saw Father John when he died. Later on Brian also died, but, unlike Father John, Brian did not join her during her postmortem existence. Later in the session Bridey contradicted herself and said that she did not watch Father John die, but she emphasized that his death was not painful. He "just died in his sleep." He then visited Bridey and they "talked."[22] Virginia does not relate any details of her postmortem conversation with Father John. In particular, she does not mention telling him that his prediction about going to purgatory had not been fulfilled. Bernstein did not question her on this subject, but he was curious about how people talk to one another after death:

MB: How did you talk to each other?
BM: Just like . . . we always did.
MB: I see. The others could hear you?
BM: Yes, they could hear me.
MB: But the people on earth, like Brian, could not possibly hear you?

At this stage Bridey pointedly replied (the book prints her exclamation in italics):

They won't listen![23]

Bernstein then questioned Virginia about where Father John is "now." I assume that "now" refers to 1952:

Do you have any idea where Father John could be now? Is he living on this earth?
I don't know . . . He's living. He lives.
He lives?

---

20. *The Search for Bridey Murphy*, op. cit., p. 145.
21. Ibid., p. 171.
22. Ibid., p. 172.
23. Ibid., p. 152.

He lives.
How do you know?
I just . . . know that he lives.
But do you know *where* he lives? Do you have any idea where he lives?
No . . . I don't know.[24]

After Brian's death there was no point in staying on in their Belfast home. She therefore went back to Cork to visit her older brother Duncan who was still alive. Bridey's mode of transportation from Belfast to Cork was somewhat unusual. In answer to Bernstein's question she said that she simply "willed" herself to Cork and there she was in her old family home. Apparently the change of place was not instantaneous, but it took her "just almost" no time to get to Cork.[25] As in the case of her husband, Bridey did not succeed in making her presence known to Duncan. Duncan was terribly old and ill. Bridey would stay by his bed and talk, but Duncan never noticed her and of course he also did not answer any of her questions. Eventually she witnessed Duncan's death, but, like Brian, Duncan did not join her. Fortunately, she had better luck with her younger brother who had died as a baby. There was of course a recognition problem. Bridey had to tell her baby brother who she was. Bernstein here inserts an editorial explanation pointing out that "presumably the baby would not have recognized the sixty-six-year-old woman" whom he had last seen when she was a little girl. On the other hand, Bernstein explains that Bridey "recognized" the baby brother at once since he "apparently still looked the same."[26] After the baby brother had been informed that the sixty-six-year-old woman was his sister they had an animated conversation. He told Bridey that he remembered her and Duncan but not their mother or the house in Cork. He did clearly remember that Duncan would tip over his little cradle and he would fall out. This is all that Bridey recalled about the meeting with the baby brother during the first session. During the second session, when Bernstein brought the subject up again, there were more details about the poor baby's "rolling out" of his cradle and their mother's wrongfully blaming Bridey for the event. She also supplied more details about the brother's appearance. While Bridey had grown into an elderly woman, the baby brother had also changed. However, he had not become an elderly man. He was now a little child but definitely no longer a baby. When he had died he could not yet talk but now when Bridey met him he could. To the question of how he was dressed, Bridey answered "no clothes." As we shall see in Chapter 9, the question of astral attire has posed serious problems for the theory. It would greatly simplify matters if astral bodies were always naked, a view championed by Dr. Crookall who was perhaps the most famous of all astral explorers. However, it remains to this day a minority position. Bridey also met her father, but there is no mention of her meeting any of her other relatives, friends, or acquaintances.

24. Ibid., p. 172.
25. Ibid., p. 174.
26. Ibid., p. 147.

The meeting with her father is mentioned indirectly as Bernstein questioned her about any new emotional ties:

> Did you have any attachments of any kind, any family attachments, relatives?
> No.
> No marriages?
> No.
> I see. Do relatives stay together?
> No. No . . . we . . . it was . . . no, my mother was never with me. My father said he saw her, but I didn't.
> Oh, you didn't see your mother?
> No.
> Your father, though, told you that he saw her.
> Yes.[27]

This is all we are ever told about Bridey's father and mother. To a skeptic who knows that the real Virginia was grossly neglected by her biological parents and totally abandoned by them at the age of three, her responses will not come as a surprise.

Bernstein extracted from Bridey the admission that she had realized that *she* was not dead although she knew that her body had died. One would have expected him to ask her in what form she had survived—whether she had become a pure mind or whether she had acquired a new body. No such questions were asked, but it is clear that if Bridey and other inhabitants of the interregnum world had any bodies, they must have been of a strange kind. For one thing they appear to have lacked sex organs. At the opening of the third session Bernstein brought up the question of whether people are divided into men and women in the postmortem world. Bridey's answer was yes but that there was no difference between males and females.[28] Bernstein asked Bridey how she could tell that "a man was a man and a woman a woman," to which, as so frequently, she answered, "you just knew." I am not sure how one is to construe Bridey's answer here, but perhaps the most plausible interpretation would be that in the postmortem world people had bodies without sex organs and their being men or women can be determined by the way they talk and by what they say about themselves. In addition to lacking sex organs, the postmortem individuals also seem to lack sense organs.

> Did you have a sense of smell, and touch, and hearing, and seeing?
> Did you have all those senses? In the astral world could you touch things?
>
> No.[29]

---

27. Ibid., p. 173.
28. Ibid., p. 182.
29. Ibid., p. 175.

Bridey consistently denied that one could smell or touch things in the postmortem world, but she volunteered the information that "you could see" and also that "you could hear."

Bernstein had first used the expression "astral world" during the second session. "While you were in this spiritual world," Bernstein asked Bridey, "did you hear any-one call it the astral world?" At first Bridey just repeated the phrase "astral world." So Bernstein asked again, "Did you ever hear that name?" The answer was "Yes, I've heard that." It is not surprising that, as a student of the occult, Bernstein should have been familiar with the term "astral world." On the other hand it may seem anachronistic that Bridey, too, was familiar with it. As far as I know, it did not become widely used in any English-speaking country, even among occultists, until the time of Madame Blavatsky (1831–1891), the founder of Theosophy. However, it may be argued that Bernstein was here interrogating Virginia rather than Bridey and it is certainly not impossible that Virginia Tighe had heard this expression before. The world inhabited by Bridey and her fellow-survivors was a drab and altogether miserable place, much inferior to the regular life of people on earth. It is true that there were no fights and wars in it, but there were no interesting events at all. Above all, there was no love or hate. There was of course no sex. Bridey also emphasized that there was no eating and no sleeping and hence, it seems, not even any dreaming. There really was nothing to do. "How did you spend all your time?" Bernstein asked in one place. "Oh . . . just waiting," was Bridey's answer. Nevertheless, when Bernstein asked Bridey if she liked where she was, the answer was yes. Bernstein became more specific:

> Was it better than your life on earth?

This time the answer was "No" and it was followed by a series of complaints:

> It wasn't full enough. It wasn't . . . just . . . couldn't do all the·things . . . couldn't ac-complish anything and . . . couldn't talk to anybody very long. They'd go away . . . didn't stay very long.[30]

Becoming exasperated by the drabness of the astral world, as it was portrayed by Bridey, Bernstein finally asked:

> Well, didn't anybody in this spirit world ever teach you anything? Didn't you ever go to school, or didn't anybody ever give you any instructions of any kind?[31]

The answer was "No." In one of his editorial comments Bernstein remarks that when Bridey reported that in the astral world one could not talk to anybody very long, her voice had become plaintive, almost pained. He adds that "numerous listeners" to the

---

30. Ibid., p. 147.
31. Ibid., p. 153.

tape recording suggested that, without realizing it, Bridey "might well have been in purgatory after all."

While living in this dreary realm Bridey had one gift not possessed by people on the earth, except of course some "psychics" celebrated in the tabloids whose predictions are usually so vague that they are compatible with almost anything that happens. Bridey could predict the future of life on the earth. Bernstein evidently thought that Bridey might have possessed such a faculty while she lived in the astral world. "Could you look at the people on the earth," Bernstein inquired, "and see what was going to happen to them?" It should be remembered here that, as I reported earlier, hypnotic subjects, particularly those in a deep trance, are highly suggestible. Virginia obviously felt that Bernstein wanted her to display precognitive powers and, not surprisingly, her answer was "Yes." "You could see the future?" Bernstein persisted. "Yes." Bernstein then asked for an example which elicited the following speech:

> I saw a war . . . some man there said there was going to be a war. It was before I was born . . . before I was born. And he . . . he said . . . be a war . . . there was a war before I was born . . . they could see people knew what was going to happen . . . if you were there.[32]

Bernstein portentously inserts an editorial note reminding the reader that Bridey Murphy MacCarthy died in 1864 and that Virginia Tighe was born in 1923. The point of this note evidently is to make the reader believe that during her interim existence Bridey-Virginia had the precognitive ability to predict the Great War of 1914–19. Virginia-Bridey's "prediction" is just as vague as the predictions about disasters and assassinations regularly appearing in the tabloids, but in her case there is the further obvious objection that the person making the "prediction" is not the astral predecessor of Virginia, but the Virginia lying on the couch who knew only too well that, not long before she was born in 1923, there had been a World War.

As a reincarnationist Bernstein was naturally interested in the way in which Bridey had gone about selecting her new body—the body of a girl born to parents in Wisconsin. In response to Bernstein's question of how she became born again, she babbled in her usual way: "I was . . . oh, I was just . . . I don't know how it happens, but I just remember that suddenly I wasn't . . . just in a . . . just a state . . . then I was a baby."[33] Did anybody "select" her new body? Virginia did not know. Bernstein then asked a pertinent question:

> How did you know what body, how did you know what country to go to, how did you know all those things? Who took care of all those details?[34]

---

32. Ibid., p. 184.
33. Ibid., p. 148.
34. Ibid.

Virginia, alas, did not have the desired information. "It just seems like it just happens
. . . I remember just being a baby again."[35] Even the inarticulate college students of
the late 1980s and 1990s who avoid libraries like a plague could have done better than
that. Bernstein in one place told his readers that Virginia could not have picked up her
knowledge of Ireland from books since she never read any books. I find the last of
these statements entirely believable. Virginia Tighe has usually been described as an
"attractive and vivacious housewife" and I have no reason to question this description. In the 1970 *Newsweek* article noted earlier she certainly did not appear de-
mented. In her trance states, however, she seems like a mentally retarded person. In
any event, Bernstein was acutely disappointed that Virginia was "never able to relate
the details of the rebirth process" and he adds that other subjects he has hypnotized
since then have also failed to "throw any light on this issue." He adds reassuringly
that other—unnamed—investigators claim "somewhat better results." Fortunately
some later "investigators" have been able to describe this process in great detail.[36]

The Case Remains "Controversial"

During the last fifteen years or so numerous cheap paperbacks have appeared in
which reincarnation is championed. The authors are thoroughly disreputable but apparently there is money in such books and they are published by companies not generally associated with fostering belief in the occult. In these books it is asserted either that Bridey Murphy is a famous case that demonstrates reincarnation or, more
modestly, that it is "highly controversial." It is sad having to report that even some reputable writers continue to see merits in Bridey Murphy often for years after the
event. Francis Story, the English Buddhist whom we already met and whom we shall
meet again several times, accepted it without the slightest demurrer. Professor
Ducasse, who was a totally honest man and a fine scholar and who convincingly
demonstrated the fraudulence of the Hearst exposé, naively accepted the case itself.[37]
Ian Stevenson who, as a trained psychiatrist, knows something about the unreliability of hypnosis, dismisses hypnotically recalled past lives as cryptomnesia, but does
not extend this dismissal to the Bridey Murphy case. While not accepting it as proving an earlier life in nineteenth-century Ireland, he believes that some of Virginia's
memories must have been acquired "paranormally."[38] The favorite line of the more
educated reincarnationists and of writers who pretend to be above the battle is that al-

---

35. Ibid.
36. See Chapter 15, pp. 248ff.
37. *The Belief in a Life After Death* (Springfield, Ill., 1961), chapter XXI.
38. *Children Who Remember Previous Lives,* pp. 45, 281–82. Stevenson refuses to regard the case
as an instance of cryptomnesia, but all his statements appeared before he could have read the article by
Melvin Harris which contains the information about the Irish exhibitions in Chicago and other mid-west-
ern cities.

though there are indeed weaknesses in the Bridey Murphy case, it is far from closed. This view is defended by Gina Cerminara, a psychotherapist whose *Many Mansions* (1950) is the most readable exposition and defense of Edgar Cayce's work. In a later book—*The World Within* (1957)—she denied that the Bridey Murphy case had been demolished. "It may be years," she wrote, "before all the evidence has been accumulated and thoroughly examined."[39] A similar verdict is offered by the unnamed and disingenuous authors of the Time-Life volume *Psychic Voyages* (1987) which I quoted earlier. "The final judgment," they write, "is yet to be delivered."[40] The facts here presented seem to me to show that the final judgment *has* been delivered. The case is utter and total rubbish. I am happy to say that most intelligent people who tried to familiarize themselves with the relevant facts reached the same conclusion. Unfortunately this does not mean, as we shall see shortly, that regressions to past lives ceased or that reincarnationists stopped appealing to hypnotic regression as "dramatic evidence" for their position.

Perhaps the recent spate of hypnotically derived charges by children that they were sexually abused by their parents and other adults, which have resulted in horrendous miscarriages of justice, will at last convince even believers in reincarnation that hypnotic memories cannot be trusted.[41]

---

39. *The World Within*, p. 22.

40. Ibid., p. 118.

41. For an excellent and moving survey of these cases see Martin Gardner's "The Tragedy of False Memories," *Skeptical Inquirer,* Fall 1994. One of the most terrible of these cases is described in detail in Lawrence Wright, *Remembering Satan: A Case of Recovered Memory and the Shattering of an American Family* (New York, 1994). The victim in this case is a perfectly decent (and pious) policeman from Olympia, Washington, who is currently serving a life sentence. It should be added that not all the bogus abuse charges are hypnotically produced. Other methods employed by the "therapists" are guided imagery, drugs, and dream interpretation.

6

More Hypnotic Regressions and "Progressions"

The Interplanetary Regressions of Sir(?) Alexander Cannon

At the end of Chapter 9 of *The Search for Bridey Murphy,* just as the Bridey Murphy story proper gets underway, Bernstein mentions that the idea of regressing somebody to a time before her birth had not occurred to him until, just before returning from New York City to his home in Pueblo, Colorado, he had picked up a copy of *The Power Within* by the "widely known English psychiatrist, Dr. Sir Alexander Cannon."[1] The title page of the book lists the following impressive degrees and distinctions after the author's name: K.G.C.B., M.D., D.P.M., M.A., Ph.D., F.R.G.S., F.R.S.A., Hon. F.B.P.S., etc. The "etc.," it should be noted, is not another degree but refers to distinctions of which we are informed elsewhere. Thus, G. L. Playfair, a well-known contemporary parapsychologist and author of *The Indefinite Boundary* (1976), a book that defends reincarnation, respectfully refers to "Sir Alexander Cannon" and describes him as a "member of the executive council of the British Medical Association and the Society for Psychical Research."[2] The only biographical sketch I have been able to discover appears in Volume 1 of the *Encyclopedia of Occultism and Parapsychology.*[3] Cannon was born in 1896 and the date of his death is surmised as 1963. He studied occultism and yoga while traveling in India and Tibet. To his more mundane titles he added "Kushog Yogi of Northern Tibet" and "Master-the-Fifth of the Great White Lodge of the Himalayas." After several positions in Hong Kong he became psychiatrist and research scientist at Colney Hatch Mental Hospi-

---

1. Morey Bernstein, *The Search for Bridey Murphy,* pp. 124–25.
2. G. L. Playfair, *How To Work Magic* (London, 1985), p. 257.
3. *Encyclopedia of Occultism and Parapsychology,* 2nd ed. (Detroit, 1985), pp. 206–207.

tal in Great Britain and later established the Isle of Man Clinic for Nervous Diseases. He also became psychiatrist for the London County Council, but here he ran into trouble when, in his book *The Invisible Influence* (1933), he claimed that he was levitated over a chasm in Tibet, together with his porter and luggage. To the best of my knowledge no other levitator ever claimed to be able to include porters and luggage in the levitation. Upon the publication of this story the London County Council dismissed him from his position as psychiatrist on the grounds that he was unfit to be in charge of a mental hospital. Cannon was, however, reinstated after bringing action for wrongful dismissal. He subsequently set up in private practice as a Harley Street specialist. It is presumably here that he carried on his assorted regressions.

The Power Within, the book that so impressed Morey Bernstein, contains a chapter entitled "Reincarnation Outflanks Freud." Although most of the chapter is devoted to reincarnation and hypnotic regressions, other topics are also treated. Sir Alexander was an ardent champion of panpsychism, the view that all things, including those we normally regard as purely physical, are also mental. Cannon's own colorful presentation deserves to be quoted:

> It is a mistake to suppose that minerals and chemicals have no life. Everything in the Universe is alive if only we knew it. . . . Chemicals can be poisoned or injured, metals get tired, so that razor blades need to be given a rest, motor-engines will "give up" under too prolonged stresses, and tuning-forks lose their vibratory power and period after prolonged use. Machines and tools are living things: have you not heard an expert say that a tool must be properly handled to give of its best? Window glass is subject to disease, especially stained glass, and the disease will spread from pane to pane by a process of infection. Metals can also become diseased by infection and, in fact, the list of such correspondence in nature is never ending.[4]

Cannon obviously was not a tennis player or he would have added that tennis balls lose their bounce because they get so tired. And surely everybody knows that clothes and all kinds of household articles deteriorate because of aging and weariness. Earlier in the chapter Cannon had discussed both suicide and capital punishment. He is opposed to both. His reason for opposing suicide is not altogether clear. He tells us that "so far from ending his miseries," suicide would plunge a person "into a dilemma ten thousand times worse than the one from which he seeks to escape." I do not at all see why that should be so and it should be noted that Cannon did not believe in the Judeo-Christian view that suicide is sinful and will be punished by God in the next world. On capital punishment he is more convincing. If I understand him, he argues that since death is not the end, the criminal who is executed does not really lose his life and hence he is after all not punished. This is a splendid argument and I shall from now on use it when discussing the subject with believers in capital punishment who also believe in life after death. I am not, however, at all sure that this argument was

---

4. Alexander Cannon, *The Power Within* (London, 1950), pp. 181–82.

actually intended by Cannon. It was suggested to me by one or two sentences in the text. His habitual style is best described as emotionally charged gibberish and it is anybody's guess what he means, if he means anything.

By 1950 when his book was published Sir Alexander had conducted 1382 "reincarnation sittings." Many of his patients, he tells us, have received "great benefits" from "discovering hidden complexes and fears which undoubtedly have been brought over by the astral body from past lives."[5] His case histories are among the most exciting of any past-life regressionist. In one of them a "business gentleman of undoubted capabilities" suffered from an inexplicable phobia about using elevators. Hypnotic investigation revealed that several centuries earlier, as a Chinese general, he had fallen to his death from a great height. In another case a woman was regressed to several previous lives all of which ended tragically. In 98 B.C.E. she had a male body and was a slave on a Roman galley. She was thrown into the water in chains and was eaten by crocodiles. It stands to reason that such a harrowing experience would leave a trace even after two thousand years. We are not informed about the symptoms from which the unfortunate lady suffered, but whatever they were, we may be sure that Sir Alexander succeeded in removing them.

Perhaps the most fascinating case concerns an interplanetary regression. A patient who was regressed to life on the planet Venus offered much valuable information about life there. In answer to the question what "went on there" she replied that "instruction in the art of living was the main activity." Unfortunately, she did not offer any information as to how this instruction was applied. The only way to find out, short of sending an expedition to Venus, would be to regress other subjects who have also lived on Venus and ask them appropriate questions. The patient told Sir Alexander that the light on Venus was constant and extremely brilliant, so brilliant in fact that our Earth was regarded as the "dark planet" there. She also supplied the surprising information that "even the trees were metallic in appearance" on Venus. As a panpsychist, Cannon could not of course see anything wrong in the idea of metallic trees.

Cannon concludes the chapter with the observation that "we have lived on this earth before, and *ad interim* between our Earth lives, we have also inhabited other planets," Mercury and Venus being the "favorites."[6] One might object that life would not be easy on these planets since their atmospheres contain no oxygen. What is more, the surface temperature on Venus is 475° C; on Mercury the temperature is 400° C on the sunny side and −170° on the night side. But these are pedantic details which only a niggling skeptic would bring up.

Interplanetary regressions, the discovery of life on Venus and Mercury, and levitations together with porter and luggage were by no means Cannon's only feats. He also had the gift, which he shared with St. Francis Xavier (who resurrected no less than eight bodies), and with Jesus himself, of bringing the dead back to life. His resurrection technique is described in *Sleeping Through Space* (1938):

5. Ibid., p. 170.
6. Ibid., p. 185.

Administer a severe kick with the knee between the shoulder blades at the same time shouting in (the) left ear "Oye," "Oye," "Oye." It is rarely necessary to repeat the operation before life is again resumed, but this can be repeated up to seven times in long-standing cases.[7]

In an article, written eleven years later for the *British Journal of Medical Hypnotism* and suitably entitled "Some Hypnotic Secrets," he tells what to do with difficult hypnotic subjects:

If the patient wakes up at all before I have got my hypnotic sleep suggestions home to him, I place both of my thumbs on his carotid arteries vagus nerves and carotid body firmly . . . until he is "off" again.

The author of the generally sympathetic article in the *Encyclopedia of Occultism and Parapsychology* remarks that "the unfortunate patient stood a fair chance of being strangled, but doubtless he could be resuscitated by the redoubtable doctor's 'Oye, Oye, Oye' technique."[8]

I cannot decide whether Cannon was mad or a fraud. It is possible that he was both, with madness predominating. Mad or fraud or both, he sure was fun, which is more than can be said for Bernstein. In fact the only good thing I can say for Bernstein is that without him I would never have discovered Sir (?) Alexander and his assistant, the Dame of St. Hubert.

Note on Cannon's Titles

Readers may want to know the reason why I inserted the question mark after "Sir" when referring to Alexander Cannon. As I was writing this section it occurred to me that Cannon had not really done anything that would have induced any British government to recommend him for a knighthood. I also began to wonder about Playfair's claim that Cannon had been a member of the executive council of the British Medical Association. I wrote to the Central Chancery of the Order of Knighthood at Saint James' Palace in London and received the following answer from its secretary, Lt. Col. Anthony Mather, OBE dated February 20, 1995:

Unfortunately I have been unable to trace your Alexander Cannon as having been knighted. However, if you find any further information which you think would be of some use I will of course look through the records held here at the Central Chancery once again.

---

7. *Encyclopedia of Occultism and Parapsychology,* op. cit.
8. Ibid.

The answer from the Information Officer of the British Medical Association (dated September 8, 1994) was similarly negative. She enclosed Medical Directories from 1955 and 1962 and wrote as follows:

> He claims to have been a member of the "BMA Specialist Psych. Gp." but I can find no support for this in the BMA Archives, nor any reference to it in the Council lists for that period.

The Preface of *The Power Within* contains an acknowledgment to "Rhonda de Rhonda, F.R.G.S., Dame of St. Hubert, for being one of the chief hypnotic trance subjects." This is a great name and a great title. I verified that Rhonda de Rhonda really existed, but inquiries with the British and Belgian embassies in Washington and the Archdiocese of New York have not yielded any evidence that there is an order of St. Hubert. This is too bad because Rhonda de Rhonda would undoubtedly have been an admirable Dame of this order.

Voltaire and the Beheading of Shirley MacLaine

The real objections to the Bridey Murphy case were not widely known in 1956, but the public at large seemed to accept the bogus Hearst exposé as definitive. This did not prevent numerous past life regressionists from plying their trade and in America, especially California, they were not wanting for willing and eager subjects. If we are to judge by the frequency with which they were mentioned in the tabloids, in *Fate* and also in more respectable publications like *Time,* the two outstanding regressionists in the United States were Ralph Grossi and H. N. Banerjee. According to *Time,*[9] Grossi, a hypnotist based on Pittsburgh, was hired by the *National Enquirer* to fly to Hollywood to explore the earlier lives of movie and television celebrities. The stars are easy to hypnotize, Grossi remarked, simply because they are such positive thinkers. The *National Enquirer* of March 13, 1984, reported some of the explorations of this "famed expert." The least tedious of the regressions is that of Glenn Scarpelli who revealed that in the middle of the eighteenth century he was an English actor named Richard Lawrence. He then suddenly launched into a near-perfect recital of Hamlet's soliloquy. After he was brought back Glenn exclaimed that he had never studied *Hamlet.* Grossi not unexpectedly concluded that Glenn had in fact lived as Richard Lawrence, adding that "this further proves the existence of life after death."

Grossi may be said to belong to the "anything goes school." A much better known member of this school is the previously mentioned Indian regressionist H. N. Banerjee. I first came across him in an article in *The Star* of April 4, 1980, which featured a report on the work of Ian Stevenson and one of his birthmark cases that I will

---

9. September 10, 1984.

discuss in Chapter 10. Banerjee is shown with the actress Ann Miller who is convinced that she had an earlier life as the Egyptian queen Hatshepsut who ruled in 1500 B.C.E. Even as a child Ann Miller felt an "eerie link" with Egypt and when she saw a statue of Queen Hatshepsut at the Metropolitan Museum in New York she knew that this was her former self. She subsequently visited the queen's tomb and "knew instinctively" the location of the queen's missing body. To her astonishment it was indeed recovered a few days later in the location specified by Ann. Banerjee, wearing a benign smile which clearly indicated that he would certify any past life of a movie star, reassured Ann that her story was entirely plausible. "I am convinced that her story is true. She always had a strong unexplainable feeling for Egypt." The same article also informs us that in a previous life Cher, looking very beautiful, was an advisor to an Egyptian king and that Susan Strassberg lived in Ancient Rome as a Christian who was thrown to the lions. Ann Miller seems just right as an Egyptian queen, but Susan Strassberg, who happens to be a highly intelligent woman, could really have done better. What fun is there in being a Christian and especially one who is eaten by lions?

Banerjee is the coauthor and author respectively of two "classical" works on reincarnation: *Lives Unlimited—Reincarnation East and West,* published by Doubleday in 1974 and written in conjunction with Will Oursler, a well-known journalist of an earlier generation, and *Americans Who Have Been Reincarnated,* published by Macmillan in 1980. I cannot describe the former of these better than by quoting a paragraph from the book's jacket:

> Moving from the most secluded reaches of Tibet, where reincarnation has long been regarded as a fact of life, to the legendary island of Atlantis, from the trances of Bridey Murphy to the visions of Edgar Cayce, the authors explore the different approaches to "other lives" taken by Buddhists, Hindus, Tibetans, and Western believers. Their discoveries will bring even the most skeptical readers into the heart of the search for the human soul.

On the cover of the second book Banerjee is identified as Executive and Research Director of the Schofenberg Research Foundation, Kingfisher, Oklahoma, and Director of Research, India Institute of Parapsychology, Jaipur, Rajastan, India. A letter I sent to him at the Schofenberg Foundation was returned to me with a note that he had gone back to India where, we may be sure, he is carrying on his valuable work. Banerjee tells us in *Americans Who Have Been Reincarnated* that belief in reincarnation is a tradition "as American as baseball and apple pie" and he asserts that many famous Americans, including Benjamin Franklin, Walt Whitman, Henry David Thoreau, Henry Ford, General Patton, and J. Paul Getty were reincarnationists. What he says is true about the last three on this list, but I am not so sure about the first three. In any event, the book carries ringing endorsements from several of the best-known tabloid occultists, including Sybil Leek, Jess Stearn, Brad Steiger, and Gina Cerminara whom we already met in the last chapter. Banerjee was one of the first to treat people by a form of past-life therapy that he called "para-analysis" and which is said to be a help in the cure of everything from migraine to unwanted personality traits. The highlight of Banerjee's book is undoubtedly the chapter in which he describes the five past lives of Glenn Ford, a prominent Hollywood actor of the 1950s and 1960s. In the sessions with Banerjee, Ford discovered previous lives as a piano teacher in Scotland in the early 1800s and as a member of Louis XIV's cavalry. Some years later, with the help of another regressionist, Ford recalled lives as a cowboy, a British sailor in the seventeenth century and a Christian by the name of Flavius who was thrown to the lions in the Coliseum. I would not be surprised if he met Susan Strassburg there. Ford claims that the regressions conquered his fear of death.

Prominent among other stars who have had earlier lives are Loretta Lynn, Sylvester Stallone, and, needless to say, Shirley MacLaine.[10] Loretta Lynn had no fewer than six previous lives. In one she was a Cherokee princess, in another an Irish woman and in a third a rural American housewife. These she discovered on her own. In 1980, as a result of hypnotic regressions, she discovered three more lives—as the wife of a bedridden old man, a male restaurant employee in the 1920s, and as a maid in the royal household of one of the King Georges of England (she does not remember which George). She had an affair with the king, but she also got involved with one of his courtiers. "The king's best friend kept grabbing me and making love to me behind the king's back," she told John Leo, "and I was afraid to tell the king about it because they were such buddies." The king died before Loretta but then she was choked to death by the courtier. I find this difficult to understand. I would have thought that the king's demise would be welcomed by the lovers who now had no fear of discovery. Stallone thinks he may have been a monkey in Guatemala, something I find entirely credible, and also a wolf. He told Leo that he feels a strong kinship with wolves and that he has been able to go up to them in the wild without being harmed. He also had a previous life as a human being. It occurred during the French Revolution. Stallone "feels sure" that he was guillotined by the Jacobins.

Shirley MacLaine obtained the information about her previous lives not by hypnotic regression but during acupuncture and chiefly by consulting trance mediums in California, Sweden, and Peru. All of them turned up the same facts—that she had lived many times before, both as male and as female. "I was definitely a prostitute in some lifetime," she is quoted as saying. "It is no accident that I played all those hookers." Her most tragic life was undoubtedly as a court jester during the reign of Louis XV. The king personally decapitated her "for telling impertinent jokes." "I watched my head rolling on the floor. It landed face up and a big tear came out of one eye." It may be of some interest to point out that in Voltaire's *Century of Louis XV* there is no mention of any beheading of a woman by the king. Voltaire had the utmost loathing for Louis XV for personal as well as ideological reasons and he would never have suppressed such a juicy royal crime if it had really occurred. Perhaps

---

10. John Leo, "Reincarnation Is Alive and Well in Hollywood," *Time*, September 10, 1984, p. 68.

Shirley meant Louis XIV, but Voltaire also wrote *The Century of Louis XIV* and there is again no mention of a beheading of anybody by the king. Voltaire did not write about Louis XVI, but as everybody knows, this ill-fated monarch's only connection with beheadings was the loss of his own head.

"Reincarnation International"

Ever since the early years of the century Great Britain has been fertile territory for past-life regressions. It is not easy for somebody living in the United States to keep track of all the fascinating reincarnations occurring in the British Isles. Fortunately, in January of 1994 a quarterly entitled *Reincarnation International* began to appear in London, which contains all the information that a reincarnation enthusiast could desire.

I discovered this remarkable publication through an announcement available at the library of the American Society for Psychical Research. The opening paragraph of the announcement will give an idea of the scope of this new publication:

> Have you lived before? Do you share with Sylvester Stallone a belief that you were beheaded during the French Revolution? Perhaps your past-life roots go back to Egyptian times like Tina Turner who may even have been Queen Hatshepsut Maat-ka-Ra. Or is your past as colorful as that of the late Judge Christmas Humphreys who was certain he had been sentenced to death some 3,300 years ago during the reign of Egypt's Ramses II for making love to a Virgin of Isis.

Christmas Humphreys, it will be recalled, was the prosecutor (not judge) who spoke so cruelly about children suffering from genetic illnesses and handicaps. His unjust death sentence in Ancient Egypt may well have been the cause of his mean-spiritedness. As for Tina Turner, she should be informed that Ann Miller has a prior claim on Queen Hatshepsut.

Roy Stemman, the publisher and editor of *Reincarnation International* warns against uncritically taking hypnotic regressions at their face value:

> The power of the mind *is* incredible and there is no doubt that our subconscious has the ability to imagine and invent—particularly under hypnosis—in a way which we still do not fully understand. For that reason, I believe it is wrong for people who are hypnotically regressed to an apparent past life to take it at face value, as many do, without checking its veracity. They need to assess the evidence very carefully before they can speak with confidence about having lived in a previous incarnation.

Fortunately, however, many cases can be supported by independent verification:

> The work of Dr. Ian Stevenson has added considerably to our knowledge and he is now studying cases in which a person appears to have been reborn carrying physical marks which coincide with the cause of death—such as a bullet wound to the head.

By the time I am writing this chapter, four issues of *Reincarnation International* have been published and for the most part they do not disappoint. In spite of the cautious disclaimer I quoted a moment ago, *Reincarnation International* belongs to the anything-goes school. The very first issue contains a totally uncritical article about Bridey Murphy with pictures of Bernstein, Virginia Tighe, and other participants. The case is celebrated as a great breakthrough. This article was something of a bore, but it must be said that every issue contains exciting reincarnation news from all over the world. John Mack's *Abduction: Human Encounters with Aliens* (1994) is sympathetically reviewed by the editor in the July 1994 issue. I had not known that in addition to being an abductionist Mack is now also a believer in reincarnation. According to the review, Mack told *Esquire* that by using a special breathing technique he discovered his previous life in sixteenth-century Russia in which his four-year-old son was decapitated by Mongols. The review also mentions the story of Donna Bassett, a skeptical writer who went to Mack claiming that she had been abducted. Mack was easily fooled, but his supporters claim that she had indeed been abducted. One obviously cannot win against these people.

By far the most exciting issue to date is number 4 (November 1994). It tells us that Princess Diana believes that she once was a nun. In the same issue there is the sensational story of a German airman, killed in the Battle of Britain, who was reborn in Scotland and who has established contact with his surviving German co-pilot. There is also a full illustrated report of a reincarnation conference in Oslo, attended by, among others, Dr. Raymond Moody, the *Life After Life* celebrity; Satwant Pasricha, Ian Stevenson's loyal associate whose investigations I will discuss in Chapter 16; and an orthodox rabbi from Minneapolis who has established contact with the souls of some of the victims of the Holocaust.

Perhaps the most enjoyable story, discussed in every issue so far, is that of Jenny Cockell, an English housewife, forty-one years old, who had a previous life as Mary Sutton in Malahide, a small town north of Dublin. Jenny has told her story in *Yesterday's Children,* a book that by 1994 had gone into a third printing. She has been the subject of a television documentary and has spoken about her past life and her children from that life in numerous television, radio, and press interviews. She and her "former oldest son," Sonny, have even appeared together on the "Donahue" show in New York.

The story of Jenny's discovery of her previous incarnation is altogether remarkable. As a child Jenny had oppressive dreams in which she was a woman named Mary lying in a hospital bed, mortally ill, and full of anxiety about the children she was leaving behind. She had "always known" that the period of her previous life was from 1898 to the 1930s and that it took place in Ireland. Studying a map of the Irish Republic she was mysteriously drawn to Malahide. With the aid of a number of hypnotic regressions and a series of dubious inferences everything was solved. A Mary Sutton in Malahide had died at the appropriate time and left numerous children behind who were not properly cared for by their father, an alcoholic who was given to violent fits. Most of Mary Sutton's children are now in their sixties or seventies and Sonny, the oldest, happily accepted Jenny as his mother. Some of the others appear to be luke-warm, but they are at least friendly, whatever they may think in private. Jenny's quest, Roy Stemman observes, "has lifted a huge burden of guilt from her shoulders—guilt apparently carried with her from a previous life."[11]

The articles and interviews in *Reincarnation International* are profusely illustrated and several of the photos are priceless. One shows Mary Sutton, who looks exceptionally beautiful, with her daughter Phyllis in 1927, when Phyllis was two years old. Below it is Jenny, looking young and handsome, with Phyllis, very grim and ancient with a shock of white hair. On the same page is a picture of Jenny with her oldest son, Sonny. There is not the slightest physical resemblance. He is quite small, totally bald, and looks like a man in his mid or late seventies. Jenny clearly feels great tenderness for Sonny. Although he may be much older than she, chronologically speaking, he is "really" over twenty years younger and in much need of maternal affection. This case is pure joy, worthy of the Marx Brothers or Woody Allen. Incidentally, Jenny thinks that reincarnations are a "normal thing." She remembers several other lives, especially one in Japan immediately preceding her life as Mary Sutton. Unfortunately all the children from that life must have died long ago and there will not be any happy reunions.

Futurology

In recent years past-life regressionists have extended their activities to exploration of future lives. It is reasoned that, if hypnosis can regress a person to a period before he was born, it can also "progress" him to a period after his death. In their future lives the subjects would of course be familiar with the state of the world at that time and all kinds of interesting things might be learned that cannot be discerned by ordinary means. There is just one catch. The "progressionists" almost never show any interest in the near future. People are progressed to future centuries when all of us, including the skeptics, will be safely dead.

The late Helen Wambach was not only a leading past-life regressionist; she was one of the stars of the tabloids and one of the "authorities" to whom Shirley MacLaine appeals for a scientific underpinning of her investigations. She was a leading contributor to *Psychic,* a magazine devoted to "New Realities," and the author of two widely circulating books, *Reliving Past Lives* (1978) and *Life Before Life* (1979). By 1977 she had reached such celebrity status that James Crenshaw, a prominent occultist writer whom we shall meet again in the chapter on Kübler-Ross, wrote an entire admiring article about her work for *Fate.* Even outside occult groups Wambach's work has occasionally been treated with respect. In *Death, Society, and Human Experience,* a psychology and sociology text, the second edition of which was published in 1981,

---

11. *Reincarnation International,* January 1994, p. 14.

Robert J. Kastenbaum treats Wambach seriously as one of the two leading reincar-nationists, the other being Ian Stevenson.[12] It should be added that in a memorable déjà vu experience in 1966 Wambach discovered a previous life in the eighteenth century as John Woolman, a Quaker preacher, who had been a crusader against slavery.[13]

Wambach's futurological findings were published in the *National Enquirer* in May 1982. "Amazingly," we were told, all subjects progressed into future lives between 2100 and 2300 agreed on what they saw—"a frightening world devastated by a nuclear holocaust and pollution and devoid of vegetation." How they survived is not clear, but perhaps they had taken sufficient provisions into their space vehicles since half of Wambach's subjects were "inside space colonies orbiting around the earth." Fortunately after 2300 conditions on the earth "had" greatly improved. Nevertheless, many of those progressed were by then living on other planets. "Amazingly," we are also informed, "people from outer space had been helping in the evacuation of the earth."

Before leaving Dr. Wambach I should mention that, as behooves a leading figure in the immortality movement, she herself had a moving near-death experience in 1981. It was reported in *The Globe* of December 13, 1983, along with numerous other similar and equally remarkable visits to the next world. We are told that Helen "slipped into the afterworld during surgery." In the operating room her father appeared to her. "A warm glow spread through my body," she told *The Globe,* "and my father was bathed in a white light." Her father "looked" at her and told her that it was not yet time to join him. "You still have much work to do," he said and Helen promptly returned to this life. It is not entirely clear how she recognized her father or how, having lost his original body including the eyes, he could "look" at her. I gather that he had not yet begun a new incarnation and was living in the astral world which Bridey Murphy had found so tedious. Helen's visit no doubt greatly improved his mood.

One of my favorite progressionists is Dr. Bruce Goldberg, a talented comedian who, when I corresponded with him in the mid-1980s, was a dentist in Baltimore and also had a practice in past-life therapy. As I mentioned previously he has moved to California and now confines himself to treating physical and psychological complaints by means of hypnotic regressions as well as progressions. In his *Past Lives, Future Lives* (1982), a book that easily solves all the most difficult metaphysical problems, he reports numerous exciting progressions. He admits that progressing a person is much more difficult than regressing him and explains this as due to the fact that all of us have been "programmed to believe that the future hasn't occurred yet." This is evidently a serious error. In spite of this widespread prejudice, Dr. Goldberg frequently succeeds in progressing his subjects into distant centuries. He reveals in some detail what life will be like in the year 2542. Some altogether remarkable

---

12. In 1984 Prentice Hall published a wretched little book by Kastenbaum, *Is There Life After Death,* in which he shows himself to be a convert to reincarnation and totally distorts, whether by design or ignorance, the case of the unbeliever.

13. *Reliving Past Lives,* op. cit., pp. 1–2. See also Banerjee, *Americans Who Have Been Reincarnated,* op. cit., pp. 64–66.

changes will have taken place by then, especially in such areas as transportation, farming, and the dissemination of information. Dr. Goldberg made his discoveries by progressing a young man from Baltimore named Larry who in his future life became Zeku, the son of a scientist by the name of Lus-Lus who was in charge of constructing an underwater city. The progression gets really exciting when Dr. Goldberg asks Zeku how people moved around in 2542. The answer, to use *National Enquirer* terminology, was "startling": "You could be beamed from one place to another, which consisted of disassembling the molecules of your body and reassembling them at the other transportation center at your destination"[14] Unfortunately the technique of "disassembling" and "reassembling" the molecules of the body is not described. I hope that mistakes were not frequent at the destination, especially as far as brain-molecules were concerned. Zeku had equally "amazing" information about the size of fruits:

> Farming had undergone tremendous change. Very large forms of vegetation were developed by geneticists, resulting in fruits the size of cars. Lasers were used to divide and process the foodstuff.[15]

What is not explained is how these giant fruits were delivered or stored. No doubt there were by then refrigerators the size of baseball stadiums to accommodate the new giant apples, peaches, and strawberries. As for transportation, perhaps the fruits were temporarily shrunk to the familiar size in the store and then returned to their real size upon reaching the customer's home. Undoubtedly the highlight of technological improvement concerned the new methods of transmitting information to the public. Newspapers disappeared. Instead there was the "information pill." This timesaving device "contained all the new scientific achievements, new items of general interest, and all of the latest advancements."[16] New information pills were available every day and my guess is that, in addition to the scientific information, they also contained all the latest gossip. The information pills were swallowed just like other pills, and here for once one could be sure that all the new ideas were really digested. Dr. Goldberg in his modesty has not realized that he himself constitutes the best evidence for reincarnation. His comic gifts are quite in the same league as those of Fatty Arbuckle and Ben Turpin. I do not for a moment believe that such a stupendous talent can be explained by ordinary genetics. The only adequate explanation would be in terms of one or more previous lives of assiduous labor, or else the hand of God.

Much as I admire Drs. Wambach and Goldberg, I must register one complaint. I wish that they would give us information about the near future, perhaps the next two decades or even the next two years, especially in such matters as nuclear disasters and the conquest of disease. Stock market quotations would also be welcome. I venture

---

14. Bruce Goldberg, *Past Lives, Future Lives,* pp. 163–64.
15. Ibid., p. 264.
16. Ibid., p. 165.

the guess that they and other hypnotic explorers of the future will not comply and that they will continue to confine their progressions to distant centuries.

The preceding paragraph was published in the first of my articles on reincarnation in *Free Inquiry* in the fall of 1986. Since then my request for short-term predictions has been fulfilled. In *Mass Dreams of the Future,* published by McGraw-Hill, Chet B. Snow, who was Helen Wambach's main assistant during her final years (she died in 1985) and who may not unfairly be described as her spiritual heir, has offered numerous predictions about events in the 1990s. Snow was hypnotically progressed by Helen Wambach during a "fateful October 1983" session. Wambach took Snow past his July 1998 birthday and "on to the end of that fateful year." Snow observed dreadful disasters wherever he looked:

> . . . unlike 1997, it now seemed as if the world had collapsed and everything that had been important before no longer mattered.
>
> I immediately knew that large chunks of the former West Coast had quickly sunk into the Pacific ocean as several earthquakes and volcanic eruptions had decimated the "Ring of Fire" borderlands surrounding the Pacific earth plate. It might be more accurate to say that the ocean had come rushing up into the California valleys as the bottom had literally fallen out at key coastal junctures, shaken by the seismic activity. Water stretched as far inland in some areas as parts of Nevada and Arizona.
> . . . Apparently the entire Pacific area had been wracked with storms and various Earth changes: quakes, volcanoes or land sinks. On the opposite side of the continent there had also been some flooding and quakes, but in general the land had risen instead of falling into the sea.[17]

Wambach then asked how things were going in Japan and received a horrifying reply:

> Japan as a country doesn't exist any longer. A lot of it's fallen into the sea.
>
> It was the same when she asked about human casualties resulting from all these cataclysms.
>
> "How many people have died as a result of these wars and natural disasters?" she asked.
>
> "Millions," was my immediate and laconic reply.
>
> Although my voice sounded so calm, that simple word, a mere number but with what implications, shocked my conscious mind, which was monitoring the experience as always. I thought, "I must be mistaken!" But sadly a feeling that this is a minimal figure remains with me long after that fateful October 1983 session and I must stand by that answer, hard as it is to accept rationally.[18]

The "Soviets," who presumably reemerged after the 1991 breakup of their country, behaved atrociously during these commotions:

---

17. *Mass Dreams of the Future,* 11, 13, 15.
18. Ibid., p. 15.

Instead of moving with immediate humanitarian relief, the Soviets had taken advantage of our temporary helplessness to take over West Berlin and most of West Germany. Yugoslavia was being undermined by a vicious civil war into which Soviet-led troops from Hungary and Czechoslovakia had intervened. Washington had protested vainly and had again cemented alliances with Great Britain, France and Italy but could do little else.[19]

It is reassuring to know that in spite of all these cataclysmic disasters Snow himself remains optimistic about the future of the human race. As a comedian he is not in Bruce Goldberg's league. Where Goldberg is joyously absurd, Snow is deadly dull. His gloomy forecasts show only one thing: it is wisest to confine hypnotically derived predictions to the distant future.

The Journal of Regression Therapy

It must not be thought that Snow has shown the slightest repentance about the forecast that Soviet troops would overrun West Berlin and most of West Germany in 1997. Quite the opposite: he takes credit for his remarkably accurate prediction. The July 1995 issue of *Reincarnation International* has a two-page article in which Snow relates various highlights of his career. He tells of his past-life therapy with Helen Wambach in the course of which he was taken back to Atlantis and also to Egypt where he was stabbed in the back. He then turns to the political situation in Europe (1995) and with brazen effrontery he implies that his prophesies have been fully confirmed:

> I was able to look forward in time and see some things which are already coming true
> in the mid-1990s and these were published in the book 10 years ago. Already the Yu-
> goslavian situation is where it is, the Russians are looking much less nice—there's
> a real political difficulty there which could well come to the surface again, as I saw.[20]

It is obvious that one cannot argue with somebody like Snow. One can only be thankful that the world does not contain too many people with brains like his.

Snow is evidently regarded as a major figure among reincarnationists both in England and the United States. *Reincarnation International* for July 1994 features his picture together with a short article singing his praises. Entitled "Tomorrow Today" the journal expresses pleasure over the visit to London by "Dr. Chet Snow, best-selling author of *Mass Dreams of the Future*." (It is total news to me that this book has ever been a best-seller.) The article goes on to list numerous lectures and seminars Snow was about to give in England. It concludes by mentioning that since 1984 Snow

---

19. Ibid.
20. P. 22. The editor of *Reincarnation International* sees nothing wrong with Snow's claim that his predictions have been confirmed.

has led more than 300 "transformational" seminars around the world and is also a past-president of the California-based "Association for Past Life Research and Therapy" (APRT). For some years the association has been publishing the *Journal of Regression Therapy* which has had numerous well-known reincarnationists on its editorial board, including Edith Fiore, Raymond Moody, and C. Norman Shealy. The spring 1989 issue contains a rousing review of *Mass Dreams of the Future* by Hazel Denning who seems to be the guiding spirit of the journal. The book is described as a "monumental work" and Snow as "another prophetic voice pointing the way to changing history and creating a future world of harmony and peaceful coexistence." The progressions of Snow and other of Wambach's subjects reported in *Mass Dreams* provide the strongest evidence that there will be a "decline of the world's population up to 95% within a couple of generations, followed by renewed growth thereafter." Like Snow, Denning engages in "apocalyptic thinking":

> Using the astrological concept of the "Great Tropical Year" as a model of historical Time cycles, Dr. Snow argues that part of our current Apocalyptic thinking may spring from man's subconscious memories of the Great Flood which sank Atlantis around 12,500 years ago. Is the planet preparing for a repeat performance of that or some similar cataclysm as we pass from the Age of Pisces into that of Aquarius?

Needless to say, Denning was delighted that Snow devotes an entire chapter to UFOs, Star People, Walk-ins, and out-of-body experiences.

Denning's review of Snow's book is entirely representative of the level and viewpoint of the articles and reviews in the *Journal*. Every New Age extravaganza, however farfetched, is actively promoted. One of the favorite topics is "spirit releasement therapy." According to releasement therapists human beings are frequently "taken over" by one or more "discarnate" beings. The spirit is usually that of a dead person who has not yet moved on to higher regions. According to the description of a course offered by the Discovery Center on the West Side of Manhattan, of all places, seventy to a hundred percent of the population are affected or influenced by one or more spirit entities. The leading authority on this topic is Edith Fiore whose "classic" *The Unquiet Dead*, published by Doubleday in 1987, is enthusiastically reviewed in the spring 1987 issue. The book contains descriptions of "spirit entry," ways to detect spirit possession and, most important, the technique of "depossession." In the fall 1986 issue there is a fascinating article by Louise Ireland-Frey entitled "Clinical Depossession: Releasement of Attached Entities from Unsuspecting Hosts." The author tells us that she frequently speaks to the spirits and occasionally asks them for advice. If a session lasts over two hours she finds it wise to terminate it and requests the spirits within the client to remain inactive until the next session. She asks them to answer through the fingers if they understand her. Only once has there been more than a brief pause before an affirmative answer was given. On some occasions two entities were in disagreement within the patient—one was willing to say yes

while the other said no. "Much to the host's puzzlement and discomfort," such conflicts are not rare.[21] From another writer I learned that occasionally spirits attach
themselves to the therapist during the session and then we are really in a pickle. However, appropriate coaxing can usually overcome the most obstreperous spirits. Not
only mental but also physical conditions can be cured by depossession. The fall
1987 issue has an article by Dr. (Ph.D.) Hiroshi Motoyama, a Japanese depossessor,
which is summarized in the table of contents as follows:

> Dr. Motoyama relates the process of resolution of a severe intestinal condition in a
> man who in a previous lifetime had drawn the attachment of an angry feudal lord.
> Working through the karmic relationship and releasing the attached spirit restored the
> suffering man to health. Dr. Motoyama outlines the necessary steps in transcending
> such karma.

It may be noted that Edith Fiore is also interested in abductions by space aliens. In
1989 Doubleday published her *Encounters* (Doubleday), which is favorably reviewed
by Hazel Denning in the October 1990 issue. The conclusion of her book which has
been unfairly neglected outside abduction circles deserves to be quoted in full:

> I feel that the discovery of visits to our planet Earth by beings from other worlds and
> their interactions with humans is the most exciting and significant happening of the
> twentieth century.

"Channeling," made popular by Shirley MacLaine, is not short-changed. Chet
Snow reviews John Klimo's "standard" book on the subject in the spring 1989 issue. I
need hardly tell the reader that he finds it "outstanding." If properly used, channeling
can "open one to more self-awareness, both as a spiritual being and as part of a greater,
living Whole." Snow was particularly intrigued to discover that "everyone from God
to Jesus Christ to extraterrestrials, group souls, and the 'elementals' from plants and
minerals have thus voiced their opinion at one time or another,"[22] which seems to be
Snow's convoluted way of saying that all of them have been sources of channeling. I
should add that Klimo, the author of the standard book, is also an occasional contributor to the *Journal.*

Denning, Snow, Fiore, Motoyama, and Klimo are daring and original thinkers, but
nobody is quite in the same class as Dr. Bruce Goldberg, the futurologist we met in a
previous section. In the October 1990 issue we learn that in 1989 he retired from den-
tistry "to give his full time to hypnotherapy, a field in which he is recognized as an authority." We also learn that he is a life member of the APRT and president of the Los
Angeles Academy of Clinical Hypnosis. In case any reader wishes to become his patient or "client," let me add that his new practice is located in Reseda, California. The

---

21. *Journal of Regression Therapy,* Vol. 1, p. 100.
22. P. 81. Klimo's *Channeling* was published in Los Angeles in 1987.

same issue of the *Journal* publishes a sensational article by Dr. Goldberg entitled "Your Problem May Come from Your Future: A Case Study." I believe that never before has anybody been cured by treating the future cause of his present trouble. This is truly mind-boggling, but it will seem incredible only to those of us who believe that time is real and who fail to realize that the future *is* now. Dr. Goldberg begins the article by objecting to John Gribbin's remark in *Time Warps* (1980) that hypnosis researchers had failed to investigate future lives. Dr. Goldberg protests that he has been doing progression therapy for no less than thirteen years "to help patients overcome habits, phobias, and other self-defeating sequences that began in a *future* lifetime."[23] He then offers the case history of a patient by the name of Pete who had a hand-washing compulsion and who was also haunted by the number eight and the name Teresa. Dr. Goldberg effected a complete cure by progressing Pete to the year 2088 when Pete (now called Ben), who was at that time a technician in a nuclear facility in Tulsa, Oklahoma, committed a horrendous blunder resulting in a meltdown, which contaminated the entire Tulsa area and also led to the death of a skeleton crew and of Ben himself. Ben died in August 2088. The eighth month in the year 2088 had obvious associations to the number 8. Ben also worked in the "Teres-Alpha unit" which spells out as Teresa, the name that had been haunting Pete for most of his life. Pete is totally recovered and if he is going to be a technician in an atomic installation in 2088, he will be doubly careful never to commit any horrendous blunders. He is going to tune in to a different "frequency" and in that way avoid the dreadful events in the future to which Dr. Goldberg had progressed him. "I like this case," Dr. Goldberg concludes, "because it illustrates the principle that the future is now. We can change the future, but we must perceive it first."[24]

I hope that the reader will realize what a colossal breakthrough Dr. Goldberg has achieved in showing that mental (and also, I suppose, physical) illnesses can be due to what *will* happen to a person. He has opened up a rich field for novel diagnoses and treatments. I would not be surprised if in future centuries he will be referred to as "the sage from Baltimore." In the meantime, a Nobel Prize for Medicine and a fellowship in the Royal Society would surely not be out of place. However, our admiration for Dr. Goldberg's gifts must not blind us to the incoherence of his story. There cannot be two different futures for Pete in Tulsa or anywhere else in the year 2088. He either will die in the meltdown of the atomic energy plant or he will not die such a fiery death at that time. Dr. Goldberg's talk about different "frequencies" leading to different futures is pure verbiage. Knowledge of the future *as it will really be* cannot result in altering the future. Knowledge of what *would happen* if certain conditions are fulfilled can help to avoid what *would have happened* if these conditions had been fulfilled. Even if we allow the possibility of progressing somebody into the future, the individual could not observe a *merely hypothetical* future, just as in the present one cannot perceive a merely hypothetical person or object. Richard Nixon had two daughters and I suppose that he could have had a son, but it is impossible for anybody

23. *Journal of Regression Therapy,* 1990, p. 21, Dr. Goldberg's emphasis.
24. Ibid., p. 29.

to perceive the merely possible son. Avoiding conditions which would have brought about a certain undesirable result is not changing the future, and regardless of what Dr. Goldberg or anybody else may say, the future is not now.

It is a good thing that Hitler did not have Dr. Goldberg's gift. By having himself (or one of his associates) progressed at the time of Pearl Harbor to VE Day, he might have decided not to declare war on the United States and the world would have suffered vastly more damage than it did.

Does Past-Life Therapy Work?

By 1977 past-life therapy had become sufficiently faddish to be written up in the "Behavior" section of *Time*.[25] The most interesting cases in this article come from the patients of Morris Netherton, a therapist practicing in Los Angeles. One of them concerns Nancy Shiffrin who suffered from writer's block. This was traced back to the seventeenth century when she recalled being on trial for heresy. She had hidden an incriminating diary from her persecutors. Three hundred years later she was still "hiding the book." After therapy with Netherton she overcame her block and can now finish books. In fact she is listed along with Netherton as coauthor of *Past Lives Therapy* (1978), one of the first full-length books on the subject. Another patient, Diane Strom, whose picture is reproduced in the article, complained about anxiety over financial problems when she was in fact well-off. Netherton's diagnosis was that she had a fear that nobody would help her when she was in trouble. She relived her birth in the course of which she struggled with the umbilical cord that was wrapped around her neck. In another regression she saw her son trampled by a horse. She ran into town for help but nobody came to her assistance. We are not told whether Diane Strom was freed from her irrational fears about money or, if she was, whether no other symptoms took their place.

Time quoted two critical opinions. One came from the well-known English psychiatrist Anthony Storr who saw in past-life recollections nothing more than instances of cryptomnesia which, I am sure, is true but does not explain their alleged therapeutic effectiveness. The comments by Alexander Rogawski, former chief of the Los Angeles County Medical Association's psychiatry section, were far more derogatory. "It's a mystic takeoff on psychoanalysis—one of those fads that come and go like mushrooms." The popularity of past-life therapy proves only that "suckers are born every minute and customers can be found for everything." I fully agree that suckers are born every minute and that probably most patients in past-life therapy fall into this category. However, such a sweeping dismissal is not satisfactory because we know, *not* from the writings of believers, but of completely skeptical psychologists that the technique occasionally does achieve results; and it is an interesting question why this should be so if reincarnation is a myth and hence all past-life recollections illusions.

---

25. October 3, 1977.

In an extremely interesting and valuable article[26] Jonathan Venn, a psychotherapist from Baltimore, reports his treatment, lasting for sixty sessions, of a twenty-six-year-old patient who was suffering from hypochondriac chest pains. Venn uses hypnosis but is not a believer in reincarnation. One of Matthew's complaints (Venn refers to the patient as Matthew) was that he could not cry. This was traced back to his father's striking him for crying and threatening to strike him again if he did not stop. In the third session, apparently without urging from Venn, he regressed to the personality of a French pilot supposedly killed over Belgium in 1914. His name at that time was Jacques Gionne Trecaultes. He "remembered" being machine-gunned through the chest by a German pilot. He cried, moaned, yelled, sweated, and clutched at his chest for half an hour. Matthew also "relived" four other lifetimes and "previewed" two future lives and he ostensibly communicated with persons living on another planet. He came to believe in the reality of these other lives, especially that of Jacques, for which he presented the most vivid details.

When they were checked, most of Matthew's "memories" turned out to be false. Nevertheless the hypochondriacal symptoms disappeared and Venn also reports that Matthew's family and social relations greatly improved. According to Venn, Matthew improved not because he remembered having been shot through the chest in a previous life but because of the release of strong, taboo emotions and the relationship with his therapist. "The release of strong emotions," Venn writes, "was made possible by the rapport and by the past-life fantasy, precisely because it *was* a fantasy. It provided sufficient distance from reality for Matthew to release his tears."[27] I think that all of this makes good sense although a number of facts have not been explained, for example, why the patient felt the need to regress to earlier lives and why he should enact the particular fantasies that enabled him to cry. I have not met Venn, but he strikes me as a warm and highly intelligent man, vastly superior to the kind of person connected with the APRT. Matthew had no fewer than sixty sessions with Venn and if I am right about Venn's emotional and intellectual character, the experience of being accepted by such a person must have had a healing effect, as Venn himself is quick to point out.

Three questions remain. First, did Matthew's improvements last? Assuming that they lasted, how many patients treated by this method show significant improvements? And, finally, does the success of past-life therapy prove that the traumatic events "remembered" really took place? I do not know the answer to the first two questions, but there is no doubt about the third, which is the only one strictly relevant to our concerns in this book. Successful treatment by past-life therapy does not prove the reality of past lives: there is no *a priori* reason why the discharge of repressed emotions can be beneficial only if it is accompanied by veridical memories.

---

26. "Hypnosis and the Reincarnation Hypothesis: A Critical Review and Intensive Case Study," *Journal of the American Society for Psychical Research,* October 1986.

27. P. 422, Venn's italics.

✿❧❀❧✿

7

Spontaneous Memories of Earlier Lives

✿❧❀❧✿

Throughout the ages claims have been made by or on behalf of certain individuals that they could recall previous lives. These memories or ostensible memories differ from hypnotic regressions in that they occur to the person in his waking life and, furthermore, they are not provoked by an artificial stimulus. "I have been born many times, Arjuna," says Krishna in the Bhagavad Gita,

> and many times hast thou been born. But I remember my past lives and thou hast forgotten thine.[1]

It is widely believed by Buddhists that yogis have the power to remember entire past lives, and not only recent ones, but all those in which they inhabited a human body. In his Preface to the fourth edition of the *Tibetan Book of the Dead,* the editor, an American anthropologist by the name of W. Y. Evans-Wentz, who was a convert to Buddhism, insists that the belief in reincarnation need not be taken on faith. On the contrary, it has a "sound basis" in the "unequivocal testimony of yogis who claim to have died and reentered the human womb consciously."[2] Similarly, Swami Nikhilananda, the editor of the abbreviated version of the Upanishads whom I quoted earlier, rejects the theory of annihilation partly because it is inconsistent with "the intuitive and direct experience of the seers regarding the indestructibility of the soul."[3]

In Buddhist scriptures the Buddha is frequently credited with remembering an unlimited number of his own earlier lives and also with the power to intuit the details

---

1. IV, 5.
2. P. v.
3. P. 58.

99

of the past and future incarnations of other human beings. In the Sanyutta-Nikaya the Buddha is reported to have made the following claim:

> I, brethren, according as I desire, can remember my divers former lives, that is today, one birth, or two, or three, or four, or five births, or ten, twenty, thirty, forty, fifty births, or a hundred, a thousand, or even a hundred thousand, or even more.

John Hick, to whose *Death and Eternal Life* I am indebted for this information, mentions the Buddha's alleged recollection of life as an immensely rich and powerful king in

> a royal city surrounded by seven ramparts of gold, silver, beryl, crystal, agate, coral, and gems; this surrounded by seven rows of palm trees made of similar precious stones and metals; his magnificent palace; his 84,000 wives, chief of whom was the Pearl among Women; his 84,000 dependent cities; his 84,000 elephants.[4]

For a preacher of asceticism these are rather remarkable collections. I have often wondered where space could be found to house 84,000 wives, not to speak of 84,000 elephants. Hick points out that there is no credible historical evidence that the real Buddha ever made such claims and he adds that details of his past incarnations "belong to the rhetoric of fairytale rather than to historical reality."[5]

Reincarnationists habitually list numerous famous men and women in history who supposedly had spontaneous recollections of earlier lives. The list usually includes Pythagoras, Empedocles, Ovid, the Emperor Julian the Apostate, Swedenborg, Goethe, and Alexander Dumas Fils. They also include in their list the somewhat less famous Madame Blavatsky and Annie Besant, the first two leaders of the Theosophical Society. Empedocles, Swedenborg, Dumas, and the two theosophist ladies really belong on this list, but in the case of the others the evidence is rather dubious or nonexistent. Pythagoras did believe in reincarnation and he may well have claimed to recall previous lives, but the only evidence for this are two paragraphs in Diogenes Laertius, a notoriously unreliable purveyor of gossip and hearsay, and one of Ovid's poems in which Pythagoras is made to recall his participation in the battle of Troy as a brave soldier by the name of Euphorbus.

Julian the Apostate (331–363) is invariably said to have remembered being Alexander the Great. Julian was raised as a Christian but abandoned Christianity as a result of his philosophical studies. He was a just and noble ruler who tried to return the empire to the practice of religious toleration. His early death proved a boon to the persecuting Christians, and I would not at all be surprised if the rumor about his "recollection" was started by Julian's Christian enemies to suggest that he was mad. In any event, even reincarnationists admit that it is nothing more than a story. Goethe

---

4. *Death and Eternal Life*, p. 333.
5. p. 380. The earlier passage is quoted by Hick on p. 379.

did on several occasions express sympathy for "metempsychosis," but the only evidence that he claimed to remember having lived before is the following statement: "Surely, I must have lived already before the Emperor Hadrian, for everything Roman attracts me with inexpressible force." Paul Siwek, a Catholic opponent of reincarnation, devotes a chapter of his *The Enigma of the Hereafter* (1952) to these "memories of the 'initiated.' " Siwek rightly ignores the claims about Ovid and Julian but he takes all the others very seriously and tries to discredit the value of their ostensible memories on the ground that these persons were known to be either psychotic or else exceedingly unbalanced. This seems to me a misguided approach for the simple reason that, as C. D. Broad remarked in a different context, showing that a person is "cracked" does not by itself provide a good reason for supposing that what he claims is false.[6] I should also remark in passing that Siwek fails to show in some cases, especially those of Empedocles and Goethe, that the individuals were either mad or highly disturbed. There are much better strategies of dealing with the reincarnationist appeal to spontaneous memories.

Perhaps nobody in history has had spontaneous memories spanning a longer period than Annie Besant (1847–1933), whom I already briefly mentioned in the chapter on Karma. According to her biographer, Theodore Besterman,[7] she remembered animating the mineral world, ascending to the vegetable kingdom, eventually becoming a monkey. She was born into human form around 600,000 B.C.E. In her first human incarnation, she was a male savage who led warlike expeditions. She reincarnated more than fifty times. More recently she was the Egyptian philosopher Hypathia, who was killed by Christian fanatics. Finally she became Giordano Bruno, the pantheistic philosopher and supporter of the Copernican theory who was burnt in Rome in 1600. I have not been able to discover who she was between her death at the stake and her rebirth in nineteenth-century England.

Annie Besant was immensely famous in her own day. Brought up in a suffocating Anglo-Catholic family, she contracted a disastrous marriage with the Rev. Frank Besant. After the dissolution of the marriage, she became an ardent freethinker and leading figure in the National Secular League, an atheistic organization headed by Charles Bradlaugh. In 1877 she and Bradlaugh were tried for selling *The Fruits of Philosophy*, a pamphlet on contraceptive methods written in 1832 by Charles Knowlton. They were found not guilty of publishing an obscene libel, a verdict which resulted in the legalization of birth control in Britain. Annie subsequently became a prominent socialist, serving for some years on the executive committee of the Fabian Society. She was greatly admired by people of the most varied backgrounds. William James called her "that high-souled lady,"[8] and Pandit Nehru, who had known her

---

6. In discussing the argument for the existence of God from religious experience Broad observes that "one might need to be slightly 'cracked' in order to have some peep-hole into the super-sensible world." (*Religion, Philosophy and Psychical Research*, London, 1952, p. 198).

7. *Mrs. Annie Besant* (London, 1934), pp. 214–21.

8. *Varieties of Religious Experience* (New York, 1961 reprint), p. 37.

when he was a child, spoke of her as "the most magnificent lady"[9] he had ever met. In 1889, she was converted to theosophy and, upon the death of Madame Blavatsky in 1891, she became the leader of the majority faction of the Theosophical Society. She did not wholly retire from politics in her later years, becoming an ardent champion of the movement for Indian independence. She died in India, convinced that she would be swiftly reborn.

The occultist literature of the late nineteenth and early twentieth centuries is filled with accounts of memories for which "remarkable" independent corroboration is claimed. However, it is only with the arrival of Ian Stevenson on the scene that this kind of evidence has acquired an investigator and spokesman whose presentations deserve to be taken seriously. Born in Montreal in 1918, Stevenson obtained his medical degree at McGill University. He eventually specialized in psychiatry and at the age of thirty-nine obtained an appointment as professor of psychiatry and neurology at the University of Virginia Medical School in Charlottesville. As the Carlson Professor of Psychiatry, a post to which he moved some years later, he founded the Division of Parapsychology, whose director he has been ever since. Stevenson is generally distrustful of hypnotic regressions and all the cases he has studied are of the spontaneous variety. He has also been interested in other areas of parapsychology, but his fame rests exclusively on work bearing on reincarnation. In his early publications he did not take a definite stand, but in more recent years he has come out as a very ardent supporter of reincarnation. It should be remarked that he is an excellent writer and that the presentation of his cases is always lucid, systematic, and extremely detailed. Ian Wilson, one of his critics, acknowledges that Stevenson has brought "a new professionalism into a hitherto crank-prone field."[10] The present book contains numerous criticisms of Stevenson's various claims. I therefore wish to record that I have the highest regard for his honesty. All of his case reports contain items that can be made the basis of criticism. Stevenson could easily have suppressed this information. The fact that he did not speaks well for his integrity.

Stevenson got involved with one adult spontaneous-recollection case that caused something of a stir in England in the early 1970s and to which I will turn shortly. However, the bulk of his cases concern small children, and they have a fairly uniform pattern. These children usually begin making statements between the ages of two and four about coming from a home and place different from those in which they are living. They recall altogether different parents and most of them speak of having lived as adolescents and adults. Some also recall their death, often a violent one, in their preceding life. Children vary greatly in the quantity of their utterances and the rich-

---

9. See G. S. Jones's review of Anne Taylor's *Annie Besant: A Biography* (1992), *London Review of Books*, May 27, 1993, p. 17. Anne Taylor's book contains a fascinating description of life among the radical intellectuals during the last decade of the nineteenth century. Other recent biographies are A. Nethercot, *The First Five Lives of Annie Besant* (London, 1961), the same author's *The Last Four Lives of Annie Besant* (London, 1963) and Rosemary Dinnage, *Annie Besant* (Middlesex and New York, 1986).

10. *Mind Out of Time*, p. 48.

ness of the details they recall. The volume and clarity of the statements usually increase until the age of between five and six. After that there is less and less mention of a previous life and by the age of eight the memories have in most cases faded completely. During the period when the child remembers his early life he often behaves in strange ways. The strange behavior, Stevenson notes, is consistent with the character and occupation of the remembered person. However, none of this would be particularly impressive and even begin to be evidence of reincarnation if the children's recollections could not be corroborated. Often indeed they cannot be, and Stevenson dismisses such cases as not deserving further consideration. However, in several cases, which form the subject matter of his books, there has been extensive corroboration. Research shows that the person the child remembers to have been did in fact exist and many, though usually not all, descriptions of the experiences, acts, and relationships turn out to be correct. This at least is what Stevenson maintains; and if one reads his books and articles without knowing what the critics have to say, one can hardly fail to be impressed.

The adult case in which Stevenson became prominently involved concerned an elderly Englishman by the name of Edward Ryall, who wrote a letter to the *Daily Express* in May 1970 saying that he had clear and extensive memories of a life in the seventeenth century as a West Country farmer by the name of John Fletcher. The letter was published and came to Stevenson's attention. Stevenson corresponded with Ryall and paid two visits to his home. He became convinced of the authenticity of Ryall's recollections and encouraged him to write a book about his previous life. Ryall's book, *Second Time Around*, appeared in 1974, with an introduction and supplementary notes by Stevenson. The case caused so much interest that in 1976 the British Broadcasting Corporation devoted a program to it. Participating in the program, the bulk of which was reprinted in *The Listener* of June 3, 1976, were Ryall himself, Stevenson, and two skeptics—John Taylor, professor of mathematics at London University, and John Cohen, professor of psychology at Manchester. Ryall came off very well, parrying all hostile questions, though he quite expectedly failed to convince the skeptics of the genuineness of his recollections.

What are we to make of Stevenson's work? I will discuss the cases of the children in Chapter 16 after I have presented the arguments against reincarnation. There are certain general reasons for rejecting them as evidence for reincarnation that equally apply to all cases of ostensible memories of past lives. These general reasons cannot be adequately stated until the arguments against reincarnation have been discussed. However, aside from these general reasons, there are also more specific, and extremely damaging, objections to Stevenson's investigative methods. Here I wish to say a few words about the denouement of the Ryall case.

Ryall was eventually exposed as either a hoaxer or the victim of delusions, or, very possibly, a combination of the two. Credit for his exposure belongs to Michael Green, an architectural historian whose role will be explained in a moment, Renée Haynes, editor for the British Society of Psychical Research and an Oxford history graduate, and to Ian Wilson, whose *Mind out of Time*, a book I quoted previously, presented the full details of the story for the first time. I should remark in passing that *Mind Out of Time*, a book hardly known in the United States, is far and wide the best work on reincarnation that I have seen. Many of the most famous reincarnation cases are minutely examined and on the basis of meticulous research all of them are found wanting.

From the start, Ryall's book failed to convince most readers. It simply did not have the ring of truth. It did not read like a series of recollections but rather like erotic fiction embellished by some period details. Renée Haynes in her book *The Seeing Eye* (1976) and in several subsequent articles pointed out numerous anachronisms. She and Ian Wilson found that while some of Ryall's recollections did check out, others of a crucial character did not. The main of these was that the parish records of Weston Zoyland do not list any John Fletcher for the period of Ryall's story. They do not record his marriage to a Cecily Fuller or the death of his father or his mother or of Fletcher himself or the baptism of his two sons, all these being events mentioned in Ryall's book. What finally proved the undoing of Ryall's claims were the investigations by Michael Green, the Inspector of Ancient Monuments and Historic Buildings for the Department of Environment in London. Green found Ryall's statements about his house and farmlands extremely vague. He began corresponding with Ryall, who displayed great uneasiness at having his claims for the first time submitted to a real expert. After much evasion and prevarication he finally answered Green's request to mark on a large-scale map that Green had sent to him the location of his lands and to supply details about the construction of his house. It should be mentioned parenthetically that Ryall claimed to have had recollections of his earlier existence throughout his life and they were not only not fading but becoming clearer and more specific. When Ryall finally replied, he placed the farmlands on a location that had been open marshland until 1800, and the house he described was not a style nor was it made of material found in that part of England in the seventeenth century. It is only fair to add that part of Green's opinion has been questioned by another expert in the period. In an article in the January 1986 issue of the *Journal of the Society for Psychical Research* Stevenson reports that he has obtained a contrary opinion on this subject from Dr. Robert W. Dunning, editor of the *Victoria History of Somerset*. According to Dr. Dunning, it is quite possible that in the last half of the seventeenth century a farm existed at the edge of Western Zoyland at the site indicated by Ryall. Even if Dunning is right all the other grounds for skepticism remain and they are quite sufficient to warrant a negative verdict on the case.

Ryall died in 1978 and Stevenson went on defending him for a number of years. However, in the end he admitted, somewhat grudgingly, that the case was not as strong as he had originally thought. In an interview in the September-October 1986 issue of *Venture Inward*, a periodical published by the Association for Research and Enlightenment, the organization that promotes the ideas and writings of Edgar Cayce, Stevenson remarks that he does not now regard the case as "enthusiastically" as he had ten years earlier. He concedes that the absence of any John Fletcher in the parish records is damaging, but he does not refer to Michael Green's correspondence with Ryall, which has seemed to most readers to expose the latter as a faker, Dunning's contrary opinion notwithstanding. Stevenson's surrender is in fact far from total. "What we may be dealing with," he tells the interviewer, "are perhaps some real memories of a previous life which Ryall then . . . embellished rather like a historical novel." Stevenson evidently invested so much emotion and time in this case that he cannot let go of it. I earlier praised his honesty. I cannot do the same for his judgment.

8

The Conservation of Spiritual Energy

The argument to be considered in this chapter has been widely used ever since conservation principles in physics became known among the general public. The basic idea is stated in a passage by the late rocket scientist Werner von Braun, which Thomas Pynchon placed at the head of his novel *Gravity's Rainbow*:

> Nature does not know extinction; all it knows is transformation. Everything science has taught me and continues to teach me, strengthens my belief in the continuity of life after death.

I do not know whether von Braun believed in reincarnation or the traditional Western form of survival, but if his reasoning is sound it would also prove life before birth. I will quote three statements of the argument by reincarnationists, one by a nineteenth-century American, the other by contemporary Buddhists. The following is the formulation by E. D. Walker:

> Nothing is either lost or added. There is no creation or destruction. . . . The law of conservation of energy holds in the spiritual realm as in physics. The uniform stock of energy in the universe neither declines nor increases, but incessantly changes. . . . Science allows no such miracle as the theological special resurrection, which is contrary to all experience. But it recognizes the universality of resurrection throughout all nature, which is a matter of common observation. The idea of the soul as a phoenix, eternally continuing through myriad embodiments, is adapted to the whole spirit of modern science.[1]

---

1. *Reincarnation: A Study of Forgotten Truths,* op. cit., p. 25.

V. F. Gunaratna, a Buddhist philosopher, after informing his readers that "thought, like matter, is energy," proceeds to assert that, since it is energy, it cannot be destroyed or annihilated. A few pages later in the same work we are again assured that, being a form of energy, thought "cannot be lost or destroyed." It goes on producing its results, and they in turn produce theirs, "though not necessarily in the same plane or sphere."[2] What we call life, according to J. A. Storey,

> is a combination of physical and mental energies. . . . When the physical body is no more capable of functioning, energies will not die with it, but continue to take some other shape or form which we call another life.[3]

Perhaps the fullest statement of the "principle of the conservation of spiritual energy" is contained in "Ten Reasons for Believing in Immortality," a sermon delivered at the Community Church in New York in 1929 by John Haynes Holmes (1879–1964), one of the leading liberal Protestants of his time. Holmes begins by stating the conservation principle of physics in its pre-Einsteinian form, in which what is conserved is simply energy and not mass-energy. This is a detail that is of no consequence to our discussion. "The gist of this doctrine," Holmes writes, is "that nothing in the universe is ever lost. All energy is conserved." No matter what transformations take place, "the energy persists if not in the old form then in a new one," and the sum total remains the same. Holmes has no doubt that the conservation principle can be applied to the "spiritual world." Just as physical energy does not simply appear and disappear, so "intellectual or moral or spiritual energy" does not simply come and go:

> We would laugh at a man who contended that the heat in molten metal, which disappears under the cooling action of air or water, had thereby been destroyed. Why should we not similarly laugh at a man who argues that the personality of a human being, which disappears under the chilling influence of death, has thereby been annihilated?

The soul of man "is just as much a force in the world as magnetism or steam or electricity," and if the cosmic law of conservation "forbids the destruction of the latter," it must also "forbid the destruction of the former." In this way we are led to the conclusion that human beings must survive the death of their bodies:

> What prevails in the great realm of matter can be only an anticipation of what must equally prevail in the greater realm of spirit.[4]

---

2. *Rebirth Explained* (Kandy, Sri Lanka, 1980), pp. 16 and 38–42.

3. *Rebirth* (Buddhist Publication Society, Kandy, Sri Lanka, 1971). J. A. Storey must not be confused with the previously mentioned Francis Story.

4. Holmes is arguing for life after death as conceived by Christians, but he was a friend of Gandhi and a sympathetic student of Indian thought and would in all probability not have objected to the use of his argument as a defense of reincarnation. All quotations are from pp. 257–58 of P. Edwards and A. Pap (Eds.), *A Modern Introduction to Philosophy* (Third Edition), where Holmes' sermon is reprinted.

Before going any further it should be emphasized that the defenders of this argument are dualists. They are not talking about ordinary energy but about a special form of it that is not recognized by physicists—"spiritual energy"—an energy that exists in the "greater realm of spirit." A materialist who regards thought as a secretion of the brain or who maintains that mental events are identical with brain states could quite consistently regard them as energy in the physical sense or at least as mass, which is convertible into energy. Such a claim is not open to a dualist.

The most obvious objection to this argument is that there is no such thing as spiritual energy. If we accept dualism, as the defenders of the argument do, then thought is *not* a form of energy. It may be related to energy in various ways, but it must be *sui generis* or else we are back to some form of materialism. If the expression, "spiritual energy" really referred to energy of some kind, it would have to be quantifiable. It would then be entirely possible to select a unit of this energy, say a "spir," and it would not be absurd to ask such questions as "Into how much heat or electricity can the spiritual energy now present in this person's mind be converted?" It would be possible to convert spiritual energy into kinetic or chemical energy and it would in principle be possible to establish appropriate transformation formulas. Evidently, none of the writers I have quoted would regard such transformation formulas as a possibility.

Let us ignore this objection and grant for the sake of discussion that "spiritual energy" refers to something that is real but not physical. This would not be of any help to the supporters of the argument. The conservation principle has been shown by physicists to hold only for physical energy. If there is a nonphysical energy, we have no right whatever to say that the conservation principle applies to it. Incidentally, if we allow the concept of "spiritual energy," there would be no reason to disallow a concept of "spiritual entropy"; and just as *usable* physical energy is constantly lost, so the same might well be true of spiritual energy.

Even if we waive all these objections, the argument would still prove nothing to the point. The conservation of physical energy does not guarantee the continued, much less the eternal, existence of particular entities. It is quite consistent with the destruction of houses, mountains, stars, and of course plants and animal bodies. What evidence is there that if our minds were indeed composed of spiritual energy, and if this energy were indestructible, that our *individual* minds exist for ever? It appears that versions of the argument had already some currency in the eighteenth century, quite a long time before the first formulation of conservation principles by physicists. We may infer this from the fact that Hume offered a critical discussion of it in his "Of the Immortality of the Soul," the essay mentioned in Chapter 1. "Admitting a spiritual substance to be dispersed throughout the universe," he wrote, we have no right to exclude the possibility that it "may be continually dissolved by death"[5] and take on forms or modifications that would be of no interest to us, that is, which would in no sense be continuations of *us*.

---

5. See P. Edwards (Ed.), *Immortality,* p. 135.

As for von Braun's solemn pronouncement that "nature does not know extinction," the proper comment is that it is specious rhetoric. Nature "knows" plenty of extinctions. Dinosaurs are extinct and so are a great many other species. And what is true of "nature" equally holds for the human world. The library of Alexandria was burnt down by a mob of Christian fanatics in 391 C.E. and many of the books in it, including all the works of Democritus, were lost forever. Similarly, many priceless art treasures were destroyed during the last war. And what about the Watergate tapes whose text had been erased and the Iran-Contra documents shredded by Oliver North and his secretary? Examples can be multiplied indefinitely. Defenders of the argument occasionally say such things as, "If death is really the end, where does the consciousness of the individual go?" The skeptic can reply without any absurdity that consciousness goes nowhere—it just ceases to exist. Such an answer is entirely appropriate in a great many completely uncontroversial situations. As they age, singers frequently lose the special sheen of their voices. It clearly makes no sense to ask where the sheen has gone and the same is true of shadows that have disappeared. The fact that the sheen of a voice or a shadow has not gone anywhere does not entail that they still exist and are indestructible.

9

The Astral Body

Lunatic theories may be divided into those that are dreary and those that are fun. Heidegger's assorted pronouncements about death, if taken literally, are prominent specimens of the former. One of the most enjoyable examples of the latter is the theory of the astral body, to which I briefly referred in Chapter 1. When we turn to what I call the "interregnum" problem—the question of how a person subsists in the interval between death in one regular body and birth in a new one—it will become clear that invoking the astral body is a natural and by no means illogical move. Professor Geddes MacGregor, who as a professional philosopher has a much better grasp of questions relating to personal identity than other reincarnationists, is ready to champion the astral body in spite of its "occult" associations. Most forms of reincarnationism are indissolubly linked to the astral body, as their protagonists readily admit, and I will try to show that this by itself is a sufficient reason for rejecting them. Reading about the astral body has given me so much pleasure that I would like to be able to say something kind about it. Unfortunately I cannot oblige. On examination the theory turns out to be just as hopelessly absurd as it seems at first sight to all sane people.

What is the astral body and why should anybody believe in its existence except that it helps the cause of reincarnation? The astral body, in the words of the late Dr. Robert Crookall, who until his recent much-lamented death was generally regarded as the foremost astral theorist, is a "nonphysical, 'second' body that is the 'double' or duplicate or the physical body."[1] The more primitive and philosophically illiterate believers frequently identify it with consciousness or the soul, but this is clearly absurd since consciousness and the soul (regardless of whether these are treated as the

---

1. "Out-of-the-Body Experiences and Survival," in J. D. Pearce-Higgins and G. S. Whitby (Eds.), *Life, Death, and Psychical Research* (London, 1973), p. 67.

same thing) do not possess size, shape, and location the way the duplicate of our physical body would have to do. Dr. Crookall realizes that the astral theory must seem "incredible to 'common sense' people," but this only means that they are unfamiliar with
the extensive evidence in its favor.

Bilocations

This evidence is twofold. In the first place, "innumerable men, women, and children
have . . . had the experience of leaving their [regular] bodies temporarily and eventually reentering them." The subjects of these experiences frequently observe the second body, of whose existence they are not conscious most of the time, since in waking life "it is normally 'in gear' with the physical."[2] Dr. Crookall is here referring to
out-of-body experiences (OBEs) or what he and others tendentiously call "astral projections." The other evidence consists of the less frequent cases in which the astral
body has become "exteriorized" and has actually been observed by other people. The
latter of these phenomena are familiar to all students of the history of Christianity. It
has been reported of numerous saints that they were seen in two places at the same
time. Thus St. Anthony of Padua, whose sermon to the fishes has been immortalized
in one of Gustav Mahler's *Wunderhorn* songs, knelt to pray on Holy Thursday of 1226
in the Church of St. Pierre du Queyrrix at Limoges and at that very moment appeared
at the other end of the town at another service. Sister Maria Coronel de Agreda, a seventeenth-century Spanish nun who modestly doubted her own gifts, had telepathic
powers, was able to levitate, and underwent no less than five hundred bilocations. Just
as saints and other members of religious orders no longer levitate, so they also have
not engaged in bilocations in more recent centuries, but several secular cases have been
reported during the past one hundred and fifty years. One that is often mentioned in
the literature of occultism concerns Mme. Sagée, a schoolteacher in nineteenth-century France. Soon after her appointment, according to Dr. Crookall's account, rumors
circulated that she had been seen far from the classroom where she was engaged in
teaching. On one occasion when she was writing on the blackboard, Dr. Crookall
writes, "all the girls saw not only her physical body but also her 'double' which made
the same gestures."[3] Perhaps the most distressing event occurred when she was helping to dress one of the girls, standing behind her. The girl happened to glance in the
mirror and saw not one but two Mme. Sagées. She promptly fainted. After numerous
complaints by parents the school authorities dismissed the unfortunate teacher. No information is available on whether she had engaged in acts of bilocation before her arrival at the school or whether she continued in such acts after her dismissal.

The most famous and, in the opinion of some, the best-documented case of bilo-

---

2. Ibid.
3. Op. cit., pp. 67–68.

cation, which no champion of the astral body ever fails to mention, is that of Mr. and Mrs. Wilmot. The following is quoted from Dr. Crookall's article:

> *S. R. Wilmot* sailed from Liverpool to New York, encountering a great storm. His narrative reads: 'Upon the night following the eighth day of the storm, the tempest moderated. Towards morning, I dreamed that I saw my wife, whom I had left in the United States, come to the door of my state-room, clad in her nightdress. At the door she seemed to discover that I was not the only occupant of the room, hesitated a little, then advanced to my side, stooped down and kissed me, and, after gently caressing me, quietly withdrew.
>
> Upon waking, I was surprised to see my fellow-passenger, whose berth was above mine, but not directly over it, leaning on his elbow and looking fixedly at me. "You're a pretty fellow!" he said at length, "to have a lady come and visit you in this way!" I pressed him for an explanation, which at first he declined to give. At length he related what he had seen while lying wide awake in his berth. It exactly corresponded with my "dream." I questioned him about it, and on three separate occasions he repeated to me the same account of what he had witnessed.
>
> The day after landing, I went to Watertown, where my children and wife had been for some time. Almost the first question my wife put when we were alone together was, "Did you receive a visit from me a week ago last Tuesday?" "A visit from you?" I said. "We were more than a thousand miles at sea!" "I know it," she replied, "but it seemed to me that I visited you." "That wouldn't be possible," I said. "Tell me what makes you think so."
>
> My wife then told me that, on account of the severity of the weather, she had been extremely anxious about me. On the night previous, the same night when, as mentioned above, the storm had just begun to abate, she had lain awake thinking of me. About 4:00 A.M. it seemed to her that she went out to seek me. Crossing a wide and stormy sea, she came at length to a low, black steamship whose side she went up; then descending to the cabin, passed through it to the stern until she came to my state-room. "Tell me," said she, "do they ever have state-rooms like the one I saw, where the upper berth extends further than the under-one? A man was in the upper berth, looking right at me. For a moment I was afraid to go in, but I soon went up to the side of your berth, bent down and kissed you, and embraced you and then went away."
>
> The description given by my wife of the steamship was correct in all particulars, though she had never seen it.[4]

The details of the case, supported by various documents, were published in the *Proceedings of the Society for Psychical Research*, Vol. 7 (1891), and they have ever since been cited as evidence for the existence of an astral body. The independent corroboration of three witnesses, only one of whom (Mr. Wilmot) had any interest in psychical phenomena, was too remarkable to be explained in any other way. Professor C. D. Broad, who did not believe in the astral body, nevertheless called it a "very strange story" and took it seriously enough to devote several pages to it in his *Lec-*

---

4. Op. cit., pp. 71–72.

tures on Psychical Research. Susan Blackmore has gone to the trouble of studying the original documents in the archives of the Society for Psychical Research. After one reads the results of her investigation the case looks a great deal less impressive than it did when reported by Dr. Crookall or even by Professor Broad. What made the case so impressive was the apparent corroboration of Mr. Wilmot's dream by the testimony from Mr. Tait, the passenger in the other berth and from Mrs. Wilmot. Mr. Tait was dead by the time the case was written up twenty-seven years after the event occurred, and his corroboration is available only in a letter from Miss Wilmot, Mr. Wilmot's sister, who also traveled on the *City of Limerick*. As for Mrs. Wilmot, the details of her supposed corroboration all come from Mr. Wilmot. She reported merely that she had had a "dream" that left her with a vivid sense the next day of having visited her husband. She at no stage asserted that she remembered flying over the ocean to the *City of Limerick* or that she recalled, in a dream or otherwise, walking into his stateroom and kissing him. Equally important, she at no time claimed to be aware of the peculiar features of the berths in the stateroom. Since she knew about the dangerous storm and since another steamship had been reported lost, she was understandably anxious about her husband, and this seems to be a perfectly natural explanation for the dream she did report. It should be added that the Wilmot case is generally regarded as the best-supported case on record of a bilocation as well as an OBE in which a person could accurately perceive objects at a great distance from her physical body.[5]

Out-of-Body Experiences

Bilocations are a myth, but out-of-body experiences or OBEs are very real and there is not the slightest reason why a person who rejects the *theory* of the astral body should deny their reality. The term "out-of-body experience" has been simply and clearly explained by Blackmore as referring to "an experience in which one seems to perceive the world from a location outside the physical body."[6] There is surely no question that many people in many countries at many different times have had such experiences. These experiences have certain common features: the individual can travel at enormous speed, he can penetrate material objects like walls, roofs, and human bodies as if these were not there, and he is not noticed by others. The last does not of course apply to bilocations, but I am disregarding these here. Certain further characteristics asserted to belong to all OBEs, both by Dr. Crookall and other astral theorists, are not in fact universal. The most important of these is the observation by a person of his second or duplicate body. Celia Green in her book *Out-of-Body Ex-*

---

5. Susan Blackmore's discussions are found in "Are Out-of-Body Experiences Evidence for Survival?" *Anabiosis*, December 1983, and in a letter in the same journal, 1984, pp. 169-171. Professor Broad speculated that the person seen by Mr. Tait was Miss Wilmot who may have entered the stateroom while she was in a daze.

6. *Beyond the Body* (London, 1982), p. 1.

periences (1968) reports many cases in which the person perceived himself as a blob or globe, a flare or a point of light, or in which he simply "looks" at his original body and has no sense of possessing another one in the place from which he is looking. Some astral travelers have reported seeing an extremely elastic silver cord connecting the astral body to the sleeping physical body. It is also the belief of many astral theorists that, if the silver cord or "astral cable" is broken, the person must die. When a person dies, the cord breaks and this enables the astral body to leave for other regions. The supposed universality of the observation of the silver cord during OBEs has frequently been cited as conclusive evidence that they cannot be hallucinations. For this reason it should be emphasized that many reports of OBEs are on record without mention of a silver cord or, for that matter, any connecting link. Dr. Kübler-Ross, whose remarkable adventures are the subject of Chapter 12, has not once reported seeing such a cord. Many of Celia Green's subjects do not report such a cord, and no astral cable appears in many of the OBEs reported in other cultures.

Needless confusion has been produced by an ambiguous use of the phrase "astral projection." In one innocent sense it just means the same as OBE, and in *this* sense a person who denies the existence of the astral body does not deny the existence of astral projections; he objects to one particular explanation or interpretation of astral projections. Often, however, the term has been used to refer to the separation of the astral from the physical body, and of course in this sense, but only in this sense, an opponent of an astral body must deny the reality of astral projections. Charles P. Tart, a California psychologist, who is a warm friend of the astral body, evidently has some difficulty in stating the position of skeptics. "The current physical science belief system," he writes, "defines such experiences as meaningless and not at all as indicating the existence of any kind of soul." To this Tart adds the reflection that "the physical science world view is neither psychologically satisfying nor scientifically sound." The former of these defects is presumably the result of its leading to only one conclusion: "death is the end for each of us."[7] I do not believe that Tart really means "physical science," for physics has nothing to say, one way or another, about OBEs or about the astral body. What he presumably means is the *philosophy* of empiricism, which has often been espoused by physicists and other scientists. The appropriate comment is that an empiricist would emphatically *not* deny the reality of OBEs. He would question whether they, or anything else, provide sufficient evidence for the astral body. Susan Blackmore, who has probably studied the subject more exhaustively than anybody else, lists a number of possible explanations of OBEs and treats the theory of the astral body as just one and in many ways the least plausible of the competing explanations.[8] If, as we shall see shortly, this theory can be independently shown to be absurd, it would at once be ruled out of court.

Dr. Crookall, the aforementioned doyen of astral theorists, was interviewed a few

---

7. "Out-of-Body Experiences," in J. White (Ed.), *Psychic Explorations* (New York, 1974), pp. 353–54.

8. *Beyond the Body*, op. cit., especially Chapters 4 and 21.

years before his death by Martin Ebon, one of the leading psychic explorers in the New York City area. From all the thousands of cases with which Dr. Crookall was familiar, he picked an OBE by William Gerhardi as "perhaps the most complete and convincing on record." It should be explained parenthetically that very many of Dr. Crookall's correspondents were persons with little education, but Gerhardi (1896–1977) was a well-educated and talented novelist whose works received high praise from outstanding literary figures like H. G. Wells and Bernard Shaw, among others. In 1934 he published a thinly disguised autobiography with the title *Resurrection*, in which he described his astral adventures. In the interview with Martin Ebon, Dr. Crookall produced extensive quotations from this book for which there is no space here. In the article cited earlier he offers the following summary:

> Gerhardi used his released "double" as an instrument of the Soul—he used it to see, to will, to reason, etc. He set himself to accumulate proof that he was really freed from his physical body, in a nonphysical body, and that it was no dream. He said "what evidence, what more evidence?" He went about noting which windows were shut, etc., matters that he could check when he re-entered his body. This he did and then thought, "We have a duplicate body, all there and ready to use, the almost-indistinguishable double of the physical body. It seems that, for the first stage of survival at least, we already have a body neatly folded away in our physical bodies, always at hand in case of death, or for special use."[9]

Dr. Crookall concurs with Gerhardi's reasoning. "If a man can leave his physical body temporarily and continue to exist as a self-conscious being," he told Martin Ebon, "the fact would prove a strong presumption that eventually when he comes to leave his physical body, i. e., to die, he will then also continue to exist as a self-conscious being in that second body."[10]

An Astral Grand Tour of the Next World

The most obvious objection to believing in the astral double is that, aside from bilocations, which are difficult to take seriously, there is not the slightest observational evidence for its existence: nobody has observed it with his senses and no scientific instrument has ever detected it. This is indeed a valid objection, but I think that there are more basic considerations that justify us not only in not believing in the astral body but in *rejecting* it. To explain these considerations and to show the full absurdity of the astral theory I will present the case of Dr. George Ritchie, a Virginia psychiatrist whose astral trip in December 1943 has frequently been hailed as one of the great events in astral history. The *Time-Life* volume, *Psychic Voyages*, devotes the opening two and a half

---

9. Op. cit., p. 70.
10. M. Ebon (Ed.), *The Evidence for Life After Death* (New York,) p. 116.

pages of a chapter entitled "At the Portal of Death" to Dr. Ritchie's trip and tributes to his epoch-making experience have come from many quarters. Thus Dr. Raymond Moody, who dedicated his best-selling *Life After Life* to "George Ritchie, M.D. and, through him, to the One whom he suggested," has called Dr. Ritchie's astral adventure "incredible," "fantastic," and "startling," and he credits his own research into "post-mortem" experiences to his meeting in 1965 with this remarkable "clinical professor of psychiatry at the School of Medicine . . . who had been dead, not just once but on two occasions about ten minutes apart."[11] (Dr. Ritchie has never been a clinical professor of psychiatry, and he was "dead" once and not twice, but it sounds better the way Moody puts it.) Canon Pearce-Higgins, coeditor of the abovementioned *Life, Death, and Psychical Research*, takes a special interest in those who have been to the Be-yond—who, in the words of the seventeenth-century metaphysical poet Henry Vaughan, have "peeped into glory"—speaks of Dr. Ritchie in glowing terms as one such peeper. His "most remarkable projection," his "round-the-astral-world trip," was an experience of "immense range" and can be described as nothing less than "apocalyptic."[12]

The story of George Ritchie's apocalyptic experience was first publicly told in *To Live Again*[13] by the late Catherine Marshall, the author of a number of inspirational books, some of which sold millions of copies in the 1950s. Dr. Ritchie's story is con-tained in a chapter entitled "Is There Life After Death?" Catherine Marshall admits that ultimately a person has to base his belief in the hereafter on faith. "Final proof as the scientist means proof," she writes, is not available, "not yet in our day."[14] However, our faith is greatly aided by the account of experiences like those of Dr. Ritchie. The ex-perience is attributed to "a physician with a large practice in Richmond, Virginia."[15] Although Dr. Ritchie's full name is not given, the physician is referred to as George and is described as a good friend. His story, she writes, "is one of the most astonish-ing I have ever heard." Had she "gotten the story second hand," she might "have doubted its validity," but, knowing her "physician-friend as well as she does," she can-not disbelieve it. It is emphasized that the account George gave to Catherine Marshall is incomplete. After relating a conversation with Jesus, George is quoted as saying: "A lot more passed between us—I've never felt free to tell anyone the rest of it."[16]

A much more detailed account appeared in the December 1970 issue of *Fate*, one of the most widely read occultist periodicals in the United States. (This, incidentally, is the account on which Canon Pearce-Higgins bases his enthusiastic remarks.) The article is entitled "I Found Life Beyond Death." Dr. Ritchie's name is again withheld. At the end of the article a note is inserted informing the reader that "the editors first heard this wonderful experience at the May 1970 Spiritual Frontiers Fellowship

---

11. *Life After Life* (Harrisburg, PA, 1976), p. 18.
12. Op. cit., pp. 229ff.
13. New York, 1957.
14. Op. cit., p. 214.
15. Op. cit., p. 197.
16. Op. cit., p. 201.

Spring Conference held in Chicago." They were so "impressed by the speaker's sincerity and conviction" that they felt they had to bring his testimony to the readers of *Fate*. They then add that "because of the author's professional standing, he requests we identify him only as a graduate of a Virginia medical school and a practicing psychiatrist." In this article Dr. Ritchie once again emphasizes that he "has not been given permission to tell this whole experience."[17] It is hinted that the author of this prohibition is Jesus or some other supernatural source.

It appears that at some time between 1970 and 1978, when Dr. Ritchie decided to write a book about his experience, the supernatural author of the prohibition relented. Perhaps he was so impressed by the sales of Moody's book that he felt it would be unfair if Dr. Ritchie, who after all had *had* the kind of experience about which Moody only wrote, were prevented from sharing in the income that can be derived from stories about explorations of the next world. In any event the prohibition was lifted and in 1978 Dr. Ritchie's *Return from Tomorrow* was published by Chosen Books, a company formed by Catherine Marshall and her second husband, Leonard LeSourd. There is no indication in the book that any portions of Dr. Ritchie's story are still withheld from the reader.

In December 1943 George Ritchie was a private in the U.S. Army, stationed at Camp Barkley in Texas. Because of the shortage of physicians it was arranged that George would be released from his Army duties to take an accelerated degree at the Medical College of Virginia in his hometown of Richmond. He was supposed to catch a train to Richmond on December 20, but a few days earlier he became ill with pneumonia. During the night of December 20 his temperature was 106.5, and he collapsed while his chest was being x-rayed. Early in the morning the physician on duty, getting no pulse, respiration, or blood pressure, pronounced George dead and asked the ward boy to prepare George's body for the morgue. A few minutes later the ward boy begged the physician to make an attempt to resuscitate George. This he did by injecting adrenaline into George's heart muscle, and George gradually came back to life. George remained on the critical list for five days but eventually made a complete recovery.

George Ritchie himself has always been totally convinced that his resuscitation was the result of divine intervention. In a notarized statement several years after the event, Dr. Donald Francy, the commanding officer at Camp Barkley, stated:

> Private George G. Ritchie's . . . virtual call from death and return to vigorous health has to be explained in terms of other than natural means.[18]

In an interview in the *Toronto Star* in October 1970, Dr. Ritchie proudly displayed this testimonial and observed with becoming modesty that he could still not "fully fathom" why he of all people was "chosen to return to life."

During the time when he was thought to be dead, Dr. Ritchie says that he re-

17. P. 49.
18. *Return From Tomorrow* (from now on abbreviated as RFT), p. 81.

members undergoing a succession of remarkable encounters. After lapsing into unconsciousness, he found himself sitting at the edge of his bed and looking with distaste
at a body closely resembling his own. George was still intent on catching the train to
Richmond. In the corridor he met a sergeant who was carrying a tray with medical instruments. George told him to watch out since they were about to collide. The next moment the sergeant went right through George without either of them feeling anything.
Before he knew it, George was outside the hospital flying at great speed in the direction of Richmond. At one stage, when he reached the town of Vicksburg, he descended to the ground, but discovered, much to his astonishment, that he was unable
to touch any objects. He tried to start a conversation with a man who was walking toward an all-night cafe. The man did not answer George's questions. George then
tapped the man's shoulder but his fingers went right through him. George realized that
he had become a "substanceless" being and that it was pointless to proceed to Richmond and he therefore decided to return to the hospital. After a series of harrowing experiences in the course of which he tried to talk to nurses, orderlies, x-ray technicians,
and physicians, but was never once noticed by any of them, he finally found the small
isolation room in which he had "died." He was acutely puzzled when he saw his own
dead body lying in bed and realized that he had two bodies looking exactly alike:

> I could see this body lying there on the bed but I was the being that was, in every way,
> shape and form, just as big as the one on the bed.[19]

Before long, an intensely luminous being made of nothing but light appeared, and
George at once realized that he was in the presence of Jesus, the son of God. Dr.
Ritchie makes it clear that this Jesus was no "weakling" or "sissy," but on the contrary
"the most totally male Being" he had ever met. During a momentous conversation
about the "point" of life, which was carried on in thoughts rather than in words,
George began to fall in love with Jesus. All the familiar symptoms of an amatory attachment were present. George realized that he "did not want to leave Him—I knew
that I never wanted to be without Him again."[20] When, finally, George returned to life
on the earth he was heartbroken and felt and acted like a lover who had been separated
from his beloved. Writing twenty years after the fateful meeting with Jesus he remarks:

> The cry in my heart at that moment has been the cry of my life ever since: Christ,
> show me Yourself again.[21]

The rest of the story concerns the grand tour of the next world that so greatly impressed Canon Pearce-Higgins and Dr. Moody. Here at last a human being could see

---

19. *Fate*, p. 45.
20. Ibid., p. 47.
21. Quoted from Dr. Ritchie's contribution to J. E. Weiss (Ed.), *The Vestibule* (Port Washington, NY,
1972), p. 67.

for himself what hell and heaven were like. Dr. Ritchie is after all a psychiatrist who can tell delusions from veridical experiences, Canon Pearce-Higgins observes, and we have Dr. Ritchie's own unqualified assurance that he saw the real thing. The hellish regions came first. George witnessed the dreadful tortures suffered by suicides, alcoholics, violently angry types, and sexual perverts. It must be emphasized that all these dead people had lost their regular bodies and were now living in their astral doubles. What is more, their punishments were intimately connected with the "lack of solidity" of their astral housing. The violent types, for example, appeared to be "writhing, punching, and gouging" and they were obviously out for blood. Yet, since they "had no substance," there never were any injuries and the frustration was unbearable. The same was true of the sexual perverts, who were "tied up in all kinds of lewd relationships" and performing "sexual abuses in feverish pantomime." Perversions that George had never dreamed of "were being vainly attempted all around." The attempts were of course vain since none of these beings could make physical contact. There is a striking similarity between some of Dr. Ritchie's recollections and Dante's descriptions in the *Inferno*. I have no doubt that this similarity is wholly accidental, unless, of course, Dante's astral body also paid a visit to the next world.

The heavenly spheres were much less exciting. In one area George was shown "astro-laboratories" in which scientists who wore "loose-floating hooded cloaks" appeared to be engaged in some "vast experiment." Enormous buildings stood in a beautiful sunny park. The scene reminded one of a well-planned university, but what George saw was so magnificent that comparisons with anything on earth were quite "ridiculous." George was eager to know what kind of experiment was being conducted and he turned to Jesus for information. Although "Knowing flamed from Him like fire," Jesus did not oblige with an answer. "No explanation," George writes, "lighted my mind." What he received, however, was infinitely more precious than an explanation. As before, Jesus communicated "love, compassion for my ignorance, understanding that encompassed all my non-understanding."[22] With all due respect I cannot approve of how Jesus handled this situation. If I ask a teacher for information on a topic which I do not adequately understand I would not deem love and compassion for my ignorance a suitable response. Surely there is a time for love and a time for information; and just as information is no substitute for love, so love is no substitute for information.

Later George was introduced to a realm inhabited by composers, painters, and inventors. The music was of extreme complexity and George realized that "Bach was only the beginning," an opinion that would be endorsed by many earthbound music lovers. Although the astro-scientists and the astro-artists seemed extremely serene and totally devoted to their work, something was clearly missing from their lives. What was missing, George realized, was the love of Jesus. They were indeed single-mindedly pursuing the truth, but this very pursuit seemed to distract them "from the Truth

22. *RFT*, p. 70.

Himself . . . standing in their midst."[23] Finally, George saw "infinitely far off" a city of light. This was the highest region and in fact it *was* Heaven. It was populated by beings who had truly been saved and who were composed, like Jesus, of nothing but light. Nothing is said about the shape of these beings. These "radiant beings," George reasoned, were former inhabitants of the earth who, unlike the suicides, the alcoholics, and the perverts, and also unlike the selfless scholars, "had indeed kept Jesus [as] the focus of their lives." They had "looked for Him in everything," and they had done this "so well and so closely that they had been changed into His very likeness."[24] All of a sudden, for reasons we shall never know, two of the radiant beings "hurled themselves across that infinity with the speed of light" toward the location occupied by George and Jesus, but, disproving Einstein's special theory of relativity, George and Jesus "drew away still faster." This was effectively the end of the grand tour. Suddenly the travelers were back in the hospital room in Texas. Jesus intimated to George that he must resume his life on earth. George was desperate and begged Jesus not to leave him, but Jesus would not relent. He did however make George's reentry into his physical body as painless as possible by "spiritually anesthetizing" his "psychic being." George then lost consciousness and he knew nothing more until he woke up again on the morning of December 24.

Just like Dr. Moody and Canon Pearce-Higgins, I am greatly impressed by the majestic sweep of this tour. However, I must register a sense of disappointment as well as consternation. It is not clear why there had ever been a supernatural prohibition if *Return from Tomorrow* really tells all. I had been hoping for some juicy theological revelations, but the book contains nothing the least bit heretical or unorthodox and I do not see how any religious group could be offended by any part of Dr. Ritchie's story. The only people who might take offense are manufacturers of alcoholic beverages and advocates of suicide, but they would have been just as put off by the revelations that had already been communicated in the article in *Fate*.

Subsequent Corroborations

Ever since his "wonderful" experience took place, George Ritchie has been totally convinced that he really visited the next world in the company of Jesus Christ. However, he realizes that some of his readers will remain skeptical. Dr. Ritchie and his supporters believe that if we take into account some facts about his character and his training and above all if we are informed about two momentous confirmatory events, which occurred in 1944 and 1952, all doubts will be allayed.

In an earlier section I quoted a remark by Canon Pearce-Higgins to the effect that, as a psychiatrist, Dr. Ritchie may be expected to be able to distinguish fantasy from

---

23. Ibid., p. 71.
24. Ibid., pp. 72–73.

fact. Dr. Ritchie himself is in full accord with the Canon. In his psychiatric practice, he informs us, he has had occasion to study dreams and hallucinations. He has had several psychotic patients who were hallucinating and "there is just no resemblance" between the delusions of these patients and his own experience. Since some critics may raise the question of his sanity, Dr. Ritchie also tells us that before he could begin his training as a psychiatrist he was put through a severe "grilling" by every senior member of the psychiatry staff at the University of Virginia. He mentioned his meeting with Jesus to them quite openly. "What the eminent doctors made of it," he writes, "I don't know, but after hearing me out, every one of them judged me both sane and emotionally stable."[25] In addition to Dr. Ritchie's sanity and his experience as a psychiatrist we should also keep in mind the "enormous—indeed central—effect" of the experience on his life. The words I just quoted are Moody's,[26] but Dr. Ritchie himself repeatedly asserts the same thing. Let others explain it as they please, he remarked to Catherine Marshall, "I only know that it remains the most vivid experience of my life—from that day on I've not been the same person."[27] "This experience," he repeats twenty years later, "was the most entirely real thing that's ever happened to me."[28] He goes on to say that he has "bet his life" on the assumption that the experience was veridical. Everything he has done in the last thirty years—"becoming a doctor, becoming a psychiatrist, all the hours of volunteer work with young people each week"—all of it "goes back to that experience." Surely a delusion could not do that, it could not "govern a man's entire life."[29]

Skeptics will hardly be impressed by these considerations. The fact that a person is sane does not mean that he can never become the victim of a delusion. Perfectly sane people begin to suffer from delusions if they are subjected to starvation, extended periods of sleeplessness, or any number of other unusual conditions. It should be remembered that at the time of his experience George was extremely ill and that his brain, which had not died, was in Canon Pearce-Higgins' words, "very fevered." Furthermore, although Dr. Ritchie's experience may be significantly different from certain classic delusions of paranoid schizophrenics, this does not mean that it cannot have been a delusion. Paranoid delusions are surely not the only ones that occur. As for the Canon's assertion that, as a psychiatrist, Dr. Ritchie may be presumed to be able to distinguish fantasy from fact, it should be pointed out that quite a few psychiatrists, including some extremely brilliant and famous ones, did suffer from delusions; and obviously they did not recognize the delusional nature of their experiences. Just as it is agreed among sensible people that a lawyer who handles his own case has a fool for a client, so a psychiatrist is least likely to detect his own delusions or uncover his own unconscious motives.

25. Ibid., p. 17.
26. Foreword to *RFT*, p. 10.
27. *To Live Again*, op. cit., p. 201.
28. *RFT*, p. 16.
29. Ibid.

It is futile to discuss the question of whether it was really the meeting with Jesus that caused Dr. Ritchie to become a kind and compassionate physician. I doubt that he would have become a criminal or a drug addict if he had not met Jesus and perhaps he would have become a kind physician even without undergoing his tremendous experience. Many self-centered adolescents have turned into useful and responsible adults without undergoing any mystical experiences and many people have become "doctors and psychiatrists" and done useful volunteer work although they did not meet Jesus in the course of a postmortem experience. However, even if all of Dr. Ritchie's virtues were the effect of his experience, this would not have the slightest tendency to show that the experience was veridical. There is no evidence whatever that only veridical experiences can have powerful or beneficial effects on a person. Logicians refer to the notion that a belief must be true because it is the result of admirable motives or false because of its disreputable origin as the "genetic fallacy." There is a similar fallacy that could be appropriately named "the fallacy of effects," in which it is thought that a belief must be true or an experience veridical because it produces desirable effects. It appears that Dr. Ritchie and his supporters are guilty of this fallacy.

I now turn to the two later events which, in the opinion of Dr. Ritchie, clinch his case. The first concerns the atomic submarine developed by the late Admiral Rickover and his associates. Dr. Ritchie has given two accounts of this event. In the article in *Fate* he tells us that in his visit to the scientific laboratories of the next world he had seen the astral scientists work on "some sort of instrument panel." Then, "ten years after this experience," he happened to see in *Life* magazine a picture of the *Nautilus*, the first atomic-powered submarine. On seeing this picture, Dr. Ritchie "felt the hair creep up" on the back of his neck. For he had seen "them" (i.e., the astral beings) "working on it in 1943 in one of those technical laboratories." This account of the illustration in *Life* is neither accurate nor entirely clear. It turns out that the illustration is not of the *Nautilus*, but of the second atomic submarine and no instrument panel of any kind is visible. By the time he wrote *RFT*, he had evidently done some checking, and this time the description is quite accurate. He now tells us that the issue of *Life* appeared in December 1952, almost exactly nine years after his meeting with Jesus. On the page in front of him, he writes, was a drawing of "a gigantic sphere-shaped structure cut away to reveal men and machines inside it."[30] Among the objects visible in the drawing was a moving crane mounted on steel girders, a huge circular tank, turbines, stairs, catwalks, and in one corner a small control room. According to this account, nothing happened to the hair on the back of his neck when he saw the picture in *Life*. Instead, his "fingers suddenly tightened" and his "heart pounded" in his throat. These symptoms of agitation were the result of his "certainty" that he had "seen all this before." He was also certain that not recently, but, "years ago" he had "stood staring not at a drawing of this enormous sphere but at the thing itself."[31] Then he read the following text supplied by the author of the article in *Life*:

30. Ibid., p. 119.
31. Ibid., p.120

Last week the Atomic Energy Commission partially lifted the veil of secrecy and allowed *Life's* artists to make a drawing of some details of the prototype of the second US atomic submarine engine and the strange house that holds it. The building, now going up near Schenectady, N.Y., will be the world's largest man-made sphere, . . . the two hundred and twenty-five foot steel shell.[32]

The article explained that the scientists would build the submarine inside the sphere and then submerge it for tests in the huge tank. Dr. Ritchie says that he was now utterly baffled. For he had never been to Schenectady. Moreover, what he recalls having seen was the finished product whereas the picture was of a submarine about to be built. At last Dr. Ritchie remembered where he had seen the finished and operating atomic submarine. It was "in that tranquil campus-like realm" inhabited by astral beings who were dressed like monks. Needless to say he was extremely puzzled by this realization and he could see that many intriguing questions might be raised about the relation between the realm of the discarnate physicists and our own world. Without Jesus as his guide, he did not think it safe to follow up these questions. However, he could not help wondering whether "philosophers are right when they say that certain ideas seem to drop into widely scattered areas of the world from 'somewhere' simultaneously."[33] I don't have the faintest idea which philosophers hold the strange notion about the "scattering" of ideas in different places. Nor, if Dr. Ritchie is right, were the ideas "scattered" simultaneously in the present case: the idea of the atomic submarine evidently occurred in the next world several years before it came to scientists on the earth. In any event, it was this occurrence that led to Dr. Ritchie's decision to start speaking out in public about his "encounter with Christ."[34]

The other corroborative event has to do with the location of an all-night cafe in Vicksburg, Mississippi. There are again two accounts of this event and they are inconsistent in quite crucial respects. In the 1970 article in *Fate* the account is offered as a postscript to the main story. After his brush with death, George was sent to medical school in Richmond, but because had had not done well in certain subjects he was dropped from the special program and reassigned to active duty. In September 1944, according to this account, he and another student who had also been dropped, drove back to Camp Barkley. They took the straight route that led through Memphis, New Orleans, Dallas and Fort Worth to Abilene. Suddenly, as they were driving into Vicksburg, George "recognized the place" and said to his companion who was at the wheel: "If you will drive one block further down the street you will find a white all-night cafe on the corner." His companion expressed acute surprise since he was under the impression that George had never before been to Vicksburg. George replied enigmatically "in one sense I haven't." His companion drove on and, true enough, at the end of the block there was the all-night cafe, which George had seen the night he

32. Ibid.
33. Ibid.
34. Ibid., p. 121.

had "died and left his body." As further independent confirmation Dr. Ritchie tells us that if we look at a map we will find Vicksburg on the straight line connecting Richmond and Abilene. "Of course" he had taken this straight-line route in his "astral body back in December 1943." He seems particularly impressed by this story. "I like to add this postscript," he writes, "because I think it helps some of you to believe."

In view of Dr. Ritchie's care in supplying documentary support for the medical facts of his story, I had hoped that he would also have obtained a notarized statement from his traveling companion concerning the events in Vicksburg just related. If we turn to the much more detailed account supplied in *RFT*, we find that no such document could have been obtained for the simple reason that the conversation reported in *Fate* never took place. This time we are informed that George set out from Richmond not in September but in October of 1944 (which is not a point of significance except to cast doubt on the general trustworthiness of Dr. Ritchie's memory) and there is not "*a* traveling companion," but "three other medical students" who had also failed to stay in the program.[35] A student by the name of Pete was at the wheel while the other three, including George, were "watching for signs to the bridge which showed on our map."[36] Pete was driving down a street in the direction of the river. "Any signs?" he asked George who was supposed to keep an eye on the left. George was so agitated that he could not answer. His mouth was feeling dry and his stomach was tight. Something about the layout of the town seemed uncannily familiar. In this account George does not make any predictions to the others on what they would see. Instead he tells us at great length about what went on *in his mind*. He "knew" that he had never been in this place, and yet he "knew exactly" how the streets would intersect and how the shoreline would look. All at once he "knew for sure" that a few blocks ahead there would be a white frame building with a red roof and the word "cafe" in neon lights. As George was carrying on these reflections a sign appeared indicating that they would have to take a left turn to get to the bridge. George asked Pete to go straight another two blocks, explaining that he thought that he had recognized something. George's excitement now knew no bounds. It was too good to be true— he was getting firsthand confirmation of the objective reality of his astral adventure:

> My heart was hammering too hard to speak. A block ahead, on my side of the car, on the corner, was a white all-night cafe with a red roof. The neon letters over the door were turned off in the bright daylight but the Pabst sign was still propped in the righthand window.[37]

On his lap George had a map and with his finger he traced a straight line due east from Abilene across Louisiana to Vicksburg, Mississippi. This did it. If there had been any doubts before there could not be any now. A voice inside him was "shouting":

---

35. Ibid., p. 96.
36. Ibid., p. 97.
37. Ibid., p. 98.

So it was here! Vicksburg, Mississippi. Here was where I stopped in that headlong bodiless flight. Here I stopped, and thought, and turned back.[38]

Except for the difference in the date, the discrepancies between the two accounts of the Vicksburg episode are by no means insignificant, but on the contrary quite crucial to its value as corroborative evidence. It should be noted that Dr. Ritchie himself has not offered one word of explanation of these inconsistencies. A critic would suspect that the conversation reported in the first account was concocted. It was safe to do so since the article was unsigned. Once the author's name was revealed it became possible for readers to try and discover the identity of the traveling companion and query him about the content of the conversation in Vicksburg. If the book should become a bestseller like Moody's, an inquiry of this kind would not at all be unlikely. It therefore became safer to make the prediction a silent one. I prefer the more charitable explanation that Dr. Ritchie's memory had played him a trick in the lecture printed in *Fate* and that when he prepared a book about his experience, he made a more resolute effort to recollect all the relevant experiences as carefully as possible. Memory lapses and embellishments in the course of telling a story are very human and are not reasons for moral outrage, but in the present case they lead to an important criticism. If in 1972 Dr. Ritchie "remembered" a conversation that never took place, how can we trust his memory of 1978 about exactly what went on in his mind thirty-four years earlier? I imagine that Dr. Ritchie would wish his 1978 account in *RFT* to be regarded as definitive. It has to be emphasized that this account offers no corroborative evidence whatsoever for Dr. Ritchie's view that his great experience was a real objective trip and not an extended fantasy. In the account in *Fate* we had a spoken prediction in the presence of another person, which was subsequently verified. Now there is no conversation and *no spoken prediction*. Instead there is a great deal of agitation—George's mouth was feeling dry, his hands were "sweating," his stomach was tight and his heart hammering—and a very full report of George's *state of mind*. The absence of a spoken prediction is crucial. Without testimony that such a prediction was made, and verified, the Vicksburg episode does not provide a shred of evidence for Dr. Ritchie's case.

I will offer a suggestion as to what may in fact have happened, which seems to me much more credible than Dr. Ritchie's account. George had gone through an exceedingly difficult and lonely year in 1944. He had not made good in medical school and he was about to be shipped overseas, which was not a pleasant prospect. Throughout this time he had been thinking about his "wonderful" experience and the love that was streaming from him to Jesus and from Jesus back to himself. He was evidently longing for some kind of "objective" confirmation that the meeting with Jesus was not just a dream. He was therefore prone to déjà vu experiences that would supply the needed rational support. When he and his companions drove through Vicksburg the sights of the place including the cafe seemed familiar and were at once interpreted as identical

---

38. Ibid., p. 99, Dr. Ritchie's italics.

with certain of the objects "seen" in the early phase of George's astral trip. The various physiological changes—if they really happened—made the whole thing emotionally all the more impressive to him. It seems to me entirely possible that there was not even a silent prediction about the location of the all-night cafe. When it came into view it seemed familiar as did other objects in Vicksburg. The prediction was then retrospectively supplied when George came to think about and "remember" the excitement during the passage through Vicksburg. The more often the story was told the more convinced George became that he really had made such a prediction.

The Vicksburg "corroboration" calls for one further comment. In both of these accounts Dr. Ritchie seems tremendously impressed that his map showed Vicksburg to lie on the straight line between Richmond and Abilene. Both he and the editors of *Fate* imply that this fact clinches the case. There is, however, a simple question that evidently never occurred to any of them: how did George Ritchie's astral body know the route from Abilene to Richmond? Not even migrating birds and airplanes always take a straight line course, but they at least have assorted navigational devices at their disposal. What were the navigational devices available to George Ritchie's astral body? What previous flight training did it have? Similar questions can and should be raised about most other astral travelers. The astral body is supposed to be an exact replica of the regular one, the only difference being that it has no mass and is not publicly observable. Lack of "substance" surely does not automatically provide it with the infallible ability to reach a given destination. The question does not perhaps, arise in connection with William Gerhardi, whose astral travels were confined to his home, but it certainly arises about most of the other trips described in the literature. We shall see in Chapter 12 that Dr. Kübler-Ross claims to have paid an astral visit to friends in San Francisco observing their meal from outside their window. How did she manage to get to San Francisco, from Virginia without maps or other aids? And what about Mrs. Wilmot who was flying over a stormy ocean dressed in nothing more than a nightgown? She did not even know the exact location of the steamer on which her husband was traveling. Neither Dr. Ritchie nor other astral travelers should be taken seriously until they can answer these and similar questions.

The other corroborating experience is even more ludicrous. Setting aside any possible discrepancies in Dr. Ritchie's two accounts, one cannot avoid reflecting on the utter inappropriateness of an atomic submarine in the heavenly or near-heavenly abode of the selfless astral scientists. Where are the oceans in their land? Furthermore, since they are apparently not afraid of being attacked and since they do not engage in warfare of any kind, what possible use could such a contraption have for them? They are supposed to be vastly more intelligent than human beings on earth. It is scarcely credible that they would spend their time and energy in the production of objects for which they have no use. We may, I think, conclude that whatever George Ritchie saw in the astro-laboratories, it was not an atomic submarine. There seems to be a much more plausible explanation for Dr. Ritchie's "recognition" experience in December 1952 than his assumption that he really visited the next world and saw the astral scientists work on an atomic submarine. His autobiographical remarks in *Return from Tomorrow* make it clear that by this time he was irking to "go public"—to tell the whole world about his experience. Being basically a shy man he needed a new corroboration to fortify himself. He became once again prone to déjà vu experiences and the hair on the back of his neck became ready to creep up. I have little doubt that if no atomic submarine had ever been invented or if Dr. Ritchie had never come across any illustration of it, some impressive "recognition" would have been forthcoming sooner or later confirming in his mind the veridical character of the original experience.

What we have here is by no means uncommon in stories about the supernatural. The published reports read impressively at first, but the closer we get to the reported situation, the greater the justified misgivings; and when one gets very close, the whole tale evaporates. We saw this in the case of Mr. Wilmot and we have now seen it in the case of the Vicksburg flip-flop. In honor of Dr. Ritchie and Mr. Wilmot I propose to refer to this phenomenon—the hiatus between the original claim and the actual evidence—as the Ritchie-Wilmot syndrome. In later chapters in the present book we shall meet several additional illustrations. I am not in this book concerned with miracles in the theological sense, but it might be noted that much the same is found when one tries to investigate the evidence for the miracles of the various religions.

Astral Tribulations

I will now offer five considerations for rejecting the astral theory. They show that we have good reason for believing that there is no such thing as an astral body, that even if it did exist it would not be a second body of the person who is supposed to possess it, and finally that it cannot be of any use for the purpose of survival after death.

THE PROBLEM OF ASTRAL ATTIRE

I am not aware of a single case of bilocation in which an astral double was observed without clothes. When St. Anthony of Padua preached in two different churches in Limoges at the same time he was wearing his usual clerical robes during both sermons. As for Mme. Sagée, the nineteenth-century French bilocationist, she surely shocked her students sufficiently by appearing in two places without being naked in either one of her apparitions. Mrs. Wilmot's visit to her ailing husband greatly shocked the prudish Mr. Tait, the occupant of the upper berth, but he did not assert that she came in the nude. On the contrary, all parties agreed that she was wearing her nightgown. In some reports of "private" OBEs, in which the traveler's astral body is not publicly observable, the double was naked, but in most of them it did wear garments just like those worn by regular bodies. Now, the clothes worn by astral doubles cannot be ordinary, physical clothes; the astral bodies lack the solidity that would keep the clothes in place. The only alternative seems to be that they are astral clothes, but where are astral clothes manufactured and how do they suddenly appear on the scene when a bilocation or a private OBE occurs? Incidentally, what did George Ritchie wear when, after running out of the hospital, he flew through the air and descended in Vicksburg for an aborted meeting with a stranger and during his tour in the company of Jesus?

In one of his most intriguing books, *The Next World—And the Next*, given to this world in 1966, Dr. Crookall has brought together the opinions of astral scholars on this topic. The book incidentally also deals at length with the fascinating questions of the precise location of "Hades" (the next world) and of "Paradise" (the world after the next world). Dr. Crookall reports a number of cases in which the astral body was indeed naked but invariably became mysteriously clothed when the person felt embarrassed. This does not suggest to him that we are dealing with dreamlike experiences but rather that the laws of the astral world differ from those of the familiar physical universe. In any event, the great majority of astral bodies wear clothes that look just like those worn by their physical counterparts. Dr. Crookall favors the view of the anonymous author of *Life Beyond the Grave*, a work published in London in 1876 that appears to be based on unimpeachable messages from the Beyond. This anonymous author wrote that "there is a spiritual duplicate to every physical object," and Dr. Crookall is quick to point out that "if this is the case our clothes possess etheric (astral) doubles that are invisible to the physical eye."[39] Substantially the same position has been advocated by the early theosophist leaders Annie Besant and Charles Leadbeater, who maintain that, although the astral world is richer than the ordinary physical world in that it contains many objects that do not correspond to anything in the physical world, the astral world does contain an accurate copy of every regular physical object. This is an ingenious theory, but when its implications are worked out it may perhaps seem slightly farfetched. It would mean that every time somebody produces something, he also produces an astral copy of that thing. A carpenter who builds a set of bookshelves is really building two sets, the regular one he sells to his customer and an astral copy he sells to nobody. And the same of course applies to everything. A dentist, for example, who fills a tooth is really filling the tooth he thinks he is filling as well as its astral duplicate, and when I am writing these lines I am really writing them twice at the same time. This is too much. I would rather believe that all astral bodies are always naked and that we are deluding ourselves when we observe them clothed. If it were not needed for reincarnation one might almost be tempted to give up the astral body.

THE QUESTION OF MEMORY TRANSFER

The problem of astral clothes, though tricky, is not the worst difficulty facing astral believers. Another has to do with the known dependence of memories on the brain. George Ritchie's astral body is supposed to have made the grand tour while his reg-

---

39. *The Next World—And the Next* (London, 1966), p. 38.

ular body was out of action. Memory traces of the experiences during this trip were produced in the astral brain and *not* in George's regular brain. They could not have been produced in the regular brain since the regular body was not in the various places visited during the trip. However, it is the George Ritchie with the regular body who, ever since he awoke from unconsciousness on December 24, 1943, has claimed to remember the events that took place during the visit to the next world. How could the appropriate memory traces have been produced in George's regular brain? Do astral brains by some kind of sympathetic magic produce duplicate traces in regular brains upon "reentry"? If they do not, the astral theorist is condemned to the view that here, but not in the case of any other genuine memories, the person can remember the events without appropriate memory traces in the brain. Even if there is an astral brain with memory traces, clearly nobody has or can have the slightest evidence that they produce duplicate traces in the regular brain at the moment of reentry. The alternative that here and only here a person can remember without memory traces in the brain goes against everything we know about the physiologically necessary conditions for memories. The difficulty seems fatal either way. This objection may not faze astral theorists who, along with other occultists and also more respectable believers in survival, seriously believe in what they call "extra-cerebral" memory. In Chapter 17, in which I discuss the dependence of consciousness on the brain, I will explain why all such talk should be dismissed as absurd, but only if it is not absurd could there be a reply to the difficulty just mentioned.

SYNCHRONIZATION

The next problem for the astral believer is that of synchronization between the regular and the astral body, not just between the two brains. It will be remembered that the astral body is supposed to be an exact duplicate of the regular body. If the astral body leaves the regular body of a boy aged ten, it will look just like the boy looks then; if it leaves the body of the same person at the age of eighty, it will look like the regular body at the age of eighty. The astral bodies of men will look like the regular bodies of men and the astral bodies of women like the regular bodies of women. If a boxer has just been punched in the face resulting in a flattened nose and the loss of three front teeth, his astral body will show the same flattened nose and the same gap in his mouth. If the boxer retires and eats a great deal so that he becomes enormously fat, his astral body, too, will be enormous. If a woman in her prime, with soft and unblemished skin, were to take an astral trip, the skin of her astral body would be soft and fresh. However, if the same woman were to take a trip many years later when her skin has become parched and wrinkled, this would also be true of her astral double. Astral believers prefer to state their theory in very general terms and usually flinch when such specific consequences are derived from it, but there is no doubt at all that these and similar statements about the appearance of astral doubles are really implied by the theory.

Now, the question that at once arises is how this exact synchronization is achieved. Except when it is released for a journey, the astral body resides inside the regular body. However, the exact state of the regular body at any given time is very largely the result of its movements and of influences upon it coming from its environment. To secure the synchronization required by astral theory we will have to postulate that corresponding to every physical act and movement there occurs an astral act and movement. Corresponding to every ordinary breath, every normal meal, every physical exertion, every conversation, every sexual act, every injury, there must occur a corresponding astral process. Surely no sane person can believe that this happens. One would think that while it is safely "tucked" away inside the regular body, the astral body cannot do anything at all. But this is not all. One of the key propositions of astral theory which we have met on several occasions makes most of the external influences on the astral body quite impossible. I am referring to all events in the person's life involving physical contact. According to the believer, the astral body cannot touch or be touched by another body, physical or astral. When our prize fighter had his nose flattened and three of his teeth knocked out, the corresponding damage to his astral body was *not* possible. Similarly, insofar as eating involves physical contact between various parts of the body and the food consumed, it cannot have an astral counterpart, and there is no way of explaining how the astral body becomes enormous if the regular body overeats.

THE IDENTITY PROBLEM

Allowing all the highly questionable factual reports and interpretations on the part of astral theorists, it may be questioned whether the astral body can be identical with the person whose life it is supposed to continue after death. Suppose for the sake of argument that somebody had a rabbit living inside of him and that the rabbit escaped after the person's death. This would surely not amount to the person's survival. Now let us suppose that while I am asleep my astral body left, "materialized" the way people do in the course of bilocations, and then committed a murder. After the murder he dematerialized and returned to his residence inside my regular body. Surely *I* could not be charged with murder. My astral body and not I, who was sleeping at the time, is the culprit. The most I could be charged with is giving shelter or asylum to a murderer.

THE ASTRAL BODY, TOO, MUST DIE

Let us for the sake of argument grant that all of us possess an astral body. There are two reasons for supposing that it cannot help the cause of survival. The first is the evidence we have that our consciousness depends for its existence on the regular body and especially the regular brain and not on any other body or brain. I will discuss this in Chapter 17. The second reason I will spell out now. Astral philosophy teaches that, except for its "lack of solidity," the astral body is an *exact* double of the regular one. Without this assumption the theory would not explain the facts or alleged facts of bilocation. However, if the astral body is an exact duplicate of the regular body it must die along with the regular body. This entirely reasonable conclusion seems to have escaped all astral theorists. If the regular body died as the result of a brain tumor or as the result of being shot through the heart, the astral brain and the astral heart must have been similarly injured. It is evident that if a person is to survive death he will need some other vehicle.

10

Telephone Calls from the Dead, Birthmarks, and the *Modus Operandi* Problem

In this chapter I am concerned with the evidence for reincarnation based on certain birthmarks and birth defects which, according to a number of writers, can only be explained on the assumption that they are the result of wounds sustained in an earlier life. Before I present the birthmark evidence, I will discuss the rather different and much more enjoyable question of telephone calls and tape recorded messages from the dead.

Telephone Calls from the Beyond

For many years I have been an avid reader of assorted tabloids—*The National Enquirer, The Midnight Globe, The Star, The National Examiner, The Sun,* and *News of the World.* Some people read these journals for secular reasons, they are titillated by stories about the private lives of movie stars, famous athletes, and other celebrities, and they also usually like to look at the pictures of beautiful models. My own reasons are of a more spiritual nature. The editors of the tabloids seem to be especially addicted to occult phenomena and they not infrequently feature reports about the next world. Among the leading citizens of the Beyond who have been contacted and who have supplied exciting information are Elvis Presley, Marilyn Monroe (who is eager to return to *this* world), Grace Kelly, Jack Benny, and Adolf Hitler (who has expressed regret over his treatment of the Jews and who has put the blame on Göring and Goebbels). Goering and Goebbels, I should add, have not been contacted for their side of the issue.

In my days of innocence I had been under the impression that all telephone calls originate from citizens of this world. When therefore I saw a banner headline in the *Midnight Globe* of March 20, 1979—"Phone Calls from the Grave"—I assumed that some coffins are now equipped with cellular telephones and that the calls referred to were made by persons who had been buried by mistake. However, this being the *Midnight Globe*, no such purely material phenomenon was referred to. The phone calls were from people who had really died and were now living in the Beyond. One of the most carefully documented cases concerned a New Jersey woman named Marie D'Alessio. After dreaming that a friend was in danger, Marie decided to call her. The account in the *Midnight Globe* then continues:

> They spoke for several minutes, and Marie hung up reassured. Days later she learned the friend she had been speaking with had been dead for six months.

A case with a tragic ending involved Mrs. Elsie Pendleton of Palos Verde, California. In February 1975 Mrs. Pendleton was awakened in the middle of the night by a phone call from her mother who had died six months earlier. The mother's voice repeatedly gave the warning "Tell Scott, No!" Scott was Mrs. Pendleton's teenage son who had been very close to his grandmother. This remarkable case not only involved a telephone call from a dead person but also a written message. For, the next morning, when Mrs. Pendleton woke up, she found a scratch pad on her night table with the message "Tell Scott, No!" in the unmistakable handwriting of her late mother. The reader will hardly be surprised to hear that a short time later Scott was killed in a car accident while taking part in a senseless prank.

These and several other cases are cited from a major work on the subject—by two "top psychic researchers," D. Scott Rogo and Raymond Bayless, *Phone Calls from the Dead*—published in 1979 by Prentice-Hall. The *Midnight Globe* quotes Dr. Gertrude Schmeidler, a professor at the City College of New York, in support of the high standing of the authors. They are "devoted contributors to psychic research" and we can "disregard the possibility that this book is a spook or a fraud." *Phone Calls from the Dead* was followed in 1981 by *The Case for Life After Death* by Elizabeth McAdams and Bayless. The book deals, among many other fascinating topics, with voices from the dead on tape, the photographs of "spirits," and "mysterious phone calls from the dead." As "scientific" parapsychologists, the authors are careful not to claim too much. They concede that it is not possible to reach conclusions about life after death with complete certainty, but they regard an affirmative answer as highly likely, considering all the manifold reports in support of it. In the chapter on telephone calls they discuss the suggestion that the calls are "produced by our own minds psychokinetically" and conclude that the calls are from the dead who, in spite of being dead, are "self-aware, intelligent entities with their own motives, drives, and intentions." [1]

The Rogo-Bayless volume has achieved the status of a classic on heavenly phonology, but it would be a mistake to think that such calls are rare. The bibliography of their book mentions numerous articles in *Fate* and its British counterpart *Light*

---

1. P. 133.

reporting similar phone calls. These articles are mainly from the 1960s and 1970s, but many years earlier, in 1921, F. R. Melton, a British psychical researcher, had published a pioneering work, *A Psychic Telephone*, which, I believe, is the first work on the subject.

The *Midnight Globe* stated quite accurately that both Rogo and Bayless had published numerous books prior to their work on supernatural phone calls. Rogo was particularly prolific and exceedingly well informed about all areas of psychic research. He is the author of *Parapsychology: A Century of Inquiry* (1975), a very useful survey of the subject, and of *The Search for Yesterday* (1985), a paperback defending reincarnation. I corresponded with him in the 1980s not, I hasten to assure the reader, to obtain information about the Beyond (I already had a great deal of such information from the writings of Drs. Kübler-Ross, Moody, et al.), but about certain statements in his book on reincarnation. I was therefore shocked to learn from his father that he had been murdered in 1991. So far as I know, the case has not yet been solved, but one cannot help hoping that Rogo will call before long, either one of his friends or the Los Angeles police department, since he might have valuable clues. Surely his change of residence does not exempt him from his civic duty to supply the police with all the relevant information in his possession.

Tape Recorded Messages

Voices from the Beyond have not infrequently been recorded even without benefit of the telephone. The McAdams-Bayless treatise has a chapter entitled "Voices and Raps on the Tape Recorder," which describes the research of Attila von Szalay and the "noted European philosopher and author" Dr. Konstantin Raudive. An impressive article on the subject appeared in *The Star* of July 28, 1980, entitled "Voices from the Grave on Tape Bring New Proof of Life After Death." It deals with the work of Mrs. Sarah Estep and the German "psychologist and veteran researcher" Dr. Fidelio Koeberle. Mrs. Estep who has a degree from the Mary Washington College of the University of Virginia has recorded no less than 15,000 messages from the dead during the six years preceding publication of the article in *The Star*. On the basis of these messages she has formed a definite idea of what life is like in the Beyond:

> They say it's pretty and indicate that there are houses but no food. They have said that family relationships continue if you let them and that you can be met by friends and loved ones who have also passed on.
>
> Some voices have come through and said that they are sick. Others have said they feel very good. They indicate there are doctors, nurses and healers over there.

These descriptions agree fairly well with what Elvis Presley said many years ago to the *National Enquirer*, that life in the Beyond is pretty much the same grind as on earth. Since Mrs. Estep mentions that some of the inhabitants of the Beyond are sick, I cannot help wondering if they ever die and, if so, what happens to them after their death there. Do they move on to a Super-Beyond?

Mrs. Estep's research has the wholehearted endorsement of Hans Holzer, the author of numerous books on occult topics and founder of the Center for Paranormal Studies in Los Angeles. "There is no question in my mind," Holzer is quoted in *The Star*, "that this is valid proof of life after death." There is no other way of explaining the "thousands of tapes, many of which contain specific messages from clear, intelligent voices." Dr. Fidelio's collection consists of thousands of voices, speaking a great variety of languages, not only German, French, English, and Swedish, but also several Indian dialects. The messages give information that Dr. Fidelio did not possess and they sometimes speak in languages with which he is not familiar. There is no doubt that the voices "come from the dead." Eight years after the article in *The Star*, Mrs. Estep offered detailed accounts of her contacts with the Beyond in *Voices of Eternity*, a book which reproduces her conversations with the dead via radio, telephone, and television. She not only possesses proof of the reality of reincarnation, precognition, and clairvoyance, but also knows that UFOs come from Alpha Centauri.[2]

I have no doubt that if one were to investigate the stories by the various writers in *Fate* and *Light* and the cases cited by Bayless, Rogo, McAdams, von Szalay, and the others, they would speedily collapse. This is the usual fate of such "startling" tales. Such an investigation is, however, not at all necessary because there is a very basic reason for rejecting these reports. This is what I call the *modus operandi* problem, the impossibility of specifying a credible way in which the telephone calls or the taped messages could have been transmitted by the dead. The *modus operandi* objection is a very powerful one and, as we shall see in this chapter and later in the present book, its destructive ramifications are widespread.[3] I will explain it in some detail after I outline the birthmark evidence for reincarnation in the next section.

Birthmarks and Birth Defects

According to Stevenson "birthmarks and birth defects" are "some of the strongest evidence in favor of reincarnation." These birthmarks and birth defects "correspond to wounds or other marks on the body of the related personality." In some cases there is a "correspondence" between internal diseases of children and similar diseases from which the "previous personalities" suffered. Stevenson concedes that he has to rely to a large extent on the memories of the surviving friends and relatives of the de-

---

2. For more details about the work of Mrs. Estep and other investigators of voices from the dead see Chapter 5 of R. A, Baker, *Hidden Memories*, op. cit. This splendid book provides highly plausible explanations of how the delusions of psychic investigators like Mrs. Estep, Dr. Fidelio, and Dr. Raudive are produced.

3. Its application to most contemporary forms of belief in God is explained in "God and the Modus Operandi Problem," the Postscript to the present book.

ceased individuals for information about the location of the wounds or other marks on the bodies. There may be a temptation on the part of the informants to "harmonize" the memories of the wounds with the observations of the birthmarks on the children's bodies, but Stevenson is confident that his informants are generally reliable. In any event he tells us that he has overcome this objection in about thirty cases by obtaining autopsies and other medical records of the deceased individuals.[4]

Stevenson regards these birthmarks as such strong evidence because they are objectively observable and because the only serious alternative explanation—that of "a psychic force on the part of the baby's mother that influences the body of the embryo or fetus within her"—can safely be ruled out. He observes that this alternative explanation is "almost as mindstretching for the average Westerner as reincarnation" and he adds that in twelve of his cases it can be "firmly excluded" since the child's parents had not heard of the "identified previous personality" until after the child's birth.

Because of the importance that he attaches to birthmarks, Stevenson tells us in *Children Who Remember Previous Lives* (1988) that he has reported a large number of such cases in "volumes now in preparation." Apparently a four-volume work on this subject with profuse illustrations exists but has not appeared so far. In *Death and Survival* (1992) Robert Almeder, a devoted disciple, refers to "the current publication" of Stevenson's *Birthmarks and Birth Defects: A Contribution to Their Etiology* by Paragon House of New York. Jeffrey Iverson, a British admirer who has called Stevenson "the Galileo of the twentieth century" also lists Stevenson's book on birthmarks in the bibliography of *In Search of the Dead* (1992). This time the publisher is given as University Press of Virginia and the date as 1991. Inquiries with both publishers produced the information that they had published no such book and were not planning to publish one.

Although Stevenson's multivolume work on birthmarks has not been published, several of the case histories he has reported do include, as an essential part of the evidence for reincarnation, details about the birthmarks of the individuals and their alleged relation to wounds and illnesses of the earlier bodies. I will briefly discuss the case of Corliss Chotkin, Jr. It will serve as a useful illustration of the kind of evidence that so greatly impresses Stevenson. It is a typical Stevensonian case and the objections to it would, with some minor adjustments, apply to all the others.

The case concerns three members of a Tlingit family in Alaska. The Tlingits are committed believers in reincarnation. Victor Vincent, an elderly fisherman, told his niece, Mrs. Corliss Chotkin, Sr., that he would be reborn as her son. This sort of thing sounds fantastic to most Western ears but not to believers in reincarnation. Victor Vincent died in the spring of 1946 and eighteen months later Mrs. Chotkin gave birth to Corliss who has been claimed to be the reincarnation of Victor Vincent. When Vic-

---

4. I am confining the discussion to Stevenson's presentations because he has written more extensively on birthmarks than any other reincarnationist. A briefer treatment is found in Story, op. cit., pp. 160 ff. and 276–78.

tor told his niece that he would be reborn as her son he showed her two scars from minor operations. One was near the bridge of his nose, the other on his upper back. He told her that she would recognize him in his new life by birthmarks on her child's body which would correspond to his two scars. According to Mrs. Chotkin, this is exactly what happened. Corliss had two birthmarks that were exactly at the sites of the scars that Victor Vincent had shown to her.

Stevenson entered the case in 1962, over fourteen years after Corliss's birth. By this time, according to Mrs. Chotkin, the birthmarks had shifted from their original location. However, they remained very visible and one of them specially impressed Stevenson. After describing its size and location, Stevenson remarks that "its resemblance to the healed scar of a surgical wound was greatly increased by the presence at the sides of the main birthmarks of several small round marks that seemed to correspond to positions of small round wounds made by needles that placed the stitches used to close surgical wounds."[5] There was other evidence that Corliss was identical with Victor Vincent. One of Mrs. Chotkin's aunts related a dream she had shortly before Corliss's birth that Victor Vincent was coming to live in the Chotkin's home. Mrs. Chotkin "was certain" that she had not previously told her aunt about Victor's prediction. Corliss "spontaneously" recognized a number of people whom Victor Vincent had known including his widow. Mrs. Chotkin also said that Corliss mentioned two events in Victor's life about which "she did not think he could have obtained information normally." It is not clear that she described these events to Stevenson, and in any case Stevenson does not tell us what they were. Furthermore, Corliss showed several behavioral traits similar to those of the late Victor Vincent—they both stuttered, they combed their hair in much the same way, they had a passionate interest in boats, and they had strong religious propensities. Both also were left-handed. As in the Asian cases which form the main body of Stevenson's work, Corliss made few remarks about his previous life as he grew older, and by the time Stevenson first met him in 1962, at the age of fifteen, he told Stevenson that he remembered nothing about it. He gradually lost the stutter that had formerly afflicted him. Stevenson last saw him in 1972 when he enjoyed good health and was working contentedly in a pulp mill near his home.

The main objection to this and all similar cases is of course that there is no conceivable way in which the scars of Victor Vincent could have been transferred to the body of Corliss. I will get to this in a moment. However, it also needs to be observed that the case is evidentially very weak in several other respects. To begin with, all the parties are believers in reincarnation and furthermore all significant statements originate with Mrs. Chotkin about whom Stevenson has told us next to nothing. It is notorious that even otherwise reasonably honest persons cannot be trusted when it comes to claims relating to their religion or some cause they deeply believe in. Writers on the history of the miracles of Christianity have spoken of "religious" or "pious" lying, but I would prefer to call it "religious confabulation." It should be noted that Stevenson

---

5. *Children Who Remember Previous Lives*, p. 58.

did not hear the prediction made by Victor Vincent and that he did not see Victor Vincent's scars. It is difficult to believe that Mrs. Chotkin made up the story of the prediction, but it is very possible that she was mistaken in her recollection of the exact nature and location of the scars. (Incidentally, Stevenson does not tell us whether Corliss also had a birthmark near the bridge of his nose.) Mrs. Chotkin was "certain" that she had not previously told her aunt anything about Victor Vincent's prediction, but all of us, even when we are not engaged in a matter of great emotional significance, are certain of having said or not having said things when the opposite is the case. As I shall explain more fully in Chapter 16, "spontaneous recognitions" of friends and relatives of the deceased are easily produced by various hints and clues. As for the "two events in the life of Victor Vincent about which Mrs. Chotkin did not think Corliss could have obtained information normally," I would like to remind the reader about the cases of remarkably accurate memories by hypnotized subjects of events in the remote past about which they "could not have obtained information normally." It always turned out that they could and did obtain the information normally. I see no reason to suppose that the same is not true in the present case. I will not comment at this time on the significance of the gradual fading of Corliss's memories of a previous life since I will discuss this question fully in Chapter 16. Stevenson always passes off this gradual forgetting by the children as of no significance, but it seems to me to be highly significant and greatly weakens the evidential value of all these cases.

As far as I know birthmarks are cited as evidence only among some of the cultures in which belief in reincarnation is prevalent. It seems to me very likely that in many of the birthmark cases there are no predictions (or else they are retrospectively invented) such as the one made by Victor Vincent. What happens is that when a child is born with some birthmarks, the parents or other interested parties try to remember or look for somebody who died fairly recently and of whom it was known that he had wounds whose location corresponded to the location of the birthmarks of the child. This would explain why the autopsies or other medical records might confirm this part of the stories. I should add that in looking for the previous person, the Tlingits, or more generally the believer in reincarnation *and* in the transmission of scars, would not be behaving in a fraudulent or dishonest fashion. *He* is not trying to prove reincarnation. He already accepts it and, given his assumptions, it makes perfectly good sense to proceed as he does. However, for somebody who does not share his assumptions, the search for the dead person with wounds in the right places shows the worthlessness of such cases as evidence for reincarnation. The view that the Tlingits and other believers in birthmark transmissions tend to look for the original body is not something I can prove, but it seems to be eminently reasonable and does not burden us with fantastic and even incoherent explanations.

The Modus Operandi Problem

None of the critical considerations just mentioned is fatal to the view that the birth-marks on Corliss's body are evidence that he is the reincarnation of Victor Vincent. What is fatal to it and of course to the general claim that wounds and illnesses may be transmitted from a dead person to a child or an embryo is that there is no con-ceivable way in which such a transmission could take place. How are the scars picked up, how are they going to be stored for a period of varying length, and how are they going to be imprinted on the successor body? It should be noted in passing that there cannot be any genetic transmission, not only because acquired character-istics cannot be inherited, but also because the new and the old bodies are not in the same genetic line.

Stevenson shows some awareness of this problem. He postulates a "nonphysical" body, which is going to survive the death of the regular physical body. This non-physical body which is identical with our mind will pick up the scars and imprint them on the embryo. I discuss Stevenson's nonphysical body in detail in Chapter 15. Here I will simply say that it closely resembles the astral body we met in the last chap-ter. The objections to accepting Stevenson's theory as an answer to the *modus operandi* problem are threefold. In the first place, as we already saw and as we shall see later specifically in relation to Stevenson's version of the astral body, there is no good reason for believing that such an entity exists. Second, and most important, Stevenson's nonphysical body is not the sort of thing to which physical scars could be transferred and which could do any imprinting on the embryo. Finally there is the problem of size. In most cases the scars on the old body are probably bigger than the embryo's entire back at least during the earlier stages of pregnancy. Even if we sup-pose that the imprinting takes place just before birth or right at birth, the scars can-not possibly be imprinted in their original size. Are they specially shrunk for the oc-casion? If so, how and when does the shrinking take place?

To avoid any misunderstanding I should emphasize that nothing I have said rules out the acceptance of causal theories just because it is not *known* how the cause produces the effect. A famous illustration is the story of the analgesic effects of as-pirin. Aspirin itself was first developed in the 1890s by a German chemist who was attempting to relieve his father's painful, crippling arthritis. The evidence soon be-came overwhelming that aspirin relieves pain and also works as an anti-inflammatory drug, but the mode of its action was unknown. It was not until 1971 that John R. Vane showed aspirin to block the production of prostaglandins, hormones released when cells are injured or stimulated by other hormones.[6] An intriguing and as yet unsolved recent case concerns the connection between "vertex baldness" (a bald patch on top

---

6. There is some doubt that Vane's theory gives the complete answer. For details on the history of aspirin and related drugs and also for doubts about the completeness of Vane's theory see G. Weissmann, "Aspirin," *Scientific American*, January 1991.

of the head) and heart attacks. A team of physicians at Boston University found that, in men under fifty-five, vertex baldness is significantly correlated with heart attacks. According to the statistics they compiled, the more extensive the baldness the higher the risk of heart attacks. For men with mild or moderate vertex baldness the risk was about 40 percent greater than for men with a full set of hair. The risk goes to 340 percent for men with severe vertex baldness. A particularly interesting case that I do not wish to discuss in detail because it would lead to controversial issues that are not relevant to the subject of the present book is that of the *modus operandi* of the repression of emotions like love, rage, and fear. It is widely agreed that such repressions, especially in childhood, lead to all kinds of neurotic difficulties in later life. Assuming that this is so, how exactly do the repressions produce the unfortunate results?

None of these and countless other causal theories are inherently objectionable because we *can* describe possible *modi operandi* in language that is not meaningless or self-contradictory and because the *modi* do not violate well established laws. By contrast, the claims that telephone calls or taped messages were received from the dead or that birthmarks have been transmitted from a deceased body violates one or both of these requirements. It has to be emphasized, because it is sometimes forgotten, that nobody has ever observed the imprinting of the scars at either end and, what is more basically troublesome, such imprinting cannot in principle be observed because the second body cannot be seen, heard, or in any other way, noticed.

I will return to several of the questions touched on in the preceding paragraphs in the chapter devoted to what I call the interregnum problem, the question of what a person is like between incarnations. It will become clear there that the *modus operandi* problem is fatal not only to the birthmarks argument but to the entire reincarnation theory. By the way, I do hope that Stevenson's four-volume work will find a publisher. He seems to me a sincere, but deluded man and he does deserve his day in court. What is more, publication of the book would give pleasure all around. Stevenson and his supporters would be delighted. As for the publishers, I do not believe that they would lose any money. Given the state of education in the world, especially the United States, there will be plenty of believers or would-be believers to buy such a profusely illustrated defense of reincarnation. As for myself, it would be a joyous occasion for additional comments about this absurd nonsense in a later edition.

Dr. Kübler-Ross, Dr. Moody, and the New Immortality Movement

On Death and Dying

Dr. Kübler-Ross definitely belongs in this book. She is an ardent believer in reincarnation and she not only believes in the astral body but is an astral traveler of the first rank. In an earlier chapter I quoted her completely untroubled acceptance of déjà vu experiences as proof of reincarnation. I described her there as the most uncritical person in the history of the world. My account of various episodes in her career as a champion of immortality will show that I was hardly exaggerating.

Of all the friends of the occult discussed in the present book Kübler-Ross is the only one who has some genuine achievements to her credit and a few words are in order about her work with dying patients that has brought her well-earned acclaim. She was catapulted into fame as the result of her book *On Death and Dying*. Published in 1969, it became a durable best seller. *On Death and Dying* is rich in ideas and observations and evidently the work of a person of unusual sensitivity and compassion. In this book Kübler-Ross advanced her famous theory about the five stages—denial, anger, bargaining, depression, and acceptance—through which dying patients typically pass. It is clear that she regards acceptance of death by the patient as something highly desirable and implies that those who do not reach this stage have not achieved as much as one could hope for. Some of these conclusions have been challenged both by religious and by secular critics. However, there has been practically unanimous approval of Kübler-Ross's discussion of the special needs of dying patients generally ignored both by physicians and by the patients' families. The reviewer in the *Journal of the American Medical Association* concluded that *On Death and Dying* offers "insight and understanding so that all those who have contact with the terminally ill can do more to help them." It should be emphasized that *On Death and Dying* contains no speculations of any kind about life after death. We now know that at the time of writing the book, Kübler-Ross was already carrying on conversations with messengers from the next world, but it would have been impossible to infer anything of this kind from the purely secular content of the book. The last two pages, which are particularly moving, could well have been written by an outright unbeliever. "There is a time in a patient's life," Kübler-Ross writes, "when the pain ceases to be, when the mind slips off into a dreamless state, when the need for food becomes minimal and the awareness of the environment all but disappears into darkness."[1] At this time many relatives become greatly upset and find it difficult to remain with the dying person. Speaking from extensive firsthand experience, Kübler-Ross insists that the moment of death is "neither frightening nor painful, but the peaceful cessation of the functioning of the body. Watching the peaceful death of a human being reminds us of a falling star; one of the million lights in a vast sky that flares up for a brief moment only to disappear into the endless night forever."[2]

In the years following 1969, Kübler-Ross wrote many articles and gave numerous lectures repeating the message of her book and she became widely regarded as the leading figure in what was frequently described as the "thanatology movement." In 1976, Dr. Robert Gibson, the president-elect of the American Psychiatric Association, remarked:

> I know Dr. Ross, and I cannot find words to express fully my tremendous admiration for her contributions to our understanding of the final stages of life. Her research in death and dying is remarkable. It will have enduring value for decades to come.

When Kübler-Ross testified before the Special Committee on Aging of the U.S. Senate on August 7, 1972, the chairman, Senator Frank Church, as well as other members of the committee were highly respectful and deferential. Senator Charles Percy spoke of her as his "distinguished constituent."

"One Hundred and Ninety-Three Clear-Cut Cases from All Over the World"

As far as I know, Kübler-Ross's first published statement of her belief in life after death, expressed in rather muted language, came in a short essay in 1973 in *To Live and To Die—When, Why and How*, a volume dealing with various bioethical problems. This book had a very limited circulation, but by that time Kübler-Ross had become a television celebrity and in several of her appearances in the years after 1973

---

1. *On Death and Dying* (New York, 1969), p. 273.
2. P. 276.

she openly proclaimed her total assurance not only that human beings survive death, but that this conclusion had now been established by the most extensive empirical evidence. One of her fullest discussions of the subject appeared in the December 1975 issue of *People*, a mass-circulation magazine specializing in stories about the private lives of movie stars and other public figures. The editors of *People* must have believed that a defense of immortality by a superstar like Kübler-Ross would make just as good copy as details about the latest Hollywood sex scandals. The article was prominently advertised on the front cover. It bore the title "Life After Death? 'Yes, Beyond a Shadow of Doubt,' Says the Eminent Dr. Kübler-Ross." Readers were informed that Dr. Kübler-Ross had agreed to discuss her "new and controversial findings" about life after death with Linda Witt of *People*. Underneath a picture of Kübler-Ross, "the famed Swiss-born psychiatrist" is quoted as saying "I know as certainly as I am sitting here that there is life after death." Linda Witt was interested in how Kübler-Ross reached her conclusion. "I have always felt something significant happens a few moments after death," Kübler-Ross replied. At that time, she continued, most of her patients "got the most fantastically peaceful expressions, even those who had struggled terribly with death." She then turned to the subject of death visions:

> I wondered, "To whom do people talk on their deathbeds?" My own father talked to his father who had been dead thirty years, and then turned back and spoke rationally to me. We label this "hallucinations," as if once we superstitiously put a label on it, it is taken care of.

I must interpose a defense of our classifying experiences like those of Kübler-Ross's father as hallucinations. There is nothing the least bit "superstitious" about it. In calling an experience a hallucination we mean two things: that the object experienced by the hallucinating individual is not also perceived by other suitably placed observers and that scientific instruments would not obtain data of the kind received when a real object is present. The deathbed vision of Kübler-Ross's father *was* a hallucination in this sense. Kübler-Ross evidently believes that the question "to whom do people talk on their deathbeds?" presents a special problem to the skeptic. This is not so. The answer is quite simply that the dying person talks to nobody, but mistakenly believes to be addressing a real person.

Three and a half years earlier Kübler-Ross herself had no difficulty answering a similar question in the case of one of her dying patients who was suffering from delusions. In the course of her testimony before the Senate Committee on Aging she described in great detail the case of a twenty-eight-year-old mother of three children who was dying of a disease of the liver. Her husband had spent all his savings and incurred heavy debts to pay doctor and hospital bills. She was constantly going in and out of hepatic comas. In her despair the woman went to a faith healer who convinced her that she had been cured by him. Kübler-Ross entered the case when the patient was confined in a hospital room at the end of a long hallway, furthest away from the nursing station. Except for Kübler-Ross, she never had a visitor, not even her husband, and spent her time talking about God's miracles and the faith healer who had cured her. On one of her visits Kübler-Ross found the patient lying on her bed smiling, with her arms still beside her body. "What in the world are you smiling about?" Kübler-Ross asked her, "Don't you see these beautiful flowers that my husband surrounded me with?" the woman answered. Kübler-Ross explains that there were no flowers to be seen and then, without any hesitation, describes the experience as a delusion. "It took me a while," she told the Senators, "to appreciate that this woman realized that she could not live without some expression of love and care, hopefully coming from her husband." To go on living, Kübler-Ross continued, the patient had to "develop a delusion of flowers sent to her by her husband." If Kübler-Ross's father was not *merely* hallucinating but was in fact talking to an inhabitant of the next world, this is something to be shown by detailed evidence and cannot be taken for granted just because he was not insane. In any event, Linda Witt did not seem to be too impressed and asked: "What would you describe as your first positive evidence?" Kübler-Ross answered:

> About seven years ago, a patient who had been declared dead despite heroic last-minute resuscitation efforts spontaneously came alive three-and-a-half hours later. She shared with me how she felt: she had floated out of her physical body and watched herself being worked on. She described in minute detail the resuscitation team—who was there, who wanted to give up, who wanted to continue, who told a joke to relieve the tension. This gave me my first clue.

This was only the beginning. Since then, Kübler-Ross proceeded, she has obtained "193 very clear-cut cases from all over the world, both religious and nonreligious people." All the subjects "experienced the same thing." There was one particularly remarkable case. We are told that the person had been clinically dead for no less than twelve and a half hours. These remarkable cases and all the other relevant material was to be published "in a year or so." The forthcoming book would contain "hard numbers and hard data." Without mentioning any names, Kübler-Ross refers to "friends from many fields of science"—physicists, "people in electronics," and a new species described as "super-neurologists"—who are collaborating with her and who have confirmed her findings. These "great scientists working on the project" supply the "cross-verification" that is so important to the skeptical mind.

Before continuing with the presentation of Kübler-Ross's views, a few observations are in order. I am writing this account in 1995, twenty years after the Kübler-Ross interview in *People*. The book which was to contain "the hard numbers and hard data" has not appeared and there are no signs that it is going to appear. Kübler-Ross has never disclosed the names of any of the physicists, electronic experts or super-neurologists who "cross-verified" her conclusions. The only "scientist" Kübler-Ross ever mentions is Robert A. Monroe, a leading instructor in "astral travel" about whom I will have something to say later in this chapter. Whatever we may think about the value of Monroe's work, he is, by his own account, a retired businessman and not either a physicist, engineer, or neurologist, super or otherwise. It is also worth pointing out that the patient who provided Kübler-Ross with her "first positive evidence" for life after death had not suffered brain-death. If she had, she would not have been able to talk intelligently to Kübler-Ross after her resuscitation. We are entitled to assume that throughout the period of her "death" the brain could register stimuli similar to those it received while the patient was fully alive. It is totally illegitimate to infer, as Kübler-Ross evidently does, that in such cases consciousness continued although the body was dead. Since the brain was not dead, these cases do not have the slightest bearing on the question of whether consciousness continues to exist after the body has died. As for the stories about patients who were revived without apparent brain damage after having been clinically dead for several hours, these are strictly for the birds and for readers of the *National Enquirer*. No reputable physician on earth, Catholic, Protestant, Islamic, Jewish, or atheist, will take them seriously for one moment. In the opinion of all physicians other than Kübler-Ross, a person's brain is *irreversibly* damaged if no blood is supplied to it for periods *very* much shorter than those mentioned by her.

Most of the rest of the interview in *People* concerned the details of the next life as disclosed in the experiences of the 193 "clear-cut cases." Without exception all reported that the next life is unbelievably wonderful. The experience is the same, "no matter what the cultural background" of the individual. They all "describe a feeling of peace, beautiful, indescribable peace, no pain, no anxiety." After "virtually shedding their physical bodies, as a butterfly comes out of a cocoon," the patients became "perfect, completely whole." By this Kübler-Ross means that, in the course of their postmortem experiences, these people found that their maimed or disease-ridden bodies had suddenly been restored to full health. A young man, for example, "whose leg was cut off in an automobile accident floated above the crash scene and observed the rescue effort, and recalls his leg being intact." One should spell out the implications of this last statement. Kübler-Ross does not have "a shadow of a doubt" that this young man visited the next world and that the same is true of all her other "clear-cut cases." Since these subjects are not hallucinating, it is evident that what survives is not only the mind but also an *intact* body. This intact body cannot be the old body since that body is *not* intact. Kübler-Ross does not maintain that the young man's postmortem experience miraculously restored the severed leg in his ordinary human body. Moreover, in the case of people who are not resuscitated, the ordinary body does die and *is* irreversibly damaged. It is not surprising that Kübler-Ross should have become an ardent champion of the astral body. The indescribable peace is not the only blessing reported by Kübler-Ross's subjects. While they were dead they also achieved "a high understanding." The transition to the next life, furthermore, is not unpleasant at all and it is carried out in the company of friends or relatives:

Whomever you most loved in life who preceded you in death is there to help you make the transition, and you talk to them. It is a transition, as dramatic as cutting the umbilical cord. But the important thing is that you don't go through it alone.

After reaching the next world, with their bodies whole and their minds vastly improved, the clinically dead individuals not unnaturally "resented, sometimes bitterly, the attempts to bring them back to life." For what they were coming back to was not only life in a lower realm, but it was for them a "dreadful existence" with "cancerous bodies" or "amputated limbs."

Kübler-Ross and Dr. Moody

In the fall of 1975 Mockingbird Books, a small Virginia company, published *Life After Life,* a slim volume by Raymond Moody, Jr. When this book was published, Moody was totally unknown. He had been a teacher of philosophy in a small college in Virginia for a short period. Subsequently he decided to become a psychiatrist and when *Life After Life* appeared he was in his fourth year at the Medical School of the University of Virginia. The greater part of Moody's book consists of a collection of "postmortem" reports, accounts of experiences by people who had been close to death or who had actually been declared dead and had been resuscitated. Although Moody did not claim that these reports proved or were any kind of evidence for belief in life after death, both the title of the book and numerous of his remarks made it clear that he was indeed a supporter of immortality. *Life After Life* became a major best seller. After the initial hardcover printing, it was republished in two separate paperback editions. According to a survey in *Publishers Weekly* of September 25, 1978, no less than three million copies were in print at that time.

Life After Life had an introduction by Elisabeth Kübler-Ross. After complimenting Moody—"this young scholar"—on his courage in making his findings available to the general public, she asserts, without any qualifications, that Moody's research provides clear-cut evidence for belief in life after death. She tells us that she was engaged in similar research, compiling accounts of patients "who died and made a comeback" totally against the expectations of their physicians. The accounts she has compiled "very much coincide" with the reports presented by Moody. She then issued a warning that Moody was likely to be attacked from two quarters. He was going to be criticized by the less open-minded members of the clergy who prefer to make the topic of life after death "an issue of blind faith" and who are liable to accuse Moody and herself of "selling cheap grace." Kübler-Ross predicted that Moody would also be criticized by physicians on the ground that this kind of study is "unscientific." Needless to say, Kübler-Ross rejects all such criticisms. She tells us that both in religion and in science we must have "the courage to open new doors" and employ new "scientific tools" such as those used by Moody and herself to explore as vital a topic as the reality and nature of survival after death. In conclusion Kübler-Ross expressed special pleasure that Moody's book should appear just as she herself was "ready to put her research findings on paper."

By the spring of 1976 the sales of Moody's book as well as the lectures and television appearances of Kübler-Ross had become newsworthy. The *New York Times, Newsweek,* and various other publications featured articles about the new "scientific" immortality movement. The subject was deemed important enough by the *New York Times* to devote to it a paragraph in the section on "Ideas and Trends" in the Sunday edition of April 25. This paragraph was a summary of a lengthy report in the *Times* of April 20, entitled "New Studies of the Dying Process Provide Impetus for Scientific Inquiries on the Question of Life After Death." On July 13, *Newsweek* devoted a whole page in its section on "Ideas" to the activities and publications of Kübler-Ross, Moody, and other luminaries of the new movement. Both articles mention some critical reactions, but they are entirely respectful. Kenneth A. Briggs, the author of the article in the *Times,* went out of his way to emphasize the high standing of Kübler-Ross in the medical world. "The question of whether there is life after death, long the province of theologians, psychics and ordinary speculators," Briggs opens the article, "has recently become a subject of investigation among members of the scientific community." The major impetus to this investigation was "supplied by the noted psychiatrist, Dr. Elisabeth Kübler-Ross, whose studies of the dying process have been widely circulated and highly acclaimed." It is Dr. Kübler-Ross's "high standing" among health professionals and the general public that has helped to focus "immediate attention" on this new claim in support of life after death.

The new immortality movement has been hailed with undiluted enthusiasm by the various tabloids—*The National Enquirer, The Midnight Globe,* the *Star,* and other newcomers to this genre—which seem to be the favorite literature of millions of semi-literate Americans. Nowhere else are Moody, Kübler-Ross, their original allies, and various newcomers of the 1980s quoted more frequently or with more unqualified admiration. It would, however, be a mistake to think that the appeal of the movement has been confined to publications which, to put it mildly, do not pursue serious scholarly objectives. Entirely respectable publications have featured articles praising the new movement as a necessary and healthy antidote to the skepticism of the scientific establishment. As an illustration I will refer to an article in the *Hastings Center Report,* a bimonthly published by the Institute of Science, Ethics and the Life Sciences at Hastings-on-Hudson. This periodical deals primarily with bioethical questions and many of its contributors are persons of high standing in the academic community. The *Hastings Report* of October 1977 contained an extremely sympathetic article on the great current interest in survival or, as the author calls it, "the public passion for immortality." The article bears the title "Beyond Death: The Rebirth of Immortality." The author, Michael Marsh, is identified as "a philosopher working on a book about immortality."[3] Marsh

---

3. Marsh's *A Matter of Personal Survival* was published in 1985 by the Theosophical Publishing House.

regards Kübler-Ross, Moody, and their associates as serious thinkers whose influence is entirely salutary. The article is in effect a review of five books, all in varying degrees favorable to immortality, published during the preceding four years. The first is Moody's *Life After Life,* the second *The Human Encounter with Death* by Stanislov Grof and Joan Halifax whose work is discussed in Chapter 13 and which, like Moody's book, has an introduction by Kübler-Ross. The main purpose of Marsh's article appears to be a protest against what he takes to be the attitude to the subject of immortality of "nearly all the world's intellectual establishment." The philosophers, scientists, and other intellectuals, who make up this establishment, assume without discussion that there is no life after death. This "accepted wisdom" holds "to a reductionist world view in which humans are nothing but complex animal organisms; [and] organisms are nothing but temporarily organized matter." Among "the people who count," Marsh goes on, the idea of immortality appears "not only foolish, but taboo and undiscussable." However, no matter what the world's intellectuals may think, the idea of immortality will not die. Marsh refers to a 1976 Gallup Poll in which 69 percent of Americans say they believe in life after death. He adds that the taboo on the discussion of immortality is "slipping" and mentions the popularity of Kübler-Ross and Moody as evidence for this slippage. At the end of the article Marsh observes that "the prestige of America's establishments, including the scientific one, has dwindled." Marsh applauds this development and remarks that "authoritarian pronouncements" (by the scientific establishment) "about what can and cannot be true no longer stops sensible people from looking for themselves." The new immortality movement, which has lifted the taboo on discussions of life after death, has brought about a situation in which "we may once more wonder and explore."

Moody and His Critics

In January 1977, *Readers' Digest* reprinted major portions of *Life After Life* under the title "Life after Death—The Testimony Mounts." The editorial introduction assured the reader that the near-death experiences that are recounted by Moody "with scientific detachment" were "nothing less than fantastic." By 1977 Moody had apparently obtained his M.D. and in a biographical footnote we are told that he "is currently on leave of absence from a psychiatric residency at the University of Virginia Hospital and is writing a sequel to *Life After Life* . . . scheduled for spring publication." The sequel, an even slimmer volume than the original, *Reflections on Life After Life,* was published in June of 1977.[4] It is best described as a non-book. Chapters are separated from one another by four or five blank pages. The type is large and the margins are unusually wide. Several chapters consist of little more than extensive quotations from writers like Plato and William James which are very interesting but of dubious

---

4. *Life After Life* will now be abbreviated as *LAL* and *Reflections on Life After Life* as *Reflections.*

relevance. The book numbers one hundred fifty pages, but Moody's own contributions would not amount to more than forty or fifty pages in a normal book.

Since publishing *LAL* and *Reflections* Moody has become a "past life therapist," treating patients by having them recall the traumatic experiences in earlier lives that are supposed to be responsible for their psychological problems. More recently he has developed a technique of calling up deceased friends and relatives by gazing into mirrors. I will briefly discuss this bizarre concoction in the next chapter. Here I am only concerned with Moody's work as it is reported in the first two books.

In *LAL* Moody bases himself on fifty cases of people who were resuscitated after having been pronounced clinically dead (i.e., after their heart had stopped beating) or who in the course of accidents or illness had come very close to death. By the time he wrote *Reflections* he claims to have accumulated three hundred cases. Moody interviewed all these subjects and one wonders how much time he could have devoted to the interviews. It should be remembered that during this period he was also completing the studies for his medical degree. I will explain later on why, in my opinion, Moody cannot be trusted and why his work cannot be regarded as scientific in even a very charitable sense of the term. However, several features of "the near death experiences" reported by Moody have also been observed by people who are trustworthy and who have no axes to grind. It is not unreasonable to conclude that near-death experiences (NDEs) really possess several of these features. The real question is whether this provides any evidence whatever for survival.

In his excellent and insufficiently known article "Psychology and Near-Death Experiences,"[5] James E. Alcock offers a concise summary of the ideal case or "theoretically complete model experience" of Moody's subjects:

> At the moment of greatest physical discomfort, the patient hears the physician pronounce him dead, and he hears an uncomfortably loud ringing or buzzing sound. He feels himself being drawn rapidly through a long tunnel. He notices that he has a new body with powers very different from the old one, and may even see his old body lying on the bed with the resuscitation team gathered around it; but his vantage point is outside and above his body. He catches sight of dead relatives and friends and encounters a "being" of very bright light, a "loving, warm spirit." This spirit helps him to panoramically review the events of his past life. He is overwhelmed by feelings of love, joy, and peace. . . . Finally, he comes to some kind of barrier, but is made to turn back and go, reluctantly, back into his body. Following resuscitation, he is emotionally very moved and is no longer afraid of death.

Moody does not claim that all of these elements are present in all NDEs but he asserts that many of them are present in many experiences and some elements are pre-

5. *Skeptical Inquirer,* Spring 1979, pp. 27–28. Gerd H. Hövelmann's "Evidence for Survival from Near Death Experiences—A Critical Appraisal," in P. Kurtz (Ed.), *A Skeptic's Handbook of Parapsychology,* is another extremely valuable critical discussion of the work of Moody, Osis-Haraldsson and other champions of near-death experiences, including several not covered in the present book.

sent in all. Moody does not explicitly claim that the survival-hypothesis is the best explanation of this uniformity, but such an argument is certainly suggested in both of his books. If this is a misunderstanding, it is one that Moody evidently delights in and has incidentally, or not so incidentally, made him a wealthy man.

It is not clear how Moody selected his sample. What is clear is that his subjects, or returnees, as I prefer to call them, are totally uneducated and devoid of the slightest capacity for self-criticism. These primitive returnees are regularly met by reception committees of deceased friends and relatives, but the same is not true of educated persons who have had NDEs.[6] They seem to have been shamefully neglected by their friends and relatives. Incidentally, Moody's returnees do not talk like ordinary mortals, but the way uneducated people are imagined to talk by bad novelists and screen writers.

Before going further, it should be emphasized that by no means are all NDEs euphoric. It is almost inconceivable that Moody is not aware of this fact, but there is never the slightest allusion to it in his books. According to an editorial in the *Lancet* (the official journal of the British Medical Association) of June 24, 1978, the NDEs of a sizable proportion of returnees were of a gruesome kind. "Of male survivors of cardiac arrests," we are told, "80 percent had dreams of violence, death and aggression, such as being run over by a wheelchair, violent accidents, and shooting their way out of the hospital only to be killed by a nurse."[7] The frequency of terrifying or at least highly unpleasant NDEs is also emphasized by Robert Kastenbaum who, after presenting numerous "negative" instances, remarks that they "can be collected by the bushel—there just is no market for them."[8]

What do people look like in the Beyond? Moody offers a good deal of information about the likeness of the returnees, but none at all about their "receivers." Some returnees experience themselves as pure minds ("they were not in any kind of 'body' at all"), but most of them had new bodies which had the properties, familiar from astral literature, of being penetrable and able to move at enormous speed. Moody refers to these as the "spiritual" bodies. The spiritual body, we are told,

> has a form or shape (sometimes a globular or amorphous cloud, but also sometimes essentially the same shape as the physical body) and even parts (projections or surfaces analogous to arms, legs, a head, etc.). Even when its shape is reported as

6. E.g., E. A. Rodin (a neurologist from Michigan), "The Reality of Death Experiences—A Personal Perspective," *The Journal of Nervous and Mental Disease,* May 1980, J. J. Preisinger, Jr. (a California psychiatrist), "My Near Death Experience," *Free Inquiry,* Winter 1990–91, and A. J. Ayer (the British philosopher), "What I Saw When I Was Dead" in P. Edwards (Ed.), *Immortality* (New York, 1992). Rodin returned to the topic in "The Reality of Death Experiences: A Reply to Commentaries," *Anabiosis,* February 1981. In both of his pieces, Rodin insists that such experiences do not constitute evidence for survival.

7. This summary is quoted from P. and L. Badham, *Immortality or Extinction?* op. cit., p. 84. The *Lancet* editorial is based on "The Survivors of Cardiac Arrest" by R. G. Druss and D. S. Kornfield, *Journal of the American Medical Association,* July 31, 1967.

8. "Happily Ever After," *Human Behavior,* September 1977, reprinted in R. Kastenbaum (Ed.), *Between Life and Death* (New York, 1979), pp. 19–22.

being generally roundish in configuration. it is often said to have ends, a definite top and bottom, and even the "parts" just mentioned. . . . Words and phrases which have been used by various subjects include a mist, a cloud, smoke-like, a vapor, transparent, a cloud of colors, wispy, an energy pattern. . . .[9]

I personally would have no objections to becoming a globular cloud, but I hope that members of the reception committee do not assume this form too often since there would be serious recognition problems. There is also of course the question of attire which we mentioned in the last chapter and about which Moody offers no information. His returnees do not tell us about whether they see themselves dressed or naked and they also supply no information about the attire of the receivers.

One of the most enjoyable of Moody's tales concerns the omniscient returnees whom he discovered in the period between writing his two books. These people told Moody that "they got brief glimpses of an entire separate realm of existence in which *all* knowledge—whether past, present, or future—seemed to coexist in a sort of timeless state."[10] They had attained "a moment of enlightenment" in which "they seemed to have complete knowledge." Unfortunately our earthly language cannot adequately convey this strange experience. Moody's subjects commented that "this experience was ultimately inexpressible," that the words they were using after their return were "at best only dim reflections of the reality"[11] they were trying to describe.

In spite of these language difficulties, several of the omniscient returnees were quite expansive on the subject. One woman, with whom Moody had an "extended interview," is reported as follows:

It seemed that all of a sudden, all knowledge—of all that had started from the very beginning, that would go on without end—that for a second I knew all the secrets of all ages, all the meaning of the universe, the stars, the moon—of everything. . . . This all-powerful knowledge opened before me. It seemed that I was being told that I was going to remain sick for quite a while and that I would have other close calls. And I did have several close calls after that. . . . I had been granted the universal secrets. . . . I do have the memory of once knowing everything.[12]

Readers of these accounts are likely to hold out high hopes that the omniscient subjects will share some of their newly obtained knowledge. If they know everything then they also know the causes and cure of Alzheimer's Disease, nephritis, and schizophrenia, to mention just three particularly terrible diseases that are so imperfectly understood in the present life. What a boon to mankind these postmortem experiences could turn out to be! One might expect Moody to publish the answers to these problems in spite of his passionate concern for the privacy of his subjects. Alas, there is

---

9. *LAL,* p. 38.
10. *Reflections,* p. 9, my italics.
11. P. 10.
12. Ibid., pp. 10–11.

a rub: the returnees forget everything—every answer, every solution, every new bit of knowledge they acquired during their stay in the Beyond. All his returnees agree, Moody regretfully notes, that "this feeling of complete knowledge did not persist after their return; that they did not bring back any sort of omniscience." This formulation does not fully convey the loss they suffered. It is not just that they don't bring back omniscience: they don't bring back a *single* answer. The lady, who during her sojourn in the next world, knew "all the secrets of all ages" found herself, on her return, ignorant of the secret of any age. "They"—it is not clear who "they" are—had told her that if she chose to return to the present life, the "all-knowing knowledge" would be "erased." Just as "they" had predicted, she cannot "remember any of it." She does, however, "have the memory of once knowing everything."[13]

Critical readers of Moody at once raised questions about the authenticity of his reports. From the very beginning he resolutely refused to allow any inspection of his files in order to protect the privacy of his subjects. In his second book he addresses himself at some length to the complaints of his critics. He realizes that he has made "extraordinary" claims, but he will not budge:

> It will continue to be my policy not to use names. There are several reasons for this. People have come to me under the assumption that I would not be using their names. I want to continue this practice so that I can continue collecting accounts which people might not give me if they felt that they would be identified. It might well make more tantalizing reading if I were to print a picture of a person and give out his name and address, as one might do in a newspaper article. However, this would not make my study more credible from a scientific point of view.[14]

This is obviously a total evasion of the demand for documentation. Nobody asked Moody to print photos of his subjects or give their names and addresses. What any scientifically disposed critic would demand is the opening of Moody's files to a committee of impartial and trained investigators, who would then also have an opportunity to talk to Moody's subjects. This is a far cry from having their names and photos displayed in print. Moody has never shown the slightest inclination to allow such an investigation.

The reasons Moody gives for not opening his files are an insult to the intelligence of his readers. If a medical researcher claims to have successfully tested a new drug on a number of patients he is only too ready to show his data to other researchers. He does not back off on the ground that he will not give the names or publish the photos of his patients. Moody's claims are much more sweeping and have far wider implications than the claims of most medical pioneers. If he really had the evidence, if all the people he refers to really exist and if they told him what he says they did, and if his interviewing techniques are above-board, he would throw his files wide open; he would welcome and indeed demand an investigation of his data.

---

13. Ibid.
14. *Reflections*, p. 82.

The suspicion is not that none of Moody's subjects exist or that he has "made it all up," a charge by skeptical questioners which Moody mentions. The suspicion is that he has fudged his data so that the cases would exhibit a far higher degree of similarity than what was actually reported. I have already mentioned the fact that his subjects do not talk like real human beings. This made me at once suspicious. There are also remarks attributed to them that seem innocent enough but which make one wonder about the authenticity of the reports. I will give one example. In *LAL* he professes to quote a subject who was allegedly cured of his fear of death by his postmortem experience:

> When I was a little boy I used to dread dying. I used to wake up at night crying and having a fit. . . . My mother would talk to me and tell me, "No, that's just the way it is and we all have to face it." She said that we all had to do it alone and that when the time came we would do it all right.[15]

Ordinary people do *not* talk like this if only because it is glaringly false that everybody "dies alone." The writings of Heideggerian existentialists frequently contain this pretentious nonsense, though I am sure that in their private life they also do not make these pronouncements: they know perfectly well that some people die alone and some do not.

I will give two further illustrations of what I can only call Moody's "bad faith." In Chapter 9 I quoted his claim that Dr. Ritchie was a "clinical professor of psychiatry" and that he had had not one but two near-death experiences ten minutes apart. It will be remembered that Dr. Ritchie was never a "clinical professor of psychiatry" and that he had one and not two near-death experiences. Moody did not mention Dr. Ritchie by name but it is clear that he was the "professor" referred to. At the time of making this statement Moody could hardly know that Dr. Ritchie would write a book of his own where the real facts were going to be revealed. Even more dishonest is Moody's use of a passage from *A History of the English Church and People* by the Venerable Bede, an English monk who lived from 673 to 735 C.E. Moody asserts that this "return from the dead story . . . resembles in many respects those heard today."[16] Unfortunately for Moody, some of his readers are familiar with the writings of Bede. Paul and Linda Badham, the authors of *Immortality or Extinction,* who are meticulous scholars, tell us that "Moody has made Bede's story fit his scheme, by the simple expedient of omitting all the copious data in Bede which conflict with it." Bede's account is primarily concerned with the torments of hell, but Moody does not mention this. The Badhams conclude that "if this case, which is of course the only one readily available for public checking, is a typical example of the way Moody handles his material then this casts serious doubt on his reliability."[17]

What about the similarities between the near-death experiences reported by

---

15. *LAL,* p. 68.
16. *Reflections,* p. 66.
17. *Immortality or Extinction?* (London, 1982), p. 87.

many subjects all over the world including some who have no connection with Moody—the tunnel, the light, and the euphoria? Don't they show that the experiences are "veridical" and not delusions and hence don't they support the survival hypothesis? The answer is that they do not. There is a very good explanation for these similarities in purely physiological terms. In the article I mentioned earlier Dr. J. J. Preisinger, Jr., a California psychiatrist, describes a freak accident that very nearly cost him his life. He fell from the roof of his home and crashed onto a cement step-edge near the entrance. His chest was caved in and his lungs had been punctured. He was unable to breathe and thus could not produce any sound. He also could not move his lower body. He would have died if he had remained in this position for more than ten minutes, but fortunately his wife appeared just in time to save him. While he was facing death he had a Moody-type experience:

> Succumbing to the lack of oxygen, I began to feel progressively more euphoric. Time seemed to be suspended; I felt that I was floating through a long, dark grey tunnel, the end of which was illuminated by a brilliant white light. I had wispy flashes of events from my life. I saw many vague, shadowy people along the length of the tunnel, but could not identify any by name. I knew this was the end and did not even think in terms of regrets since I felt such a sublime great pleasure.[18]

Preisinger's wife impulsively put her hands under his shoulders and began to lift him. His ribs "popped back out and into place." The noise aroused Preisinger and initiated "a sensation of speedy reversal from the glowing light, back through the tunnel." Just like Moody's subjects, he felt keenly disappointed at the loss of his sublime euphoria.

Preisinger offers a physiological explanation of his experience that is accepted by most critically trained persons, but apparently not by Moody:

> When oxygen to the brain is reduced, as happens during the administration of anesthesia, drowning, and in altitude sickness, a great euphoria results, along with confusion and disorientation. People with hypoxia (decreased and insufficient oxygen) have the feeling that they have little or no concern as to the consequences of the deprivation. . . . The instability of the temporal lobe of the brain, the major area that produces visual hallucinations, can well account for the light and tunnel visions. Shutting off oxygen intake to the brain when we are dying serves to eradicate the pain that most humans falsely believe to be intrinsically associated with death.[19]

Years later Preisinger told Moody about his close call but, not surprisingly, Moody did not accept the explanation. Hypoxia (or anoxia) does not by itself explain all features of every particular NDE. This is so because people differ from one another and the circumstances in which NDEs occur vary widely. However, there is not the slight-

---

18. *Free Inquiry,* Winter 1990–1991, p. 51.
19. Ibid.

est need to suppose that the individual visited the next world and it seems clear that any meetings with dead relatives are hallucinations.[20]

Kübler-Ross, Osis, Haraldsson, and Grof

It is not surprising that other leading figures in the new immortality movement should have turned to Kübler-Ross for endorsements and introductions to their books. One of the best known of the "scientific" apologists for life after death is Karlis Osis, a prominent parapsychologist, whose publications on the subject go back to 1961. The article in *Newsweek* gave an account of the work of Osis, suggesting that it was equal in significance to that of Moody and Kübler-Ross. On June 15, 1976, the *National Enquirer* contained pictures of Kübler-Ross and Osis side by side, describing them as "top scientists" and "leading experts on death and dying." In 1977 Osis, together with his associate Erlendur Haraldsson, published *At the Hour of Death,* a work defending belief in life after death on the basis of a survey and statistical analysis of deathbed visions similar to the one experienced by Kübler-Ross's father.

Kübler-Ross opens her introduction to *At the Hour of Death* by recommending the book to all "researchers and scientists" who have questions about "the newly flourishing and widely publicized research on death and life after death." This "newly flourishing research" is parenthetically identified with Moody and herself. She then compliments the authors on their courage to investigate an area which is viewed with suspicion in our "secular and skeptical world" and "which was still very much taboo a few years ago" when their study was begun. Not only did Osis and Haraldsson investigate a neglected area but, what is more important, they came up with the right answer. Kübler-Ross is pleased to hail their work "as yet another confirmation of existence after 'death.' " She puts quotation marks around the word "death" because, in her opinion, Osis and Haraldsson have demonstrated that "death is not an end but a new beginning, simply a transition into a higher state of consciousness." The research of Osis and Haraldsson also shows, like Moody's and her own, that, contrary to the parochial prejudices of many religious believers, *all* human beings are guaranteed admission into God's garden. "All men are alike at birth and death," she remarks and it is not the "denominational label," but the quality of a person's religion that will help him in the transition to the next world.

The year 1977 saw also the publication of *The Human Encounter with Death* by Dr. Stanislav Grof and Joan Halifax, who was at that time Dr. Grof's wife. I will discuss the work of Grof and Halifax in detail in Chapter 13. Here it is sufficient to explain that they base their defense of belief in survival primarily on certain experiences

---

20. For a fuller discussion of the physiological and psychological causes of NDEs see Susan Blackmore, *Dying To Live* (Amherst, N.Y., 1993) and various articles by Ronald K. Siegel, especially his "Life After Death" in G. O. Abell and B. Singer (Eds.), *Science and the Paranormal* (New York, 1981).

of dying patients who had been given LSD or other psychedelic drugs." Aside from much praise for Dr. Grof who is throughout treated as "the author" of the book (as if Joan Halifax did not exist) and who is described as a "talented writer and an extremely bright and well-read researcher," Kübler-Ross uses her Foreword to state some of her own most cherished convictions. She alludes to the fact that in the 35,540 "death observations" compiled by Osis, only 10 percent of the subjects were conscious during the hour preceding their death. All the others had been "drugged." She then states her "personal opinion that our heavy emphasis on 'drugging' patients prior to their death is a great disservice to them and to their families." Fear of death can be eliminated if the patient does not merely *believe* but possesses *knowledge* that death is a transition to another and superior "plane." This knowledge can be obtained by dying patients if only they are allowed to remain fully conscious during their last moments on the earthly plane:

> Patients who were not heavily medicated in their final hours were able to experience these blissful states prior to their transition, resulting in a knowledge (rather than a belief) of a waiting, loving presence of another being.[21]

Since the whole of Chapter 13 is devoted to the work of Dr. Grof there is no need to discuss it at this stage. Something should however be said about the notion that deathbed visions constitute evidence for life after death. The underlying idea seems to be that a person who is dying is close to the next world and hence has a better view of it than people who are young and in good health. James Boswell, who had a morbid obsession with death, made it a practice to attend executions, some of them of is own clients for such crimes as sheep-stealing, in the hope of hearing the condemned man's last words which might be a description of the next life. James H. Hyslop (1854–1920), the first secretary-treasurer and research officer of the American Society for Psychical Research, expressed the same idea in a paper included in his *Psychical Research and the Resurrection* (Boston, 1908). "If there be such a thing as a transcendental spiritual world and if we actually survive in our personality after death," Hyslop wrote, "we might naturally expect some connection between the two sets of cosmic conditions, at least occasionally." It would not be unreasonable to expect these "connections" to take place at the time at which a person crosses from one world to another.[22]

Another of the predecessors of Osis and Haraldsson was Sir William Barrett (1844–1925), a distinguished Irish physicist who also had a lifelong interest in psychical research. He was one of the founders of the *Society for Psychical Research,* its president in 1904, and the editor of its journal from 1884 to 1899. The founders of the Society for Psychical Research were well aware of deathbed visions. F. W. H. Myers, cofounder of the society and perhaps the most influential psychical researcher

---

21. Foreword to Grof and Halifax, *The Human Encounter with Death* (New York, 1977), p. vii.
22. P. 94.

of the nineteenth century, briefly alludes to this topic in his monumental work, *Human Personality and Its Survival of Bodily Death.* However, neither he nor most of the other figures in psychical research during the half century following the establishment of the British Society saw much significance in deathbed experiences. Unlike Myers, Barrett was greatly impressed by deathbed visions. In *On the Threshold of the Unseen* (1917) Barrett declared himself totally converted to the view that on some occasions dying patients establish contact with the next world. "The evidence seems indisputable," he wrote, "that in some rare cases, just before death, the veil is partly drawn aside and a glimpse of the loved ones who have passed over is given to the dying person."[23] In 1916, when he was seventy-two years old, Barrett married Dr. Florence Wiley, a well-known gynecologist and obstetrician who shared his interest in psychical research and, more especially, in deathbed visions. She assisted him in his last book, *Death-Bed Visions,* which was published in 1926 shortly after his death. Barrett and Lady Barrett continued their communications for twelve years after his death with the assistance of several well-known mediums. Barrett's messages from the Beyond were published in 1937 in Lady Barrett's *Personality Survives Death.* Neither she nor the Rev. R. J. Campbell, who contributed a Foreword to the book, had any doubts that the messages recorded by Lady Barrett really emanated from Sir William. It may be interesting to note that one of the persons he met in the next world was F. W. H. Myers. In one of the sessions, he is quoted as saying "Myers and I are learning many things together," adding modestly "and I from him." There is no mention of whether Sir William succeeded in converting Myers to his view on the evidential value of deathbed visions. In the early years of the century messages from Myers were received with great frequency, but there has been nothing by or about him since the publication of Lady Barrett's book. I hope that the absence of any message does not mean that he died.

Osis and Haraldsson's *At the Hour of Death* is a culmination of work begun in the late 1950s. Osis had been an assistant of Eileen Garrett, a well-known English medium who spent the last decades of her life in New York as publisher and editor of *Tomorrow,* a quarterly devoted to psychical research. Eileen Garrett was evidently a fascinating woman. According to Osis she "literally lived between two worlds, being able to see identifiable images of dead relatives around visitors to her office while remaining fully functional in the physical world."[24] Mrs. Garrett had known Sir William Barrett personally and encouraged Osis to proceed with a systematic survey of deathbed visions. Many of the earlier reports had been based on statements by relatives of the dying patients. Osis thought that more reliable results would be achieved by conducting a survey of medical personnel. In 1959 and 1960 he sent a questionnaire to 5,000 physicians and 5,000 nurses. Six hundred and forty of these were returned. The respondents reported 1300 deathbed apparitions. Osis writes that 190 of

---

23. 3rd English edition, p. 160.
24. *At the Hour of Death,* p. 17.

the respondents were subsequently interviewed "in great depth." The details of this investigation are described in *Deathbed Observations by Physicians and Nurses,* a monograph published by the Parapsychology Foundation in 1961. In 1962 Osis became director of research at the American Society for Psychical Research, whose leading spirit he has been ever since. With the financial backing of Chester F. Carlson, the inventor of the Xerox machine, Osis substantially expanded the American sample, receiving a further 1,004 responses. Subsequently, in conjunction with Erlendur Haraldsson, a parapsychologist from Iceland, Osis undertook a similar investigation in India.

Osis and Haraldsson are not afflicted with any sense of false modesty. Their investigation, they tell us early in the book, "is the first truly scientific research into experiences of the dying at the hour of death."[25] They are prepared to grant that the "knowledge" they "brought back" is not the last word and that "subsequent explorers" will make further discoveries when "they apply new ingenuity, more rigor, and more resources than we pioneers could."[26] Although future explorers may improve on their results, Osis and Haraldsson are convinced that they have attained "new insights into the mystery and meaning of death." What Osis and Haraldsson found is "both surprising and hopeful." The evidence provided by their interviews "strongly suggests life after death."[27]

As the conscientious scientists they aspire to be, Osis and Haraldsson are eager to stress a certain tentativeness about their conclusions. They tell us that they now possess a "thoroughly plausible, though tentative, picture of postmortem existence." When Osis and Haraldsson speak of a "tentative" picture they do not mean that they entertain any doubt about the truth of what they constantly call the "afterlife hypothesis."[28] That human beings survive death is beyond serious doubt. Certain features of the afterlife are also established beyond all question. It is, for example, a "finding loud and clear" that the vast majority of dying patients are guided to the afterlife by close relatives.[29] What we are as yet ignorant of—and what may perhaps be clarified by future explorers with their greater ingenuity and resources—are the later stages of the next life. Unfortunately the data collected so far do not contain the reports of "prolonged excursions" into the next life. We do indeed have "many descriptions of the initial stages of postmortem existence," but nothing, alas, about "what happens the next day, or the next evening."

Osis and Haraldsson are convinced that their work revolutionizes our picture of the universe, but they are not at all sure that it will be received with sufficient seriousness either by the "scientific community" or by the leaders of the various religious congregations. Osis and Haraldsson are deeply disappointed at the lack of interest by

---

25. *AHD,* p. 2.
26. Ibid., p. 18 3.
27. Ibid.
28. *AHD,* p. 5.
29. Pp. 184–85

religious leaders in paranormal phenomena. They also deplore the preoccupation on the part of so many well-known theologians and clergymen with social issues. It is too bad that they "are obsessed with this-world [sic] concerns and political actions."[30]

Osis and Haraldsson are of course quite right that in recent decades many religious people and the leaders of many sects have been much more concerned to help the poor and sick, to fight social discrimination and irrational laws like those against voluntary euthanasia than to contemplate the alleged beauties of the next world. Some, like the present writer, regard this as great progress, but Osis and Haraldsson would rather restore religious believers to a "sense of the eternal."[31] After all, what is seventy or eighty years in this life compared to an eternal life in the Beyond for which, thanks to them, to Kübler-Ross, and to Moody, we now possess incontestable evidence! Moody, incidentally, is a great admirer of the work of Osis and Haraldsson. On the jacket he is quoted as calling the book a "major contribution to the scientific study of the question of postmortem existence." I am writing this paragraph eighteen years after the publication of *At the Hour of Death* and it is evident that their message has fallen on deaf ears. Scientists do not show the slightest interest in deathbed visions and religious leaders continue to busy themselves with social and political ones.

Let us look at some cases that are typical of those on which Osis and Haraldsson base their grandiose claims. The following case concerns a sixteen-year-old American girl who had just come out of her coma. She remarked to the nurse who supplied this information:

> "I can't get up," and she opened her eyes. I raised her up a little bit and she said, "I see him, I see him. I am coming." She died immediately afterwards with a radiant face, exultant, elated.[32]

Osis and Haraldsson emphasize that the girl's consciousness was "very clear" and that therefore a brain-disturbance can be ruled out. More significant, however, are the girl's radiance and exultation. This hardly fits in with the hypothesis that death means destruction. "What," ask Osis and Haraldsson, "could possibly make a sixteen-year-old girl 'exultant' and 'radiant' when giving up a life still unfulfilled?"

Not all patients are eager to make the transition to the next life; but whether they are eager or not, whether their prognosis for recovery is favorable or not, once the apparition has appeared, they die anyway. Thus we are told of a college-educated Indian man in his twenties who was recuperating from mastoiditis, that he was doing very well, and that both he and his physician confidently expected a recovery. Alas, the patient had an apparition and died almost instantaneously. In the words of the Indian respondent:

---

30. Pp. 203–204.
31. *AHD*, p. 34.
32. Ibid.

He was going to be discharged that day. Suddenly at 5:00 A.M. he shouted, "someone is standing here dressed in white clothes. I will not go with you!" He was dead in ten minutes.[33]

This last apparition does not seem to fit in with the claim of Kübler-Ross, Moody, and Osis and Haraldsson that the guides are always beneficent beings. The same is true of some of the "mythological or historical religious figures" who appear during deathbed visions. In America, and among Christians in India the religious figures who most frequently appear are Jesus and the Virgin Mary.

No Hindu is on record as having met either the Virgin Mary or Jesus Christ. However, Hindus frequently meet "Yamdoots," who are supposed to be the representatives of the merciless divinity, Yama or Yamaraj, the god of death. Hindu patients sometimes refuse to follow the Yamdoots into the next world, but their opposition is usually futile. One such patient, of whom we are told that his consciousness seemed to be clear, although his temperature was above one hundred and three degrees, is reported to have exclaimed:

"Somebody is standing there! He has a cart with him so he must be a yamdoot! He must be taking someone with him. He is teasing me that he is going to take *me*! But, Mamie, I am not going; I want to be with you!" Then he said someone was pulling him out of bed. He pleaded, "Please hold me; I am not going."[34]

The patient's pleas were ignored. For, as we are also told, "his pain increased and he died." It should be observed that Osis and Haraldsson regard this case as no less veridical than the cases in which patients are "radiant" and "exultant" before the end. I cannot refrain from commenting that the Yamdoot was clearly guilty of murder. If he ever returns he should be apprehended and tried for his crime.

This is perhaps the place to observe that the patients could not have identified the divine beings they supposedly met. A Christian patient in India developed chest pains and shortly thereafter "saw Christ coming down through the air very slowly. Christ . . . waved his hand that he should come to him."[35] How could this patient possibly know that it was Jesus who was coming down through the air and waving at him? A housewife who, in the course of a deathbed vision, sees her late husband is in a position to identify the hallucinated person; and the same is true of the other deathbed visions of friends and relatives. But the patient who saw Jesus and the various Hindu patients who were called by Yamdoots did not meet these divine beings during their earthly careers. What they did see here on earth are statues, pictures, and other images of these divinities. The conclusion seems irresistible, that the patients who meet Jesus "recognize" him because the hallucinatory figure resembles the statues, pictures, and other

---

33. P. 44.
34. Ibid., p. 90.
35. Ibid., p. 65.

images with which they are familiar. Even if it is granted that Jesus and the Yamdoots exist and that they reside in the Beyond, we have no ground for supposing that the dying patients met them in the course of their deathbed experiences. I am reminded of a trial some years ago in which a follower of the Rev. Sun Myung Moon sued a "deprogrammer" for having abducted him. The Rev. Moon claims to have talked to Jesus, Moses, and Buddha and he has also asserted that Jesus once approached him for aid in "the salvation of the universe." In reply to a question by the defense attorney how he recognized Jesus he said that he did it "from holy pictures."

James Alcock has pointed out serious defects in the questionnaires that were given to nurses and physicians which were bound to result in unreliable and confusing data. Aside from this, the responses could not be more than anecdotal evidence of the weakest kind for what the patients experienced. Moody at least interviewed the subjects, but Osis and Haraldsson were getting reports "about the observer's impressions of what a patient was experiencing in a situation that occurred in all likelihood years before."[36] Furthermore, no attempt was made—presumably none was feasible—to ascertain the background and possible bias of the nurses and physicians who responded to the questionnaires.

Even if all these misgivings are waived, there remain formidable objections. The reasons Osis and Haraldsson give for dismissing naturalistic explanations are incredibly feeble and flimsy. The fact that only Christians meet Jesus and the Virgin Mary while only Hindus meet Yamdoos and Krishna would indicate to any person with minimal common sense that we *are* dealing here with culturally conditioned hallucinations. According to Osis and Haraldsson this view is contradicted by the fact that religious patients do not meet such "traditional middlemen" as priests, brahmins, or rabbis. Among Western patients not a single dead clergyman acted as an "otherworldly envoy" and only five of the Hindus were met by gurus. The simple reply to this is that most believers have a vastly higher regard for their divinities than for the "middlemen" of whose human foibles and limitations they are well aware. Osis and Haraldsson cannot wholly deny the relevance of cultural conditioning. Cultural forces we are told do not cause the deathbed visions. They are "powerful enough to sensitize or inhibit patient's seeing certain kinds of phenomena."[37] If "sensitize" means anything here, the statement would imply that Jesus, the Virgin Mary, Krishna, the Yamdoots and a large number of other holy figures really live in the Beyond and that cultural conditioning determines which of these will be selected by a given patient.

Perhaps the weightiest objection was put forward by James F. McHarg, a British psychiatrist, in his review of *AHD* in the *Journal of the Society for Psychical Research*.[38] McHarg points out that although Osis and Haraldsson reasonably exclude a number of specific medical possibilities, "they do not even mention the most im-

---

36. Alcock, op. cit., p. 29.
37. *AHD*, p. 92.
38. September 1978, pp. 185–87.

portant of all—cerebral anoxia." We already met this condition in the last section and it would clearly account for the sense of peace and happiness that many dying patients experience. It is also, McHarg points out, a well-known cause of visual hallucinations.

I have left one final very basic criticism to the end, one that applies equally to Moody and to Osis and Haraldsson. If any of the near-death experiences are taken as evidence for survival, they presuppose the reality of the astral body. The people who meet Moody's subjects and those who come to take away the dying patients of Osis and Haraldsson cannot have their old bodies—these were cremated or decomposed in some fashion. However, they do have bodies even if some of the more primitive patients call them "spirits." Moody and Osis and Haraldsson are great believers in the astral body, but as we found in Chapter 9, there are fatal objections to this belief and any theory that requires one to assume the existence of astral bodies is thereby condemned as absurd.

Students have asked me who is worse, Moody or Osis-Haraldsson. The answer is that each is worse than the other: Moody is more evasive and slippery, Osis and Haraldsson are more inane. The fact that Kübler-Ross has championed such people is by itself quite an indictment; but we shall see in the next chapter that worse was yet to come.

A Note on Later Champions of Near-Death Experiences

The new immortality movement is only a side issue in the present book, but in fairness I should mention the work of two of Moody's successors—Kenneth Ring, a psychology teacher at the University of Connecticut, and Michael Sabom, a cardiologist from Atlanta. Ring's contributions to human knowledge were published in two books—*Life at Death* (New York, 1980) and *Heading toward Omega* (New York, 1984). The former has a moving introduction by Moody, the latter by Kübler-Ross who describes Ring's book as "masterful." Sabom's *Recollections at Death* (New York, 1982) concludes on a reassuring note: "Does the near-death experience represent a glimpse of an afterlife?" Sabom asks, "Could the mind which splits apart from the physical brain be, in essence, the 'soul,' which continues to exist after final bodily death?" The answer given on the last page of his book is a ringing "yes." Those who had a near-death experience "were touched by some ineffable truth encountered face to face at death's chosen moments."[39] Extracts from Ring's two books appeared in the *Midnight Globe* in 1980 and 1984. The last of the three installments in 1984 is accompanied by the information that Lucille Ball had direct contact with the spirit world, that Lee Strassberg appeared to Ellen Burstyn just twenty-four hours after his death, and that Barbra Streisand's father "reached out from the spirit world" to send her a message during a séance. Ring's book is on the same level and the *Midnight Globe* is a fitting outlet for his reflections.

---

39. Pp. 185–86.

Ring believes that some of the subjects of NDEs have special access to the future. "Virtually all the near-death survivors state or imply," Ring told the *National Enquirer,* "that major geophysical and meteorological changes will begin during this decade." There is going to be an increase in earthquakes, volcanic eruptions and "massive geophysical changes." The dates supplied by the survivors were 1984, 1985, and 1988. Perhaps the most disturbing forecast, with no date given, concerns Florida which is going to break off from the mainland. Fortunately, however, the distant future presents a happier picture:

> The world will survive and all these catastrophes will be followed by a new era, . . . marked by human brotherhood, universal love and world peace.[40]

Ring insists that these prophecies cannot be illusions. In an interview published in the September-October 1981 issue of *Expansion,* a journal devoted to "psychic growth" and "changing patterns of consciousness," he remarks that "these people, who report a planetary review, seem to be tapping into some slice of the future." There is such a "genuine similarity" and "commonality" in their forecasts that it cannot just be a matter of chance.

I confess that I find some of these prophecies extremely scary, especially when considered in conjunction with the Snow-Wambach predictions of the dire fate of California and Nevada which I reported in Chapter 6 and the equally frightening forecast about the destruction of New York endorsed by Dr. Kübler-Ross which we will meet in the next chapter. It would not be a bad idea if Ring, Snow, Kübler-Ross and of course Dr. Bruce Goldberg were to pool their data and supply futurological information to presidents, prime ministers, and especially to the governors of endangered states like California, Florida, Nevada, and New York so that preparations for mass evacuations can be made before it is too late.

---

40. *National Enquirer,* August 17, 1982.

12

The Fantasies of Dr. Kübler-Ross

The Materialization of Mary Swartz

In 1978 Kübler-Ross disclosed some of her most spectacular evidence. In its issue for May 1 of that year, *Newsweek* devoted an entire section to the subject of "Living Dying." Kübler-Ross's work is prominently described in several of the articles. "Some thanatologists," we are informed, "are making efforts to find more positive images of death—as a passage to another life rather than as a wall through which no one passes." These efforts hinge on reports of people who have had "near death and other out-of-body experiences" suggesting that "the psyche, or soul, can function independently of the body." Although there is "widespread skepticism in the scientific community," investigations of the paranormal phenomena are continuing "largely because of the influence of the charismatic Kübler-Ross." Drawing on "the enormous moral capital she has accumulated as a counselor of the dying," Kübler-Ross is staking her reputation and investing much of her time and energy in validating the gospel of a benign life after death. Kübler-Ross is then quoted about the hostility of her critics. With evident relish she reports that the more she goes "into this after-death research, the more some scientific people want to shred me to pieces." Kübler-Ross has no doubt that her ever-increasing evidence will eventually rout the opposition.

Kübler-Ross told the *Newsweek* reporters of "visits" she has received from "materialized" dead patients. Only one of these is described in any detail. She reports that nine years earlier a dead patient by the name of Mary Swartz had suddenly appeared in her office. Kübler-Ross has no doubt whatever that the visitor was the "materialized" Mary Swartz and not an imposter and she is totally certain that she herself had not become the victim of a delusion. Knowing that her medical colleagues would not believe her account, Kübler-Ross asked her visitor to write a brief note to a mutual friend and sign it. Next to a photo of Kübler-Ross, *Newsweek* displays the beginning of this letter, written on University of Chicago stationery. "Hello there," it says, "dropped in to see Dr. Ross. One of two on the top of my list." No information is given as to the identity of the "mutual friend" and we are also not told whether Mary Swartz visited the other person on top of her list. My guess is that she did not. Otherwise the mutual friend would surely have come forward with what would be powerful evidence in support of Kübler-Ross's belief that her experience was not a delusion.

Kübler-Ross did not tell the *Newsweek* reporters all the details surrounding this event. It turns out that Mary Swartz was "Mrs. S." about whom Kübler-Ross had written at some length in her contribution to Jess E. Weiss's *The Vestibule*.[1] The purpose of this book, which was published in 1972, was "to establish with more certainty that there is an after life, thereby alleviating fully or to a degree, the sting of death." Kübler-Ross's contribution is entitled "The Experience of Death" and more than half of it is taken up with the story of Mrs. S., though not one word is said about her subsequent materialization. Mrs. S. had been one of the patients interviewed by Kübler-Ross and the other participants of the workshop on death and dying whose investigations had formed the basis of *On Death and Dying*. When Mrs. S. was interviewed by Kübler-Ross and her associates she was in her fifties and had been ill with Hodgkin's disease for twenty years. She had been introduced to Kübler-Ross as "the woman who cannot die" and the two of them spent many hours talking together. Mrs. S. had been in the Intensive Care Unit of several hospitals, usually in critical condition, but each time she recovered sufficiently to go home and carry on with her work as mother and housewife. Her husband was a schizophrenic whose mental state had been deteriorating in recent years. He had become abusive toward their son and frequently beat him without provocation. When Mrs. S. met Kübler-Ross the son was a little over fifteen. Her "only unfinished business on this earth," as she put it, was to provide for the boy. She had made arrangements to place him with relatives after his sixteenth birthday. Mrs. S. expressed her conviction that she could hold out until the boy turned sixteen. After that everything was going to be all right. She was discharged from the hospital six months before her son's birthday and then returned for her last stay five months later. She specially requested to talk once again to Kübler-Ross's seminar. She was eager to tell them about an episode she had not mentioned previously. Weakened by internal bleeding she had lost consciousness during one of her earlier hospital stays. The nurses and doctors believed that she had died and attempted to revive her. She herself had floated out of her body and, from a few feet above, she had observed the attempt to resuscitate her. The doctors gave up after a while. Mrs. S. awoke as an orderly wheeled her body to the morgue. She lifted the bedsheet off her face and the shocked orderly turned around and wheeled her back to her room. When she was released from the hospital a few weeks later, nobody discussed the incident with her. She now felt

---

1. Port Washington, NY, 1972.

that she had to talk to somebody about the event and wanted to know if she was psychotic. She was grateful for the assurance that she was definitely not insane. Mrs. S. lived on until a few days after her son's sixteenth birthday. She had obviously left a very deep impression on the members of the seminar.

The connection between Mrs. S. and the materialized Mary Swartz became clear in an interview with Kübler-Ross published in *Fate* magazine in April 1977. *Fate* is probably the leading occultist periodical in the United States and I am sure that nobody will fault its editors for an excess of skeptical caution. As far as I can judge, *Fate* publishes anything and everything so long as it favors beliefs in survival, precognition, astrology, UFOs, and whatever else is fashionable among occultists. The interview with Kübler-Ross follows the feature article entitled "Apparition Shocks Mae West." Other articles in the same issue are "The Girl With Green Bones," "The Flaming Fate of Dr. Bentley," and "Philippine Psychic Surgery." James Crenshaw, the interviewer of Kübler-Ross, appears to be a wholehearted believer in psychic phenomena to whom materializations of dead people are entirely familiar. Kübler-Ross told Crenshaw that not long after the death of Mrs. S. in 1968 she was in a state of turmoil. In her account of what transpired at that time it becomes evident that Mrs. S. is the same person as the Mary Swartz whose materialization Kübler-Ross had described to the *Newsweek* reporters. The strain of working with terminal patients, Kübler-Ross told Crenshaw, had become too much for her and she had decided to devote herself to another branch of medicine. It was shortly before she was going to announce this decision that Mrs. S. made her postmortem appearance. Kübler-Ross was in the hospital corridor near the elevator. She was just going to tell a minister friend that she had decided to give up her work with dying patients. It was at this crucial moment, before Kübler-Ross had said anything about her decision, that Mary Swartz materialized, not as an apparition, but "as a solid three-dimensional living human being." I gather that the minister was not aware of the dead woman's reappearance on earth in spite of her three-dimensional solidity. Mary Swartz asked Kübler-Ross if she could talk to her for a few minutes. The request was granted and after the minister had entered the elevator, the two women walked to Kübler-Ross's office. I will give the rest of the story in Kübler-Ross's own words:

> She leaned over my desk and told me she had come for only two reasons; one was to thank us. The second was that she wanted me to promise her that the work would continue. I promised.

The timing of Mary Swartz's visit was extremely propitious. Who knows—if she had not materialized when she did Kübler-Ross might have abandoned her work with dying patients!

Kübler-Ross, according to her account, was "totally shocked" by the appearance of Mary Swartz since she did not believe in "anything like this" at that time. Needing some proof of the materialization she asked her visitor to write a note to a colleague who had participated in the seminar. Mary Swartz gladly obliged. "With a knowing smile on her face she wrote a short greeting to my friend and afterward walked out of the office." *Fate* is full of stories of materializations. In the very article about Mae West that precedes the interview with Kübler-Ross, we are told that an old friend of the actress by the name of T. J. Kelly had materialized on "a beautiful white couch" in her Hollywood apartment some ten years after his death. James Crenshaw could therefore reassure Kübler-Ross that her experience was by no means unique. In one respect, however, it seemed to be unprecedented. "It is possibly the first case on record," Crenshaw concluded, "in which an apparently solid spirit figure, appearing spontaneously, has been induced to give a handwriting sample."

The Badhams, whose views about Dr. Moody's untrustworthiness I quoted in Chapter 11 and who refer to Kübler-Ross as "the doyen of all researchers in this area whose imprimatur in the form of a foreword is sought by all her fellows," find the story of the materialization of Mary Swartz totally incredible. Kübler-Ross, they write, "says she has talked with a ghost and persuaded the ghost to write a letter which she has framed on her wall." This they cannot accept:

> Such a report is not merely contrary to nature, but also contrary to all that the Society for Psychical Research has discovered in its investigations of 1684 cases of alleged apparitions. Whatever we are to make of such phenomena, one thing is common to all cases ever investigated by the SPR: apparitions leave no physical traces behind them.[2]

Here I must defend Kübler-Ross. Who is to tell in advance what apparitions can or cannot do? Kübler-Ross's story is certainly "contrary to nature," but perhaps some apparitions can leave traces behind them and it may take a powerful personality like Kübler-Ross to bring out this capacity. In any event, Kübler-Ross would deny that Mary Swartz was merely an apparition.

Kübler-Ross evidently had no difficulty in persuading James Crenshaw that Mary Swartz had returned from the dead. People who are guided by stricter standards of evidence than the contributors to *Fate* will not be so easily impressed. There are many puzzling aspects of Kübler-Ross's story. The first thing that struck me was the absence of any report from an impartial expert identifying the handwriting in the letter as that of Mary Swartz. Furthermore, it is mentioned that she reappeared as a "solid three-dimensional human being." If this is so, she must have been just as visible to other observers. Did the minister with whom Kübler-Ross was talking as Mary Swartz appeared also see her and has he supplied a notarized statement to this effect? Mary Swartz is supposed to have walked out of Kübler-Ross's office just like any ordinary human visitor would. In that case she could have been seen by other people in the building. Did anybody in fact see her? Kübler-Ross tells us that she was "totally shocked" since she did not at that time believe in the return of the dead. Nevertheless she had the presence of mind to ask for a note on University of Chicago

---

2. Op. cit., pp. 87–88.

stationery. Would it have been too much to ask Mary Swartz to stay a little longer so that she could also be introduced to some of the unbelievers who work at the University of Chicago? Perhaps Kübler-Ross was indeed too excited to think of this additional method of confirmation. However, it should be remembered that Mary Swartz appeared in order to influence Kübler-Ross's decision on a matter of great importance. This means that during her postmortem existence she has means of determining what is going on in Kübler-Ross's life. For several years after 1975 Kübler-Ross was in much difficulty because of her vigorous defense of belief in life after death. She used to say that the scientific establishment was trying to "shred her to pieces." Presumably Mary Swartz knows all this and knows that Kübler-Ross's critics are quite mistaken. Why then has Mary Swartz, who was so devoted to Kübler-Ross, not returned for other visits? Why does she not reappear and have herself seen, touched, photographed, fingerprinted, and perhaps checked for special birthmarks?

These considerations together with Kübler-Ross's admission that she was in a state of extreme turmoil will lead a rational person to conclude that the visit of Mary Swartz was a hallucination. There are of course more general reasons. The Badhams rightly observed that Kübler-Ross's report is "contrary to nature." I take this to mean that no credible *modus operandi* for the resurrection of Mary Swartz's body and its transportation to the University of Chicago Medical School can be specified: how can a body that has been cremated or rotting in the grave for ten months constitute itself into a living person? And there is also the evidence discussed in Chapter 17 that a person's consciousness depends on her brain.

Before leaving the story of the reappearance of Mary Swartz I should mention that the aforementioned Raymond Moody has devised a method that allows suitable subjects to meet deceased friends or relatives by gazing at a mirror in what Moody calls an "apparition chamber." At one end of this chamber Moody placed a mirror four feet tall and three-and-a-half feet wide on the wall. At the other end he put an armchair whose legs had been removed. Moody's subjects, who were carefully selected in order to get the most promising material, were subjected to a day of brainwashing which Moody calls "facilitation" before they began their mirror gazing. To his own great surprise most of the subjects did see deceased friends or relatives in the mirror. When Moody himself tried to summon up his late maternal grandmother whom he had loved dearly, he received a visit from his paternal grandmother whom he had not loved at all. Fortunately, however, she had greatly changed for the better during her stay in the Beyond. She even looked younger than at the time of her death, younger even than, judging by photographs, she had appeared before Moody's birth. She did not appear "ghostly" or transparent, but, like Mary Swartz, "completely solid in every respect." The experience left Moody with an "abiding certainty that what we call death is not the end of life."[3] It should be mentioned that no photographers were present at any of

3. All of the quotations are from Moody's article "Through the Looking Glass," *Parade*, November/December 1993. This article is based on the book by Moody and P. Perry, *Reunions—Visionary Encounters with Departed Loved Ones* (New York, 1993).

Moody's apparition-visitations. To anybody interested in this subject I highly recommend R. C. Finucane's *Appearances of the Dead—A Cultural History of Ghosts* (London, 1982, Buffalo reprint 1986), an informative and amusing account of famous apparitions. Finucane quotes a remark by the early eighteenth-century writer Henry Bourne to the effect that "almost all the stories of ghosts and spirits are grounded on no other bottom, than the fears and fancies and weak brains of men."[4] Bourne's statement admirably expresses my own view except that I would omit the word "almost."

Robert Monroe, Instructor in Astral Travel

The *Newsweek* article in which Kübler-Ross was shown holding the letter signed by the late Mary Swartz contained the report that Kübler-Ross had now become an astral traveler. It also described at some length the work of Robert A. Monroe, Kübler-Ross's teacher, founder of the Monroe Institute of Applied Science in Afton, Virginia, and author of a widely read book on *Journeys Out of the Body* (1971). According to his own account, Monroe began having out-of-body experiences in 1958. Unpredictably and without any efforts he "found himself leaving his physical body to travel via a 'second body,' to locales 'far removed from the physical and-spiritual realities of his life.' " The last statement is taken from the back jacket of Monroe's book, which contains a chronicle of his numerous astral flights. Unlike most other astral theorists, Monroe claims that his second or astral body can establish physical contact with material objects and hence with the ordinary bodies of human beings. He reports that he paid an astral visit to the home of a woman friend giving her an astral pinch that resulted in a black-and-blue mark. Unfortunately the name of this woman friend is withheld.

According to an article by Joan Kron in the 1976 Year-End issue of *New York Magazine*, which is devoted to the theories of Kübler-Ross, Moody, Monroe, and other researchers in related areas, Monroe now claims that he can fly "in tandem" with his wife. He also told Joan Kron that a married couple who are living miles apart and who have been trained by him pay each other astral visits every night. Presumably out of concern for their privacy, Monroe does not reveal their names. It is not made clear whether the visiting astral body establishes contact with the ordinary or the astral body of the partner receiving the visit. I would assume that it is the latter's regular body that is involved. Monroe's book has a chapter on "Sexuality in the Second State," but no information is provided on whether sexual intercourse between an astral and a regular body can result in a pregnancy, regular or astral.

Monroe's assertions that his astral body and the astral bodies of those he had instructed can be seen and touched appears to imply that it is possible to photograph an astral flight, but, to my knowledge, neither Monroe nor any of the other travelers trained by him has so far come up with a photograph. Astral travelers frequently at-

---

4. Finucane, p. 165.

tach themselves to the ceiling of the room they visit. It would be most interesting to have a picture of an astral body in this position. In his book Monroe tells of a surprise visit to a friend who is quoted as complaining that Monroe hung in the air "like a filmy piece of grey chiffon." It is unfortunate that this unnamed friend did not have a camera ready at hand. Monroe told the *Newsweek* reporters that during the seven years prior to the interview he had dispatched no less than 1400 persons on astral journeys. It is scarcely credible that not a single one of all these travelers had the good sense to have himself photographed. If I were the subject of such an epoch-making experience—especially if I were attached to the ceiling—I would certainly want the whole world, and especially all scientific skeptics, to know about it.

Monroe publishes a brochure which advertises the various benefits resulting from the courses offered by his institute:

> Healing. Re-energizing yourself. Pain reduction. Dehabituation from smoking, drugs, and overeating; concentration and decision-making techniques; accelerated data-learning.

Most recently Monroe has invented a machine that eases the fears of dying patients. It does this by allowing the patients to "visit new reality systems" which in effect means visits to the next world. Professional scientists have ignored this remarkable invention, but it was enthusiastically hailed by the *Midnight Globe* of August 21, 1979. In an article entitled "Clues to Humanity's Biggest Question" which also covers the work of Kübler-Ross, Moody, and other explorers of the hereafter, Monroe is quoted as saying "My machine gives you a preview of the other world." Understandably he would not reveal the exact details of his "patented" machine to the *Midnight Globe*. *Newsweek,* however, describes it as a "signal generator which uses tape recordings of various sound pulses to induce the separation of soul from body." For Monroe, it should be explained, the separation of the soul from the body means the separation of the astral from the regular body, with the person's consciousness attached to the astral body. Monroe told *Newsweek* that during the preceding six years he had guided no less than thirty dying patients out of their bodies. He adds that only five have returned to tell of their new life in "other energy systems." On one of his own astral trips Monroe encountered a dead man who told Monroe that he had been put to work and implied that it was not work of a particularly enjoyable or exciting kind—"It's no different here from where you came from." This report totally contradicts Kübler-Ross's repeated assertion that the next life is total bliss for everybody.

In the fall of 1976 Joan Kron, the author of the article in *New York Magazine*, spent a weekend at Monroe's Institute taking his "M-5000 program." She did this in the company of twelve other men and women each of whom paid 175 dollars for the instruction. Most of the thirteen inquirers seemed entirely promising material. One was an accountant whose hobbies are religion and philosophy and who is convinced that he has been reincarnated. Among the women one was the founder of the

Louisiana Society for Psychical Research, another had recently lost her husband and had a daughter who was writing a book on ESP in dogs, and a third was sent by the *National Enquirer*. Two of the participants, a physician from Washington, D.C., and a teacher of psychological counseling, came because of enthusiastic recommendations about Monroe's work which they had received from Kübler-Ross. All thirteen participants of this group spent a total of twelve forty-five minute sessions with the appropriate electric hookup and listening to the tapes giving them assorted instructions and suggestions. Yet not one of them achieved a "lift off." One of the sessions consisted of exercises in remote viewing of a six-digit number. Nobody made a correct guess. Another tape told the trainees how to make a cotton ball rise up by means of will power, but the balls did not rise. Perhaps the absence of positive results can be put down to the inexperience of the participants, but the one long-term success about which Joan Kron heard was no more impressive. The instructor casually mentioned that one woman had taken the course in order to reach her dead son. Joan Kron was particularly interested in this claim since she had lost one of her own children. The instructor later told her that the woman had reached her dead son after "months of practice at home." Joan Kron tracked the woman down and discovered that she had not actually been able to "contact" her son. After taking Monroe's course she had had a dream in which her son appeared to her and told her not to worry about him since he still existed and was not alone. We have here another instance of what in Chapter 9, in honor of Dr. Ritchie and Mr. Wilmot, I call the Ritchie-Wilmot syndrome: again and again the claims and "reports" of occultists lead to a disappointing denouement when it is possible to trace them to their sources. I should add that Monroe and some of his students may well have experienced OBEs, but by itself this in no way shows the reality of the astral body.[5]

The Astral Adventures of Kübler-Ross

It is clear that Kübler-Ross is one of Monroe's prize students. Unlike Joan Kron and her group, Kübler-Ross caught on rapidly. Her first session was only a partial success, but it clearly showed her great innate gift for this kind of commotion. Kübler-Ross was reclining on a waterbed in an isolated room in Monroe's institute. Wires connected the electrodes on her head to a polygraph. Sounds intended to induce the appropriate mood were communicated through earphones. As the take-off signal came, Kübler-Ross speedily ascended to the ceiling. Needless to say, she was "thrilled to bits" that she had "made it up to the ceiling." I should interrupt the account of this "incredible" experience to emphasize that Kübler-Ross's speedy ascent was not visible

---

5. For a sympathetic but not uncritical treatment of Monroe's work see Chapters 6 and 12 of Susan Blackmore, *Beyond the Body*, op. cit. See also Chapter 1 of *Psychic Voyages* (Time-Life Books, Alexandria, Va. 1987).

to anybody else. Although Monroe claims that he and his students can be observed by those to whom they pay astral visits, none of Kübler-Ross's numerous astral trips was observed by anybody except herself. The only Kübler-Ross body that could be observed remained lying on the waterbed. In any event, when Kübler-Ross got to the ceiling she began to "study its layers." This was in preparation for a penetration of the ceiling and the continuation of her journey. She was already then totally convinced that one "can get through any material stuff." I gather that she studied the layers of the ceiling to find the opening through which she could propel herself from the room. Just as she was about to do this, the instructor—"this damn guy"—called her back and thereby aborted the mission. Kübler-Ross "plunked" into her regular body and no matter how hard she tried, she could not make another ascent on this occasion. Kübler-Ross was understandably "mad as heck" at the instructor. She had a heart-to-heart talk with him and tried to make it clear what an extraordinary person he was dealing with. "You don't know me well," she said.

> It takes me a long time to get into something, but once I go, I go faster than anybody else, so next time I take off, don't stop me, even if I go too fast. I'll take care of that.

Kübler-Ross was going to travel at "super-speeds" and she firmly told this excessively cautious instructor not to interfere under any circumstances.

The second trip, which took place on the following day, was a resounding success. Kübler-Ross has called it the "highlight" of her life and it is clear that she also regards it as a momentous event in the history of the world. I should mention parenthetically that these epoch-making events occurred in July 1975. Kübler-Ross has not at all been reticent about her "super-exciting" experiences. She mentioned them to the reporters from *Newsweek*, to the *Midnight Globe*, and also to the *Midnight Globe*'s rival, the *Star*. The fullest account, however, is to be found in a very long interview published in *The New Age* of November 1977. This is a monthly, published in Brookline, Massachusetts, devoted to the propagation of environmental causes, spiritual healing, "holistic health" and many of the fashionable forms of occultism. Anything favoring belief in life after death is treated with special affection. Kübler-Ross was interviewed by Peggy Taylor, the journal's editor, and Dr. Rick Ingrasci, its leading medical contributor. At the beginning of the interview there is an editorial note expressing the great satisfaction of the interviewers to have had the opportunity of talking to Kübler-Ross. We are also told that her work has taken her through "many personal transformations and experiences which are not readily understandable in the terms of our present scientific models." Kübler-Ross's ascent, to return to her second journey, was as instantaneous as the first time and on this occasion the obstreperous instructor did not dare to interfere. She took off like a rocket, going through the ceiling and into the sky. Her remark to the instructor that she "goes at super-speeds" had been no idle boast. At the outset she had given herself "the command" to go faster than the speed of light and to go "further than any human being has ever been." Apparently the "command" was not totally effective, since she did not go faster than light, but she did become the first human being to travel *at* the speed of light. After she had covered "a few hundred thousand miles," she suddenly remembered that she had failed to follow one of Monroe's basic instructions. She was traveling horizontally and not vertically. Even though her instruction had so far been minimal, Kübler-Ross mastered the situation at once. She told the *Newsweek* reporters:

> The moment I realized I was going at the speed of light horizontally, I switched and made a right-angle turn, rounded a big hill and went up. I knew I had probably gone where nobody had ever been. I felt super.

In the *New Age* interview,, she added

> Stuff like this excites me! And I went so far and so fast that nobody could ever catch up with me. I felt very safe: nobody could find me. I was really where nobody had ever been, and from then on I have no recollection.

Kübler-Ross had gone to Monroe's institute in the company of some "*very* skeptical physicians, psychiatrists, and different kinds of scientists." She does not mention whether any of her companions also succeeded in ascending from their waterbeds, but she does report a meeting with this "group of scientists" after her return from outer space. They all "stared" at her and remarked about the "total glow" that surrounded her. Kübler-Ross did recall that during her exploration of space "they" had chanted the words "shanti nilaya" at her. Kübler-Ross does not explain who "they" were and I suppose she is not herself sure of "their" identity. Some of the scientists knew that "shanti" is the Sanskrit word for "peace," but nobody in the group knew the meaning of "nilaya." Kübler-Ross even then felt that there was something prophetic about her hearing these words in outer space. The scientists were tremendously interested in getting her to recall other details of her journey. Perhaps there were astronomers among them who would have liked to obtain firsthand information about galaxies that are too distant to be explored by more conventional methods. Unfortunately, however, the scientists did not succeed in stimulating her memory. "I'm sure I didn't want to remember," Kübler-Ross remarks, "it was much too sacred to share with these strangers."

Kübler-Ross had another experience fraught with prophetic meaning during her stay at Monroe's estate in Virginia. While taking Monroe's course she was staying in his guesthouse, a building that is rather isolated. Kübler-Ross describes it as a "kooky house." Although nobody else was staying there, she had the "distinct feeling" that she was not alone. She was sure that the house was "filled with something" and that she was being observed. She was so sure of this that at first she did not even want to take a shower. By 1977, when Kübler-Ross was interviewed by Peggy Taylor and Rick Ingrasci, she had become a believer in "entities"—spiritual messengers from the next world. Speaking about her shattering experiences in Monroe's guest house two years after the events, she expresses her conviction that such "entities" had invaded the house. In her fear of the mysterious "presences" she bolted the bedroom door, but in the morning it was wide open. Kübler-Ross is quite certain that this strange event cannot be explained by reference to natural causes. It was during the second night, which Kübler-Ross describes as "the most incredible night" of her entire life, that the really strange things began to happen. This was the night after her astral journey to the outer reaches of space. She had premonitions that something extraordinary was about to happen and for a while she thought about spending the night in other quarters. Perhaps Monroe could put her up in a guest room in the main house which had not, she hoped, been invaded by mysterious presences. In the end Kübler-Ross decided to "face whatever it was that was coming." Perhaps indeed she had gone too far, but now that she had made contact with the spiritual beings who had chanted "Shanti Nilaya," she had to go all the way. She could not pull back any more. She had to "face it," because if she did not face it now, it would happen later anyway. She could not sleep. She was tossing back and forth. She was "delirious." She was "like in a fever" and then it hit her "like lightening." It was utterly overwhelming and, like many other of Kübler-Ross's recent experiences, it cannot really be described in words. Although the experience was indescribable, she managed to find words to describe it in considerable detail:

> What happened is that I went through every single death of every single one of my thousands of patients that I had seen by then. And when I say I went through their death processes, I mean this literally—I had every experience every patient ever had and the bleeding and the pain and the agony and the cramps and incredible pains and tears and loneliness and isolation—every negative aspect of every patient's death.

Not only did Kübler-Ross "literally" experience every agony of her thousands of patients, but she did so "a thousand times" over, "always in a different version but with the same agony." It can be readily understood that she could not "finish a thought" while undergoing such horrendous suffering. However, in spite of the "endless incredible agony," she finally succeeded in composing "one sentence":

> I asked for a shoulder to lean on, I was very specific: it had to be a man's left shoulder where I could put my head. And I thought if I had a shoulder, a man's shoulder to lean on, I could bear it.

The request for a male shoulder to lean on was not granted. An "incredible voice" came at her from all directions, declaring with great firmness: "You shall not be given." Kübler-Ross thereupon moderated her request. She would have been glad to receive "a hand to hold" and she did not specify that it had to be a male hand. Even this modest request was denied by the incredible voice. Kübler-Ross now became even "less choosy" and was willing to settle for nothing more than a fingertip. At this stage a great insight came to her. She realized that "this" was something she had to do alone, "not even in the presence of a fingertip." She then made her sacred commitment. "Give me whatever you have in store," she said, "and I can take it alone." This sacred commitment had a miraculous result. In the "split second" that it took her to make her affirmation, the whole agony disappeared.

This was not the end of the shattering experience in Monroe's kooky guesthouse. What followed can once again not "be put into words." Fortunately Kübler-Ross has developed a special skill for describing the indescribable and she once again had no difficulty in relating what had happened to her. After the endless agony was over she was lying in bed while the room was illuminated by a night light. She looked at her belly and could not believe what was happening. Her abdominal wall started vibrating at "a very high speed—super, super fast." What she saw was "anatomically impossible," but this does not mean that Kübler-Ross was hallucinating. The "anatomically impossible" did happen. This presumably means that biologists need to revise their views in the light of the experiences of specially endowed persons like Kübler-Ross. It should hardly come as a surprise that an individual who can travel at the speed of light has abdominal walls that can vibrate at anatomically impossible speeds. We can now see why Peggy Taylor and Dr. Ingrasci maintain that Kübler-Ross's recent experiences cannot be comprehended in terms of contemporary scientific models. Not only her abdominal walls, but various other parts of her body started vibrating at enormous speeds. After that, the closet began to vibrate; and after the closet, the walls of the room; after the walls, the whole world—absolutely every entity composing the universe. Kübler-Ross has a tendency not to distinguish between her experiences and what actually goes on in the world and I should therefore point out that, to the best of my knowledge, nobody else in July of 1975 noticed similar vibrations of all the things in the universe. After everything had started to vibrate, something "opened up" in front of Kübler-Ross. At first it looked like a vagina, but then Kübler-Ross examined the object more closely and it turned out to be the bud of a lotus flower. It had the "most incredible" colors and Kübler-Ross looked at the bud "in utter awe" while simultaneously noticing the vibrations going on in the whole room. When the flower was wide open, the vibrations stopped and "all the million molecules became one." At the same time Kübler-Ross herself merged into this giant molecule. Then she fell asleep. When she awoke she wanted to tell Monroe about her remarkable experience but did not do so because it was too "sacred" to be talked about. Later she did talk about her experiences on Monroe's estate with. some Buddhist monks and "people from India." They told her that the full meaning of "Shanti Nilaya" was "ultimate home of peace."

It is time to return to Kübler-Ross's astral activities. It is doubtful whether Kübler-Ross was in need of Monroe's instruction. A year before she met him, she had taken off on her own without the benefit of any electronic or acoustic aids. This "incredible experience" occurred during one of her exhausting five-day seminars. This seminar or workshop was attended by dying patients, by parents whose children were dying, by people who had recently been bereaved as well as by social workers, counselors, and clergymen. At the end of the last day there had been an emotionally charged ritualistic celebration. At five in the morning Kübler-Ross tried to go into her room, but a dying woman insisted that she hold her hand. Finally, at 5:30, as she was about to go to sleep, a young girl, who had been deeply moved by the proceedings, dashed into the room and asked Kübler-Ross to watch the rising of the sun with her. This was her birthday, not in a chronological sense, but symbolically, as the beginning of a new life. Kübler-Ross told her that she could watch the sun rise at the window, but she herself had to get some sleep. During the next hour and a half she found herself floating above her regular body. She was "taken care of" by "a lot of beings" who were working on her body like a team of efficient car mechanics. Each one concentrated on one "rusty" part, replacing it with a new one, so that in a short time Kübler-Ross was whole again. When she woke up she felt "super-healthy," as if she were twenty years old again. Her young visitor looked at her with amazement. She said that, while she was asleep, Kübler-Ross had looked as if she were dead. There had been no respiration or pulse although the body remained warm. She would have been worried if she had not known that this was an out-of-body experience. Kübler-Ross explains that this was the first time she had heard about out-of-body experiences. In an interview with the *Star* five years later she expressed herself with great enthusiasm about astral travel, returning once again to her first "incredible experience." "The experience of soaring free," she told the *Star*, "the beauty of colors, the ability to be any place in the world in the time it takes you to think of it, are indescribable." She added that she herself had experienced this freedom "many times." It is not only the joy of soaring free and traveling at the speed of light which makes astral journeys so enjoyable. In many of these trips one also meets altogether remarkable people or beings. In this connection Kübler-Ross alluded once again to her first journey. On that occasion, she told the *Star*, she was "lifted out" of her body by no less than ten spiritual beings who were "working to fix" her up and make her young again.

The Canadian Television Interview (1978)

Kübler-Ross has not the slightest doubt that she possesses an astral body and that her travels at the speed of light are real physical events—just as real as the space exploits of the NASA astronauts. They are just as real, but of course conducted at vastly greater speed. On October 2, 1978, Kübler-Ross appeared on a television program of the Canadian Broadcast Corporation entitled "Man Alive." In the course of this program she described another of her astral trips and she also offered some theoretical reflections on the cause and precise nature of this remarkable phenomenon. She was interviewed by Roy Bonnisteel who raised questions about the evidential value of the reports of resuscitated patients. Bonnisteel very properly observed that although the hearts of these patients may have stopped, their brains were still active. The so-called post-mortem experiences could therefore very well have been due to "residual brain activity." Instead of answering Bonnisteel, Kübler-Ross brought up the work of Monroe:

KR: You can teach people clinically and scientifically in a research laboratory to have an out-of-body experience. I—

RB: You have had it?

KR: I have done it in a laboratory hooked up on polygraphs, on a waterbed hooked up on polygraphs. You can on command, at your wish, at your desire, in a structured laboratory environment, have someone teach you to have an out-of-body experience.

To illustrate this Kübler-Ross mentioned one of her astral flights:

KR: I can wish to be with my friends in San Francisco and I can have this out-of-body experience and I can tell you what they have on their kitchen table. Now you tell me how you explain that.

RB: You can do this?

KR: Oh yes. we have done it in the laboratory to verify our own skeptical, you know, concerns.

RB: Who's we?

KR: Monroe in Virginia does that. That is his specialty.

People who love San Francisco but who are condemned to live elsewhere are likely to envy Kübler-Ross's newly acquired skill. Kübler-Ross does not need to bother with flight schedules or with trips to and from the airport. Now that she is an accomplished astral traveler she probably does not even need Monroe's assistance. Above all, it takes her practically no time to get to San Francisco. The distance from New York to San Francisco is approximately 3,000 miles. Flying with the speed of light, i.e., at 186,000 miles per second, it takes Kübler-Ross 3/186th or 1/62nd of a second to cover 3,000 miles. It takes me longer than that to walk from one end of the kitchen to the other. We shall note a little later that Kübler-Ross feels very superior to her critics. One can easily see why.

Like most other champions of the astral body, Kübler-Ross is interested in astral projection primarily because of the indirect evidence it supposedly provides for the survival hypothesis. However, she also believes that those who have mastered the art of astral travel can derive incalculable benefits right here in this life.

We can teach, for example, a quadriplegic returning from Vietnam who doesn't live, who barely exists in a VA hospital, you can teach him to have an out-of-body experience at his command, at his time, when he wants it and he can, for example, attend a football game. His physical body is in a VA hospital (and yet) he can attend a football game. He doesn't even need tickets. Or he can go to attend his child's graduation. Do you understand the clinical ramifications those things have? Why this research is significant?

Roy Bonnisteel wanted to know if astral trips had been carried out under controlled scientific conditions. This question gave Kübler-Ross an opportunity to insist once again that all her survival research is strictly scientific:

Oh yes, oh yes. We have invited eight scientists and psychiatrists from Topeka and from the Medical Foundation, very skeptical people. I have participated in it where we all went through the experience and then shared with each other what we experienced and verified with—there's tremendous amount of research going on on every single aspect of this data and, forgive me, I would not ruin my professional reputation and say things on top of my head if I wouldn't be 100 percent sure.

It is unfortunate that the "eight scientists and psychiatrists" have never been identified. It is also far from clear just what they could have "verified"—a term that is used rather loosely by Kübler-Ross. It is too bad that Bonnisteel did not draw Kübler-Ross out about the details of "the tremendous research on every aspect of this data." (Kübler-Ross's grammar is as good as her science: if "data" is singular, one wonders what the plural would be.) However, Bonnisteel did press Kübler-Ross about her astral journey to San Francisco. She did not tell him the names of her friends in San Francisco to whom she paid an astral visit. She also did not supply any information as to what she "saw" on their table and whether what she saw was identical with what the friends observed with their ordinary eyes. Bonnisteel wanted to know what she was like during the visit.

RB: When you appear to your friends in San Francisco, do you materialize?

KR: No.

RB: No?

KR: No. They do not see me.

RB: They don't see you.

KR: No.

RB: Do they know you're there?

KR: You need a—you would need an incredible amount of energy to materialize and I am not interested in that. All I needed to know for me to go through this experiment as a subject is to know if this is really true. I need to know for myself whether this is real or whether this is a projection of wishful thinking.

Kübler-Ross did not materialize on her astral trips because she was not "interested" in generating or collecting—I do not know which word she would regard as appropriate—"the incredible amount of energy" necessary for this purpose. She implies that such materializations are not at all impossible and that they are within the voluntary control of a properly trained traveler. This certainly is the view of her mentor, Robert Monroe, who, as we noted, appeared on the ceiling of a friend's apartment and who trained a married couple to pay nightly astral visits to one another. It is too bad that Kübler-Ross is not interested in materializing. Since she believes that acceptance of her views about life after death is of the greatest importance to the human race one might have expected her to be only too eager to carry out a decisive experiment which would rout the skeptics once and for all.

Kübler-Ross's remarks about "the incredible amount of energy" required for the materialization of astral bodies raises a number of intriguing questions. Who has observed the utilization of the energy in question for purposes of materialization? What kind of energy is involved? Is it heat, electricity, or chemical energy? Or is it perhaps some new form of energy not familiar to conventional physicists, perhaps a special kind that will become known as "astral energy"? Where is this energy stored? I assume that, like all energy, it can be converted into other forms. If so, could it be used to run cars or heat houses? Since incredible amounts of this energy can bring about materialization, it would appear that it can be converted into mass or at least a special kind of "astral" mass. Would such a conversion follow Einstein's famous formula concerning the equivalence of mass and energy? If not and if the conversion follows some other laws, what are these laws? I hope that these and other related questions will be answered by Kübler-Ross or by some other astral philosopher.

There is also a problem concerning the claim that during her astral journeys Kübler-Ross travels with the speed of light. How exactly did Kübler-Ross measure the speed of her motion? According to Einstein's special theory of relativity, for which there has been a great deal of experimental confirmation, it would require an infinitely great force to accelerate an object to the speed of light, which is another way of saying that such an acceleration is impossible. There is no indication that Kübler-Ross has any interest in Einstein's theories. I suppose that if she knew anything about them, she would dismiss them without any hesitation: since she traveled with the speed of light and since the special theory of relativity implies that this was impossible, it follows that Einstein's theory is wrong.

Kübler-Ross answers questions about the appearance and activities of the inhabitants of the Beyond without the least hesitation in much the same way as an experienced traveler might give information about places he has recently visited. According to Kübler-Ross, the next world is populated by all who ever lived on this earth. However, there is no time and no space (whatever this means) and hence there cannot be any problem of overcrowding. In various of her earlier statements, Kübler-Ross had already mentioned that we will be reunited with those we loved. There would seem to be a recognition problem. The inhabitants of the next world can hardly look as they did when they died with diseased and damaged bodies. What about people who were burned to death leaving nothing but ashes behind? On this topic Bonnisteel did not let Kübler-Ross off lightly.

> RB: Are they (the citizens of the next world) ever described in terms of what they are wearing? Are they wearing anything?
>
> KR: Only shortly after death they will appear like the physical bodies in order for you to recognize them. This is like an ethereal body. But you obviously know your child or your mother or father—
>
> RB: Yes, but you see, I'm wondering how they look, because a lot of people on their deathbed don't look very well. I mean, am I going to see—am I going to—
>
> KR: They look young and healthy.
>
> RB: They look young and healthy?
>
> KR: Yes.
>
> RB: At a younger age.
>
> KR: They look the way they feel would appeal to you the most.
>
> RB: Hmmm.
>
> KR: Like if you had a marvelous time with your mother when she was fifty, she looked at her best she would come to you the way she looked when she was fifty and you had the best time together. But that is their choice. They can appear any way that is the most appealing to you.

Animal lovers will be pleased to learn that animals no less than human beings are going to survive in the Beyond. I assume that they will also be able to appear as they were when they were most lovable.

> KR: After the transition if a woman has been very attached to a poodle, had no children, this poodle will, you know, come to her, to help her in this transition. We have only heard of cats and dogs. But that was not my special area of interest, I must say.

Some people are very attached to horses, some to monkeys and I believe that zoo-keepers become exceptionally fond of walruses who are among the most affection-ate animals. We also know that on occasion there has been a great deal of love be-tween human beings and whales. If dogs and cats can make it, we may assume that horses, monkeys, whales, walruses, and probably many other animals will also be re-united with their human friends. It is a pity that Kübler-Ross has not shown more in-terest in the fauna of the next world. Fortunately this gap in her account has been filled by the reports from an animal lover who has been living in the next world since October 1970. The animal lover is Dr. Alvin Daniel Matson, a Lutheran theologian who dictated his messages to his daughter, Ruth Taylor, via Margaret Flavell Tweedell, an experienced clairvoyant who is a graduate of the London School of Paranormal Psychology and Sanctuary of Healing. Dr. Matson's reports were published as *Witness from the Beyond* by a small Chicago company in 1975. The 1980 paperback reprint, carries a ringing endorsement from Kübler-Ross printed in bold red type. Dr. Matson not only met astral dogs and cats but also astral birds and insects. Astral flies, alas, are just as much a nuisance as they were on earth, constantly biting the human inhabitants of the Beyond. Dr. Matson does not tell us what happens to astral mosquitoes after they have been swatted in self defense by astral human beings. Is this their final end or do they move on to a Beyond-Beyond?

The concluding portion of the Canadian interview was largely devoted to a description and discussion of a special revelation that Kübler-Ross had experienced a few years earlier. In spite of all the staggering evidence which she had accumulated in support of her survival theories, evidence which would have overwhelmed anybody less cautious and skeptical, Kübler-Ross had not yet become utterly sure that her conclusions were correct. Although her research has been "cross-verified by many scientists and physicians across the country," there was still a "glimpse of a doubt." She could not afford to be only 99 percent sure. "As a scientist," she had to "know it 100 percent." Then "this incredible experience"—to which Kübler-Ross frequently refers as a "miracle"—occurred and it removed the last vestige of doubt. The miracle took place in the headquarters of the Rev. Jay Barham with whom Kübler-Ross was associated for several years. It was witnessed by no less than seventy-five people. Kübler-Ross assured Bonnisteel that these seventy-five witnesses were "very open-minded" and that they had "dedicated their life to service and to helping their fellow men." It is not clear how she could have known this. Anyhow, here is Kübler-Ross's description of the miracle:

> Suddenly these big feet walk by me, this enormously tall figure stands there seven foot ten and starts talking to me and tells me that this miracle had to happen to me in order to take the last shadows of a doubt out of my mind.

The enormously tall man then took Kübler-Ross's hands, quietly opened them and lifted her up. He led her into a back room saying he wanted to be alone with her for a few minutes. The remainder of the experience which was "almost humanly indescribable" is described by Kübler-Ross in the following words:

> He said that my work on death and dying was only a test if I can take resistance and hostility and my fame was a test to see if I could take fame and that my real work was beginning now and I would have to be aware that the society in which I live would try to shred me to pieces because of this and asked if I am willing to take the pain and then he looked at me in regard to all the hostility I am getting now because of this work and said always remember, should you shield the canyons from the windstorms you would never see the beauty of its carvings.

The Rev. Barham and the Four Celestial Informants

The "enormously tall" man responsible for the "almost humanly indescribable" miracle just recounted was a messenger from the next world who became one of the "spirits" concerning themselves with Kübler-Ross's welfare during her years in California. In more secular terms, he was one of four cronies of the Rev. J. Barham, a shrewd operator who must have sensed at once that Kübler-Ross was a wretched woman hungry for experiences of "indescribable love" as well as reports about what is going on in the next world.

Kübler-Ross first met Barham in 1976 and was at once tremendously impressed by him. "This man," she told the reporter from *Time* (referring to Barham), "has more gifts than you have ever seen—he is probably the greatest healer that this country has."[6] In an interview in *Playboy* in May, 1980, she is even more effusive. "The world thinks he is a nobody," she said, "but he has a greater gift for healing than anybody I have ever met. In all the traveling and the hundreds of talented people I have seen, I never met anybody with more humility or a greater gift."[7] Her teaming up with Barham and Barham's wife was "a predestined part of our commitment before we were born."[8]

The article in *Time* has a picture of Barham showing him to be a bespectacled, bald and tight-lipped middle-aged man. With his wife, Martha, he had founded the Church of the Facet of Divinity in 1975, just as Kübler-Ross was beginning not to have a shadow of a doubt about the reality of the next world. Prior to becoming a man of God and a therapist, Barham had been a sharecropper in Arkansas and then, for eighteen years, an aircraft worker in San Diego. His education is slight and, according to the reporter of the *New York Times*, he speaks in a drawl, making frequent grammatical mistakes. He is a high school dropout and has a mail-order degree in divinity. The Church of the Facet of Divinity was no ordinary church. As far as I can make out there were two main activities in which members participated. The first was a somewhat violent form of psychodrama. The second consisted of séances resulting in the appearance of spirits from the Beyond who assist in the sex therapy in which Barham specializes. I do not believe that the sex therapy angle has the slightest appeal to Kübler-Ross, but the production of messengers from the Beyond fitted in perfectly with the explorations of the next world in which she had embarked a little earlier. She persuaded her husband, a wealthy Chicago physician, to spend $250,000 for a forty-two acre site very close to Barham's ranch. There she established her new headquarters which she called "Shanti Nilaya." She now realized that when these Sanskrit words had been chanted at her in outer space, they were meant as a prophetic message about the work she was now destined to carry forward.

---

6. *Time*, November 12, 1979.
7. *Playboy*, May, 1980, p. 103.
8. Ibid.

The séances, needless to say, take place in the dark.[9] The area in which Barham and his spirits operate consists of a large meeting room as well as two small "visitation" rooms. At the beginning of a séance, Barham lies down in one of the visitation rooms and goes into a trance. At this stage the congregation engages in singing and chanting to raise the energy level. Barham's remarkable creations, it is thought, are more easily accomplished when the surrounding atmosphere is highly charged. A number of "spirit guides" or "entities" are produced by "cloning"the cells of Barham's body. Two kinds of entities are produced in this way. One group consists of the "darkroom regulars" who include all of Kübler-Ross's spirits—Salem, Ankh, Willie, and Mario. The others are cloned doubles of Barham himself. I take it that at any one time only one such double "materializes." The spirits part the curtain and move into the main room, sometimes completely naked. Kübler-Ross, who was totally sold on the reality of this cloning, explains the process in some detail in answer to a question by the *Playboy* interviewer:

> It takes two forms of energy. Number one, it takes an enormous amount of positive energy, more energy than to shoot a rocket to the moon. So it is not an ordinary kind of occurrence. If anybody in the group is destructive or negative, no guide can possibly materialize. It is very complicated. Second, it takes channel energy. A person—like Jay Barham—acts as the channel, and the guides take actual molecules out of him to clone a human being, in which form they appear. The bulk energy to create the guide who comes to visit comes from us, the group. It is a true cloning. And the more people there are in the group, the faster the materialization happens. Jay is the best channel I know, not the only one but the best. Not only does he have a huge amount of positive energy but he has the ability to put himself into this trancelike state where the guides can work on him without waking him up.[10]

As I understand it, the spirit guides are there to begin with in their nonphysical state and the cloning results in their assumption of human form.

The first mention in print of Kübler-Ross's contact with spirits occurred in an article in the March 1977 issue of *Human Behavior*. The article, suitably entitled "Mystical Portents," is by Eleanor Links Hoover and deals in a highly sympathetic way with the views of a number of contemporary psychologists who have introduced the occult into their therapeutic practice. The article opens with the information that, a short time previously, Kübler-Ross, "the eminent doctor who has revolutionized our view of death and dying," addressed a holistic medical conference in San Diego. She

---

9. It is well known that other séances are also carried out in the dark. It is amazing that the believers in spiritualism see nothing suspicious in this fact. On this subject the great Houdini said all that needs to be said: "This necessity for darkness seems but the grossest invention of the medium to divert . . . the attention of the sitters. . . . It can be supported only as a visionary, speculative superstition; an instrument to foster hallucinatory illusion and as an admirable subterfuge to cover fraud." *A Magician Among the Spirits* (New York, 1924), p. 268.

10. *Playboy*, May, 1980, p. 102.

is reported to have told a "hushed hall" of several hundred psychologists, psychiatrists, and mental health experts that "she had been visited the night before by three spirit creatures." She had asked the spirits what the most important thing was that she could discuss at the conference. "Tell them about us," the spirits replied. According to Eleanor Hoover, the audience was "stunned, electrified, supportive and, significantly, not really surprised." She then observes that the concept of "unseen forces" is now "so established in some professional and scientific circles that it raises few eyebrows." In spite of the widespread acceptance of this "concept," it is apparently not "talked about" publicly and hence it is remarkable "when someone as distinguished as Kübler-Ross shares her voices and visions with us." I do not know much about the kind of people who attend holistic health conferences, but I doubt whether Eleanor Hoover's explanation of the supportive attitude of the audience is correct. I wonder if some of them did not respond out of pity for a well-meaning woman who once made valuable contributions and had now become the victim of delusions.

Since that meeting Kübler-Ross has frequently spoken about her spirit guides. In later statements there are always four of them. We are not informed how long they have been living in the Beyond, but it is clearly suggested that they have been there for a long time, several centuries at the very least. They are therefore in an excellent position to tell Kübler-Ross what goes on in that realm. In addition to supplying invaluable reports about the nature of the hereafter, Kübler-Ross's spirits exert profound influence on her day-to-day life and indirectly on the lives of the patients treated by her and by Mr. and Mrs. Barham. Both in the 1979 interview with *People* and in a communiqué issued to the *National Enquirer* on August 26, 1980, Kübler-Ross insists that everybody possesses "personal spirits" and that everybody can "develop spirit contact." The trouble with the world is that except for herself, the Barhams, and some of the mystical psychologists mentioned by Eleanor Links Hoover, hardly anybody tries to reach his spirits. "People would be able to heal emotionally and physically," she told the *People* reporter, if only "they would get in touch with their spirits."

In the *National Enquirer* communiqué Kübler-Ross describes each of her four spirits and the roles they play in her life. The first is called Salem and he is a very special spirit. When she first met Salem, she had one of her incredible and indescribable experiences:

> I experienced this incredible love that is beyond any human description. It was a feeling of total contentment. Salem represents peace and love.

A second spirit is called Ankh. Kübler-Ross says very little about him except that he "gives wisdom." Mario, the third spirit, is responsible for Kübler-Ross's "health and safety." He appears to be a combination of body-guard and personal physician. Any time Kübler-Ross is sick "or down in the dumps," Mario comes and offers his help. Not surprisingly, Kübler-Ross regards his care for her well-being as a "big blessing." What she did not tell the *National Enquirer* is that Mario is also a lecturer on sex who is imbued with the ideas found in the writings of some of the most radical defenders of sexual freedom. The July 30, 1979 issue of *New West* contains a detailed and, as far as I can judge, extremely well-researched article by Kate Coleman entitled "Elisabeth Kübler-Ross in the Afterworld of Entities." The article is primarily about the activities of Barham, his wife, and their supernatural assistants. It appears that Mario was a regular lecturer at Barham's sex-therapy sessions. He had started out lecturing in the nude, but later he wore a long, white gown made for him by one of the women in the group. The fourth and final spirit guide is Willie with whom Kübler-Ross was already in communication in Jerusalem at the time of Jesus, but more of this later on. Willie teaches her "joy." He told her that all her life had been "work and responsibility and very little laughter and joy." He very sensibly advised her to try and have more fun. If Mario distinguishes himself by giving lectures on sex, Willie's *forte* is singing. Kübler-Ross at her lectures frequently plays a tape-recording of Willie's singing of "You Are My Sunshine." In the article in *Human Behavior* Eleanor Hoover thought that when Kübler-Ross spoke of her conversation with her spirits, she was referring to nothing more than voices and visions; and it is true that occasionally Kübler-Ross speaks of the appearance of spirits in the course of dreams. However, she also insists that her spirit guides are "very, very real," meaning by this that they are much more than visions and voices—they are three-dimensional, publicly observable beings who wear turbans, who lecture and sing, and who are also very active sexually.

Kübler-Ross insists that the world is full of spirits. Beings like Salem, Ankh, Mario, and Willie are "all around us." Every human being has "at least one guide who is never more than two feet away." Kübler-Ross apparently has this information from the spirits themselves. However, although the spirit of every person is so close physically, this does not mean that it is easy for a person to reach his spirit. "To make contact with your spirit guide," Kübler-Ross told the *National Enquirer*, "you must first get rid of negative feelings such as greed, guilt, fear and shame." I do not believe that the ability to meet a spirit has anything to do with getting rid of such "negative" feelings. To meet a spirit two conditions have to be satisfied. The first is to engage in a systematic suppression of one's critical faculties in order to achieve a state of maximum credulity. The second is to attach oneself to a brazen and totally unprincipled exploiter of human credulity. The first of these conditions is already met by many people all over the world. The second is more commonly satisfied in Southern California than elsewhere.

Kübler-Ross as Teacher of Jesus

I have already mentioned that this life is not the first one for Kübler-Ross. The earlier life about which she gives us some information was as Isabel in Palestine at the time of Jesus. She does not claim to have spontaneous memories of this life. Nor, perhaps surprisingly, does she appeal to memories obtained during hypnotic sessions. She learned of her previous life from Barham. According to participants in Barham's therapy sessions they were "taught" by him that "they had all lived during the time of Jesus and had been among His disciples." Willie, one of her spirit guides, told her that she had been his teacher in Palestine and the article in *New West* contained the further news that she had been one of "the most important" teachers of Jesus himself. The spirits who supplied this information also listed Harry Houdini as one of the teachers of Jesus. Houdini, who abominated all forms of occultism and spent much of his time exposing fraudulent psychic researchers, would have been amazed by this information. Because of her great importance in her earlier life, the Barhams as well as the materialized spirits frequently addressed Kübler-Ross as Isabel. It might be noted in passing that Gen. George Patton, Jr., and Shirley MacLaine also lived in Palestine at that time. I would not be at all surprised if Kübler-Ross met them there and if the trio were advisers to Jesus the night before the Sermon on the Mount. There were no speech writers in those days, but advice from distinguished friends was surely always welcome. I think I can detect the hand of Kübler-Ross in several passages.

On April 29, 1980, the *Star*, one of the leading American tabloids, published an interview with Kübler-Ross in which the subject of reincarnation was discussed at some length. In this interview she does not hesitate to denounce in the harshest terms other champions of reincarnation who are gravely misleading the public. She rejects all talk about "Karma" as a myth. No one, she observes, "was born to suffer" and each time an individual comes back "it is with a clean slate." She also warns the public to beware of stories about earlier incarnations as kings or queens. Her greatest scorn, however, is reserved for those "who tell you about a former life as a member of the opposite sex." Such a person is a total "charlatan." For the spirit "is created only once, as either male or female." On this last point some distinguished occultists do not concur with Kübler-Ross. Ruth Montgomery, who is in constant communication with the late Rev. Arthur Ford, quotes numerous instances in which there has been a sex change, from one incarnation to another. In one of her best-known books, *The World Before*, she reports, for example, that Richard Burton and Elizabeth Taylor were lovers in an earlier century, "but Burton was a woman and Taylor was a man." If Kübler-Ross is right, this cannot be so. It should prove a fruitful subject of discussion among believers in reincarnation which of these views is correct.[11]

What about Hitler? This topic came up in the *Playboy* interview and Kübler-Ross offers information about his future that should be of interest to everybody.

---

11. In fairness I should add that in her foreword to *Reincarnation: The Phoenix Fire Mystery*, an anthology edited by J. Head and S. L. Cranston from which I earlier quoted her endorsement of the déjà vu argument, she reverses herself. She first states her considered conviction that "those who are born again into another life will not only be born again as human beings, but will always be born again as male or female, depending on the form in which they have been created by the Source or God." However, in a footnote the editors tell us that in December 1984 Kübler-Ross sent a note to them saying that she had been wrong—"We are born as male or female each time we incarnate." What caused this change of view has not been revealed.

Playboy: When Hitler died, would he have experienced all this love and compassion? Didn't he have to pay for his evil doings?

KR: . . . your example of Hitler is a good one, because to me, Hitler is the most negative person who ever lived. But negativity can only exist in the realm of the physical person. In the realm of spiritual energy that is God-created, negativity cannot exist. It is all unconditional love. Therefore, when Hitler stands in the presence of his life and does his evaluation, he watches, with compassion, the death of the 1,500,000 people he killed at Maidenek concentration camp. He will watch the results of the constant choices in his life. He will watch this not with grief, agony and guilt, because these negative emotions do not exist. Instead of self-pity or self-loathing, he will have compassion.

Playboy: For himself?

KR: And for all the tragedy he has caused. He will have an incredible understanding of why he became the man he did, what he needed to learn; he will understand the time of history in which he lived and that supported him and pushed him in that direction. He will probably gain in understanding of human behavior far more than most human beings ever gain. And that, you must understand, will be a huge asset when he chooses how he will return in order to become a *great* leader.

Playboy: Will he inevitably come back as a great leader?

KR: Yes. He misused his powers for destruction and failed to lead a nation to its more positive, fulfilled existence. For this, by the way, he may have to wait 3000 years or 5000 years, in order to find a nation that offers the opportunity to undo all his misdeeds. Then he will probably be the greatest leader who ever existed.

Here for once I cannot go along with Kübler-Ross and her spirit guides from whom she evidently received all this information. Since the guides live there, their descriptions of the Beyond cannot be challenged by an outsider. Merely living in the Beyond, however, does not turn one into a prophet. I do not believe that people's characters ever radically change. Even if he has several hundred years of intensive psychotherapy supplemented by psychoactive drugs, Hitler is likely to remain a colossal menace. I must hope that he stays away as long as possible. I realize that the people living in the Beyond—Marilyn Monroe, Elvis Presley, Grace Kelly, and the rest—would much rather that he left and returned to the earth, but that is their problem. The *Playboy* interviewer did not inquire about the future of Stalin and Mussolini. I suppose that, by the same logic she used for Hitler, Kübler-Ross would tell us that they too will come back as great leaders, but not, I hope, for a few thousand years.

Pandemonium at Shanti Nilaya

In the late spring of 1978 several upsetting events occurred which resulted in the defection of the majority of Barham's followers. The first of the events exposing Barham occurred during a visit by Deanna Edwards, a folksinger and therapist, who had been one of Kübler-Ross's closest friends. During the first séance she attended, her personal entity, Pico, took her to one of the visitation rooms where he solicited sex. Deanna rejected his overtures. Pico thereupon insisted that she had sexual problems with her husband and that he, Pico, could help her overcome them. Deanna became furious. She could not see Pico's features in the dark, but she had her suspicions about his identity. She accepted another invitation to the dark room the next evening, fully determined to expose the fraud and to help Kübler-Ross see the truth. During the second séance she waited until an entity had been "called up" or "cloned." Not surprisingly the entity was once again Pico and Pico again invited Deanna to a visitation room. At this moment she tore the tape off the light switch and turned on the lights. What everybody could see now was Jay Barham totally naked except for a turban on his head. Pandemonium broke out with anguished cries from all corners of the room. Deanna felt that this visual demonstration would finally open Kübler-Ross's eyes, but Kübler-Ross had reached a stage of faith at which she was impervious to ordinary canons of evidence. One of the defectors from Shanti Nilaya later remarked that Kübler-Ross is "so emotionally dependent on the Barhams that she cannot see." When things had quieted down Kübler-Ross addressed Deanna in a weary, tragic voice: "Why did you do it, Deanna?" "To show you the truth," Deanna replied. "I don't believe you," Kübler-Ross said, and then repeated wearily, "Why did you do it?" Kübler-Ross had of course seen a body and face looking just like the body and face of Jay Barham, but this did not mean that Barham was a fraud. The person they had all seen was Pico, Barham's cloned or "coned" double. Apparently, like some of the other members of the group, Kübler-Ross refers to Barham's supernatural gifts of producing spirits and doubles not as "cloning" but as "coning. " There was no further discussion and the two women have not met since. After Deanna returned home, she received a letter from Kübler-Ross explaining the nature and gravity of her offense:

> As you endanger a materialized entity with electric light, so the person's (the channel's) health and well-being is endangered since they use their fibers to clone the body of the entity.

Kübler-Ross is understandably concerned about the safety of the entities who mean so much in her life, but it is worth pointing out that apparently nothing happened to Pico as the result of his exposure to light. Nor does Kübler-Ross mention any cases she has observed in which exposure to light *did* hurt any of the entities.

Kübler-Ross is not usually vicious, but she made extremely spiteful remarks about Deanna to the *Playboy* interviewer. I infer that in spite of all her protestations about Barham's honesty and genius she felt that Deanna had exposed his fraudulence.

She [Deanna] had this glorious Messiah complex that she was going to save me from this fraud, when I wanted to share with her what was the greatest gift of my life. For fifty years, I have gone my own path and certainly don't need a jerk like her with all her own hang-ups to tell me what to do.

Kübler-Ross insisted that the naked man who was seen when the light went on was not Barham but his cloned double.

Playboy: You were there during that incident?

KR: Yes and I have the whole thing on tape . . .

Playboy: We'd like to hear that tape.

KR: No. I want to keep those things for my autobiography. If I give everything away to you now, I might as well forget about writing my book.

Here, Kübler-Ross's good faith has to be questioned. If she had nothing to hide, she would surely have been willing to play the tape for the interviewer. I am writing this in the spring of 1995, fifteen years after the *Playboy* interview, and there is not the slightest sign of an autobiography or of the publication of the tape in any shape or form.

I have little doubt that the majority of the church members who were present when the lights were switched on began to have serious doubts about Barham's integrity in spite of all the talk about cloned or coned doubles. The mass defection, however, did not occur until some time after this episode. One of the supernatural entities, it appears, is a particularly unsavory individual who took a ten-year-old girl to a visitation room where he tried to seduce her. The shaken girl told her mother whose faith in Barham and his spirits was not unshakable. She complained to the police, but there was nothing the police could do since there was no way of identifying the child molester. This event undoubtedly shook many members. What finally brought about the mass defection was the discovery of a little book, *The Magnificent Potential*, by Lester A. Hinshaw which had been published in New York in 1958. According to one of the defectors, this book contained every last thing in the way of psychological theory and practice that Barham and his spirits had been preaching. Following the scene with Deanna Edwards and the charge of child molestation, this was too much for most of the members. In a bitter confrontation they accused Barham of the grossest plagiarism. Barham was asked why he did not tell the group that he had used Hinshaw's book as his source. He answered, in his usual brazen way, that the entities had forbidden such a disclosure. He was asked facetiously whether he would kill somebody if the entities demanded it and he replied, without any hesitation, that he would. In the past Barham had also shifted responsibility to the entities whenever troublesome questions were raised. On this occasion most of the followers no longer accepted his alibi. In May of 1978 a formal complaint was lodged with the California Department of Consumer Affairs in San Diego charging that the Barhams had violated the licensing rules governing psychotherapy. In this instance, too, the authorities could not take any action because what most people would call "therapy sessions" could also be construed as the religious ceremonies of Barham's church and hence were not covered by the rules licensing psychotherapy.

The defectors never questioned Kübler-Ross's integrity and they regarded her as a fellow-victim of fraud. "Everybody spoke to Elisabeth about this in dozens of meetings with her," one woman told Kate Coleman, "nothing was kept from her. She was told everything from A to Z." It was of no avail. One of those who became alarmed was Dr. Herbert Cheuvront, the president of the University of Humanistic Studies. Only three of the thirty Ph.D. students enrolled at Shanti Nilaya under the university's auspices remained after the mass defection. Cheuvront sat in at a meeting between Kübler-Ross and some of the disgruntled students. He asked her to "please validate" what she was doing. He recommended that she should contact the parapsychology department at Duke University. Kübler-Ross was not interested. "I know what I'm doing," she said. "I am right. The entities don't need proof." She expressed herself in similar language to Karen Jackovich of *People*.[12] "He [Barham] has so much integrity," Kübler-Ross said, "the truth does not need to be defended." All the complaints, she told the *New York Times*,[13] should be dismissed as coming from "vengeful defectors." Rather haughtily she remarked to the interviewer from *Time*: "Many attempts have been made to discredit us. To respond to them would be like casting pearls to swine."

The Break with Barham

As late as May of 1980 when the *Playboy* interview was published, Kübler-Ross was totally devoted to Barham and bitterly resented any aspersions on his character or on his healing powers. Something happened during the year following this interview which resulted in a breakup of the alliance. The only published information in my possession states that on June 21, 1981, Kübler-Ross fired Barham as executive director of Shanti Nilaya. This statement is part of an interview with Kübler-Ross by Joan Saunders Wixen for the Independent News Alliance. I do not know if it was ever published in a newspaper or magazine. I learned about it from the article in *Harpers* by Ron Rosenbaum which I quoted earlier.[14] The typescript of the interview was sent to me at my request by one of Kübler-Ross's assistants.

Kübler-Ross told Joan Wixen that she had been conducting her own investigation of the allegations against Jay Barham for a long time "unknown to anyone including Mr. Barham":

---

12. October 29, 1979.

13. September 17, 1979.

14. "Turn On, Turn In, Drop Dead," *Harper's*, July 1982, p. 42. This article is reprinted in Rosenbaum's *Travels with Dr. Death* (New York, 1991).

I was determined from the outset that I would never accept these allegations as truth unless they were proven beyond a shadow of a doubt, to my complete satisfaction. No one could offer such proof, so after the rumors continued, I set out on my own investigation which took many months and involved me in a first-person way, and ultimately led me to the conclusion that Mr. Barham's behavior did not meet the standards we have set for all employees of Shanti Nilaya.

Kübler-Ross does not reveal just how she carried out her own investigations which yielded the necessary "proof." Later in the discussion, Joan Wixen reminded her that she had once called Barham the greatest healer in the world. "What do you think about him now?"

Many years ago he had demonstrated great promise and a real gift of healing—but you know if these abilities are ever misused or utilized in a play for fame or power or personal gain of any kind, we quickly lose these gifts, if we ever had them. Jay Barham's healing skills declined, as verified by a December 1980 physician's report indicating that there were no measurable effects any longer on anyone he attempted to heal.

Kübler-Ross's account of why she changed her mind would be more believable if she had named the physician who examined Barham's healing powers in December 1980 and it would also be interesting to find out if any physician had testified to measurable effects of Barham's "treatments" prior to December 1980.

As far as I know, Kübler-Ross never apologized to Deanna Edwards. Nor has she ever faced the consequences for her philosophy of the unmasking of Barham. If Barham is a fraud, then presumably the four spirit guides are also frauds and then the cloning did not really occur. If this is so, what happens to the information about the Beyond supplied by the spirits and what about the miracle performed by the seven-foot-tall man which confirmed her mission for bringing knowledge about immortality to a skeptical world? What about the voice which she had heard in Monroe's guest house and which she subsequently recognized as that of Mario? And what about her life as teacher of Jesus? More generally, what about reincarnation—is it still a "fact" as she glibly asserted in her foreword to *The Phoenix Mystery*? My guess is that these are questions which Kübler-Ross simply cannot face. Later in the interview Wixen asked Kübler-Ross how she could be so certain that there is life after death. To this she received a rambling and long-winded answer. Kübler-Ross talked about "the people who have always been threatened" by her work. (I have no idea who these people are or why anybody should feel threatened.) Then we get the usual rigmarole:

The common human denominator is that people after death become complete again. The blind can see, the deaf can hear, cripples are no longer crippled after all their vital signs have ceased to exist. After death, you simply shed your physical body like a butterfly does its cocoon.

To Wixen's request for evidence Kübler-Ross replies that "After thirteen years of research it is like somebody asking you to prove the color red is red."

Kübler-Ross has a medical degree and she presumably has taken some courses in which the physiology of the brain and its relation to consciousness is discussed. It never seems to occur to her (or to most other occultists) that the dependence or at least the apparent dependence of consciousness on the brain conflicts with belief in survival. What irritates me most about Kübler-Ross's pronouncements on the subject is not so much their shrillness and their dogmatism but the staggering ignorance of science and philosophy which they betray.

"Isn't She Wonderful?"

In the second half of 1984 Kübler-Ross moved her headquarters to a farm near Charlottesville, Virginia, which she had bought from her friend, Dr. Raymond Moody. According to the Winter 1984/85 issue of *Vital Signs*, a publication of the International Association of Near Death Studies, Kübler-Ross "now spends most of each year traveling worldwide to lecture and present the 'Life, Death, and Transition' workshops which have earned her the personal respect and affection of hundreds of thousands of participants." The Spring 1985 issue of the same publication contains a report of a lecture given by Kübler-Ross at the University of Connecticut on April 12, 1985. "Despite their having sat for two hours on bleacher seats," we are told, "the audience appeared rapt as Kübler-Ross described how, in twenty years of working with dying patients, she has documented twenty thousand near-death experiences." Kübler-Ross appears to believe that if we have twenty thousand cases of NDEs this is greater evidence for life after death than if we only have a handful. This is of course totally fallacious. If NDEs can be adequately explained without bringing in the afterlife then twenty thousand will not be any better evidence than one. If I dream every night that I am president of the United States this is no better evidence that I am president than if I have this dream only once.

The Virginia headquarters are no longer called "Shanti Nilaya" but the "Elisabeth Kübler-Ross Center." This center publishes a quarterly *Newsletter* which gives information about Kübler-Ross's activities, about the "transition," as it calls death, of friends and associates and the activities of miscellaneous occult movements. Both the *Newsletter* and an article in the *New York Times Magazine* of January 22, 1995, show that Kübler-Ross's addiction to far-out mystical causes is undiminished. The Summer 1990 *Newsletter*, picked out at random, devotes most of the last page to announcing "the great pyramid healing conference in Egypt" on December 1–8, 1990. We are invited to this conference "to join Elisabeth for a Quantum Leap Healing" and the Pyramid is described as "the greatest power place of the planet." The *Newsletter* usually contains a list of books "recommended by Elisabeth." I will quote two of the recommendations in the Summer 1990 issue:

Black Dawn—Bright Day by Sun Bear and Waburn Sun Bear predicts earth changes. What, when, and where these changes will happen in different parts of the country. What you can do spiritually and mentally to prepare yourself. Bear Tribe Publishing.

To Dance with Angels—Don and Linda Pendleton.
This book holds a key to the meaning of life on planet Earth and all that lies beyond. Structured around a series of in-depth interviews with this Grand Spirit through the medium, Thomas Jacobson. Published by Zebra Books.

In the *Times Magazine* article, which nobody interested in the Kübler-Ross phenomenon should miss, the author, Nathaniel Rosen, tells us about apocalyptic predictions, quite similar to those of Chet Snow, which Kübler-Ross endorses without hesitation. Rosen had seen an old-fashioned horsedrawn carriage in her garage. "That's for after the earth changes," Kübler-Ross explained to him. She then showed him the "Future Map of the United States" mailed out by the "Earth Changes Report" and dated 1998–2001. California has become an island and much of the mid-West has been destroyed. Rosen told Kübler-Ross that he was from New York. She shook her head sadly. "You should move," she said, "this is one of the places that is not going to make it." As I already observed at the end of the last chapter, such predictions are extremely frightening. The only safe places left seem to be Atlantis and the Beyond; and, given the nature of some recent arrivals, I am not so sure about the Beyond. Kübler-Ross no longer has the four spirit guides supplied by Barham, but she still has her "spooks" or "guardian angels" who whisper advice and explanations to her. Nevada will disappear in the coming cataclysm. The spooks told her that this is punishment for all the nuclear testing that took place there.

Kübler-Ross has great difficulty accepting reality when reality is not pleasant. Her husband, who divorced her during the Barham years, died in 1994. Needless to say she expects to be with him in the next life. "To my mind," she told Rosen, "when you're married, you're married for life. That's my philosophy. So even after he married that young Lou-Lou, he was still my husband. In other words the divorce was not real." Emmanual Ross, the late husband, is not here to tell his side of the story. I am not at all sure that he would want to be reunited with Kübler-Ross in the next world. He evidently preferred a young Lou-Lou to an elderly astral traveler in this world and he may well feel the same way in the hereafter.

There have not been introductions to occultist books in recent years, but several of the new "spiritual" books carry Kübler-Ross's ringing endorsements on their covers. *The Extraordinary Life and Influence of Helena Blavatsky*, a hagiography by Sylvia Cranston, a fanatical reincarnationist, receives the following tribute:

An impressive book about a fantastic and enlightened lady. I am only sorry she lived a century too early. How I would have loved to work with her, be inspired by her, and have traveled and talked with her!

Unless Madame Blavatsky has already left the Beyond for another incarnation on the earth, Kübler-Ross should have an opportunity of meeting her after her "transition." I would love to be present at such a meeting. Other books that have been significantly aided by Kübler-Ross's support are the recent best sellers *Closed to the Light* by the pediatrician Melvin Morse, *Embraced by the Light* by Betty Eadie, and *The Celestine Prophesy* by James Wesfield. All three authors, needless to say, are enthusiastic admirers of Kübler-Ross.

In the January 1995 interview in the *Times Magazine* Kübler-Ross speaks with the same total certainty about a blissful life after death as she did in the Barham days. "It's just the most beautiful thing that can ever happen to you," she told Rosen who explains that there was "a look of beatific conviction on her creased face." Kübler-Ross showed him the framed picture of a patient of hers who had died. She was an attractive young woman who had been paralyzed from the waist down. Kübler-Ross quite casually offered the consoling reflection that "she is on the other side now, dancing and singing."

The day after the interview Rosen met Kübler-Ross again at the Shenandoah Valley Airport. People kept rushing over to embrace her. "Isn't she wonderful?" asked a woman who was X-raying Rosen's suitcase. There is no evidence that these people were freaks or fanatical occultists. They seemed like under-educated, very average, middle-class Americans. It is not clear whether their adulation is for the work with dying patients or for Kübler-Ross's message that death is not the end. Perhaps it is for both. The question will undoubtedly be asked why skeptics like me do not leave Kübler-Ross alone. It will be said that people are happier if they can believe that death is not the end and in any event Kübler-Ross's message is harmless.

I do not agree that her message is harmless. It is certainly not dangerous like the messages of political fanatics—racists, Jew-baiters, people advocating the killing of physicians performing abortions, or creationists who would suppress the teaching of Darwin. It is harmful in a more subtle way. It lowers intellectual standards. In effect, if not in intention, it preaches that we should, at least in religious matters, believe whatever pleases us. The avoidance of pain is not the only good. There is also a value called "truthfulness." One of the great achievements of the human race is the scientific outlook and the readiness to accept highly unpleasant conclusions if they are supported by the available evidence. "Where traditional beliefs about the universe are concerned," Bertrand Russell wrote in one of his last books, "craven fears . . . are considered praiseworthy, while intellectual courage, unlike courage in battle, is regarded as unfeeling and materialistic." There can never be a good excuse, he goes on, "for refusing to face the evidence in favor of something unwelcome. It is not by delusion, however exalted, that mankind can prosper, but only by unswerving courage in the pursuit of truth."[15]

---

15. *Fact and Fiction* (London, 1957), p. 46.

13

Dr. Grof, LSD, and the Amorous Snake-Woman

Dr. Grof, LSD, and the Spring Grove Program

We already briefly met Dr. Grof in Chapter 11 as one of the recipients of a Kübler-Ross Preface. If Dr. Kübler-Ross is the most credulous person who ever lived, Dr. Grof has a strong claim to second place. He is a fervent believer in reincarnation and in the law of Karma. He also believes in an Ultimate Divine Principle, in panpsychism, and in the possibility of communicating with the dead. He believes that "transpersonal" experiences, by which he primarily means various mystical states induced by LSD, can convey "instant intuitive information about any aspect of the universe in the present, past, and future." These experiences imply that

> in a yet unexplained way, each human being contains information about the entire universe, has potential experiential access to all its parts, and in a sense *is* the whole cosmic network.[1]

In the course of these transpersonal experiences human beings can "identify" with the consciousness of animals, plants, or inorganic objects and processes. It is even possible "to experience consciousness of the entire biosphere, of the planet as a whole, or of the entire material universe."[2]

What has particularly endeared Dr. Grof to many occultists is his militant and indeed quite fanatical opposition to what he calls "the scientific worldview based on

---

1. "Survival After Death: Observations from Modern Consciousness Research," in G. Doore (Ed.), *What Survives?* (Los Angeles, 1990), p. 26.

2. Ibid., p. 25.

philosophical materialism," which teaches that "consciousness . . . is a product of the brain and thus critically dependent on its integrity."[3] The target of most of Dr. Grof's polemics is this scientific world-view that is embraced by most "sophisticated Westerners." The materialistic philosophy dismisses the belief in an afterlife as the product of primitive fears of individuals who have been denied the privilege of scientific knowledge."[4] Such a philosophy is both "pessimistic" and "nihilistic" and Dr. Grof is most definitely not a pessimist. On the contrary, he is a disciple of Dr. Pangloss, believing that all is well or, as he puts it in one place, that "everything is as it should be." The main reason for including Grof in the present book is of course his defense of reincarnation, but, as in the case of Kübler-Ross, I will also discuss several of his other pronouncements.

Grof was born in 1931 in what was then Czechoslovakia. He first became acquainted with LSD in 1955 when he was a medical student at the Charles University School of Medicine in Prague. He was working at that time as an assistant to Dr. George Roubicek who had been the first to call LSD to the attention of psychiatrists in Czechoslovakia. During 1955 and 1956 Grof observed the reactions of psychiatric patients to whom Dr. Roubicek had administered LSD and in 1956 he had his own first LSD session. We are not informed by Dr. Grof how many other sessions he had, but in an interview with Maya Pines he explained that he developed "religious insights" as a result of his own experiences while under the influence of the drug.[5] After graduating, Grof worked for a number of years in the Psychiatric Research Institute in Prague on a project in which a carefully selected group of seventy-two patients with various psychogenic disturbances, mostly chronic neuroses and psychosomatic illnesses, were treated with the aid of LSD. Grof soon abandoned the view, widely held at that time, that LSD was nothing more than an agent producing a "toxic psychosis." On the contrary, he came to regard LSD as a powerful therapeutic tool. It was a "catalyst" bringing to the surface "unconscious material from various deep levels of the personality."[6]

In 1965 Grof was invited to take part in an international conference on the use of LSD in psychiatry at Amityville, Long Island. He subsequently lectured elsewhere in the United States and during this tour he was offered a fellowship by the Fund for Research in Psychiatry in New Haven, Connecticut. In 1967 Grof permanently left Czechoslovakia to join a research group in the Spring Grove Hospital Center in Catonsville, Maryland. In 1963 the so-called Spring Grove program had initiated research into the use of LSD as an adjunct in the psychotherapy of alcoholics and neurotic inpatients. In 1968 the research was broadened to administer LSD to terminal cancer patients in the hope of alleviating their physical and emotional distress.

Before turning to Dr. Grof's work with terminal patients it should be mentioned

---

3. *The Human Encounter with Death* (from now on abbreviated as *HED*), written in conjunction with Joan Halifax (New York, 1977), p. 7.

4. *HED*, p. 6.

5. Maya Pines, *The Brain Changers* (New York, 1972), p. 86.

6. *Realms of the Human Unconscious* (New York, 1975, from now on abbreviated as *RHU*), p. 19.

that the psychiatrists and psychologists connected with the Spring Grove program were not the first investigators to administer LSD to dying patients. The earliest pioneers were two Chicago physicians, Eric Kast and Vincent Collins who used LSD with fifty cancer patients to find, in their own words, "an analgesic medication which would diminish the patient's suffering and permit him to participate in life with heightened intensity." Kast and Collins found LSD to be significantly more effective than either demerol or dilaudid, two of the most widely used narcotics with such patients. Kast and Collins also observed that some of the patients

> displayed a peculiar disregard for the gravity of their situations, and talked freely about their impending death with an affect considered inappropriate in our western civilization, but most beneficial to their own psychic states.[7]

In 1964 and 1965 Kast directed two further studies of the treatment of terminal cancer patients with LSD. In the first study there had been next to no counseling. In the later studies the use of LSD was combined with psychotherapy. The later studies confirmed the beneficial results of LSD both as a pain-reliever and as an agent "lifting the mood and the outlook" of a sizable percentage of the patients. Seventy-two percent of the eighty patients studied in the third investigation said that they had received valuable insights. In the conclusion of his report of the third study, Kast remarked:

> Patients who had been listless and depressed were touched to tears by the discovery of a depth of feeling they had not thought themselves capable. Although short-lived and transient, this happy state of affairs was a welcome change in their monotonous and isolated lives, and recollection of this experience days later often created similar elation. . . . In human terms, the short but profound impact of LSD on the dying patient was impressive.[8]

Kast suggested that LSD produces an "attenuation" of the ability to anticipate future events. It is known that LSD interferes with the ability to concentrate and "to form and manipulate symbols." Patients cease to be concerned about their impending death largely because they are unable to think seriously about it. LSD acts as a pain reliever because it diverts the patient's attention to other sensations. He resembles a preverbal infant "who flutters from one pleasureful experience or fantasy to another, oblivious of consequences."[9] Grof has nowhere challenged these conclusions. He admits that LSD can distort the subject's perception of the world. Although he is a firm believer in ESP and tells us that LSD subjects can be "unusually accurate" in their awareness of "the sitter's ideation and emotions without even looking at him," more

---

7. E. C. Kast and V. J. Collins, "Lysergic Acid Diethylamide As an Analgesic Agent," *Anesthesia and Analgesia*, 1964, p. 291.

8. Eric Kast, "LSD and the Dying Patient," *Chicago Medical School Quarterly*, 1966, pp. 86–87.

9. Eric Kast, "Pain and LSD-25: A Theory of Attenuation of Anticipation," in D. Solomon (Ed.), *LSD: The Consciousness Expanding Drug* (New York 1964), p. 243.

often than not the subject's claims are mistaken.[10] I emphasize this because Grof has a tendency to forget the reality-distorting effects of LSD when he gets carried away about the wonders of transpersonal experiences.

The Spring Grove treatment of terminal patients differed from Kast's investigations in a number of ways. In the first place there was far greater emphasis on psychotherapy. The patients received an average of ten hours of counseling during the two weeks prior to the LSD session and an average of three further hours of counseling during the week after. Patients were encouraged to give in to their feelings during the LSD session and to confront areas of emotional conflict. Perhaps, most significantly, they were told in advance of the "peak experience" which they were liable to have. Although Abraham Maslow—the psychologist who coined the term "peak experience"—as well as a number of other writers on the subject quite explicitly denied that peak experiences always necessarily involve a religious element, most of the Spring Grove psychologists appeared to equate peak experiences with religious experiences in which the individual makes contact with a transcendent reality. In any event, peak experiences were definitely encouraged by the members of the Spring Grove team who believed that they had great therapeutic value. Perhaps the least important difference concerned dosage. Kast had routinely used 100 micrograms. The Spring Grove psychiatrists used a dosage ranging from 200 to 500 micrograms. It was found that there was no dependable relationship between the depth of the experience and the dosage given to the patient. Some patients receiving low dosages had dramatic peak experiences, while others receiving high doses did not.

The Spring Grove group published several papers summarizing the results of their work with dying patients. They were least impressed with the pain-relieving effects of LSD. It was in the area of emotional functioning that LSD seemed to have the most pronounced results. The following conclusions are quoted from a report by four of the leading members of the group:

> We have noted decreased depression, anxiety, and fear of death, while observing increased relaxation, greater ease in medical management, and closer interpersonal family relationships with more openness and honesty. . . . It has been our clinical impression that the most dramatic therapeutic changes followed sessions in which the patient experienced an intense psychedelic peak experience. . . . Profound experiences of this kind were described by approximately 25 percent of the patients in this study. These patients were often those who seemed most completely free of a fear of death following their sessions.[11]

From 1967 on the work with dying patients at Spring Grove was directed by Walter Pahnke who had a degree in medicine as well as divinity. Pahnke drowned in 1971

---

10. *RHU*, p. 190.
11. W. A. Richards, Stanislav Grof, Louis Goodman, and Albert Kurland, "LSD—Assisted Psychotherapy and the Human Encounter with Death," *Journal of Transpersonal Psychology*, 1972, p. 142.

and was succeeded by Grof.[12] Although he does not have a degree in divinity, Grof was even more eager to obtain a religious or "conversion" experience in his patients. Maya Pines, who spent some time at Spring Grove, reports that Grof felt "no qualms about inducing religious experiences through drugs, in people who might otherwise never have any." In reply to one of her questions he said: "I don't think we are inducing religion—I believe it is an intrinsic part of human nature. The only question is whether or not we get in touch with it."[13]

The Therapeutic "Dyad"

"A new dimension was added to the endeavors" of the Spring Grove group in 1972 when "Joan Halifax joined the team as co-therapist and anthropological consultant."[14] These are the modest words of none other than Joan Halifax and Dr. Grof. On the jacket of *The Human Encounter with Death* Halifax is described as a "medical anthropologist, specializing in psychiatry and religion." We are also told that she is "presently (1977) working with the mythologist, Joseph Campbell." Not surprisingly, the jacket carries a lengthy endorsement from the same mythologist. I should remark in passing that I would consider any praise from this purveyor of mush a kiss of death.[15] Within *HED* Halifax is described as practicing an "orientation" called "visionary anthropology." Listed first among the practitioners of "visionary anthropology" is Carlos Castañeda. If Castañeda is typical of this orientation it might be more accurately described as fictitious anthropology.[16] In any event, when Joan Halifax joined the Spring Grove team it became possible for her and Dr. Grof to combine their backgrounds "in experimental psychiatry and medical anthropology" and to view the

---

12. Readers will be relieved to hear that Pahnke is not really dead. During a LSD session not long after his disappearance, his wife Eva, "had a very powerful vision of Walter and carried on a long and meaningful dialogue with him." Dr. Grof, whose account I am quoting, is totally convinced that Pahnke's reappearance was not a delusion. Pahnke asked Eva to return a book to a friend telling her the name of the friend and the location of the book. Eva did as she was told insisting that she had had no previous knowledge of book or friend ("Survival After Death: Observations from Modern Consciousness Research," op. cit. , p. 30). On the basis of what is usually found when such tales are investigated a skeptic will suspect that we have here an instance of the Ritchie-Wilmot syndrome.

13. *The Brain Changers*, op. cit., p. 89.

14. *HED*, p. 25.

15. Readers may be interested to learn that Joseph Campbell was also a pro-Nazi and violently anti-Semitic. The details can be found in two articles by Brendan Gill in the *New York Review of Books,* September 28 and November 9, 1989.

16. Castañeda is the author of *The Teachings of Don Juan: A Yaqui Way of Knowledge* (1968), and several other books supposedly based on conversations with Don Juan, his Yaqui mentor. These books had a large circulation and were praised by numerous reviewers. One of them was accepted as a doctoral dissertation by the anthropology department at UCLA. Castañeda was exposed as a faker in Richard de Mille's *Castañeda's Journey: The Power and the Allegory* (1976). *See also* the interesting correspondence in several issues of the *Zetetic (Skeptical Inquirer)* in 1977.

data from a "broad cross-cultural perspective." Grof and Halifax from now on worked as a "therapeutic dyad" and their exchange of opinions resulted in a "process of interdisciplinary cross-fertilization."[17] "Dyad" sounds like the name of a bird and, as we shall see shortly, Grof and Halifax pounced on dying patients like a couple of voracious birds when trying to convert them to a religious view of life prior to their LSD sessions.

One of the prime pieces of evidence for reincarnation offered by Grof are experiences of some of the dying patients during LSD treatment. The sessions are preceded by a preparatory period of two or three weeks in the course of which the patients had a number of discussions with Grof and Halifax. Many of these conversations "focus on philosophical, religious, and metaphysical issues." This, we are told, is hardly surprising, since "the confrontation with one's own physical impermanence" can accentuate interest "in the spiritual and philosophical dimensions of existence." Grof and Halifax evidently regard themselves as extremely broad-minded since they are not trying to foist any *particular* religion on the patients. Psychedelic experiences frequently have "important religious or mystical dimensions." It is therefore essential for the patient to obtain "clarification . . . of the role of religion and spirituality in human life."[18] Equally, the patient's "confusion regarding conflict between various creeds" must be removed. Those who distrust all religion can be reached by emphasizing that "the spiritual experiences in psychedelic sessions usually do not take an orthodox religious form." They do not "involve a personified godhead, a pantheon of intermediary saints, and formalized ritual procedures." "The focus of psychedelic spirituality," is "the awe and wonder one experiences when confronted with the creative forces of nature and the many mysteries of the *universal design*."[19] Furthermore, the "spiritual feelings" are

> associated with the dilemma of time and space, origin of matter, life and consciousness, dimensions and complexity of the universe and human existence, and *the ultimate purpose underlying the process of creation* [my italics].[20]

Grof and Halifax want to impress the reader with their freedom from parochialism or any narrow prejudices. They therefore add that the psychedelic religious experience frequently "involves elements totally alien to the individual's own religious tradition." A Christian or a Muslim, we are assured, "can discover the law of Karma" and become an ardent believer in reincarnation, and a rabbi may become converted to Zen Buddhism.

Grof and Halifax seem to be quite unable to realize that there could be an intelligent and well-informed human being who not only rejects religious ritual and belief in a personal godhead but who equally denies or questions the existence of a "universal design." I have no idea what is meant by "the dilemma of time and space"

---

17. *HED.*
18. Ibid., p. 29.
19. Ibid., my italics.
20. Ibid.

—one of many exceedingly obscure expressions which make their appearance in the Halifax-fertilized later writings—but questions of the origin of life and consciousness seem to be strictly scientific questions on which religious experiences, inside or outside LSD, cannot possibly shed any light. As for "the ultimate purpose underlying the process of creation," I feel obliged to inform Grof and Halifax that there are many renowned philosophers and scientists who, I am quite sure, have thought about these issues at least as much as they, and who have concluded that just as there is no "universal design," there is also no "ultimate purpose" and that the material universe was *not* created.

I am reminded of an experience I had when I became naturalized in the spring of 1956. The court clerk, after warning the assembled new citizens or would-be citizens that this was their last chance to admit any false statements in their application for naturalization, decided to give a philosophical lecture to his captive audience. He described the United States as a religious nation and contrasted it favorably with such "atheistic" states as the Soviet Union, Nazi Germany, and Fascist Italy. He then added that in America the most diverse religions were tolerated and that the new citizens were welcome to profess whatever religion they pleased so long as they were believers in *some* religion. The only ones not welcome were "the followers of Hegel" who reject all religion. I have often meant to write a letter to this gentleman enlightening him about the supposed atheism of Nazi Germany and Fascist Italy and the religious views of Hegel and the majority of his followers. However, what I found particularly galling was the assumption that religious freedom in the United States does not extend to unbelievers and that a person cannot be both a loyal American subject and an agnostic or atheist. I feel the same revulsion at the narrowmindedness of Grof and Halifax. I do not believe in brainwashing, not even of dying patients and not even when the intentions of the brainwashers are noble. (Do not most brainwashers think that they are acting in the interest of those whom they are indoctrinating?) Grof and Halifax tell us that they "clarify the role of religion and spirituality in human life" for their patients. What they mean, of course, is that they try to convince the patients of what *they* take this role to be. Do they also mention what Lucretius, Hume, Bertrand Russell, and Freud believed about the role of religion?

Bertrand Russell once described the religious indoctrination of defenseless children as "dastardly." Much the same applies to attempts to subject defenseless cancer patients to such indoctrination. Grof and Halifax not only misuse their position but also betray their own insecurity. Why cannot they leave the patients alone and just explain that they may have strange and intensely emotional experiences as a result of the administration of LSD?

When Grof and Halifax discuss the hopeless plight of unbelievers who have realized the inevitability of death, their views are indistinguishable from those of the most ignorant and bigoted religious fanatics. Kübler-Ross, in her valuable little book *Questions and Answers on Death and Dying*, written before she became a full-time apologist for survival, remarks that she has worked with only four "genuine true athe-

ists" and that "they died with amazing peace and acceptance, no different from a religious person."[21]

Grof and Halifax, basing themselves on purely *a priori* grounds, adopt a totally
different position. After mentioning the "existential dilemma," which human beings
face when they come to realize that "there is no escape from physical death" and that
they will sooner or later "have to leave this world bereft of everything that they have
achieved and accumulated," they at once assume that there is only one way in which
this dilemma can be overcome. The solution is "transcendence," which in this context is another word for survival after death:

> The crisis is resolved when people find referential points beyond the narrow bound-
> aries of the physical organism and limitations of their own life spans. It seems that
> everyone who experientially reaches these levels also develops convincing insights
> into the total relevance of the spiritual dimension to the universal scheme of things.[22]

I have news for Grof and Halifax. There have been a great many unbelievers, famous
ones as well as many others, like the patients mentioned by Kübler-Ross, not known
to the public at large, who did not believe in survival or a "universal scheme" and who
faced death with courage and serenity.

Psychiatrist and Metaphysician

In this chapter I am not primarily concerned with an evaluation of Grof's psychiatric
theories, but some of the passages quoted in later sections will not be intelligible without a brief account of his ideas in this area. Grof believes that neurotic and psychotic
disturbances are largely the result of birth trauma or what he calls "perinatal phenomena." "By "perinatal" Grof means experiences occurring "around" birth—during
birth or immediately preceding or immediately following biological birth. Although
very few psychiatrists support such a theory, Grof is by no means alone here. Similar views were expressed long ago by Otto Rank and more recently in England by
R. D. Laing and Frank Lake and in the United States by Arthur Janov and Thomas
Verny. Grof believes that in LSD sessions his patients can reexperience perinatal traumas and that this produces beneficial results. More recently when the use of LSD became illegal Grof has claimed to be able to induce similar reexperiences by means of
what he calls "holotropic" therapy. The holotropic technique is described in various
of Grof's later books, especially in *Beyond the Brain* (1985). It involves Eastern
breathing techniques accompanied by percussive music.

There are some grounds for questioning whether it is possible to remember a
birth trauma, with or without the aid of LSD. These doubts are due to what we know

---

21. *Questions and Answers on Death and Dying* (New York, 1974), p. 159.
22. *HED*, p. 47.

about the immaturity of the fetal brain and to recent research on the sensory and cognitive capacities of newborn children.[23] I should add that the reliving of a birth trauma might have beneficial effects even if the memory is illusory, but in fact there is no credible evidence that this is so. In a review of *Beyond the Brain*, Richard Morrock observes that some of Grof's enormous claims might be easier to accept if Grof "had included a few figures concerning how many of his patients are cured of specific symptoms, as opposed to those who are not or who developed new ones."[24] My own impression is that Grof has no talent for any kind of psychotherapy. His eyes are too firmly focused on the supernatural to allow any real interest in the mundane problems of most patients. One also cannot help wondering about his own contact with reality when reading his repeated declarations that "everything is as it should be" (which I will discuss later in this chapter), not to speak of his irresistible attraction to various occult fancies, about astral bodies, "group consciousness," communications by and with the dead, and many more. It is necessary to emphasize that even if Grof were right in his perinatal theories and even if his regressions produced significant therapeutic benefits, this would not prove anything about reincarnation or any of his "transpersonal" claims.

Grof's work with dying patients came to an end in 1973 when he received an appointment as "scholar-in-residence" at the Esalen Institute in California where he has been living ever since. Grof continues to be a prolific author and he is evidently regarded as a major star in the occultist firmament.

Joan Halifax, the visionary anthropologist, has disappeared from the later books. She has been replaced by Christina Grof who seems to be a somewhat gentler soul, but the religious fanaticism, especially in the books written by Grof on his own, is unchecked. The hatred of "materialistic" science is greater than ever, leading Grof to make some bizarre claims. "Those who complete the death-rebirth process," we are informed, "connect with intrinsic spiritual sources and realize that a mechanistic and materialistic world view is rooted in fear of birth and death."[25] The fear of death, I would have thought, inclines people to become believers in survival rather than "materialists." We are also told that materialists and other believers "suddenly see their entire picture of reality and general strategy of existence as false and inauthentic."[26] Materialistic philosophers and scientists have frequently taken pains to study all sides of basic issues and, in at least one fairly obvious sense, it is they who are authentic. It is believers like Grof and Halifax who shun the writings of the other side and they are the ones who are most naturally characterized as "inauthentic."

It is only fair to add that at least one well-known and respected scientists has taken Grof's theories about birth traumas seriously. In the last chapter of *Broca's*

---

23. For details see Barry L. Beyerstein's extremely valuable "The Brain and Consciousness: Implications for Psi Phenomena," *Skeptical Inquirer*, Winter 1987–88.

24. *Skeptical Inquirer*, Spring 1986, p. 279.

25. *Beyond the Brain*, p. 49.

26. Ibid.

Brain (1979) entitled "The Amniotic Universe" Carl Sagan not only endorses Grof's perinatal theories but engages in wild and wooly speculation about how perinatal experiences may cause cosmologists to adopt different theoretical models. There is also an extremely confused discussion of the existence of God claiming that atheism is no more tenable than belief in God. I admire some of Sagan's work, but this chapter must be regarded as an aberration.

This is perhaps the place to mention that John Mack, the Harvard psychiatrist who not long ago published *The Abduction: Human Encounters with Aliens*, a widely discussed book about alien abductions, consulted Grof during his journey into mysticism and silliness. According to an article by Steven Rae in the *New York Times Sunday Magazine*, Mack met Grof in 1987 at a United States-Soviet conference of physicians at the Esalen Institute. In the course of this fateful meeting between two kindred spirits Mack had a session with Grof which he found "revelatory." "I profoundly became in touch," Mack is quoted, "with the loss of my mother as an infant and my father's grief at the time."[27] It is not clear whether the treatment produced any result beyond putting Mack in touch with his feelings of loss. My guess is that it did not or we would have been told. It would be wrong to blame Grof for Mack's subsequent "development" or what many of us would describe as his subsequent descent. According to Rae, he "plunged" into Eastern philosophy and Shamanism and eventually linked up with Budd Hopkins, the "father" of the UFO abduction movement. I do not recall any explicit endorsement of UFO abductions by Grof, but the bibliography of the *Stormy Search for the Self*, a book written by him in conjunction with Christina, has a bibliography with sections on "Kundalini Awakening," "Past-life Experiences and Karma," "Channeling," and "Experiences of UFO Encounters and Extra-terrestrial Contact." I do not believe that Grof ever heard of an occult theory he did not like. My guess is that if he does not actually believe in alien abductions, he at least takes this nonsense quite seriously.

At the end of the Preface to *Realms of the Human Unconscious* Grof mentions a grandiose five-volume work on which he was embarking. *RHU* was to be the first volume and *HED*, which was then in active preparation, was to be the second. The fifth and final volume, which was never written, was to "focus on the philosophical and spiritual dimensions of the LSD experience, with special emphasis on ontological and cosmological issues." It was to describe in detail "the surprisingly consistent metaphysical system that seemed to be emerging from the experimentation with psychedelic substances."[28] It is evident that this volume was to be the culmination of Grof's work and that he regards himself above all as a metaphysician. Even in the absence of this culminating volume we possess a pretty clear idea of the highlights of Grof's "surprisingly consistent metaphysical system"; and the remaining sections of the

---

27. Stephen Rae, "John Mack," *New York Times Magazine*, March 20, 1994.

28. *RHU*, p. xvii.

present chapter are devoted to an examination of these highlights which include of course a defense of survival after death in general and reincarnation in particular.

"The Supreme and Ultimate Principle"

A section near the end of *RHU* is entitled "Consciousness of the Universal Mind." Grof tells us that this consciousness is one of the "most profound and total experiences observed in LSD sessions." The individual "senses" that he has "experientially encompassed the totality of existence." Not only does the individual sense that he has "encompassed the totality of existence," but he also "feels that he has reached the reality underlying all realities and is confronted with the supreme ultimate principle that represents all Being." In this experience, it becomes apparent that matter, space and time are "illusions." These illusions as well as "an infinite number of other subjective realities have been completely transcended." Besides being "transcended," matter, space, time, and the infinite number of other realities have been "finally reduced to this one mode of consciousness [i.e., the universal mind] which is their common source and denominator."[29]

A great deal of this will not seem particularly strange or novel to students of Eastern mysticism or to those familiar with the system of Absolute Idealism as expounded in the writings of Hegel, Fichte, F. H. Bradley, and Josiah Royce. Returning to the Universal Mind, it is a "formless, dimensionless and intangible principle" and is "characterized by infinite existence, infinite awareness . . . and infinite bliss."[30] In a later work, the Universal Mind is also referred to as the "supracosmic Void" and we are told that it is "the mysterious primordial emptiness and nothingness that is conscious of itself and contains all existence in germinal form."[31] We are evidently face to face with something colossal, tremendous and overwhelming: "even a short experiential exposure to it satisfied the subject's intellectual, philosophical, and spiritual craving."[32]

It is hardly surprising that such a "profound transcendental experience" should have all kinds of desirable effects on the individual fortunate enough to have undergone it. For one thing, it has "a very beneficial effect" on his physical and emotional well-being. It is regrettable that none of the physical and emotional benefits are spelled out. The experience also—and Grof seems to regard this as at least equally important—creates "in him a keen interest in religious, mystical and philosophical issues, and a strong need to incorporate the spiritual dimension into his way of life."[33] Among the "important concomitants" of the experience there are "intuitive insights" into "the Buddhist concept of the wheel of death and rebirth" and "the process of cre-

29. Ibid., p. 203.
30. *RHU*, p. 204.
31. *Beyond the Brain* (Albany, NY, 1985), p. 131.
32. *RHU*, p. 204.
33. Ibid., p. 208.

ation of the phenomenal world as we know it."[34] Cosmologists and really all of us will be disappointed to learn that the details of the "creation of the phenomenal world" are not revealed.

In the course of this supreme experience "all the questions that have ever been asked seem to have been answered" and "there is no need to question any further."[35] Although the subject of the experience has the answers to all questions he cannot communicate them to the rest of us. The experience itself is "boundless, unfathomable, and ineffable" and as a consequence "verbal communication and the symbolic structure of our everyday language seem to be a ridiculously inadequate means to capture and convey its nature and quality."[36]

The inability of Grof and the other privileged subjects to communicate any of the answers produces a feeling of being let down in me similar to what I experienced when Moody told us that his omniscient woman had forgotten everything she had learned during her visit to the Beyond. Among other things I should have loved to know if in the year 2542 there were giant apples, peaches and strawberries as asserted by Larry-Zeku who had been progressed into the future by the inimitable Dr. Bruce Goldberg. More seriously, if, in spite of the "ridiculous inadequacy" of language, we can ask a certain question, then we should surely also be able to express the answer, *if we have it*. It is always the same with these prophets of the ultimate: they make grandiose claims, but when we press them for something concrete, we are left empty-handed. I am reminded of a story told by Bertrand Russell in his "Outline of Intellectual Rubbish."[37] In northern New York State in the early nineteenth century, a prophetess, who lived beside a lake, announced to her followers that she possessed the power of walking on water and that she was going to demonstrate it the next morning. At the stated time the followers assembled at the lake. "Are all of you totally persuaded that I can walk on water?" she asked the faithful and with one voice they replied, "We are." In that case, she responded, "there is no need for me to do so."

All Is Well

Another fruit of the supreme experience—though I gather that it is also obtained by lesser LSD experiences—is the insight that the world "is a fascinating and basically friendly place." In *HED* Grof and Halifax proceed, quite evidently approving this sentiment of their patients, that "everything in the universe appears perfect, exactly as it should be."[38] The same point is made by Grof on his own in *RHU*. He there tells us that in the "ecstasy exemplified by the feeling of cosmic unity," the subject "finds it

---

34. *RHU*, p. 204.
35. Ibid.
36. Ibid., p. 203.
37. *Unpopular Essays* (New York, 1950), pp. 110–11.
38. *HED*, p. 211.

difficult to see any negative aspects in the world and in the very structure of the cosmic design; everything appears perfect, *everything is as it should be.*"[39]

To take care of the objections of unenlightened skeptics Grof quotes from one of the lectures given by Baba Ram Dass (who was once known by the more prosaic name of Richard Alpert): "The world is absolutely perfect, including your dissatisfaction with it and your efforts to change it."[40]

Grof is entirely satisfied with this evasive double-talk and amplifies it in the following passage:

> This attitude toward the universe does not have to result in inactivity and passive acceptance of the status quo. It is compatible with a creative life style, striving for self-actualization, and various reformatory tendencies.[41]

A few days before I am writing this paragraph the newspapers reported the case of two neo-Nazi adolescent skin-heads who murdered their parents as well as their younger brother. After that they picked up a stray dog, put firecrackers in his mouth and blew him up. I wonder how Grof would reconcile his doctrine that all is well with this event—or billions of others. He does not show the slightest interest in social or political questions, but even he has probably heard of Auschwitz and of Bosnia. I wonder if he would care to present his cheerful message to Auschwitz survivors or to the citizens of Sarajevo.

There is no sense in arguing with a person who lives in the same world as the rest of us and who believes that everything is as it should be. What he needs is not a refutation but help. I would send Dr. Grof a copy of *Candide* but I do not think that he would get the point.

Group Consciousness

One of Grof's favorite transpersonal experiences is what he calls "group consciousness." It is claimed that during LSD sessions the subject can identify with the whole of certain groups. Grof's descriptions of these experiences are very similar to the account Kübler-Ross gave of her shattering and "indescribable" experience in Monroe's guest house in the course of which she "went through every single death of every single one of her thousands of patients a thousand times over." In an LSD session, Grof writes,

> it is possible to experience the totality of suffering of all the soldiers who have ever died on battlefields since the beginning of history, the revolutionary fervor of all the Communists of the world obsessed by the idea of overthrowing the capitalist

---

39. *RHU*, pp. 106–107, my italics.
40. Ibid., 107.
41. Ibid.

regimes, or the tenderness of all mothers loving their children and feeling concerned about their well-being.[42]

As if this were not enough, the LSD subject can also, "in an extreme form" of this phenomenon, "experience his consciousness expanding to encompass every member of the human race—indeed, all of humanity."[43] When I first read these claims I found them utterly incredible. In the first place, even allowing for changes in time scales, it would take the patient much too long to experience the tenderness of every tender mother who ever lived. Neglecting the tediousness of such a task, which would be liable to drive the subject to utter distraction, it just cannot be done within a single LSD session, even if it was as long as ten or twelve hours. Has Grof visualized what reproducing or witnessing all these experiences would amount to? Millions of American mothers, millions of African, British, French, German, Austrian, Russian, Polish, Czech, Lebanese, Persian mothers; billions of Indian and Chinese mothers, to mention a few major subgroups. And what about mothers of past centuries all the way back to the first recognizably human mothers? Furthermore, how could the subject (or Grof) ever be sure that every last mother had been included? Suppose 10,000 million mothers had been included in the experience. Would it not be possible to miss out on another, perhaps in Albania or Afghanistan or Brazil or Nairobi?

The capacity for group consciousness was also possessed by one of the terminal patients whose "psychedelic biographies" Grof and Halifax supply in *HED*. Suzanne, the patient whose tragic fate I will describe later in this chapter, and who had been able to travel out of her body even before her treatment by Grof and Halifax, suddenly, in her second LSD session, displayed this remarkable gift. After her emotions rapidly changed from "metaphysical loneliness" (whatever this means) to "striving for reunion" and from murderous rage to passionate love, she

> felt a deep identification with all of the mothers who have ever given birth and all children who have ever been born; then she subjectively became all of them. Through birth and death, she appeared to be connected with all of suffering humanity, millions and millions of people crying in pain. She was crying with them and at the same time *was* them, experiencing the ecstasy of this union in agony.[44]

Later in this session we are told that Suzanne

> became the mother of all the men who have ever been killed in all the wars in human history. As she became all these mothers and all these children, she felt that she was growing inside of herself and trying to give birth to herself.[45]

---

42. *RHU*, p. 180.
43. Ibid.
44. *HED*, p. 87.
45. Ibid.

One has to be firm and must not allow oneself to be intimidated by the fervor of Grof's claims. We may allow that under LSD human beings may have strange and liberating experiences—something to which less mystical writers than Grof have testified. However, it is nonsense to say that Suzanne *was* all the millions of people who have been crying in pain. It should be emphasized that Grof does not merely mean what is usually meant when a person says that he can identify with a given group. If I have been accused of a crime I did not commit (or even if I have not) I might say that I can identify with all the many people who have been the victims of false accusations. I would mean that I have a feeling or sensation which is qualitatively identical or very similar to the feelings which I believe the other members of this class to have experienced. Grof means nothing so simple and straightforward.

Grof and the Amorous Snake-Woman

Grof and Halifax are fully convinced of the possibility of time travel. We must not allow ourselves to be "brainwashed into accepting the simple-minded concept of one-dimensional time and three-dimensional space." Grof is quoting a Czech psychiatrist here who was reporting his experience during an LSD session:

> It appeared to me rather obvious that there are no limits in the realm of spirits and that time and space are arbitrary constructs of the mind . . . A single second and eternity seem to be freely interchangeable.[46]

In any event, time, as experienced under LSD, is something quite different from the ordinary clock time of our waking lives; and there is no reason to regard our ordinary time as more real. "The person in an unusual state of consciousness," Grof and Halifax write, "experiences time in a way that is quite different from our everyday perception of clock time." During several minutes of clock time, LSD subjects can

> experience entire lifetimes, centuries, millenniums, even aeons. Similarly, a dying individual can relive his entire life within several seconds and within minutes of clock-time he can experience an entire cosmic journey.[47]

Grof and Halifax appear to have no doubt that we can quite literally go back into the past and also forward into the future. As noted in Chapters 5 and 6, hypnotic regressionists believe that these feats can be accomplished by means of hypnosis. Grof and Halifax think that it can be done by means of LSD. In the course of "ancestral experiences" the subject relives experiences of his parents and grandparents. One woman, a fifty-year-

---

46. *RHU*, p. 187.
47. "Psychedelics and the Experience of Death," in Arnold Toynbee, et al., *Life After Death* (London, 1976), p. 158.

old psychologist whom he calls Nadja, "became her mother" and experienced events that took place during her mother's childhood. The mother was alive and fully confirmed the accuracy of her daughter's "memory." Grof insists that Nadja could not possibly have known about these events prior to the LSD session. On occasions, ancestral experiences "reach back many generations or even centuries." Such experiences are by no means without psychological value. On the contrary, they are "usually associated with interesting insights: the subject can relate the archaic elements to his present personality and become aware of their influence on his everyday behavior." Even more significant insights are obtained from the "actual reliving of episodes . . . specific and rich in concrete detail" from the lives of one's more immediate ancestors. As a result of these experiences some patients achieved a new understanding of some of their "personal problems and conflicts." They realized that these problems were not primarily "intrapsychic problems," i.e., the result of their own early experiences, but could be traced back to "friction points, incompatibilities, and incongruencies between their maternal and paternal lineages."[48]

Not only can a person "become" his human ancestor, he can also "identify" (whatever exactly this means) with animals on various levels of phylogenetic development. The animals with whom LSD subjects most frequently identify are mammals, reptiles, birds, amphibians, and various species of fish. Occasionally they also identify with insects, snails, octopuses, and jellyfish. The identification process is "complex and authentic" and includes "size, body image, a variety of specific physiological sensations, particularly emotions and instinctual drives, as well as unusual perceptions of the environment." The person who has such an experience may get an "illuminating insight into what it feels like when a snake is hungry, when a turtle is sexually excited, when a hummingbird is feeding its young, or when a shark breathes through its gills."[49]

One of the identifications with an animal which Grof reports in detail concerns Renata, a patient suffering from "extremely serious neurotic and borderline psychotic symptoms." During one of her sessions Renata became a reptile:

> At one point in her session, Renata had a sense of complete identification with a female of a species of large reptiles that became extinct millions of years ago. She felt sleepy and lazy as she rested on sand by a big lake and basked luxuriously in the sun. While experiencing this in the session, she opened her eyes and looked at the therapist, who seemed transformed into a good-looking male of the same species; her feelings of laziness immediately vanished, and she experienced a strong sexual arousal and attraction. According to her description, these feelings did not have anything to do with human erotic and sexual excitement; it was a quite unique and specific "reptilian" interest in and attraction to the opposite sex. Any notion of the mouth, genitals, or other parts of the body that might interest her in a human partner was completely missing. She was absolutely fascinated by scalelike facets that

---

48. *RHU*, p. 163.
49. Ibid, p. 172.

she visualized on the side of the therapist's head. One large field of this sort seemed to have a shape and color that she found irresistible; it appeared to be radiating powerful sexual vibrations.[50]

On consulting a friend who was a zoologist Grof learned that in certain reptiles distinctly colored areas on the head "play an important role as triggers of sexual arousal."[51] It is implied that Renata had no special zoological interest and that she could not possibly have known this fact about the sex life of reptiles.

It is not entirely clear what conclusion this story is supposed to vindicate. Grof either believes that we have here a case of reincarnation, that the soul which now inhabits Renata's body once animated that of the snake and remembers her mating habits or that Renata "tuned" into the mind of the female snake while the snake was sexually aroused. Now, I do not for a moment doubt that if Renata had been a female snake and Dr. Grof a male, she would have found him irresistibly attractive. However, aside from the fact that neither of the occultist explanations just mentioned is really logically coherent, there are two more prosaic explanations of Grof's *alleged* observations.

First, I am not at all satisfied that Renata really behaved in the way described by Grof. It seems to me quite likely that what he has given us are assorted inferences produced by his zeal to obtain a case calling for an explanation in transpersonal terms. Readers of Grof soon discover that he suffers from a chronic inability to distinguish between observation and inference. Furthermore, it is certainly true that most people are not informed about the mating habits of snakes, but it is not impossible that Renata did somehow pick up this knowledge in a natural way. If she had been asked appropriate questions under hypnosis the source of her information might well have been found. I think that the first of my explanations is more plausible.

Karmic Cyclones

It is too bad that the *National Enquirer* or other tabloids did not get hold of Grof and his snake story. We might have been treated to a headline like "Top Czech Scientist Proves Woman Was Snake." For that matter it is too bad that they apparently never heard about the reappearance of Mary Swartz in Kübler-Ross's office. This would have given us a title like "Dead Woman Visits Famed Psychiatrist." Grof's "Karmic resolutions," to be discussed in the present section, are on the same level as the snake woman and Mary Swartz's visit to Kübler-Ross.

According to Karmic theory, as understood and preached by Grof, many people found themselves in previous incarnations in situations involving "physical pain, bitterness, hatred and murderous aggression, inhuman terror and anguish, lustful passion,

---

50. Ibid., p. 173.
51. Ibid.

insane jealousy, or morbid greed and avarice."[52] Grof talks a great deal about "karmic imprinting." If we have a situation in which there is an oppressor and a victim, what gets "imprinted" on the Karmas of the victim as well as the oppressor is the "dyadic traumatic pattern" of such a negative situation. We are faced with "an unfinished Gestalt which in subsequent lifetimes requires repetition and resolution." Grof asserts that such a "karmic fixation" *cannot* be successfully worked through in an LSD session by simply allowing the patient to relive the painful emotions of the destructive Karmic scene. What is required for a "satisfying completion" is a "transcendence" of the event, "emotionally, ethically, and spiritually," which consists in an act of "final" forgiveness. This is far from easy, but it carries with it a reward of stupendous magnitude: when the resolution of a Karmic pattern takes place and the patient is liberated from its bonds, he experiences "a sense of paramount accomplishment and triumph." Frequently, we are told, the patient observes that this is the event for which he has been waiting for many centuries. Such a resolution can result in "feelings of indescribable bliss." To the subject, it appears to be "dictated by cosmic forces" and is altogether "beyond his comprehension." On several occasions the liberation was accompanied by the experience of a "gigantic karmic hurricane or cyclone" which, according to Grof, blows "through the centuries . . . tearing karmic bonds related to scenes from various lifetimes" in which the original imprint had been repeated.[53]

Perhaps Grof's most astonishing claims about Karmic resolutions occur in a section of *RHU* entitled "Significance of Transpersonal Experiences in LSD Psychotherapy." He refers there to the "powerful effect" which the activation of a past-incarnation experience can have on the patient's life during the post-session interval. If it has not been resolved during the session, the specific content of the patient's karmic pattern may influence his "perception of himself, of his present life situation, and of his social network."[54] He may experience the feeling of being "crushed by the burden of his 'bad karma' " and his life may become dominated by his desire to undo the consequences of the acts he carried out in his earlier life. If, conversely, the LSD session brought about the resolution of his Karmic pattern, it will result in "very beneficial change." In such a case "the simplification, the clarification and improvement" in his interpersonal relations will sometimes be quite "dramatic."[55] Nor is this all. In a remarkable passage Grof insists that the resolution of a Karmic pattern in a LSD session may have dramatic effects on *other* persons involving changes which could not possibly have been directly influenced by any of the patient's own actions after the session:

> Thus, various specific changes have occurred in the life and behavior of other people who were, according to the subject's description, part of a particular karmic pattern that has been worked through in an LSD session. Such individuals were not pre-

---

52. Ibid., p. 175.
53. Ibid., p. 176.
54. Ibid., p. 205.
55. Ibid., pp. 206–207.

sent in the session or aware of it, and sometimes they were not even a part of the subject's immediate life situation; they were at various distant places, and there was no real contact between them and the subject. The time of specific changes in their lives coincided exactly with the manifestation, unfolding, and resolution of the karmic pattern in the LSD session. These unusual coincidences observed in LSD work involving past-incarnation experiences seem to indicate that events in the sessions are part of a broader pattern, the scope of which transcends the energy field of the individual.[56]

The changes which occur in persons other than the LSD subject at the precise moment at which his Karmic pattern was resolved are instances of transpersonal phenomena "where the application of the principle of causality fails to bring satisfactory results."[57]

Such stories of Karmic resolutions and their remarkable consequences made interesting plots for Hollywood movies of the silent era. Nowadays, outside the works of Grof, they occur only in the pages of the *National Enquirer* and other tabloids. Speaking seriously, a claim of this kind, however sincerely it is put forward, should be *disregarded* by all sane and sober men, unless it is supported by a full list of the names of all the persons in question, their addresses past and present, and an *exact* description of the events that supposedly took place at the time of the "resolution" of the Karmic pattern during the LSD session in Grof's office in Prague. I have no doubt that if this information were supplied, it would be found either that the events in question did not occur or that they were not really so peculiar and that they can be quite easily explained without assuming any mysterious bond between them and what transpired in Grof's office. Many equally wild claims have been made in the past. Whenever it was possible to subject them to a critical scrutiny, the evidence simply evaporated. Incidentally, Grof is mistaken in thinking that the principle of causality would break down if his very nebulous view about the "broader pattern transcending the energy fields of the individual" were correct. In that case we would have to replace various accepted causal explanations with new and strange causal laws in which features of the "broader pattern" would be included among the causal factors.

This is perhaps the place to mention that his LSD observations have made Grof a champion of astrology as well as alchemy. He tells us that subjects who had previously ridiculed astrology and adopted a condescending attitude toward alchemy totally changed their outlook in the course of their LSD therapy. They then "discovered deeper meaning in these systems and gained a deeper appreciation of their metaphysical relevance."[58] Grof does not tell us what the "deeper meaning" and the "metaphysical relevance" of astrology and alchemy consist of. Grof probably believes that accepting these "systems" also involves rejection of the principle of causality. If he does, this would be another mistake. Accepting the systems would amount to replacing one set of causal explanations by others which, to most contemporary scientists, seem exceedingly strange and implausible.

---

56. Ibid., p. 207.
57. Ibid.
58. Ibid., p. 201.

Journeys into the Future

It will be remembered that according to Grof transpersonal experiences can convey "instant intuitive information about any aspect of the universe in the present, past and future."[59] Grof does not seem to have encountered any special problems about "intuitive" observations of the past as exemplified by the information which Nadja, the fifty-year-old psychologist, obtained about events in the childhood of her mother. Surely nothing would impress skeptics more than if Grof came up with similarly specific information about the future. In a section of *RHU* tantalizingly headed "Precognition, Clairvoyance, Clairaudience, and 'Time Travels' " he informs us that some of his patients, particularly in advanced sessions of LSD therapy, report witnessing "complex and detailed scenes of future happening in the form of vivid clairvoyant visions."[60] They can even hear "the acoustic concomitants" of these scenes, whether they are the ordinary sounds of everyday life or "alarming signals" like ambulance sirens or the sound of fire engines. It is notoriously difficult, if not impossible, to subject accounts of journeys into the past to any kind of objective verification. If a patient identifies with a Roman soldier or a Czech patriot living more than three centuries earlier, the subjects of the identification are not available for questioning. In the case of clairvoyant predictions, on the other hand, especially if they are about the relatively near future, we ought to be in a position to test the statements. Grof carefully refrains from saying that testing shows such LSD-inspired clairvoyant predictions to be false, but what he tells us is not very impressive. After reporting that "some of these experiences manifest various degrees of similarity with actual events occurring at a later time," he lamely declares that "objective verification in this area can be particularly difficult." Grof offers several reasons for this "difficulty." Unless such predictions "are reported and clearly documented during the LSD session, there is a great danger of contamination of data." Among the "major pitfalls" involved here, Grof lists "loose interpretation of events, distortions of memory, and the possibility of *déjà vu* phenomena during the perception of later occurrences."[61]

A critical reader will not find these remarks convincing. They are an alibi and a very feeble one at that. Since Grof himself is the person conducting and supervising the LSD session, what is to prevent him from properly recording every statement made by his subject so that there can be no question about what was and what was not predicted? What is more, the subject can be interrogated during the LSD session and pressed for more detailed information if his initial predictions were too vague. As for the "various degrees of similarity" between the scenes "witnessed" by the patient and the actual events which occurred later on, this is so vague that it applies to countless other predictions made by human beings for whom nobody claims clairvoyant powers.

---

59. "Survival After Death," in Doore (Ed.) , *What Survives?*, op. cit., p. 26.
60. *RHU* p. 177.
61. P. 178.

We have now evidently come to cop-out time. As in the case of Moody's omniscient woman and Grof's claim that experience of the Ultimate Divine Principle allows us to answer all questions, we are left empty-handed. If the LSD-inspired "transcendence of the usual limitations of time" turns out to be deceptive in the direction of the future one cannot help wondering how genuine it is in relation to the past.

The Death-Rebirth Experience

The evidence so far reported on which Grof bases his belief in reincarnation are phylogenetic memories experienced by his patients under the influence of LSD and the "karmic cyclones." However, both Grof and Halifax regard another class of LSD experiences as providing our most decisive evidence for the independence of consciousness from the brain and, more specifically, for the truth of reincarnation. These are "experiences of death and rebirth followed by feelings of cosmic unity."[62]

In various places Grof has offered general descriptions of these experiences of death and rebirth. In his experience of death the LSD patient commonly has visions of funerals, hearses, cemeteries, coffins, decaying cadavers, and dying human beings. The awareness of death is not, however, "mediated by symbolic means alone." At its "basis" it is "an extremely realistic feeling of the ultimate biological crisis."[63] The LSD subject, we are told,

> experiences final biological destruction, emotional defeat, intellectual debacle, and utmost moral humiliation. . . . He feels that he is an absolute failure in life from any imaginable point of view; his entire world seems to be collapsing, and he is losing all previously meaningful reference points.[64]

Grof calls this experience "ego death" and he tells us that many subjects confuse it with real dying. "The entire experience," Grof concludes, is "a profound firsthand experience of terminal agony."[65]

After experiencing his ego death, the LSD subject commonly has experiences in which he "feels cleansed and purged, as if he had disposed of an incredible amount of 'garbage,' guilt, aggression, and anxiety." His visual imagery frequently includes scenes from "the innocent world of newborn animals," such as parent animals feeding their young and birds hatching from eggs. The rebirth is also represented by the reaching of a high peak after a difficult assent. Occasionally, too, the subject has visions of "blinding white or golden light." The atmosphere in which this experience

---

62. *HED*, p. 19.
63. Ibid., p. 46.
64. *RHU*, p. 139.
65. *HED*, p. 46.

takes place is one of "liberation, redemption . . . love and forgiveness."[66] The person discovers in himself powerful "positive values" such as a sense of justice, appreciation of beauty, self-respect and respect for others as well as overflowing love. Grof cannot resist adding a theological interpretation, *allegedly* offered by the subject himself. The individual experiences these values "as a natural, logical and integral part of a higher universal order."[67]

Such experiences constitute a "profound encounter with one's own impermanence" and have "very complex . . . biological, emotional, intellectual, philosophical, and metaphysical dimensions."[68] Many of the patients dramatically changed "their attitudes toward dying and their concepts of death." The changed attitudes included a lessening in the fear of "their own physiological demise." They no longer dreaded this event because they had become

> open to the possibility of consciousness existing after clinical death, and tended to view the process of dying as an adventure in consciousness rather than the ultimate biological disaster.[69]

Helped no doubt in their philosophical reflections by Grof and Halifax, the patients now "begin to see death and dying as a cosmic voyage into the unknown."[70]

Chapter 5 of *HED* is entitled "Psychedelic Biographies" and contains detailed accounts of the LSD treatment of six terminal patients. All cases are moving and Grof and Halifax themselves appear *here* not as sophists and religious fanatics but as compassionate physicians. Although we had been told on numerous occasions that the death-rebirth phenomenon is practically universal among LSD patients, only two of the six individuals had such an experience. One of them concerns Jesse, an unskilled laborer aged forty-five, who was suffering from a cancer covering his face and neck. In spite of radiation and chemotherapy the malignancy was spreading rapidly. When Grof and Halifax first met him, he was suffering from a great variety of physical and emotional symptoms. He complained of severe pain, extreme fatigue, coughing, and difficulties in swallowing. He also had frequent crying spells, felt deeply depressed, and extremely anxious. His sleep was disturbed. He felt that his death was impending, but at the same time he was anxiously clinging to life. He was also much preoccupied with the "aesthetic" aspects of his illness—the disfiguration of face and neck and the odor of the bandages which were soaked with the fluid that was leaking from his ulcerations. Jesse had only one session with DPT (dipropyltrytramine, a psychedelic drug similar to LSD). During the preparation for this session he expressed his overwhelming fear of death. He entertained two contradictory notions about death,

66. *RHU*, p. 139.
67. Ibid., p. 140.
68. *HED*, p. 19.
69. Ibid., p. 20.
70. Ibid.

both of which were in different ways terrifying. He had been brought up as a strict Catholic. According to this teaching the quality of life after death depends on one's conduct here on earth. Jesse had been living "in sin" with a widowed woman for a number of years prior to the onset of his illness and to the extent to which he believed his religion, he appeared to face tortures for all eternity. However, he was not fully convinced of this teaching and also entertained the possibility that death was "the absolute end of everything, a step into nothingness and darkness, where one loses everything there is."[71] Faced with these alternatives, it is not surprising that, in spite of his terrible physical suffering, Jesse was so intensely clinging to life.

During the session Jesse repeatedly expressed his regret of having agreed to the psychedelic treatment and he did his utmost not to surrender to the experience. He felt that he would die if he gave in and allowed the feelings and images to come freely. Eventually he could not resist the effects of the drug and began to experience scenes of intense violence and destruction. He first had visions of animals of enormous size attacking him. He then witnessed "thousands of war scenes full of aggression and destruction" and other situations in which numerous people were dying. In a lone episode concluding this phase of his experience he saw junkyards "strewn with corpses, carcasses, skeletons, rotting offal, and trashcans spreading foul odors."[72] His own body, covered with cancerous ulcerations and wrapped in evil-smelling bandages, was also lying in a junkyard. All this mess and garbage was suddenly consumed and purified by the flames of a gigantic wall of fire. Along with the other contents of the junkyard, Jesse's flesh and bones were destroyed, but his soul survived the destruction of his body. He now found himself before God. In a final judgment God determined that Jesse's virtues outweighed his transgressions and sins. Jesse thereupon felt a sense of tremendous relief. He heard celestial music and angelic singing. Grof and Halifax cannot for long refrain from using mystical language and we are told that Jesse heard a reassuring message which, according to the account by Grof and Halifax, came to him "through supernatural, nonverbal channels":

> When you die, your body will be destroyed, but you will be saved; your soul will be with you all the time. You will come back to earth, you will be living again, but you do not know what you will be on the next earth.[73]

Jesse lived only another five days after the session. During this period his pain was lessened and his depression and anxiety disappeared altogether. Although it was a notion so alien to his religious background, he "emerged from the session with deep belief in the possibility of reincarnation." He now "accepted" his situation. The prospect of another incarnation freed him from the need of clinging to a body wrecked by cancer. Grof and Halifax agree that he might have lived a little longer if he had continued to

---

71. Ibid., p. 81.
72. Ibid., p. 82.
73. Ibid., pp. 82–83.

struggle against his impending death. However, his new insight made him die peacefully. He almost seemed to be "hurrying to get a new body on the 'next earth.' "[74]

The second case is about Suzanne, a thirty-two-year-old divorced mother of three children. We already met Suzanne in the section on Group Consciousness in connection with her ability to identify with "millions and millions of people crying in pain." She was suffering from advanced gynecological cancer that had spread all through the pelvis in spite of intensive radiation and a radical hysterectomy. The cancerous process invaded the nerve plexuses along the spine. This caused continuous excruciating pain which could not be adequately controlled even with morphine injections. She was facing the possibility of a cordotomy, an operation on the spinal cord consisting in the selective severing of neuronal tracts conducting pain stimuli. Such an operation involves the serious risk of paralysis of the legs and incontinence. Suzanne was deeply depressed. She developed strong suicidal impulses. The only "stabilizing factor" in her life, we are told, was "her sense that all this was happening for a reason and had some deeper meaning that was escaping her."[75] She herself attributed the origin of this feeling to an out-of-body experience which had occurred after her hysterectomy. She had experienced herself floating above San Francisco at night. During this experience all her pain had disappeared and she was experiencing "ecstasy and transcendental bliss." For a week after this episode she found that she could leave her body at will and have similar experiences, but later she became too frightened to "experiment further in this area."[76]

Suzanne had two sessions in both of which she was given 120 milligrams of DPT. The main content of the first session was a struggle to fight her way through a large mass of shiny black material which had the appearance of a mountain of anthracite coal. She eventually felt that she had "made it through" the mountain and "saw" a panorama of colors, mostly pink and gold, and "swirling galaxies." She identified the black mountain as a symbol of death and had a feeling of liberation. Although her emotional condition greatly improved after this session, there was no reduction in her agonizing pain. During her second session she experienced a whole series of death-rebirth images in numerous variations. She oscillated between feelings of being trapped and extreme loneliness and attempts at escape. On several occasions she "flashed on" what appeared to be sequences from previous incarnations. In one of these she was an African native who was killed by a spear. In another episode she gave birth to a child in medieval England. A little later she became a bird who was shot down by an arrow. In a final episode "her adult ego died while a new baby self was born."

The second session did not alleviate Suzanne's excruciating pains any more than the first had done, but her depression completely disappeared. Grof and Halifax tell us that she "radiated energy and determination." She decided to undergo the cor-

---

74. Ibid.
75. Ibid., p. 85.
76. Ibid.

dotomy in spite of the risks of paralysis and incontinence. "I do not care if I am crippled from my neck down and pee all over Baltimore," she said, "I want my consciousness clear and not absorbed by this pain." The operation was a stunning success. Suzanne's pain completely disappeared and all the dreaded side effects were avoided. Grof and Halifax did not regard Suzanne's new determination and radiant energy as the most significant result of her psychedelic sessions. "The most striking consequence," they write, was the change in her "concept of death and her attitude toward it." She no longer thought of death as "absolute blackness, nothingness, emptiness," but instead "became open to the possibility that after death part of the energy that constitutes the human being continues to exist in a conscious form."[77] In fact, she did not just regard survival as a possibility. To the evident satisfaction of Grof and Halifax, Suzanne became a fervent believer in reincarnation.

In addition to freeing Suzanne from her pain, the successful cordotomy was followed by a shrinking of the tumor. For several months she lived on in a state of remission and made plans to resume studies in psychology that had been interrupted by her illness. A little later, however, the pains returned and the tumor spread into her pelvis and legs, eventually reaching her kidneys. There was no medical help possible any more. However, "all through this painful downhill course," Grof and Halifax note with satisfaction, she was able to maintain "the insight . . . that there might be some form of existence beyond physical death, that 'there is light on the other side of that anthracite mountain.' "[78]

"Gross Matter" and a Gross Fallacy

Death-rebirth experiences are classified by Grof and Halifax as one kind of "profound encounter with death."[79] In their calmer moments they realize that, unlike encounters which "happen in reality" such as dangerous accidents, death is encountered "in a purely subjective fashion" in the course of the death-rebirth experiences occurring during LSD therapy. However, in spite of involving only a "symbolic encounter with death" these experiences have a "transcendental impact." I gather that none of the other transpersonal experiences, not even the Karmic cyclone which "blows through the centuries," produces equally deep and far-reaching transformations. "The memory," Grof and Halifax write,

> that consciousness emerged intact from the seemingly final annihilation constitutes a powerful emotional and cognitive model for understanding the process of actual death.[80]

---

77. Ibid., p. 88.
78. Ibid., p. 89.
79. Ibid., p. 190.
80. Ibid., p. 57.

Saying that the death-rebirth experience "constitutes a powerful . . . cognitive model for understanding the process of actual death" is a pretentious and evasive way of saying—what Grof and Halifax clearly believe—that it is strong evidence for survival. In any event, after such experiences it becomes

> quite plausible that consciousness and awareness are essentially independent of the *gross* matter of the body and brain, and will continue beyond the point of physical demise.[81]

Grof and Halifax quote with approval a saying by the German monk Abraham a Sancta Clara which, according to them, "clearly and succinctly" expresses the conclusion about survival supported by the death-rebirth experience. The epigram— "the man who dies before he dies, does not die when he dies"—has a paradoxical ring but is readily intelligible as stating that the man who has had a death-experience while still alive knows that he can and will survive his actual death.[82]

Since it is "quite plausible" to believe that consciousness will continue "beyond the point of physical demise" Grof and Halifax speak of death as a transition—"the final transition"[83]—a "transition in consciousness, a shift to another level or form of existence."[84] It would be wise to prepare for this transaction. It should be emphasized that Grof and Halifax do not mean dying here, i.e., the last phase of our lives, but our alleged existence after the "transition" has taken place. They greatly deplore that in the Western world "death takes the individual by surprise and finds him for the most part totally unprepared." To avoid such surprises we ought to

> familiarize ourselves with the maps of the posthumous journey, and, if possible, obtain practice and adequate training in the unusual states of consciousness that it entails.[85]

The maps of the posthumous journey, I gather, are found in the Tibetan Book of the Dead and other holy books of Eastern religions. Unfortunately Grof and Halifax do not describe the "practice and adequate training" in any detail. There is surely something particularly preposterous about the advice that we should prepare ourselves for death. The unbeliever has, of course, nothing to prepare for, but the believer, unless his belief is very specific, is faced with the "unknown" as Grof and Halifax admit when they refer to "voyages into the unknown." If reincarnation is accepted, the situation is hardly any better since we do not know how or where we will be reincarnated. It is not like preparing for war or for old age or for a hospital stay. As so much

---

81. Ibid., my italics.
82. Abraham a Sancta Clara (1644–1709) was born in Messkirch, but spent most of his life in Vienna. He was noted for his violent anti-Semitism. His birthplace was the same as that of Martin Heidegger and he was indeed greatly admired by Heidegger who was given to similarly profound remarks about death.
83. "Psychedelics and the Experience of Death" in *Life After Death*, op. cit. p. 199.
84. *HED*, p. 58.
85. *Psychedelics and the Experience of Death*, op. cit., p. 199.

else in the writings of Grof and Halifax, this talk about preparing for death is nothing but portentous posturing.

Grof and Halifax do not provide anything like a lucid and systematic statement of their argument that the death-rebirth experiences are strong evidence for reincarnation. However, the following seems to be a fair summary:

(1) Most dying patients and some other subjects have fairly uniform patterns of experience under LSD consisting of images and feelings which are symbols of rebirth.

(2) These experiences are sometimes extremely powerful resulting in conversion to belief in reincarnation.

(3) The death experience is "experientially identical with actual biological demise," with "total annihilation at all levels" and yet the person emerges intact from his seemingly final annihilation.

When stated in this way without the gushy rhetoric, it is clear that the argument is totally without merit. First of all, there is nothing like unanimity in the experiences of the patients. Only two of the six psychedelic biographies in *HED* contain anything about death and rebirth. Grof and Halifax claim that the death-rebirth experiences occur "quite spontaneously," without any programming, and "frequently as a surprise to an uninformed subject."[86] This is only partly true. Grof and Halifax do not suggest the specific images to the patients, but we saw earlier there is a great deal of intense brainwashing. Under LSD, patients are highly suggestible and they generally try to please the physician. This means that the data are contaminated. However, even if there had been no such contamination and even if the death-rebirth experiences were universal, it would not show that they are an accurate anticipation of what is going to happen after death. They could be more plausibly explained as wish fulfillments. It should be remembered that these patients knew that their death was imminent and presumably some or all of them would have liked to go on living, but freed from their pain and illness. In these circumstances similar wishes would lead to experiences with a similar content. If there are ten men on death row and they all dream of reprieves, literally or symbolically, nothing whatsoever follows about their actual reprieve. The Grof-Halifax argument is exactly like that of somebody who would say that the uniformity in content shows that all ten men will in fact be reprieved. The argument is in fact much weaker since we do not have such a uniformity. As for the endlessly repeated claim that the patients experienced death and yet emerged intact from this "total annihilation at all levels," the sufficient answer is that they only experienced "symbolic" death. They most emphatically did not emerge intact from *real* death. These cases do not provide instances of consciousness in the absence of a living brain.

---

86. *HED*, p. 209.

Grof and Halifax abusively and absurdly talk about "gross" matter. It should be noted that they thereby brand as "gross" the brains of Mozart and Einstein, all the most glorious scenes of nature, all works of art and all the beautiful bodies of animals and human beings. What *is* gross is the hiatus between the premise and conclusion of the Grof-Halifax argument for survival. The conclusion is about consciousness without a brain and the premise refers exclusively to experiences of human beings with brains. Of all the dreadful arguments for survival, this must surely be the most dreadful one—it is an utter nullity.

Neither the vividness of the experiences nor the subjective conviction of the patients in any way help Grof's case. The conversion of the patients to belief in survival no doubt proves the power of the experience, but it proves nothing else. If the evidence of the dependence of consciousness on the brain is as overwhelming as many scientists teach so that it is either certain or extremely probable that the consciousness of a human being does not persist after the death of his body—a topic we shall discuss fully in Chapter 17—then all we can say is that certain LSD experiences have the tendency to produce belief in a false or highly improbable proposition.

14

The Population Problem and Other Commonsense and Scientific Objections

In the present chapter I will present five arguments against reincarnation. The first three—what I call Tertullian's objection, the argument from Darwinian evolution, and the one from the "recency" of life—seem to me valid without qualification. The fourth, the population argument, does not apply to quite all forms of reincarnation. However, it does apply to most versions of the theory and the wild *ad hoc* hypotheses to which reincarnationists have resorted in their rebuttal show particularly well what a fanciful theory we are dealing with. The status of the fifth—the argument from the absence of memory—is more complicated. It is not valid as it stands, but for reasons connected with the criteria of personal identity it nevertheless undermines reincarnation.

1. Tertullian's Objection

This objection is a very simple and obvious one. It has been stated concisely and forcefully by the early Church Father Tertullian (c. 160–220), in Chapter 31 of his *Treatise on the Soul.* "How happens it," he asks there, "that a man who dies in old age returns to life as an infant?" Whoever continues life in a new body might be expected to "return with the age he had attained at his death, that he might resume the precise life which he had relinquished." If "souls depart at different ages of human life," Tertullian continues, "how is it that they come back again at one uniform age?"[1] John Hick, who endorses this objection, points out that babies are not born with adult egos "as they would be if they were direct continuations of egos which had died at the end of a normal lifespan."[2]

It is little less than scandalous that no reincarnationist has ever attempted to reply

---

1. A. Roberts and J. Donaldson (Eds.), *Ante-Nicene Fathers,* Vol. 3, p. 211.
2. *Death and Eternal Life,* p. 363.

to this argument. It is as if Christian theologians had never attempted to face the problem of evil. We may not be greatly impressed by their answers, but at least they did not simply ignore the problem. John Hick, who is not a reincarnationist, suggests that it might be possible to build an answer on the distinction between the empirical ego and the metaphysical soul. The empirical ego is what Kant called the "phenomenal" self. It is, in Hick's words, "the conscious, remembering, anticipating, choosing, acting self." The metaphysical soul on the other hand is an entity "lying behind or beneath or above the conscious self." Once we make the distinction between the empirical ego and the metaphysical soul the defender of reincarnation could meet Tertullian's objection by maintaining that what survives in a new body is not the empirical ego, which perishes with the death of the old body, but the metaphysical soul that is manifested in successive empirical egos each of which has to begin as a baby. To make this rejoinder more convincing a reincarnationist could refer to the difference between the age of an actor in a play and his age in real life. In a play an actor may age from eighteen to eighty, but although he himself ages between performances, every time he plays the same part he starts once again at the age of eighteen. In much the same way the metaphysical soul grows older with every incarnation although it starts as a baby in all its empirical manifestations. It should be pointed out that this answer to Tertullian is open to Hinduists and other "metaphysical" supporters of reincarnation who believe that what survives is "Atman," a transcendent principle, but that it is not available to Buddhists or Western sympathizers with Buddhism whose "Anatta" is in effect the empirical ego.

Everything in this reply hinges on the plausibility and relevance of the distinction between the empirical ego and the metaphysical soul. If the notion of the metaphysical soul is unintelligible, as many philosophers hold, or if it is not unintelligible but if there is no reason to suppose that there are such metaphysical souls, or if there are such souls but if they are not what we refer to by the word "I," the rejoinder collapses. I will return to this issue in Chapter 17. Here I will merely observe that quite plainly we do not mean anything as abstruse as the metaphysical soul when we use the word "I." What we refer to *is* the empirical ego; and it is this empirical ego that reincarnationists like other believers in immortality would like to survive. This is as true of Hindus as it is of Buddhists, whatever they say in their more "philosophical" moments. As for the analogy with the actor and the part he portrays, it should be remembered that a part or character in a play is not a human being living in the actual world. If it were then it *would* be older at every new performance. The analogy also breaks down at the other end. We have ways of determining the age of an actor, but since it is a transcendent principle that is not accessible to any kind of observation, we have no means of determining the age of the metaphysical soul. In fairness I want to stress that reincarnationists are not responsible for this analogy. It is my work—I introduced it in order to give some semblance of content to the otherwise totally obscure assertion that the metaphysical soul ages from life to life although the empirical ego always starts as a baby.

Reincarnation and Evolution

The next two objections are based on scientific findings that were of course not available to the individuals who first thought up the idea of reincarnation. Confining ourselves for the moment to the version that maintains that human beings can be incarnated only in human bodies, it seems clear that such a theory is inconsistent with evolution. In the first place, evolution teaches that the human race descends from nonhuman species and that there was a time when human bodies did not exist. The reincarnationist, however, is committed to an infinite series of past incarnations in *human* bodies. Furthermore, as we observed a little while ago, whatever believers in reincarnation may say in their more theoretical moments, in practice they refer to the empirical ego when they use the word "soul," and the empirical ego is the most highly developed form of consciousness. Now, evolution teaches that our consciousness developed gradually along with the development of the brain and the nervous system. The reincarnationist is committed to holding that no *such* development occurred since it is the same soul that migrated from body to body. He may indeed concede that there has been *some* development, that some souls have gradually grown kinder and wiser and better informed. However, this is not the kind of development postulated by evolutionary theory. It may be thought that the wilder form of reincarnation which holds that human souls may have been incarnated in animal bodies escapes this objection. This is not so. Reincarnationists defending this version do *not* teach that the sequence of bodies in which a soul is incarnated is in any way parallel to the sequence postulated by evolutionists. A human being, as we saw, can become a dog or a gnat and, at the other end, the soul may most recently have been in the body of a nightingale or a beaver.

It should be pointed out that in reincarnationist publications of the twentieth century, especially those by theosophists, the word "evolution" is constantly used in a highly eulogistic fashion. It is suggested that reincarnation is not only consistent with evolution but that it is in fact its completion and logical extension into the spiritual realm. In every reincarnation we are slightly better and wiser than in the one before and eventually we will attain perfection. Whatever may be thought about such a view, it clearly has nothing to do with evolution as this term is understood in biology. Let us grant for the sake of argument that the human race will develop into a "higher" species, whatever that may mean, and this higher species into a still higher one, and so on. Such a development in no way implies that the bodies of the members of those higher species are inhabited by souls that once lived in human bodies.

The Recency of Life

In any event, both versions are defeated by what science has discovered about the relative recency of life. It is now generally accepted that for many billions of years after the Big Bang the universe contained no life at all. Reincarnation in all forms postulates a series of incarnations stretching back into the past without limit; and this is clearly inconsistent with the facts. This objection would not apply to somebody who is prepared to say that there was a first soul or a first generation of souls which were created with the earliest men. This however raises the question of why a natural explanation of the "soul," i.e., the consciousness of the earliest men, is not sufficient and the more basic problem of what is meant by a soul-creation which I will discuss later. Even if we postulate a cyclical universe with an infinite number of big bangs, cosmic expansions followed by cosmic contractions, this would not affect the issue since in each cycle there would be a long initial period without life.

Pythagoras and the founders of Eastern religions can hardly be blamed for not knowing the facts of evolution or modern cosmology, but this does not make the objection any less cogent. As for contemporary Western believers, I have already noted that they usually are not the least bit interested in the findings of science.

The Population Problem

This is my favorite argument. One of my students once described it as "cute" and I think that this is an apt description. The reactions of reincarnationists to it are highly imaginative if nothing else and show to what length "true" believers will go to defend a cherished theory. The argument seems to me quite conclusive against the major form of reincarnationism, but, as I explain in detail at the end of this section, there are ways of escaping it. The escape is, however, achieved at the cost of being exposed to a new set of serious and indeed quite unanswerable objections.

The earliest statement of the argument is found in Tertullian's *Treatise on the Soul* in which he speaks of the "luxuriant growth of the human race,"[3] observing that this cannot be reconciled with the notion of the stationary population to which reincarnationists are committed. Tertullian did not have any figures, but we do, and the argument is becoming ever more impressive. In an article published in the July-August 1981 issue of *BioScience,* Professor Arthur H. Westing of Amherst summarized the best available information about the number of human beings alive at various times. At the time at which he wrote, the population was estimated at 4.4 billion. In 1945 it had been 2.3 billion, in 1850 1 billion, in 1650 500 million, at the time of Christ 200 million, and in 8000 B.C.E., approximately 5 million. Among other interesting calculations Professor Westing estimated that the 1981 population of 4.4 billion amounted to 9 percent of all human beings who ever lived and that it was greater than the number of people who lived through the entire Paleolithic age, a period accounting for 86 percent of the duration of human life. It should be added that in spite of famines and wars the same trend has continued since 1981. According to figures supplied by the United Nations the earth's population reached 4.8 billion at the end

---

3. Op . cit., p. 89.

of 1985, and in June of 1986 it passed the 5 billion mark. At the time of writing these lines (July 1995) the figure is 5,716,000,000. If current trends continue the total human population will be 10 billion by the year 2016.

These facts are incompatible with the less fanciful version of the reincarnation theory according to which human souls can occupy only human bodies. As we saw earlier, reincarnationism is opposed to any doctrine of "special creation" of souls. It denies that "new souls" are ever added to the world. All souls have always existed. Every birth is a *re*birth, the rebirth of a soul that has already existed. All this clearly rules out any population increase. Reincarnationists who maintain that some souls are eventually allowed to give up their earthly existence and merge into the Absolute or Nirvana are committed to the view that in the long run the population must *decrease*. Other reincarnationists imply that the total human population is stationary. In either case, whether committed to a stationary or decreasing population, reincarnationism appears to be refuted by the population statistics.

It is noteworthy that this argument has hardly ever been explicitly discussed by any of the academically respectable reincarnationists. I suspect that the reason for this is the great difficulty of finding an answer that would strike a sober person as even remotely credible. The less inhibited reincarnationists, however, have attacked the population argument with relish. Morey Bernstein, the author of *The Search for Bridey Murphy,* has an easy answer. We can dispose of the objection by bringing in the population of the astral world.

> The total number of entities both in this and the afterworld can remain the same while the balance shifts between the number of entities on earth and the number in the unseen world.[4]

If we refer to the human population on earth by the letter e and to the population of the astral or unseen world by the letter u we can answer the objection by maintaining that, although neither e nor u are constant, the total of $e + u$ never varies.

Substantially the same answer is offered by numerous theosophists who usually add that the population of the astral world vastly exceeds that of the earth. Thus Annie Besant was certain that the number of "unbodily egos" is always "enormously greater" than those who are incarnate, adding:

> The globe is as a small hall in a large town, drawing the audiences that enter it from the total population. It may be at one time half empty, at another crowded, without any change in the total population of the town.[5]

Irving C. Cooper, my favorite theosophist, some of whose fascinating ideas I mentioned earlier, takes note of the fear in some quarters that the constant increase in the

4. *The Search for Bridey Murphy,* op. cit., p. 259.
5. Quoted in Joe Fisher, *The Case for Reincarnation* (New York, 1984), p. 158.

earth's population will eventually deplete the astral plane. He therefore assures his readers that no such dire fate is in store for the astral world. It can absorb mass emigrations without serious damage, much as a giant corporation can easily absorb losses by a subsidiary here and there. Cooper's reassurance is welcome, but I wish that the astral world were a little less profligate in supplying egos to our world, especially since so many of them are sent to the poorest and most undeveloped countries.

V. H. Gunaratna, a Buddhist philosopher whose slender volume *Rebirth Explained* (1971) comes recommended by the Venerable Narada Mahathera as the "profound treatise" of a "learned writer," fully endorses the Bernstein-Cooper view that we must not focus our attention exclusively on the earth and should remember that there are "countless other world systems of which the Buddhist texts speak." We must also remember that, just as human beings may turn into animals or gods, so earlier incarnations of a human being may well have been on a nonhuman plane. "An animal or a celestial being," Gunaratna observes, "can be reborn as a human being."[6] If, as before, we represent the human population on the earth as *e* and if we refer to the animal population by the letter *a* and to the totality of gods by *g*, reincarnationism is not committed to the view that *e* is unchanging. It is committed to the very different proposition that $e + a + g$ is the same at all times. The facts of population growth do not in any way conflict with this broader view.

It might be mentioned in passing that population transfers between different realms have also occasionally received the attention of Christian theologians. In their case, however, the transfer is usually only from this world to the Beyond and not also the other way around. In the course of a sermon in St. Patrick's Cathedral in New York City during the Korean War, Monsignor William T. Greene assured "sorrowing parents" that "death in battle was part of God's plan for populating the kingdom of heaven." Not to be outdone, Dr. Geoffrey Fisher, a former Archbishop of Canterbury, denied that the hydrogen bomb was the greatest danger of our time. "After all," he reasoned, "the most it could do would be to transfer vast numbers of human beings simultaneously from this world to another and more vital one into which they would someday go anyhow."[7] Since the transfer is to a "more vital world," it is perhaps regrettable that the H-bomb has not yet been used. I suppose that Hitler and Stalin were really great benefactors of the human race in hastening the migration of vast numbers to a better life. One is reminded of the nuns in St. Augustine's day who committed suicide in order to reach paradise without delay. I have always thought that the nuns were far more logical than Augustine who "refuted" them by means of wretched arguments.

Let us, however, return to the population problem as discussed by defenders of reincarnation. Another Buddhist writer who has dealt with the population argument is K. N. Jayatilleke, who until his death in 1970 was professor of philosophy at the University of Ceylon. Jayatilleke held an M.A. from Cambridge and a Ph.D. from the

---

6. *Rebirth Explained,* op. cit., p. 80.

7. Both of these statements are quoted from *Immortality: Myth or Reality?* a pamphlet by the late Corliss Lamont, published by the author in New York in the 1950s (no date available).

University of London. Although he professed to be an admirer of A. J. Ayer and regarded himself as an empiricist, he swallowed even the most extravagant claims made by and on behalf of Edgar Cayce and he fully endorsed the Bridey Murphy case as evidence for reincarnation. Jayatilleke has a twofold answer to the population argument. Like Gunaratna, he appeals to the possibility that human beings were animals in previous incarnations. To this he adds that we must not rule out the possibility of the transmigration of souls from other planets. The Buddhist view of the cosmos holds that there are "hundreds of thousands of galaxies spread out in space" and that they include "thousands of inhabited spheres." It is entirely possible that some of the population increase on the earth is the result of invasions of human embryos by souls from these spheres. If, as before, we represent the human population of the earth as e, the animal population as a, and the souls living in human or nonhuman form on other planets as p, the unchanging totality is not e but $e + a + p$.

The second component of Jayatilleke's rejoinder has the wholehearted endorsement of Professor Geddes MacGregor, who is perhaps the most distinguished Christian theologian writing in defense of reincarnation at the present time. Holding degrees from Oxford, the Sorbonne, and Edinburgh, he is a Fellow of the Royal Society for Literature and taught for many years in the philosophy department of the University of Southern California. MacGregor admits that in Tertullian's time bringing up the population increase was "pardonable." However, now that we "know of the vastness of the galaxies and of the extreme likelihood that there are millions of inhabited planets besides our own," the objection no longer has "any force at all."[8]

The sufficient answer to all these and similar rejoinders is that they involve what I call "noxious" *ad hoc* assumptions. Not all *ad hoc* assumptions are automatically objectionable, and it will be worthwhile to explain the distinction between those that are and those that are not. The difference is essentially the same as the one between the two kinds of *post hoc* pronouncements noted earlier when discussing Karmic assertions about sins committed in past lives. All of us constantly make perfectly reasonable ad hoc assumptions in everyday life and occasionally *ad hoc* assumptions have proved highly fruitful in the history of science. The discovery of the planet Neptune provides a particularly instructive illustration of a reasonable and successful *ad hoc* assumption. Full details can be found in most histories of astronomy, but for our purposes the following brief summary will suffice. By the end of the eighteenth and the beginning of the nineteenth centuries Newtonian celestial mechanics enabled astronomers to calculate the orbits of most of the planets with very great accuracy. The orbits of two planets, however, those of Uranus and Mercury, defied all their calculations. To explain the discrepancy between the calculated and the observed orbits of Uranus, two astronomers, John Adams (1819–1892) and Urbain Leverrier (1811–1877), postulated the existence of a new planet having a certain size, shape, mass, and position in the sky. This was an *ad hoc* hypothesis in the sense that it was not based on any direct evidence

---

8. *Reincarnation As a Christian Hope* (London, 1982), p. 47.

and that its purpose was to "save" the Newtonian theory, i.e., to retain it in spite of observations that seemed to contradict it. In 1846 Leverrier requested the Berlin astronomer Johann Galle to carry out the appropriate telescopic observations, and the result was the discovery of Neptune, one of the so-called giant planets with a mean diameter of approximately 28,000 miles and a mass of 17.2 times that of Earth. The Adams-Leverrier hypothesis of a new planet was not "noxiously" *ad hoc* for two reasons: the theory that it was meant to save was itself powerfully supported by a vast array of observations and, although *ad hoc,* it was independently testable.

By contrast, the various rejoinders to the population argument are "noxiously" *ad hoc* because reincarnationism, unlike Newtonian mechanics, is not a theory for which there is powerful observational evidence—in fact of course there is none—and because the assumptions that are introduced are either, like mass immigrations from the astral world or from "other planes," not even in principle testable or, as in the case of population reductions on other planets, so vague as not to be testable in practice. It is perhaps of some interest to note that Leverrier later postulated the existence of a further planet he called Vulcan to explain the perturbations in the orbit of Mercury. However, astronomers have never been able to observe such a planet and the Vulcan hypothesis is now discredited. In the sense in which I am using the word here, the Vulcan hypothesis, although it turned out to be false, was not noxious because, like the Neptune hypothesis, its purpose was to save an empirically well-supported theory and because it was independently testable. The irregularities in the orbit of Mercury, incidentally, were not explained until E. Findley Freundlich's telescopic studies (in 1911 and 1913) which confirmed Einstein's general theory of relativity.[9]

I have left for separate consideration one of Dr. Bruce Goldberg's contributions to human knowledge. Dr. Goldberg, it will be remembered, is the inspired futurologist who discovered the giant fruits and the information pill that will be in use in 2562. To answer the population problem he offers a theory that is as bold as it is ingenious. There is no reason to suppose that the same soul cannot occupy "more than one body at a time." If we modestly assume that one soul occupies three bodies, the population problem can be easily disposed of:

> If one soul occupied three bodies in the year 300 B.C., for example, and if each of these sub-souls occupied three additional bodies each, it would not be difficult to see how one soul could occupy one and a half million bodies in a matter of thirteen lifetimes.[10]

It may be of interest to note that Ian Stevenson has recently endorsed this remarkable theory as a possible way of saving reincarnation. "Human minds may split or duplicate," he writes, "so that one mind can reincarnate in two or more bodies," adding that

---

9. See Ronald W. Clark, *Einstein, The Life and Times* (New York, 1971), pp. 257–60.
10. *Past Lives, Future Lives,* op. cit., p. 181.

this view is accepted by Eskimos, the Igbo of Nigeria, and numerous other groups believing in reincarnation.[11]

Unfortunately the soul-fission theory does not solve the problem. In the first place, the logic of personal identity makes it impossible for a person to occupy more than one body. Let us suppose that A's soul does "split up" and at the same time incarnates in the bodies of both B and C. On the Goldberg-Stevenson view B would now be identical with A, and C would also be identical with A. It would follow that B is identical with C, but this is absurd. If two bodies, B_1 and B_2 were to behave in exceedingly similar ways and if we had reason to believe that their sensations, feelings, and thoughts were qualitatively similar in all respects, we would still not describe them as the bodies of the same person. If, for example, B_1 were Newt Gingrich's[12] body, we would not say that Newt Gingrich also inhabited B_2 but rather that the mind associated with B_2 is Newt Gingrich's double. I do not wish to lay too much stress on this consideration here, because to defend it fully would require a long discussion and also because some competent philosophers would not agree that a person cannot be in several bodies at the same time. However, allowing such multiple occupations as *logical* possibilities, the actual facts clearly defeat Dr. Goldberg's rejoinder. "Goldberg's Law," as we may call his fission theory, is presumably not confined to the future but has always operated in the past. If this is so, we should not find five billion separate souls but a handful, perhaps a few hundred souls, each occupying millions of bodies. Yet that is not at all what we find. There are not, sad to say, millions of Newt Gingriches, George Bushes, William Rehnquists, Pat Buchanans, or, for that matter, Bruce Goldbergs.

Stevenson's conversion to the fission theory must be relatively recent. In an article published in 1974 he conceded that if "the recent increase in the world's population" continued, it would "bring difficulties for the reincarnation hypothesis," adding that these difficulties "have not reached us yet."[13] In this article Stevenson posed as a neutral observer with a sympathetic interest in reincarnation. Since 1974 the population increases have continued at an enormously accelerated pace and yet, so far from abandoning his flirtation with reincarnation, Stevenson has become an ever more convinced and forthright supporter. In *Children Who Remember Previous Lives* which was published in 1987 he has a section on "Reincarnation and the Population Explosion." He states the issue obscurely and misleadingly. The increase in the world's population, he writes, "has made some persons otherwise interested in reincarnation doubt whether there could be enough minds to animate all the human bodies that may soon exist."[14] This, it should be noted, is not the problem. It is rather

---

11. *Children Who Remember Previous Lives,* pp. 207–208.

12. For the benefit of readers in a happier time when Newt Gingrich will have been forgotten, let me explain that he was for several years after 1994 the Republican party's foremost spokesman for intolerance, divisiveness, narrow-mindedness, and contempt for the underdog.

13. "Some Questions Related to Cases of the Reincarnation Type," *Journal of the American Society for Psychical Research,* 1974, p. 400.

14. Op. cit., p. 207.

that the population increase seems incompatible with the stationary or decreasing population implied by the major form of reincarnationism. Stevenson does not now think the problem serious at all. He lists numerous "assumptions" any one of which would take care of it and he suggests that none of them is unreasonable. I have already mentioned the fission theory. Another is the assumption that "new individual human minds are created as needed and attached to human bodies." All the other assumptions are identical with those favored by Bernstein, Gunaratna, and various tabloid philosophers. It may be that "minds presently incarnated in human bodies have been promoted from incarnation in nonhuman bodies." The assumption Stevenson discusses most fully and which he seems to favor is that the interval between death and rebirth is not fixed but, on the contrary, "fluctuates from time to time." There may have been a period "when few minds were incarnated and many more were existing in the discarnate state, waiting for terrestrial incarnation, or perhaps hoping to avoid one." During a period when the interval is very great, "many discarnate minds may be awaiting reincarnation and could thus contribute to an even greater increase in the world's population than we have seen during the last two centuries."[15]

I have already discussed the fission theory and the various tabloid "assumptions," but a few words are in order about the claim that "new individual human minds" may be "created as needed and attached to human bodies." Has anybody ever witnessed such creations and attachments? If not, what would it be like to witness them? Further, do these minds come into being without a cause or are they created by some intelligent being? If so, by whom? I know what is meant by saying that a painter or a composer created a certain work of art or that a chef created a new dish, but I have no idea what is meant by creating a mind. Equally, I understand what is meant by saying that a label has been attached to a suitcase or that an artificial leg has been attached to a person who has lost his leg in an accident, but I draw a blank when told that a mind has been attached to a body. Unless the questions I have raised here are satisfactorily answered we do not have a coherent theory but mere verbiage, accompanied by certain very vague pictures. The attachment portion of this "theory" is particularly objectionable. How is a purely nonphysical entity attached to a human body? By bandaids, by scotch tape, or glue, or perhaps by means of a rope? These are not purely facetious questions: they help us see that a certain word which has a clear meaning in one familiar context has been transferred to a new context where it has none. It should be noted that Stevenson here takes seriously the "special creation" theory of conservative Christians which was ridiculed by Ducasse and other reincarnationists. What is more, reincarnationists are worse off than the Christians since, as believers in God, the latter have at least an answer to the question of who is creating the minds. Not that the theory becomes more intelligible by bringing in God.

The population difficulties can be avoided by somebody who is prepared to offer a drastically modified version of reincarnationism. Professor Ducasse never dis-

---

15. Op. cit., p. 208.

cusses the population objection, but at the end of his article "Life After Death Conceived As Reincarnation" he refers to such a revised position. Speaking of the Bridey Murphy case (of which he was a vigorous champion) and the spontaneous recollections of earlier lives by certain children, he observes that, if these cases are as strong as their supporters maintain, they are evidence for the view that "reincarnation, whether general or not, occurs at least sometimes." Ducasse leaves this question open; but, according to Stevenson, some Turkish believers are quite definite that only those who die a violent death are reborn.[16] Somebody who holds the view that reincarnation occurs but that it is not universal could quite consistently admit the population growth without invoking any of the noxious *ad hoc* assumptions. He would maintain that, while the origin of some human beings has to be explained in terms of the transmigration of souls, the origin of many (perhaps most) human beings is of a natural kind. By this I mean that the latter subclass of the human race is *entirely* the result of biological reproduction. Such a position could then also explain population growth in the usual way, by references to biological and social factors.

There is something appealing about the modesty of this revised position, but it is easy to see why it has not commended itself to most believers in reincarnation. It does seem more than an *a priori* prejudice to hold that all human beings have the same kind of origin: they are either all the result of a divine infusion of a soul into an embryo or they are all the result of transmigration or they are all produced in a purely biological fashion. Furthermore, many of the arguments for reincarnation, if they were valid, would show that *all* human beings are the reincarnation of previously existing souls. Finally, somebody taking this position is faced with the unenviable task of supplying criteria allowing us to tell who among human beings is naturally produced and who is the result of reincarnation. It occurs to me that those reincarnationists who also believe in the law of Karma, which in effect means most of them, would no longer be able to offer Karmic explanations for the apparently unjust suffering of human beings who did not have previous lives. Without criteria to tell who did and who did not have a previous life, this, in effect, would mean that such Karmic explanations would not be available for anybody. Considering the Buddhist pastor's "reassurance" to the mother whose child had been born crippled, this might be all to the good.

The Absence of Memories

This is surely the first consideration that occurs to almost anybody in the West when hearing about reincarnation: if reincarnation were a fact we ought to be able to remember our past lives, but we do not. A famous statement of this objection occurs in the *de Rerum Natura* of Lucretius:

---

16. "Characteristics of Cases of the Reincarnation Type in Turkey and Their Comparison with Cases in Two Other Cultures," *International Journal of Comparative Sociology,* 1970, p. 4.

If the nature of the soul is immortal and makes its way into our body at the time of birth, why are we unable to remember besides the time already gone, and why do we retain no traces of past actions? If the power of the mind has been so completely changed, that all remembrance of past things is lost, that, methinks, differs not widely from death; therefore you must admit that the soul which was before has perished and that which now is has now been formed.[17]

In reply, some reincarnationists have denied the premise of the argument. They have pointed to memories during hypnotic regressions and also to spontaneous memories like those of Edward Ryall or Stevenson's children. We have already shown that the former of these are illusions. The case of Ryall and various earlier "memorizers" was briefly discussed in Chapter 7 and in Chapter 16 I will offer a detailed examination of the children who formed the subject of Stevenson's investigations. It will be seen that spontaneous memories are also spurious.

There is a second reply to the argument. Now, the premise is not questioned but it is said that the conclusion does not follow. The mere fact that we cannot remember something does not prove that it did not occur. To quote C. J. Ducasse:

If absence of memory of having existed at a certain time proved that we did not exist at that time, it would then prove far too much; for it would prove that we did not exist during the first few years of the life of our present body, nor on most of the days since then, for we have no memories whatever of the great majority of them, nor of those first few years. Lack of memory of lives earlier than our present one is therefore no evidence at all that we did not live before.[18]

Ducasse does not address himself to the question of why we cannot remember our past lives, but various other reincarnationists have attributed it to the shock of death or the shock of rebirth or both. Thus León Dennis, a leading French occultist of the early twentieth century who is described by Ellen Wheeler Wilcox, the book's translator, as a "great spiritual philosopher," offers the following explanation:

We have already given a summary of the cause of forgetfulness. It is the rebirth itself—the act of reclothing a new organism, a material envelope, which in its turn plays the part of an extinguisher. By the divination of its vibratory state the spirit, each time it takes possession of a new body, of a virgin brain devoid of all images, finds itself incapable of expressing the memories accumulated in anterious lives.[19]

---

17. H. A. J. Munro (trans.), III, lines 670–78.

18. *Nature Mind and Death,* p. 492.

19. *Life and Destiny,* p. 153. Ellen Wheeler Wilcox seems to be forgotten, but when I was an undergraduate she was frequently mentioned as the worst poet who ever lived. At the beginning of *Life and Destiny* she inserts one of her poetic productions which is unlikely to change her reputation. In the Introduction to the American edition of the book, Ms. Wilcox mentions that she was greatly helped in the translation by messages from her late husband. Her Introduction is a most enjoyable piece of writing containing many other jewels.

A saner explanation is offered by Francis Story:

> For the most part it is better for unenlightened humanity that the griefs and errors of
> the past should be obliterated. If this did not happen, the majority of people would
> be crushed beyond hope of rising by the accumulated horror of past lives, and the
> "will-to-live" would not survive in them.[20]

If a reference to "past lives" were omitted, Story's remarks could be accepted by people who do not believe in reincarnation. It is really a very wise remark, quite in the
style of Voltaire and Nietzsche.

Ducasse is clearly right and the argument fails for the reason stated by him. However, it would be shortsighted to leave the matter there. Bodily continuity and memory seem to be the two major constituents of personal identity. If a later person, B,
whose body is obviously not identical with that of an earlier individual, A, also fails
to remember experiencing or doing anything as A, B cannot be said to be the same
person as A. The total absence of memories, even of the possibility of bringing any
memories back by means of hypnosis or free association, does not destroy identity if
the individual has the same body. However, if we do not have the same body, and of
course in putative reincarnation cases we do not, the absence of memory does destroy
personal identity: nothing that could constitute identity is left. Suppose I assert that
I am the same person as Julius Caesar, but I do not remember any of my experiences
as Julius Caesar. What could this possibly mean? How does my alleged identity with
Julius Caesar differ from nonidentity? To quote Leibniz:

> What good would it do you, sir, to become king of China on condition of forgetting
> what you have been? Would it not be the same thing as if God at the same time he
> destroyed you created a king in China?[21]

Voltaire expressed himself along similar lines:

> To rise again—to be the-same person as you were—you must have your memory per-
> fectly fresh and present; it is memory that makes your identity. If your memory be
> lost, how will you be the same man?[22]

That Leibniz and Voltaire are right can be seen if we consider why we would regard certain identity claims as absurd. F. Milton Willis, a theosophist whom we shall meet again
in the next chapter, offered numerous remarkable "identifications." Among others he asserted that Queen Victoria was identical with Alfred the Great. I doubt that anybody other
than F. Milton Willis believed in the identification of Queen Victoria with Alfred the

---

20. Op. Cit., p. 44.
21. *Philosophische Schriften,* Vol. IV, p. 300, quoted by John Hick, *Death and Eternal Life,* p. 310.
22. *Philosophical Dictionary,* Vol. 6 (London, 1824), p. 8.

Great. Suppose we were asked why we deny that they were the same person. The answer seems clear: their bodies were different and, as far as we know, Queen Victoria did not have any memories of having lived before as Alfred the Great.

I am sure that some people will at least implicitly reject what I have just said. It was widely believed among the Jews that the prophet Elijah would have to return before the coming of the messiah and several contemporaries of Jesus (and perhaps Jesus Himself) were convinced that John the Baptist was the reincarnation of Elijah. John emphatically denied that he was Elijah but this did not shake the belief of his questioners. I do not of course know what went on in the minds of John's questioners, but if they were at all like contemporaries who believe in reincarnation they probably had a vague picture of a gaseous duplicate or something similar leaving the body of Elijah and invading that of John or, suitably compressed, that of his pregnant mother.[23] The gaseous replica *is* the soul of the prophet Elijah and if it invades John's body he is Elijah even if he has no memories. The answer to this kind of picture is, of course, that there is no such replica and that, even if there were, it would not be Elijah.

Ducasse showed some awareness of this problem and in an article published in 1960 he attempted to meet it. The difficulty, he tells us,

> would be eliminated if memory of one's earlier lives should be regained in the intervals between incarnations; or at the end (if any) of the series of incarnations; or perhaps at some advanced stage in the series. For such regaining of memories would be sufficient to make "rebirth of one person" *mean* something different from "death of one person followed by birth of a different person"; although, of course, we *now* cannot tell which of these two is what really occurs.[24]

There are several things that are objectionable about this rejoinder. To begin with it is surely unwise to let the case for reincarnation rest on wild conjectures about memories during the interregnum or at the end of a series that may be going on for billions of years. However, there is also a more fundamental objection. At first it may seem plausible to maintain that we have two distinct and independent criteria of personal identity—bodily continuity and memory. This is suggested by the undeniable fact that in daily life we sometimes use the one and sometimes the other. However, reflection shows that the two criteria are *not* on par and that the memory criterion presupposes that of bodily continuity while the converse does not hold. We need a criterion for distinguishing between "false" and "true" memories. People often sincerely "remember" things which did not happen. They also of course remember things which did happen or, more specifically, they remember seeing, hearing, and doing things which they really saw, heard or did. These are "true" memories. It is evident that the memory criterion cannot help us to distinguish between such true and false memories. We have

---

23. For cases in which people actually "saw" such gaseous replicas, see my *Immortality* (New York, 1992), p. 337.

24. "Life After Death Conceived As Reincarnation," op. cit., pp. 149–50.

to fall back on another criterion and the only one that seems to be available is bodily continuity. When Goethe wrote his autobiography, *Dichtung und Wahrheit,* he "remembered" all kinds of things which, as independent evidence showed, happened to various friends. There was not here the required bodily continuity between the Goethe who wrote the autobiography and the young Goethe whose experiences were "remembered." He also remembered several conversations with Herder and these really took place. What this means is that there was the requisite bodily continuity between the later Goethe and the person whose conversations with Herder were remembered.

The following imaginary situation will bring out the priority of the bodily criterion with special force. Suppose that in 1993 we created an exact double of the great baritone Dietrich Fischer-Dieskau (we will refer to this double as Fischer-Dieskau II). Fischer-Dieskau II will have just as accurate memories about the life of Fischer-Dieskau I as Fischer-Dieskau I himself. Let us call them duplicate memories. It is, for example, a matter of record that Fischer-Dieskau sang the Brahms Requiem with Bruno Walter in Edinburgh in 1953. Fischer-Dieskau I will be able to give an accurate account of this event and so will Fischer-Dieskau II *in the first person.* A biographer of Fischer-Dieskau will get just as reliable information from interviews with Fischer-Dieskau II as he will from interviews with Fischer-Dieskau I. Nevertheless, all the statements of Fischer-Dieskau II are false since *he* did not have the experiences in question. They will be useful falsehoods corresponding to true recollections but they will not be true, for the experiences were those of Fischer-Dieskau I and not of Fischer-Dieskau II. Fischer-Dieskau II did not yet exist at the time when the event he "recollects" took place. It follows from the preceding considerations that even memories in the interregnum or at the end of a series of lives could not supply the required personal identity.[25]

---

25. For a fuller discussion of these issues see Chapter 25 of T. Penelhum, *Religion and Rationality* (New York, 1971), Chapter 6 of A. J. Ayer, *The Central Question of Philosophy* (London, 1973), and Chapters 7–9 of A. Flew, *The Logic of Mortality.* In fairness it should be added that not all contemporary philosophers would agree with the view that the bodily criterion is more basic than that of memory. H. Noonan, *Personal Identity* (London, 1989) and J. Baillie, "Recent Work on Personal Identity," *Philosophical Books,* 1993, are judicious surveys of the present state of the discussion. There is an excellent brief defense of the view advocated in the text in the contribution by Bernard Williams to a BBC discussion, "Life After Death," which is reprinted in H. D. Lewis, *Persons and Life After Death* (London, 1978). The difficulties concerning personal identity encountered by Buddhists who support a bundle theory of the self are explained in Bruce Reichenbach, "Buddhism, Karma and Immortality" in P. and L. Badham (Eds.), *Death and Immortality in the Religions of the World* (New York, 1987). For attempts by Buddhist philosophers and writers sympathetic to Buddhism to answer some of the difficulties mentioned in the text see N. Mahathera, *Karma and Rebirth* (Kandy, Sri Lanka, 1982), L. A. deSilva, *The Problems of the Self in Buddhism and Christianity* (London, 1979) and Chapter 7 of G. Parrinder, *The Indestructible Soul* (London, 1973). It would lead too far to examine whether the challenging views on personal identity and survival expressed in various of the writings of Derek Parfit, most fully in *Reasons and Persons* (Oxford, 1984), could help a reincarnationist avoid the difficulties mentioned in the text.

15

The "Interregnum":
What Happens Between Lives?

The Duration of the Interregnum

McTaggart toyed with the idea that in the periods between incarnations human beings cease to *exist*. As far as I know, no other reincarnationist has advanced this theory. The general view is that re*birth* occurs at once at death. A few reincarnationists maintain that re*incarnation* in a new body also occurs immediately but this is definitely a minority position. The great majority believe that there is an interval between the time of a person's death and the beginning of life in a new body. I propose to speak of this period as the "interregnum." I borrow this word from medieval German history where it denoted the interval between the death or abdication of one ruler and the election of his successor. In one famous case, between the death of Konrad IV and the accession of Rudolf I, the interregnum lasted no less than nineteen years which is trifling compared with some reincarnation interregna.

Estimates of the length of the interregnum sojourn vary widely. According to Francis Story and Roshi Yasutani, a contemporary Japanese Zen master whom I already quoted in Chapter 1, the usual interval between rebirth and reincarnation is six or seven days.[1] In the Bhagavad-Gita the interval is spoken of as an "immensity of years," and in the *Republic* Plato speaks of a thousand-year cycle. In the cultures studied by Ian Stevenson the duration of the interval is much smaller. Among the Tlingits of Alaska, for example, Stevenson found the median interval to be four years, and among his Lebanese cases it was no more than six months. In two of the cases discussed in earlier chapters the duration was much longer. Bridey Murphy died in 1864

---

1. See extracts from his *Eight Bases of Belief in Buddhism* in T. Kapleau (Ed.), *The Wheel of Death* (London, 1972), p. 44.

and was reborn as Virginia Tighe in 1923. This gives an interval of fifty-nine years. Edward Ryall, the Englishman whose reincarnation was discussed in Chapter 7, was born in 1902. As a farmer in the seventeenth century he died in 1685, giving us an interregnum duration of two hundred and seventeen years. It is perhaps not surprising that some of Ryall's memories turned out to be inaccurate. The figure for Ryall's interregnum is admittedly high, but by no means exceptional. We already noted that Plato speaks of a thousand years and Madame Helen T. Blavatsky, the founder of the Theosophical Society, estimates the interval between incarnations as a thousand to fifteen hundred years.[2] Joan Grant, the English psychic who was an Egyptian princess in her previous life, supplies the figure of five thousand years as elapsing between her two incarnations. The reliability of her statements is vouched for by the Rev. Leslie D. Weatherhead, an eminent Protestant clergyman who we already met in Chapter 2.[3] I can see that, given her onerous duties, an Egyptian princess would need a long period of rest, but five thousand years does seem a bit long. Five thousand years is not, however, the highest figure reported in the literature. F. Milton Willis, a leading theosophist of the early decades of this century, whom we briefly mentioned at the end of the last chapter, basing himself on "occult research by competent investigators," informs us that highly cultivated individuals, especially philosophers, experience an interregnum of ten thousand years.[4]

The Bardo Body and Its Relatives

Whether it lasts six days or ten thousand years, the interregnum presents a particularly ticklish problem for reincarnationists: just where and how do people spend the interregnum and, more specifically, what are they like between incarnations? There appear to be only two possible answers and neither is very alluring. The first is to say that a person exists as a disembodied or pure mind until he finds or chooses his new body. This is essentially the view of Plato. In more recent times it has been held by J. M. E. McTaggart and C. J. Ducasse, the two most renowned Western philosophers writing in support of reincarnation. Such a position is faced with numerous difficulties some of which we already canvassed in previous discussions. To begin with there is the question of whether statements about a pure mind are intelligible. Then there

---

2. This information is supplied by L. H. Leslie-Smith in his contribution to V. Hanson and R. Stewart (Eds.), *Karma—The Universal Law of Harmony* (Wheaton, Ill., 1981), p. 56,

3. Weatherhead, *The Christian Agnostic*, p. 314.

4. *Recurring Earth-Lives—How and Why—Reincarnation Described and Explained* (New York, 1921), p. 81. On the title page the following credentials are given for Willis: Fellow of the Theosophical Society; Member of the Order of the Star in the East; Member of the Karma and Reincarnation Legion. Appendix II of this work offers numerous "identifications" of famous persons: Ralph Waldo Emerson was once Epictetus, William Gladstone Cicero, Queen Victoria Alfred the Great, Lord Kichener William the Conqueror, and Alfred Tennyson Virgil.

is the problem of how a pure mind, devoid of sense organs, could ever locate and choose the mother of the next incarnation. Other difficulties derive from the brain-mind dependence facts discussed in some detail in Chapter 17. Finally, once a reincarnationist commits himself to the view that for certain periods a person exists without a bodily foundation, his position loses one of its most attractive advantages over the familiar Western forms of belief in survival.

The only alternative to the pure mind seems to be some sort of astral body; and this is in fact the view preferred by most reincarnationists. It is, for example, the position adopted in the *Tibetan Book of the Dead,* one of the sacred books of India, and a work much admired by such diverse figures as C. G. Jung, Paul Tillich, Stanislav Grof, Timothy Leary, and Raymond Moody, who sees in it an anticipation of his own startling discoveries. The Tibetan Book is primarily concerned with descriptions of the intermediate or "Bardo" world, and it offers detailed advice about how a person is to comport himself there. The Bardo body is substantially the same as the astral body we met in an earlier chapter. In the words of W. Y. Evans-Wentz, the American anthropologist who edited the English-language version of the Tibetan Book, it is

> formed of matter in an invisible or ethereal-like state (and) is an exact duplicate of the human body, from which it is separated in the process of death.[5]

The Bardo body has two of the supernatural attributes usually associated with astral travel. In the first place it can pass through material objects as if they did not exist. Since it is not "a body of gross matter," it has

> the power to go right through any rock-masses, hills, boulders, earth, houses, and Mt. Meru itself without being impeded.[6]

Second, it can go anywhere instantaneously:

> Thou art able in a moment to traverse the four continents round about Mt. Meru. Or thou canst instantaneously arrive in whatever place thou wishes.[7]

As was the case with George Ritchie's astral body, it cannot be perceived by live human beings, but at least for a short period after death it can see and hear "all the weeping and wailing of friends and relatives" although "they cannot hear him calling upon them."[8] The Bardo body thus possesses the remarkable ability to see, hear, and obtain other sensory information although it has no physical sense-organs, brain, or nervous system.

The bardo body with all its supernatural attributes is also regarded as the bearer

---

5. p. 92.
6. p. 158.
7. p. 159.
8. p. 132.

of a person's consciousness after death in *The Tibetan Book of Living and Dying* by Sogyal Rinpoche, a book published in 1992 which has received highly favorable reviews both in Britain and in the United States. According to a statement in the paperback reprint of 1994, 200,000 copies were sold worldwide during the first year after publication. The book has already been translated into German and French and editions are planned for Spain, Italy, Greece, and several other countries. The book contains a chapter on near-death experiences which, needless to say, are regarded as powerful evidence for survival after death. According to Kenneth Ring, an immortalist whom we met at the end of Chapter 11, it is "a masterful distillation for the West of the priceless wisdom of Tibetan Buddhism that gives us practical instruction and spiritual guidance on how to live in light of the greatest teacher of all—death." Philip Zaleski, the reviewer in the *New York Times*, echoes this sentiment, telling us that "as a guide to the Tibetan tradition and its insights into life and death, Sogyal Rinpoche is without peer." For more wisdom, he adds, "we must wait until the shroud descends." Carried away by his own rhetoric, Zaleski, who teaches religion at Smith College and literature at Wesleyan University, even compares Rinpoche with Dante. In effect, he tells us, Rinpoche "has delivered the Tibetan equivalent of 'The Divine Comedy.' "[9]

A guru or Master himself, Rinpoche is also the reincarnation of an earlier guru. He is evidently a highly active Master. He is the founder and "spiritual director" of Rigpa, a network of Buddhist centers and groups around the world. The hard copy edition of *The Tibetan Book of Living and Dying* lists Rigpa centers in Berkeley, New York City, as well as in London, Paris, Berlin, and several other countries. Rinpoche offers much helpful advice to the dead, who are not of course really dead, and to their surviving friends and relatives. His main goal seems to be the prevention of an "unfavorable" rebirth. Like other Tibetan Buddhists he recommends that the Tibetan Book be read to dead people during the period following their demise. Westerners, he tells us, frequently ask him how the dead can hear such readings. Rinpoche replies that the consciousness of the dead individual, when it is invoked by the power of prayer, can feel "exactly whatever we may be thinking or meditating on." The dead person will understand what is read to him even if he does not know Tibetan. There is no language barrier for him since "the essential meaning of the text can be understood fully and directly by his mind."[10] The clairvoyance of the dead individual which is "seven times clearer than in life" has certain drawbacks. If he listens to scheming and quarreling relatives whose only concern is to inherit as much as possible, "this can cause intense anger and hurt and disillusion" and he will then "be drawn into an unfortunate rebirth."[11] He may in fact become so "painfully disillusioned" that he will return as a ghost to haunt his heirs. Ghosts are evidently much

---

9. *New York Times Book Review*, December 27, 1992.

10. p. 305.

11. p. 303.

on Rinpoche's mind. He offers an interesting explanation of the behavior of "immensely rich people who are never satisfied," craving to take over this company or that one, "endlessly playing out their greed in court cases."[12] These greedy billionaires are inhabited by hungry ghosts. I find this a highly plausible explanation.

Rinpoche is at his best when relating miracles which appear to occur with great frequency in Tibet. My favorite is the so-called Rainbow miracle. Rinpoche tells us that "accomplished practitioners" of certain mystical exercises can bring their lives to an "extraordinary and triumphant end." As their material (as distinct from their astral) body dies, it dissolves into light and then disappears completely. Rinpoche offers some details of the death in 1952 of Sönam Nangyal who was the father of Rinpoche's tutor. Just before his death at seventy-nine Sönam asked his family not to move his body for a week. I will present the remainder of the account in Rinpoche's own words:

> When he died his family wrapped his body and invited Lamas and monks to come and practice for him. They placed the body in a small room in the house, and they could not help noticing that although he had been a tall person, they had no trouble getting it in, as if he were becoming smaller. At the same time, an extraordinary display of rainbow-colored light was seen all around the house. When they looked into the room on the sixth day, they saw that the body was getting smaller and smaller. On the eighth day after his death, the morning in which the funeral had been arranged, the undertakers arrived to collect his body. When they undid the coverings, they found nothing inside but his nails and hair.[13]

When I was a student at Columbia University I had an Indian friend by the name of Ved Perkasch Managdala (I hope he is alive and also that he is reading this book) who would regale me with similar miracles. In one of them a totally illiterate peasant in the north of India woke up one day speaking fluid Sanskrit and reciting the great Indian epics word by word. When I expressed my disbelief he assured me that the Western mind was simply incapable of appreciating such miracles. He was quite right, but I am happy to note that many Indians do not "appreciate" such tales either. He himself became a skeptic not long afterward. I cannot help wondering how many of the 200,000 Western readers, assuming they ever got this far in the book, accepted the story of the disappearance of Sönam's body.

So much for the Tibetans. Let us turn to the more high-brow reincarnationists who show some familiarity with the results of modern science. Francis Story (1910–1971), whom I mentioned earlier, was perhaps the leading apologist for Buddhism in this century. It may be of interest to note that Story was a close friend and associate of Ian Stevenson. He supplied many of Stevenson's cases during the first twelve years of the latter's research and also assisted in their analysis. A number of Stevenson's articles list Story as coauthor. In his article "What Happens Between In-

---

12. P. 113.
13. Pp. 168–69.

carnations?" to which I will return later on, he flatly asserts that during the interregnum we have a "mentally formed body," which is "of a different substance from the physical body," and which "possibly exists on a slightly different vibrational level."[14] He bases this view on information supplied by mediumistic controls, on the circumstances and contents of out-of-body experiences, and above all on the recollections of various people he knew in India and Sri Lanka who remembered not only their previous lives on earth but also what went on between incarnations.

It cannot be said that Stevenson has ignored problems connected with the interregnum. He seems convinced not only that they can be disposed of without any serious difficulty but that their solution is apt to produce dramatic changes in some of our basic concepts. Near the end of his article "Research into the Evidence of Man's Survival After Death," which appeared in the *Journal of Nervous and Mental Diseases* (1977), Stevenson observes that he has not attempted "any description of processes whereby a mind surviving death would persist in another, discarnate realm," adding that "such concepts" (by which he presumably means the "discarnate realm" and the entities residing in it) "require extensive revisions of current ideas about the mind-brain relationship."[15] His position is not substantially different from that of Story or the Tibetan Book. In one of his two fullest discussions of this topic he refers to a remark by the Buddha that all speculation about the nature of the intermediate entity is unprofitable, adding that we would do well to follow this injunction. He himself, however, does not do so. For a variety of reasons, some empirical and some philosophical, Stevenson prefers a body to a pure mind as the interim entity. In addition to transmitting memories and also various skills and dispositions to the new body without which we could hardly speak of the same person, the interim entity must also be the bearer of certain purely "physical qualities." What Stevenson has in mind here are the scars and wounds which, in his opinion, are sometimes transmitted from the old to the new bodies (see Chapter 10). Stevenson remarks that the wounds must somehow be "imprinted" on the interregnum body, which acts as a kind of stamp or "template" for the production of birthmarks and deformities on the new body.[16]

Stevenson's philosophical reason is connected with his insistence that "images have extension" and that as such they cannot exist in an unextended Cartesian mind but only "on or in something else that has extension." In a dream—the illustration is mine but I believe it would have Stevenson's approval—objects have shapes and relative sizes and positions. If I dream of Pat Buchanan sitting on a platform next to Oliver North while William Rehnquist is addressing the Daughters of the American Revolution, the dream Pat Buchanan will look taller than the dream Oliver North just as he is in real life, and William Rehnquist will appear in front of the people sitting on the platform. Such reflections lead Stevenson to the notion of mental space, which

---

14. *Rebirth As Doctrine and Experience*, p. 199.

15. *Journal of Nervous and Mental Disorders*, p. 167.

16. "Some Questions Related to Cases of the Reincarnation Type," *Journal of the American Society for Psychical Research*, 1974, p. 407.

I will discuss later on. This mental space, incidentally, seems to be identical with the other "dimension of which we are just beginning to form crude ideas," to which Stevenson referred during the BBC debate on Ryall.

Stevenson concedes that this "hypothetical intermediate body" must exist in some state "of which we know almost nothing." He does not seem to regard this ignorance as beyond remedy, and he hints in various places that his research and the research of other parapsychologists may gradually remove it. In any case, even in 1974 he thought he knew quite a few things about the nature of this body. To begin with, it

> must be composed of elements quite different from those with which we are familiar both in our ordinary perceptions and in the abstractions of physicists.[17]

Because of this difference from our ordinary bodies Stevenson calls it a "nonphysical body." Stevenson believes that it is "composed of some kind of matter," but it "must be matter quite different from what we usually mean by that term." We must also "expect" that the interregnum body "will be subject to quite different 'laws' from those which govern our familiar physical bodies."[18] Stevenson does not speak of an etheric or astral "double," but it is difficult to see how he can avoid believing in something of the same kind, especially when we reflect on the birthmarks of the new body appearing in the same locations as the scars or wounds on the old one.

When I first read the remarks just quoted I could not help wondering where the intermediate body came from. The answer to this question is given in Stevenson's 1980 presidential address to the Parapsychological Association, in which he reveals himself as an out-and-out occultist. The second body, which we have available at death, is nothing other than our mind, which we had or which we were all along. Stevenson is of course a dualist, and he calls himself a "radical interactionist," but no dualistic interactionist known to me among philosophers, of the Cartesian or the Humean variety, has ever identified the mind with a body. We are once again told that images have spatial location. Although he professes himself to be a Humean and to be a Buddhist, or at least to be highly sympathetic to Buddhism, Stevenson works with a picture of the mind as a "container" and an entity with a "structure." Since images have spatial properties, the same must be true of the mind "in" which they exist. The mind is thus "extended." Minds, he writes, "exist in a space that we can call mental space."[19] There is no need to regard the notion of "mental space" as "illogical" or paradoxical since it is nowhere written that "there can be only one space." Stevenson is convinced that "our mental patterns—not just our memories, but our purposes also—will persist after our deaths."[20] It may be noted in passing that here, for once, Stevenson speaks without any qualification in the first person as a believer in life after death.

---

17. P. 407.
18. Ibid.
19. "Can We Describe the Mind?" in W. G. Roll and J. Beloff (Eds.), *Research in Parapsychology 1980* (Metuchen, N.J., 1981), p. 133.
20. Ibid., p. 139.

Before leaving this topic, I should observe that Stevenson has in no way established what he evidently desires to show, that the mind, i.e., the second body, exists in a space that is just as objective as physical space. The Pat Buchanan of my dreams does not have any more objective existence than something utterly fantastic I may dream about, e.g., his flight to the moon by means of waving his arms. When the Pat Buchanan, the Oliver North, and the William Rehnquist of my dreams disappear, so do their spatial properties and relations. More generally, my dream-space disappears as soon as I stop dreaming. There is also of course no reason for regarding the mind as literally a "container" or having a "structure." On a Humean view, saying that an image is "in the mind" just means that it is one of the "impressions and ideas" whose succession *is* a person's mind. In Chapter 17 I will explain why I find Hume's account inadequate, but talking about the mind as a "container" and more generally as a "thing" is not going to remove its inadequacies.

Stevenson regards the "attachment" of the mind to the brain as "somewhat variable." The mind becomes "loosened" or "more detached" from the brain during dreams, when it is under the influence of hallucinogenic drugs, and during near-death experiences. He also quite explicitly advocates the view that sense organs are not necessary for what passes as sense perception. In support of this assertion, he refers to certain out-of-body experiences in the course of which the subjects displayed "paranormal cognition" and, what is particularly relevant to our topic, to "the small number of subjects who claim to remember events that they observed during an intermediate existence between death and presumed rebirth."[21] Persons belonging to these two groups have had visual experiences or "visionlike experiences" in which neither physical eyes nor "other parts of the body's neural equipment were used."[22] I will discuss Stevenson's view on the memories of life during the interregnum a little later. Here I wish to point out that he does not produce the slightest evidence that, in dreams, during near-death experiences, or in any of the other states on his list, consciousness is any less dependent on the brain than it is in the course of normal waking life. This contention is indeed a stock-in-trade of occultism, but, to the best of my knowledge, it does not have the endorsement of a single competent brain physiologist.

Womb Invasions

I have already explained why I do not believe in the existence of either a pure mind or an astral body. In the present context I am not particularly concerned to show that they do not or cannot exist. Instead, I would like to point out that, even if we allow their existence, reincarnation becomes a metaphysical theory as soon as either of these are brought in as the interregnum bearer of memories, skills, or anything else. Hence, con-

---

21. P. 138.
22. Ibid.

trary to the repeated pronouncements of reincarnationists, the theory cannot serve as the scientific explanation of *any* phenomena. This becomes particularly obvious when we look more closely at the supposed entry of the preexisting soul into the womb of its prospective mother and its "merger" or "fusion" with the physical embryo. When I first read the Tibetan Book and similar writings in which there are constant references to the intermediate person's decision to enter a certain woman's womb and then to make every effort to stay there by closing the "door" of the womb, I felt like protesting such crass invasions of privacy. Surely a woman has a right to determine who may and who may not enter her womb. However, on further reflection it was obvious that no violation of the woman's rights had occurred and that the women whose wombs had supposedly been invaded were really not being victimized at all. For not only does the woman herself feel nothing, but at the time of the supposed entry no outside observer could notice anything either. The invasion of the woman's womb by the reincarnating soul is obviously altogether different from the insertion of a diagnostic or surgical instrument, which is both experienced by her and observed by outsiders. An entry that is not even in principle noticeable is indistinguishable from the absence of an entry. It should be remembered that, if reincarnation is a fact, such womb invasions *are* occurring all the time, along with every pregnancy.

The emptiness of all statements of this kind is also evident from the fact that the reincarnation theory is not of the slightest use to an embryologist. It is of no more use to him than the notion of Karma is to a geologist. A geologist cannot explain or predict earthquakes any better if he believes in the law of Karma than if he does not. Similarly, an embryologist who believes in womb invasions by preexisting souls cannot explain or predict any embryological facts any better than one who does not.

In the section on the choice of parents in Chapter 1 I briefly referred to Story's "thought force" which is supposed to drive the soul to the womb of its prospective mother. Story wrote extensively about the relations of Buddhist concepts to modern science, especially genetics. He asserted with some pride that Buddhist notions supplement "the stock of scientific knowledge" without in any way "resorting to the supernatural for an explanation."[23] In addition to "thought force," Story uses such terms as "the etheric body," "thought accretion," and "mental energy potential." I take it that all of them are meant to refer to the same thing. For Narada Mahathera, another leading Buddhist philosopher, what is missing from the biologist's account is "karma-energy." In *Karma and Rebirth* Mahathera writes:

> According to Buddhism, there are three factors necessary for the rebirth of a human being, that is, for the formation of the embryo in the mother's womb. They are: the female ovum, the male sperm, and the karma-energy. . . . This karma-energy is sent forth by a dying individual at the moment of his death. Father and mother only provide the necessary physical material for the formation of the embryonic body. With regard to the characteristic features, the tendencies and faculties lying latent in the embryo, the

---

23. Op. cit., p. 248.

Buddha's teaching may be explained in the following way: the dying individual, with his whole being convulsively clinging to life, at the very moment of his death, sends forth karmic energies which, like a flash of lightning, hit at a new mother's womb ready for conception. Thus, through the impinging of the Karma-energies on ovum and sperm, there arises, just as a precipitate, the so-called primary cell.[24]

A little reflection shows that the Buddhist notions referred to by Story and Mahathera can no more add to the "stock of scientific knowledge" than any of the supernatural concepts of Christians and Jews. Let us for a moment consider the traditional Christian view that at conception God infuses a soul into the mother's womb which combines with the physical embryo to grow into a full-fledged human being. Suppose that in a particular case God forgot to infuse a soul into an embryo but that all biological conditions are exceptionally well fulfilled—the best possible genes are available (genes connected with physical health and strength and with a well-formed brain and nervous system) and along with them the best possible intrauterine environment. Surely, no intelligent and educated Christian, no matter how theologically orthodox he may be, would deny that an embryo with such splendid biological equipment and environment would be born intact physically and mentally; and if this is granted, the theory about the divine soul infusion will have been shown to be superfluous, at least for the purpose of scientific explanation. Let us next consider the case in which God does not forget to infuse the soul but in which the biological material or the intrauterine environment or both are seriously defective. As an illustration we may take genes leading to Down's syndrome or mental retardation or endogenous depression, or we may suppose that the pregnant mother is syphilitic or a heroin addict or afflicted with AIDS. Again, no intelligent Christian on earth would deny that in such a case it is likely that the child will be neither physically nor mentally intact in spite of the presence of the divinely created soul.[25]

All these reflections can be applied *mutatis mutandis* to the entities, whatever they are called, that, according to reincarnationists, invade the womb of the expecting mother. Whether it is the pure mind of McTaggart and Ducasse, the astral body of Story and the Tibetan Book, the Karma-energy of Mahathera, or Stevenson's spiritual body, it surely makes no difference whatever for what the child will be like at birth. Once this is admitted it is obvious that reincarnationist claims about womb invasions are empirically vacuous and that they cannot possibly fill any gaps or be any supplement to scientific knowledge.

It must be emphasized that unlike the ovum and the sperm the etheric body and the Karma-energy are not observable. The word "energy" may suggest that we are dealing

---

24. *Karma and Rebirth* (Kandy, Sri Lanka, 1959), pp. 2–3.

25. An intriguing dispute concerns the date at which the soul enters the mother's womb. I gather that Christian theologians offered three conflicting answers. On one view, championed by Thomas Aquinas, this happens at the time of the first movement of the fetus, on another at the first breath, and on a third when the sperm enters the egg. I cannot think of a better example of a totally meaningless dispute. How could one possibly decide the issue?

with a physical phenomenon like heat or light, but this is clearly not so since no conversion to any kind of physical energy is feasible.[26] The theories put forward by Story and Mahathera remind me of a remark made by General Alexander Haig during the Watergate hearing when he was President Nixon's Chief-of-Staff. When it was discovered that a portion of the notorious presidential tapes had been erased, General Haig suggested that perhaps the erasure was due to a "sinister force." I have always believed that the sinister force was one of Richard Nixon's hands, but in any event the etheric body and the Karma-energy have as much explanatory value as Haig's sinister force.

It should be added that at least most Western reincarnationists would concede that biological accounts are quite sufficient to explain the attributes animals have at birth, even those fairly high in the evolutionary scale. If this is granted, it surely becomes extremely implausible to say that we need a different type or kind of account for human beings, since the attributes of human beings are only an extension of those already found in animals.

Some reincarnationists like the late Dr. Raynor Johnson have science degrees but their basic outlook is totally unscientific. In *A Religious Outlook for Modern Man* (1963) Johnson first quotes Voltaire's remark that it is no more miraculous to be born twice than to be born once and then comments:

> The idea itself is not intrinsically unreasonable, for what the soul has done once, it presumably could do again for a good reason.[27]

Later in the same chapter, in reply to what he calls the "objection" that the next incarnation may be as unhappy and full of suffering as the present one, Johnson writes that "this assumption is unlikely to be sound" and elaborates as follows:

> If the soul decides once more to put forth a personality into physical existence, it is quite improbable that in the process of widening experience anything repetitive will be involved.[28]

Like other reincarnationists he cannot leave the empirical facts alone. He cannot see that there is not the slightest reason for regarding gestation and birth as anything other than purely biological processes. It is difficult to reason with people whose entire mental frame is so different from that of science and common sense.

The Fruit of Forgetfulness

Are there any ostensible memories about the interregnum and, if so, do they throw any light on what life there is like? First, a few words about hypnotically obtained

---

26. See Chapter 8.
27. P. 178.
28. P. 187.

memories. They are of course worthless as evidence in view of the general unreliability of hypnotic recollections. However, a few samples may be of interest. Many,
like those of Bridey Murphy, are tedious and for once Sir Alexander Cannon fails to
supply anything juicy. His regressions revealed a "Garden of Waiting" in which the
interregnum persons carry on their affairs. There they are protected by the "Blue Sisters" and the "White Brothers" who select our next physical body "in accordance with
what we deserve from our progression or regression in the past."[29] Sir Alexander
could surely have done better and told us something about possible involvements by
the Blue Sisters with the White Brothers issuing in green and yellow children.

Perhaps the greatest treatise on the interregnum is *Life Between Life—Scientific
Explorations into the Void Separating One Incarnation from the Next* (1986) by Dr.
J. C. Whitton, a Toronto psychiatrist, and Joe Fisher, a tabloid writer who in his earlier book, *The Case for Reincarnation* (1984), had already proved both reincarnation
and astrology and also revealed the secrets of the planet Pluto. *Life Between Life* was
highly praised in the *Journal of Regression Therapy* and also, if one can trust the back
cover, by the *Library Journal*. Based upon thirteen years of research and more than
thirty medical case histories, to quote the blurb again, Whitton and Fisher carried out
"an extraordinary adventure into the unknown." One man who had spent a number of
incarnations in a depressive withdrawn state decided to become an "amorous female."[30] Another of Whitton's patients, a woman who was evidently not quite sane,
chose her next mother "knowing that there was a high incidence of Alzheimer's disease in her family" and that there was every chance that she too would suffer from it.
Another strange woman wanted to move to higher and ever higher planes so as to "get
back to God." On this journey she would have to "drop her garment" each time she
reached a new plane until her spirit would be "truly free."[31] I suppose that the end of
this trip she was "truly" naked. It is not explained how "dropping one's garment"
raises one's spiritual standing. There are by now so many reports about the interregnum in the various paperbacks on reincarnation that the time is surely ripe for launch-
ing a "Journal of Interregnum Studies" to be followed by a "Journal of Futurology."
The natural editors for the former would be Whitton and Fisher, for the latter (who
else?) Dr. Bruce Goldberg.

I move on to the views of Story and Stevenson. On this subject Story expresses
himself with far more caution. Story ends his article "What Happens Between Incarnations?" on an entirely skeptical note. After relating a number of cases from his own
collection in which the subjects had the most detailed memories of their interregnum
existence (all of them, I should explain, being about concrete and physical meetings
with human guides right here on earth), Story concedes that "there is nothing evidential" in his reports and that "they are purely on an anecdotal level," adding that "we

---

29. *The Power Within*, op. cit., p. 184.
30. P. 47.
31. Pp. 48–49.

have no means of checking up on them as we have checked on the memories of previous earthly lives such as I have helped Dr. Ian Stevenson collect."[32] Even those who do not share Story's high opinion of the evidential value of the latter kind of case will readily see the enormous difference between ostensible memories of *earthly* happenings in a certain place at a specified time and ostensible memories of existence in an unobservable realm whose inhabitants live either as pure minds or as "spiritual" bodies and whose activities cannot in principle be observed by anybody on earth.

It is not clear that Stevenson appreciates this enormous difference. We already noted that in his presidential address he referred to interregnum memories as evidence for the view that seeing can take place without physical eyes or any neural equipment. (Stevenson never explains whether he believes in astral or nonphysical sense-organs and nervous systems.) Earlier in the same address he admitted that such memories "*rarely* contain anything verifiable," which is not surprising since "the events narrated are *not always* referable to the world of physical objects and living persons."[33] I must protest that for the reasons just indicated such memories can *never* contain anything verifiable and that they *cannot* be "referable" to the world of physical objects and living persons. In any event Stevenson thinks that in certain cases of this kind we should "listen respectfully" to what is claimed. He reasons that if the recollections of a person about a previous life on earth turn out to be "authentic," then there is a good chance that his ostensible memories about experiences during the interregnum are also substantially correct.

Readers will not be surprised to hear that the experiences that are recalled usually correspond closely either to the habits of the "previous personalities" or to expectations about the content of the afterlife based on the local religious and cultural traditions. Tlingits in Alaska tell of a ride across a lake in a canoe right after death and a subsequent return trip across the same lake just before rebirth. Indians, on the other hand, recall meetings with Krishna or Lakshmi. In Burma and Thailand such reports are much more frequent than elsewhere. Stevenson describes some recurrent themes in these reports. Quite commonly a meeting is recalled with a sage dressed in white who acts as a friend and guide and helps the interim entity in the search for new parents. There are also frequent descriptions of a fruit offered just before the new incarnation. This is the "fruit of forgetfulness," and those who eat it later remember nothing either about earlier lives or about the interregnum. The subjects who do remember the interregnum claim that they disobeyed the order to eat the fruit. I assume that, because of their notorious gluttony, Westerners almost never refuse the fruit of forgetfulness.[34]

I am sure that most sane and sober people, including, I would hope, a number of believers in reincarnation, will have no hesitation in explaining these interregnum

---

32. Op. cit., p. 199.
33. Op. cit., p. 132.
34. According to the myth of Er in Plato's *Republic* (Book X) the soul drinks the waters of forgetfulness just as it is about to enter the new body and as a result cannot remember anything that happened before.

memories as cultural artifacts that cannot be taken seriously as evidence for anything except the way in which a person's education and indoctrination shape his religious and metaphysical beliefs and various associated experiences. Stevenson is not at all prepared to accept such an explanation. "The merits of such claims," he writes, "have to be judged separately in each case."[35] Unfortunately, he omits to tell us by what criteria they are to be judged or how we could ever overcome the evidential difficulties resulting from the total unobservability of the interregnum world. It is noteworthy that Stevenson speaks in generalities. Does he seriously believe that during the interregnum some of the Thais and Burmese are offered either physical or astral apples whose consumption by their astral bodies produces forgetfulness? If he does not seriously believe this, why is he so reluctant to admit that these recollections are illusions?

What Stevenson has never seen, or what he has tried not to see, is the intrinsic absurdity of the entire notion of an interregnum existence. He has rejected the notion that human beings could exist as pure minds and choose their next parents in such a state, but he has not seen that the alternative of an astral or spiritual body fares no better. In Chapter 10 I discussed the question of how the scars and deformities of a dead body could be transferred to a spiritual body and how they could then be transmitted to the embryo. It was clear that there is no credible *modus operandi* for these transmissions. Merely raising such questions opens up a can of worms. The reincarnationist's tribulation is most obvious in the case of clearly physical characteristics, but it equally applies to anything and everything that is supposedly transmitted via the intermediate body. We have here the problem or rather the absurdity of what might be called "world-crossings."

One of my favorite examples of such an intrinsically absurd world-crossing or mixing of "planes" (to use a favorite occultist term) comes from a chapter entitled "I Was Waiting To Be Born Again" in Richard Webb's *These Came Back*. Ivonne, a commercial artist living in Hollywood, is relating what is supposed to be a set of spontaneous memories:

> There I was, sitting on this fence waiting to be born again. . . . I was born into this body on a ranch in Las Cruces, New Mexico. . . . I was a girl, and I knew I would go into the body of the child that would be born in that ranchhouse, so I was waiting. I would walk around the place, sit on the fence, go into the house and see how things were coming along with my new mother. I picked my parents. . . . It wasn't a dream. . . . While I was sitting around waiting to be born, I had on some kind of loose robelike garment. . . . It was gray-white in color. . . . As far as getting hungry, I knew I wasn't in a physical body and food wasn't important to me. . . . I knew I couldn't be seen by my new folks or any of the people who came to visit. . . . They were solid; I wasn't. . . . When I was about to be born . . . my dad hitched up the team, put my mother in the wagon and off they went . . . to my grandparents' place.

---

35. "Some Questions Related to Cases of the Reincarnation Type," *Journal of the American Society for Psychical Research*, op. cit., p. 413.

I went along, too. Not in the wagon, but staying above it, around it. . . . All I remember of the birth was that I was outside my grandparents' house, just sort of hanging around. Then everything seemed to grow hazy and dim—and then suddenly it was just as though the lights went out. That was the end—and the beginning.[36]

The incoherence of this story is obvious: how does a nonphysical body sit on a fence, how does it walk around, and how does it wear a robelike garment? Stevenson would probably smile at the absurdity of this "recollection," but his own position is no better. He avoids such obvious nonsense only by being vague and elusive on questions of detail. The imprinting of scars on and by his spiritual body is the same incoherent world-crossing as the sitting on a physical fence or the wearing of a robe by an astral body. I would invert Stevenson's remark that we should listen attentively to a subject's recollections of his interim existence if his memories of his earlier lives on earth are (supposedly) authentic. If he has *any* ostensible recollections of an interim existence at all, this is sufficient to undermine the trustworthiness of his other reincarnation memories.

---

36. *These Came Back* (New York, 1974), pp. 116–118. Webb was a successful stage and movie actor who became interested in the occult in his later years. In addition to *These Came Back* he wrote *Great Ghosts of the West* and *Voices from Another World*. I regretted to read in the *New York Times* of June 12, 1993, that he committed suicide because of a debilitating respiratory illness.

16

More About Dr. Ian Stevenson, the "Galileo of Reincarnation"

Stevenson's Standing

The present chapter is devoted to a critical examination of the leading ideas of Ian Stevenson, whom we already met on several occasions. Stevenson is unquestionably the foremost champion of reincarnation in the world today. I briefly described the highlights of his research in Chapter 7, and I also mentioned Stevenson's impeccable academic background. Writing in the *Journal of Psychical Research* in 1986, James G. Matlock observed that, "Stevenson's work is so far superior to any other in this area, and the body of evidence he has amassed is so intriguing, that the case for reincarnation rests largely upon it."[1] It will hardly come as a surprise that Stevenson has become a hero to believers in reincarnation all over the world. It is difficult to pick up a book or pamphlet defending reincarnation and published in the last twenty- five years or so that does not refer admiringly to Stevenson's work. What may be surprising is that his work has been praised and some of it also published in respectable journals. Reviewing the first volume of his *Cases of the Reincarnation Type*, the *Journal of the American Medical Association* praised his "painstakingly and unemotionally collected cases from India in which the evidence is difficult to explain on any assumption other than reincarnation." Two of Stevenson's articles were published in *Journal of Nervous and Mental Disease* whose editor, Eugene Brody, proudly told the *New York Post* that he had received three or four hundred requests for reprints from scientists in every discipline. In the volume *Psychic Voyages* in the Time-Life series on the occult Stevenson's work is treated with great respect.

Among parapsychologists Stevenson's work has had a mixed reception. Scott

---

1. P. 230.

Rogo and Professor Chari, as we shall see, are highly critical of it. The late Louise Rhine, the widow of the more famous J. B. Rhine, wrote a friendly but also highly critical review of *Twenty Cases Suggestive of Reincarnation*.[2] John Beloff, the current editor of *Journal for Psychical Research*, is a guarded supporter of Stevenson's work. In a review of the second edition of *Twenty Cases* he writes that the book has "attained the status of a classic of parapsychological literature" and he concludes that "whether the idea of reincarnation appeals to us or not, Stevenson has made sure that, from now on, we can no longer ignore it." Beloff wonders why, since reincarnation cases are so rare that "one has to scour the world for them," one should not conclude that only some human beings reincarnate.[3] In that case, I assume that for the rest of us death is final. I earlier pointed out some of the complications of such a position.[4]

The most vocal of Stevenson's outright supporters are James G. Matlock, Satwant Pasricha and Robert Almeder.[5] Almeder's admiration for Stevenson knows no bounds. In a lengthy review of Stevenson's *Children Who Remember Previous Lives*, he tells us that this "excellent and very readable book" offers "the distinct potential for profoundly changing our way of understanding the nature of human existence and death." Stevenson's work "constitutes nothing less than a Copernican breakthrough in our understanding of human nature." In fact, "describing this book in terms such as 'excellent' or 'important' is something of an understatement."[6] One begins to wonder if our language is really adequate to describe the virtues of this work. In his recent book, *Death and Personal Survival*, which carries Stevenson's imprimatur, Almeder is quite explicit that he is claiming more for Stevenson's research than Stevenson himself. Stevenson's conclusion, he writes, is "that it is *not unreasonable to believe in reincarnation* in order to explain his best cases. While that result certainly is an incontrovertible and revolutionary finding in itself, the proper conclusion should be that it is *unreasonable to reject belief in reincarnation*."[7] In the light of Stevenson's work "the belief in reincarnation is certainly as well established as, if not better than, say, the belief in the past existence of dinosaurs." Stevenson's work has decisive implications for several philosophical issues. It helps to resolve the mind-

---

2. *Journal of Parapsychology*, 1966, pp. 263–272. (With a reply by Stevenson in the same journal in 1967, pp. 149-154.)

3. *Journal of Psychical Research*, 1975, pp. 177–179.

4. See p. 233 above.

5. I should hate to have Almeder as a supporter. We already noted his false claim that Nietzsche was a believer in reincarnation. An article of his, which was rejected by *Free Inquiry* in 1988, is listed in his 1992 book as "forthcoming in *Free Inquiry*." In Chapter 2 of his book he presents as established fact the reincarnation case of Dr. Arthur Guirdham who was thoroughly exposed in Ian Wilson's *Mind Out of Time*. Almeder mentions Wilson's book a number of times, but does not tell the reader of Wilson's exposé of Guirdham. In a devastating review of Almeder's earlier *Beyond Death* in the *Journal of Psychical Research* (April 1989) the reviewer, Michael Coleman, after listing Almeder's numerous quite outrageous distortions, remarks: "Such practices would be reprehensible in a layman, and are inexcusable in a professional philosopher." I could not agree more.

6. *Journal of the American Society for Psychical Research*, 1990, pp. 88–93.

7. *Death and Personal Survival* (Lanham, Maryland, 1992), p. 62, Almeder's italics.

body problem in favor of dualism, and it also shows that Descartes, Leibniz, and Spinoza were right in their opposition to empiricism. "The remarkable evidence uncovered and examined by Stevenson shows the correctness of 'innatism'."[8]

The Initial Presumption against Reincarnation

Let us now examine Stevenson's position and see whether it stands up to criticism. Various of our earlier discussions enable us to state a formidable initial presumption against reincarnation. A believer in reincarnation is committed to a host of collateral assumptions the most important of which I will now enumerate. When a human being dies he continues to exist not on the earth but in a region we know not where as a "pure" disembodied mind or else as an astral or some other kind of "non-physical" body; although deprived of his brain he retains memories of life on earth as well as some of his characteristic skills and traits; after a period varying from a few months to hundreds of years, this pure mind or nonphysical body, which lacks not only a brain but also any physical sense-organs, picks out a suitable woman on earth as its mother in the next incarnation, invades this woman's womb at the moment of conception of a new embryo, and unites with it to form a full-fledged human being; although the person who died may have been an adult and indeed quite old, when he is reborn he begins a new life with the intellectual and emotional attitudes of a baby; finally, many of the people born in this way did not previously live on the earth, but (depending on which version of reincarnation one subscribes to) in other planes or on other planets from which they migrate (invisibly of course), most of them preferring to enter the wombs of mothers in poor and over-populated countries where their lives are likely to be wretched. The collateral assumptions listed so far are implied by practically all forms of reincarnationism, but in Stevenson's case there is the additional implication that the memories and skills that the individual took over from the person who died and that are transmitted to the new regular body appear there for a relatively short time during childhood to disappear forever after.

If Stevenson's reports are evidence for reincarnation they must also be evidence for the collateral assumptions just mentioned. These assumptions are surely fantastic if not indeed pure nonsense; and, even in the absence of a demonstration of specific flaws, a rational person will conclude either that Stevenson's reports are seriously defective or that his alleged facts can be explained without bringing in reincarnation. An acceptance of the collateral assumptions would, to borrow a phrase from Søren Kierkegaard, amount to the "crucifixion" of our intellect.

It is of some interest to note that Dr. Eugene Brody, who published several of Stevenson's articles in the *Journal of Nervous and Mental Disease* and who appears not to see any significant flaws in Stevenson's investigative procedures, nevertheless

---

8. P. 65.

refuses to accept reincarnation because it cannot be reconciled with the body of scientific knowledge. "The problem lies less in the quality of the data Stevenson adduces," Brody writes, than "in the body of knowledge and theory which must be abandoned or radically modified in order to accept reincarnation."[9] "I am not yet ready," Brody concludes his review, "to regard the transmission of information or some aspect of 'personality' from a dead or dying brain to another brain-body in the process of conception or early development by unidentified means, over a significant time interval, as the most likely explanation for the cases which he has designated "reincarnation type.' "[10]

In a simplified form, the question before a rational person can be stated in the following words: which is more likely—that there are astral bodies, that they invade the wombs of prospective mothers, and that the children can remember events from a previous life although the brains of the previous persons have long been dead, or that Stevenson's children, their parents, or some of the other witnesses and informants are, intentionally or unintentionally, not telling the truth: that they are lying, or that their very fallible memories and powers of observations have led them to make false statements and bogus identifications.

The Holes in the Reincarnation Cases

Stevenson's cases read much better in summary than when one examines them in detail. He has admitted that all his cases, even the strongest ones, possess some weaknesses. I think that this is a gross understatement. They all have big holes, and they do not even begin to add up to a significant counterweight to the initial presumption against reincarnation.

In Chapter 10, I pointed to some of the fatal flaws of the birthmark case of Corliss Chotkin, Jr. In this section I represent the critical examinations of two other cases by previous writers, both of which have been ignored by Stevenson as well as his associates. The first of these occurs in a review of *Cases of the Reincarnation Type, Volume One—Ten Cases in India* (1975) by J. Fraser Nicol.[11] Nicol offers a detailed critique of two cases in the book under review. I will summarize the latter of these, because Stevenson himself regards it as "one of the best-authenticated" of all reincarnation cases. I agree with all of Nicol's strictures, and I will add some comments of my own.

The case concerns Jagdish Chandra who was born on March 4, 1923, in the Indian city of Bareilly. At the age of three and a half he suddenly claimed to have lived before as Jai Gopal in Benares. Stevenson regards the case as so strong because Jagdish's father

9. Review of Stevenson's *Cases of the Reincarnation Type*, Volume Two, *Journal of Nervous and Mental Disease*, 1979, p. 770.

10. Ibid., p. 774.

11. *Parapsychological Review*, 1976, pp. 12–15. Stevenson lists this review in the bibliography of *Children Who Remember Previous Lives*, but he has never replied to it.

wrote a brief account of the boy's memories for a newspaper before any contact had been established with the "previous" family in Benares. Jagdish's father, K. K. N. Sahay, was a lawyer and an ardent believer in reincarnation. After hearing the boy's recollections, he invited some "friends and members of the bar" to talk to the boy. He then published a letter in the *Leader*, an English-language newspaper, describing the boy's recollections and asking for confirmation if possible. A number of persons in Benares responded to Sahay's appeal. He then wrote additional letters to the press requesting the assistance of "some leaders of India to send their representatives," who would conduct the boy to Benares, which was about three miles from Bareilly.

Stevenson assures us that Sahay was a "person of the utmost rectitude," but in his letter to the *Leader*, he had made the false statement that he had no friends or relatives in Benares. In fact, he had a cousin and her husband living there, who could very well have told him about other families in that city. In 1927, Sahay published a pamphlet entitled *Reincarnation: Verified Cases of Rebirth After Death*. This pamphlet reproduces the following statement made by Jagdish on July 26, 1926, before a Bareilly magistrate:

> My name is Jai Gopal. My father's name is Babu Pandey. Our city is Benares. The Ganges River is near my house. The gate of the house is similar to the gate of Kuarpur in Bareilly. My brother was Jai Mangal. He was bigger than I am. He died of poisoning. . . . Babu Pandey keeps his money in an iron safe. It is on the left-hand side, sunk in the wall and high up. Babuji likes Rabri [an Indian sweet]. . . . Whenever Babuji washes his face, he massages it with clay. He has a phaeton. . . . He also has a motor car. My aunt wears gold bangles, . . . Babuji wears a ring. My aunt covers herself with a long veil. . . . The Ganges is nearby. My aunt makes bread. I wear a loin cloth when I take my bath, . . . Babuji has dark glasses. Babuji listens to the songs of a prostitute named Bhagwati.[12]

Most of what Jagdish said was found to be true. Nicol, however, points out that the magistrate asked no questions and evidently just wrote down what Jagdish said. It looks to him, Nicol goes on, like something learned by heart and recited on request. He also wonders if the Hindi word for "prostitute" is known among small children in India. Two months after Jagdish had made his first statements about a previous life, his father took him to Benares where large crowds had gathered. It will hardly surprise the reader that Jagdish was able to find the house of his former father, Babu Pandey, who denied being the father of Jai Gopal.

There are many gaping holes in this story. Stevenson tells us that when he was a young child, Jagdish was always under the protection of a servant or a member of the family. It is noteworthy that when Stevenson got to Bareilly, very long after this case had developed, he made no attempt to find the servant, assuming that he or she was still alive. Nicol asks how we can be sure that the servant may not have been the source of the boy's information. Nicol also regards the father or even the mother as

---

12. Quoted in *Cases of the Reincarnation Type, Volume One—Ten Cases in India*, pp. 151–52.

possible culprits. My own impression is that the father was the guilty party. The following scenario seems to me a far better explanation of the events than any reincarnationist assumption. At the age of three Jagdish made some innocent remarks which the father at once twisted into reincarnation memories. The cousin and her husband who were living in Benares and whose existence Sahay had tried to hide supplied him with information about a person who had died at the appropriate time. This was Jai Gopal, and Jagdish before long came to believe what his father told him, that he had lived before as Gopal in Benares. The father then began his publicity campaign, terminating in the triumphant journey to Benares. None of this is farfetched if Nicol is right in his assumption that Jagdish's statement to the magistrate had been learned by heart. Jagdish himself probably repeated the story so often that he eventually came to believe it. Incidentally, there is a possible difficulty about dates. According to one account, Gopal died early in 1924 or at the end of 1923, i.e., *after* the birth of Jagdish.

Needless to say, I have no means of knowing whether the scenario just sketched approximates what actually happened. My construction is based on what Professor Chari has revealed about the manufacture of reincarnation cases in India, and also what is known about religious or "holy" lying. I will report Chari's account in detail later in this chapter. Religious lying is a depressing phenomenon, which has been discussed by many famous philosophers including Francis Bacon, Voltaire, and Hume. I already adverted to it in Chapter 10 and I will say more about it later.

Chapter 23 of B. N. Moore's *The Philosophical Possibilities Beyond Death*,[13] an excellent book which deserves to be better known, contains a detailed discussion of the case of Sujith, which forms Chapter 7 of Stevenson's *Cases of the Reincarnation Type, Volume Two: Ten Cases in Sri Lanka* [1977]. Sujith was born in 1969 in Mt. Lavigna, a suburb of Colombo. He is reported to have started making statements about an earlier life in Gorakana, a small village seven miles south of Mt. Lavigna. Sujith mentioned a girl by the name of Kusuma in Gorakana who was able to connect some of his statements with her late uncle, Sammy Fernando. Sujith was taken to Gorakana where he reportedly recognized Kusuma, several of her relatives, and a number of other persons. From then on it was clear to the local believers that Sujith was, in fact, the reincarnation of Sammy Fernando. Moore shows in detail how Sujith could have obtained all this information by natural means. Moore also points out that Sammy Fernando died only a little more than six months before the birth of Sujith. Sujith's mother said that he was born after a seven-month pregnancy, something that has not been independently confirmed. Even if this is accepted, Moore remarks, the embryo was at least one month old before Sammy Fernando died. We therefore know that at one point Sujith was definitely not Sammy Fernando. If he later became

---

13. Springfield, Ill., 1981. Moore is a professor of philosophy at California State University in Chico, Ca. Stevenson nowhere so much as mentions Moore's discussion. J.G. Matlock, a Stevenson follower, to whom I referred earlier, mentions Moore in his extremely comprehensive survey, "Past Life Memory Case Studies" [in S. Krippner (Ed.), *Advances in Parapsychological Research 6* (Jefferson, N.C., 1990)], but offers no information about Moore's critique.

Sammy, Moore asks, "what became of the individual who earlier was not Sammy: was he, too, reincarnated?"

In discussing this case, Stevenson refers to the critics who think reincarnation cases must, "accommodate to the current orthodoxy in biology." They regard the fact of Sujith's birth before Sammy's death as a disqualifying objection to the case. Stevenson tells us that a dispute arose on this point between Rationalist and Buddhists polemicists in the newspapers of Sri Lanka.[14] "For me," Stevenson writes, "this controversy seemed concerned with a side issue. Cases of the reincarnation type, if accepted as authentic, challenge orthodox biology on assumptions far more important than the minimal length of pregnancy that can produce a viable infant."[15] If this is so Moore comments, "proof of reincarnation would require disproof of orthodox biology, and thus would require evidence even more vast than that which supports orthodox biology."[16]

I don't have the space to provide the details of another examination of a Stevenson case, to which he did offer a response. The case is that of Imad Elawar, described by Stevenson in Chapter 6 of *Twenty Cases Suggestive of Reincarnation*. A critical examination by Professor Leonard Angel, of Douglas College, New Westminster, British Columbia, appeared in the *Skeptical Inquirer* of 1994. Stevenson replied to Angel in the *Skeptical Inquirer* of 1995 and sent a full rejoinder to interested parties, including the present writer. Angel responded in the same issue of the *Skeptical Inquirer*. He has also written a longer rejoinder, copies of which can be obtained from him upon request. A full discussion of the same case is available in Angel's *Enlightenment East and West*, a book published in 1994 by the University Press of the State of New York. It would be unfair for me to comment on the merits of this critique or subsequent exchanges without an account of the details. I will merely observe that Angel confirmed in my mind the serious misgivings I already had about Stevenson's investigative methods. Even if one does not share Angel's view that the case is disastrously weak, there can be no doubt that it is highly problematic and not the sort of thing to refute "orthodox biology" or to overcome the initial presumption against reincarnation.

Wilson, Roll, and Chari

In this section I will report and evaluate the criticisms of Stevenson's work by three writers of very different backgrounds. All these criticisms make some valid points, but some are less damaging than others. I will begin with objections found in the chapter on Stevenson in Ian Wilson's *Mind Out of Time*. In Chapter 7 I mentioned

---

14. I was happy to learn that there are rationalists in Sri Lanka. I shall try to learn the names of some of them and send them copies of the present book.

15. *Cases of Reincarnation Type, Volume Two*, p. 271.

16. P. 178.

several of Wilson's objections to the Ryall case. Here I am concerned with his criticisms of the child cases. In "The Explanatory Value of the Idea of Reincarnation," Stevenson noted that, "more subjects remember previous lives in higher socio-economic conditions than in lower ones."[17] In a summary ten years later he mentioned that two-thirds of Indian subjects recalled better material conditions while one-third remembered conditions that were worse.[18] Wilson not implausibly suggests that in such cases the "memories" are produced by a wish for better living conditions. In one case, for example, a boy asked for one-third of the land of his past-life father, showing no interest in his previous incarnation when this former "father" lost his fortune and became poorer than his father in the present life. Given Stevenson's figures this suggestion would not of course account for all cases. In any event, even if it is granted that all cases are illusory, there can be no doubt that other factors are also at work. Wilson also objects that in many cases there was or easily could have been contact between the parents and persons connected with the "previous personality" about whose life the child had accurate recollections.[19]

In this connection one of the findings by William G. Roll deserves to be mentioned. Roll, who is a professor of psychology at West Georgia College, a lay Zen monk, and a leading figure in American parapsychology, appears to be an admirer of Stevenson's research. Nevertheless he cannot refrain from calling attention to certain grounds for skepticism. In his extremely erudite article "The Changing Perspectives on Life after Death,"[20] Roll notes that only in seven of Stevenson's cases were the child's statements about a previous life recorded prior to the attempts at verification. Stevenson has himself admitted that where this is not done subsequent developments may lead to embellishments of what the child is supposed to have said. Yet, in all these seven cases, the child lived "within the geographical or social circumference of the previous personality." The "close connection" between the children and the surviving friends and relatives of the previous personality "raises questions of sensory cues,"[21] by which Roll of course means "normal sources of information." He charitably "assumes" that Stevenson's investigations have ruled out such normal channels.

In fairness it should be mentioned that in some of their most recent case studies, Stevenson and his associates have tried to avoid these and other pitfalls. In "Three New Cases of the Reincarnation Type in Sri Lanka with Written Records Made Before Verifications,"[22] Stevenson and his coauthor G. Samararatne claim to possess, as the title of their article suggests, statements about previous lives made before any at-

---

17. *Journal of Nervous and Mental Disease*, 1977, p. 315.

18. *Children Who Remember Previous Lives*, pp. 215–216.

19. *Mind Out of Time*, pp. 58–60.

20. Stanley Krippner (Ed.), *Advances in Parapsychological Research*, Vol. 3 (New York, 1982).

21. P. 199.

22. *Journal of Scientific Exploration*, 1988. See also A. Mills, E. Haraldsson, and H. H. J. Keil, "Replication Studies of Cases Suggestive of Reincarnation by Three Independent Investigators," *Journal of the American Society of Psychical Research*, 1994.

tempt at verification. They also claim to have extremely strong evidence that there was no prior contact between the families in question. I concede that, on the face of it, these investigations are a significant improvement over earlier cases. However, they still have many gaping holes.

One of Stevenson's most persistent critics is Professor C. T. K. Chari, an Indian philosopher, now retired from Madras Christian University, who is not a Western materialist or positivist but a Hindu and a well-known parapsychologist. Professor Chari does not reject reincarnation, but he believes that Stevenson is incredibly naive and that his reports have no evidential value. In a number of articles Chari has given us some insight into the way Indian cases "suggestive of reincarnation" are manufactured. He points out that cases of the kind Stevenson has collected occur mostly in cultures in which there is a deeply ingrained belief in reincarnation and, what is equally significant, the *type* of reincarnation claimed fits in with the peculiar form of reincarnation belief prevalent in a given area. Stevenson cannot deny these facts and counters that while cultural factors influence the details, they do not "generate" the cases themselves. Chari insists that they are cultural artifacts, pure and simple. "A reincarnationist fantasy in the small Asian child," he writes, "starts typically in play or a gamelike situation."[23] It is then promoted (or retarded) by the conscious or unconscious beliefs, attitudes, and responses of parents, guardians, and interested bystanders. Chari calls this fantasy the Asian counterpart of the "imaginary playmate" or "fictitious companion" that has been disclosed in many Western studies of childhood. He offers the guess that we have here "two ways of a child's reaching out to the world: one by *having* an idealized object [the imaginary playmate] and the other by *being* an idealized object [an earlier life on earth]."[24]

Neither parents, nor bystanders, nor witnesses professing skepticism, and not even translators can, according to Chari, be entirely trusted when it comes to reincarnation. He mentions that Stevenson in one place considers a "culturally endorsed wave of credulity," but according to Chari, what we encounter in India and also in other countries from which Stevenson has drawn his cases is something much deeper—"subtler cultural components relatively more permanent than cyclic social phenomena such as fads and crazes."[25] Stevenson's "frankly admitted ignorance of Asiatic languages" and the resulting dependence on translators and interpreters must weaken the scientific value of his reports. I might mention here that at least two of the interpreters gratefully listed by Stevenson in his "Acknowledgements" for *Twenty Cases Suggestive of Reincarnation* are tabloid characters. One of these is none other than the past-life regressionist H. N. Banerjee, whom we met in Chapter 6 who reassured the actress Ann Miller that she had once been an Egyptian queen. The other

---

23. "Reincarnation Research: Method and Interpretation," in M. Ebon (Ed.), *Signet Handbook of Parapsychology*, p. 319. See also Chari's review-article of *Twenty Cases Suggestive of Reincarnation* in the *International Journal of Parapsychology*, 1967, pp. 217–22.

24. P. 320.

25. *International Journal of Parapsychology*, p.218.

tabloid figure is Dr. Jamuna Prasad, accurately described by Ian Wilson as an "ardent Hindu, with a particular interest in spreading Hindu belief in reincarnation."[26] Stevenson tells us that Prasad acted as chief interpreter during his second visit to India, and that he and his associates "took extraordinary pains to make the translations as accurate as they could be."[27] The *National Enquirer* for March 3, 1987, had a blaring headline on its title page—"Life After Death—Top World Expert Reveals Startling New Evidence." The "top expert" turned out to be none other than Prasad, picture and all. The "new evidence" consisted of four cases, three of which are among the ten forming the main body of Stevenson's Volume I. We are not surprised to learn that, according to Dr. Prasad, life after death is an "absolute certainty." I don't believe in guilt by association and I am convinced that Stevenson is basically an honest man, but I wish that he had employed more trustworthy interpreters. Chari's point is well-taken.

The Fading of the Memories

As already noted, before very long, Stevenson's children forget all of their memories of a previous life. "The children," he writes, "nearly always stop talking about their previous lives between the ages of five and eight." Stevenson notes that the forgetting "coincides with the age at which the child leaves his narrow home circle and begins a wider participation in life outside the home at school and elsewhere."[28]

There is surely something very strange about this universal forgetting, but as far as I know, Chari is the only one of Stevenson's critics to address himself to this puzzle. Near the end of his review of *Twenty Cases Suggestive of Reincarnation* Chari remarks that "this circumstance alone [i.e. the fading of the memories] should give us pause."[29] Chari mentions "possession" as possible explanation, and it is certainly true that a possession-theory is just as consistent with the data as the reincarnation hypothesis. If B started remembering being A at the age of three and at the age of eight forgets ever having been A, this would indeed be consistent with the view that B is really A and that we have here only one soul. However, it would be equally consistent with the view that B is not A, but that B's body was invaded by A's soul which coexisted with B's soul for five years and then left. This possession theory makes a number of outlandish assumptions, but they are no more outlandish than those made by the reincarnation theory which I spelled out in an earlier section.

In the light of Chari's remarks about the social or cultural construction of reincarnation cases another more mundane explanation of the fading suggests itself. The children gradually stop "remembering" their previous lives because they have become tired of the charade and now have better things to do. The parents, too, for that mat-

---

26. *Mind Out of Time*, op. cit., p. 87.
27. *Twenty Cases*, p. xi.
28. *Children Who Remember Previous Lives*, p. 106.
29. Op. cit p. 222.

ter, have by now derived all the publicity and possible financial advantage from the commotion. This explanation is supported by the fact that Ryall,[30] who was an elderly man when he went public with his "recollections," did not subsequently forget his previous life. For him the past life recollections had become the emotional center of his existence. They brought him the distinguished American visitor, Ian Stevenson, and they were the basis of a best-selling book which in turn led to his being the star of a BBC program. Unlike the children, he did not have better things to do. It should be emphasized that there is no suggestion that the children who forgot their past lives suffered any general amnesia and were also unable to remember events of their current lives. That the child cases are charades is fully confirmed by the experience of Dr. D. R. Barker.

The Case of Dr. Barker

The late Scott Rogo's *The Search for Yesterday*[31] is a badly written defense of reincarnation which does not contain any arguments that had not been stated equally well or better in other publications. However, because of his lifelong involvement in parapsychological activities, Rogo was able to call attention to facts which outsiders like the present writer would otherwise never have learned. One of these concerns an attempted "replication" of Stevenson's investigations by Dr. David Read Barker, an anthropologist who had done research for his doctoral dissertation in India.

Stevenson hired Barker to assist him in the analysis of some of his cases and also to undertake investigations of other cases in conjunction with Satwant Pasricha, a true and tried believer and disciple. Barker could not find a single case in which there was convincing evidence of the presence of a paranormal process. According to Rogo's account, Barker told him in August 1978 that Stevenson was pressuring him to keep silent about his results. Whether or not Barker was in fact under pressure to keep silent, he did go into print on the subject on two separate occasions. One of these was a letter in the *Journal of Parapsychology*.[32] The other was a joint publication with Pasricha dealing with the case of Rakesh Gaur in the *European Journal of Parapsychology* in 1981. In the letter, Barker described the Gaur case as "the most authentic, evidential and thoroughly investigated" of fifty-nine cases he had studied with Pasricha, and he concludes that it is "best interpreted as a result of Indian social psychology rather than parapsychology."

The 1981 article consists of three parts. The first is a report of interviews conducted by both authors, and this is followed by two separate evaluations. Rakesh Gaur was born in 1969 and claimed to recall his life and death as Bithal Das in the town

---

30. See pp. 102–105.
31. Englewood Cliffs, New Jersey, 1985.
32. 1979, pp. 268–69.

of Tonk. The major portions of the report deal with the journey by Rakesh, accompanied by his father, who was an enthusiastic champion of the case, to Tonk to make the appropriate identifications. Pasricha was greatly impressed by the evidential value of the case. Despite undeniable "discrepancies in the testimonies of the informants" she concluded that "Rakesh had somehow obtained his information about Bithal Das through some paranormal process."[33] In his section, Barker offered detailed reasons for the skeptical conclusion he had already mentioned earlier in his letter. Anybody sufficiently interested should read all three parts of the article. I have no doubt that, unless one is already a passionate believer in reincarnation, one will find Barker's conclusion vastly more reasonable. I should add that Pasricha strikes me as a person of truly staggering credulity, though not quite reaching the world championship level of Kübler-Ross or Stanislav Grof. The "identifications" performed by Rakesh remind one of nothing more than the identification scenes in *The Return of Martin Guerre* in which the charming imposter Pensette is "recognized" by most of the townspeople as the missing Martin Guerre and in turn "recognizes" them, on the whole more successfully, after they have introduced themselves. The entire 1981 article is highly instructive because it clearly illustrates Chari's view that the kind of case investigated by Stevenson is a cultural artifact and nothing else. Pasricha writes like a slightly more uninhibited double of Stevenson, and the shortcomings of his "methodology" are transparently obvious here.[34]

After Rogo's book was published, Stevenson denied that he had ever exerted any pressure on Barker. He also downgraded the extent of Barker's investigations. These statements appeared in the January 1986 issue of the *Journal of the Society for Psychical Research*. The October 1986 issue of the same periodical contains a further exchange between Rogo and Stevenson. Rogo reaffirmed all his original charges. Barker, he writes, asserted that "he had *three* negative reports on reincarnation cases in the works, but Stevenson was trying to prevent him from publishing *any* of them."[35] Rogo again reported Barker as claiming that legal threats were part of Stevenson's pressure. For his part, Stevenson again flatly denied that he ever tried to interfere with Barker's freedom to express his views. In a further rejoinder, which has not been published but which he was circulating to interested parties, Rogo remarked that Stevenson has a habit of using legal threats and informs his readers that he had filed details of four such incidents with the editors of the *Journal of the Society for Psychical Research*. Unfortunately, Barker is not available to give his version of the events. I understand that he was so shaken by the entire episode that he has left the field of parapsychology.

---

33. Pp. 405–406.

34. Stevenson has criticized me for describing Pasricha as a "true and tried believer" on the ground that she once was a skeptic and came to accept reincarnation because Stevenson's cases impressed her favorably (*Journal of Scientific Exploration*, 1994, p. 423). This is a non sequitur. A person can be a true and tried believer in something that she at one time rejected.

35. P. 470, Rogo's italics.

The Problem of Western Children

In any critical reader of Stevenson's books and articles the question almost irresistibly arises why the kind of case that seems to occur with such frequency in India and other countries in which reincarnation is part of the accepted religion does not also occur in the West. Stevenson has dealt with this question in his introduction to Ryall's book and in the article "Some Questions Related to Cases of the Reincarnation Type"[36] to which I have referred on several occasions. In the former discussion Stevenson tells us that he values the publication of Ryall's book not only because of its "intrinsic merit" but also because its publication may give courage "to other persons who feel inclined to expose what seemed to them memories of previous lives, but fear unpleasant consequences if they do so."[37] Cases like Ryall's will end "the long night of suppression of reincarnation cases in the West," a "night" that has lasted "more than fourteen centuries." In the more extended discussion in his 1974 article Stevenson first flatly denies that cases of the type featured in his books do not occur in the West. He asserts that he "now" has forty cases of children in the continental United States. Stevenson adds that cases also occur in Europe, in Central and South America, and among groups in Asia whose religions do not include belief in reincarnation. He admits, however, that such cases are reported much less frequently in cultures where the population does not believe in reincarnation, but he strongly emphasizes that this admission applies only to *reported* cases. We have no valid information, he writes, "about the actual incidence of cases," and he once again expresses his suspicion that many parents refrain from reporting signs of reincarnation behavior on the part of their children for fear of ostracism and ridicule.[38]

Both Stevenson and several of his fans and admirers have repeatedly referred to a book in preparation that is devoted to Western cases. In the General Introduction to *Cases of the Reincarnation Type, Volume One* (1975), Stevenson supplies the following information:

> In my first book of case reports I stated that I had few from the United States (other than Alaska) and also relatively few from Europe. It remains true that in relative numbers we have far fewer cases from the United States (apart from Alaska) and Europe than we have from Asia. However, the number of cases reported to me from the United States has increased markedly since 1966, and more reports have also come from Europe. Of the American and European cases, suffice it to say here that on the whole they resemble in their characteristics the cases from Asia, although the children subjects of these Western cases rarely claim to remember as much detail about the previous lives they talk about as do their Asian counterparts.

---

36. *Journal of the American Society for Psychical Research*, 1974.
37. P. 29.
38. P. 396, Stevenson's italics.

He then repeats that as of 1974 he has in the United States more than forty cases

> of the type in which the subjects began to talk about the previous lives they seemed to remember at the same young age when most Asian subjects also first express their memories. The number of fairly recently reported cases in both Europe and the United States has justified reserving two separate volumes of this series to deal with them.[39]

At the end of his review of Stevenson's *Cases of the Reincarnation Type, Volume II,* from which I quoted earlier, Dr. Brody, who is a personal friend of Stevenson, refers to the latter's "forthcoming book of cases in the United States which should be of great interest to those who have followed Stevenson's work so far."[40] Writing in 1992, Robert Almeder, the aforementioned enthusiast from Georgia, asserts that "as of 1990 there are literally hundreds of cases, varying in their degree of richness, currently under investigation and documented in Great Britain and North America."[41] I assume that Almeder is referring to cases collected by Stevenson and not by himself.

With all this abundance of material, it is surprising that no book on either American or European cases has so far appeared. All that Stevenson has given us is a meager six-page article, "American Children Who Remember Previous Lives,"[42] and six short descriptions of Western cases in Chapter 4 of *Children Who Remember Previous Lives*. In an interview published in *Family Circle* of June 1978, Stevenson had deplored the paucity of his Western cases on the ground that the children remember very few verifiable details. The 1983 article fully confirms this judgment. The six cases described in the book give a much better idea of what Western children report than the bare summary of the 1983 article.

Before going any further I should give a brief account of these six cases. Four are from the United States, one from Finland, and one from England. I apologize for the extremely boring nature of all except the last of these cases. The reader will note that all the six families involved are evidently lower middle class with very little education. I find it difficult to envisage such a case developing in a family where the parents have studied science or philosophy, and not because of any "suppression" by anybody. Stevenson explains that the accounts are drastically condensed versions of the full reports, adding that "brevity and thoroughness are not usually compatible."[43] I agree, but I would add that Stevenson's cases always read more convincingly in summary because the holes are not so clearly visible.

Erin Jackson was born in 1969 in an unnamed town in Indiana. At the age of three she started talking about an earlier life as a boy, insisted on dressing like a boy, and in engaging in boys' activities. Stevenson visited the Jackson home in 1980.

---

39. *Cases of the Reincarnation Type, Volume One*, p. 2.
40. *Journal of Nervous and Mental Disease,* 1977, op. cit. p. 774.
41. "On Reincarnation" in G. Doore (Ed.), *What Survives?* (Los Angeles, 1992).
42. *Journal of Nervous and Mental Disease,* 1983.
43. P. 286.

Erin's mother had become a believer in reincarnation by then, but she insisted that Erin's statements about a previous life were entirely spontaneous. Unfortunately, neither the location nor the period of the earlier life was ever mentioned.

Roberta Morgan was born in 1961 in an unnamed town in Minnesota. She started talking about a previous life when she was between two and two-and-a-half years old, but her mother at that time dismissed the statements as nonsense. Several years later, long after Roberta had stopped talking about a previous life, the mother became a reincarnationist and contacted Stevenson. She reproached herself for not having attempted to contact Roberta's previous family. This would not have been easy since, in Stevenson's words, Roberta "gave few clues" to the period of her previous incarnation. Roberta denied ever having died, which makes this a particularly puzzling case that should be of interest to philosophers writing about person identity: if Roberta did not die, what happened to the earlier body and who is now inhabiting it?

At the age of three Michael Wright is said to have started remembering events in the life of Walter Miller who had been his mother's boyfriend before she married Michael's father. Walter was killed in a car crash at the age of eighteen, and Mrs. Wright desperately wanted him to return. She was a great believer in reincarnation and with her mother formed a reincarnationist "enclave" in the midst of a conservative Christian community. Mrs. Wright had all kinds of psychic experiences which Stevenson does not describe, but he does complain about her credulity. He nevertheless believes that she accurately reported Michael's statements and he is not prepared to dismiss the case.

Replacing people who died in accidents and who are greatly missed seems to be a common theme in reincarnation cases, East and West. Mrs. Eastland, an Idaho housewife, had lost her six-year-old daughter Minnie in an accident in 1961. She would have given anything to get Minnie back. Both she and her older daughter, Sharon, had dreams which they interpreted to mean that Minnie would come back. In 1964 Susan was born, and when she was two, she started to talk about incidents from Minnie's life that she herself "could not normally have known about." Even Stevenson considers this case "comparatively weak," since "we cannot exclude the possibility that Mrs. Eastland had, without being aware that she was doing so, passed on some information to Susan."[44]

The remaining two Western cases are in their general features quite similar to the Eastland case. In the Finnish case of Samuel Helander, the person who died prematurely was Samuel's uncle Pertti. Both Samuel's mother (Pertti's sister), and Samuel's grandmother (Pertti's mother), were eager to get Pertti back. Pertti had died in April 1975 and Samuel was born in June 1976. There were the usual announcing dreams, and to the delight of his mother and grandmother, Samuel had numerous memories and recognition experiences, "proving" that he was indeed Pertti.

The most interesting of the six Western cases is that of Gillian and Jennifer Pollock which has also been described in considerable detail by Ian Wilson.[45] Joanne and

---

44. *Family Circle*, June 14, 1978, p. 40.

45. *Mind Out Of Time*, op. cit., pp. 19–26. Wilson's account is a great deal more skeptical than the one given by Stevenson.

Jacqueline, the adolescent daughters of John and Florence Pollock, were killed in a particularly horrible car accident in a small English town in May 1957. John Pollock was an ardent believer in reincarnation. When his wife gave birth to identical twins, Gillian and Jennifer, in October 1958, John was convinced that the twins were the reincarnations of the girls who had been killed. There were, as usual, recognitions that "could not be explained in a normal way," but there was also birthmark evidence which greatly impressed Stevenson. Jennifer, the younger twin, had two birthmarks that corresponded both in location and size to marks on Jacqueline's body. The Pollock case caused quite a stir in England. As late as 1979 the twins, birthmarks and all, appeared during the London Weekend Television's *Credo* program. Stevenson has presumably written up the case in detail in his book on birthmarks which has yet to be published.[46] In later years, the twins had no traces of any memories of a previous life, and I gather from the accounts offered by both Stevenson and Wilson that they themselves are quite skeptical about any reincarnationist explanation.

Why is there this disparity in the number and the quality of Eastern and Western cases? I don't believe that the answer is difficult to find, and it has nothing to do with suppression. In the West, we do not have a host of witnesses with an ardent belief in reincarnation who will manufacture the necessary "proofs"; and, if any such proofs were manufactured, we have numerous skeptics right on the spot who would subject them to a much more elaborate and searching scrutiny than any undertaken by Stevenson and his associates. Stevenson's remarks about the probable occurrence of reincarnation cases among Western children will come as a total surprise to child psychologists and teachers in the West who would presumably notice such claims and behavior. Several of my closest friends were kindergarten teachers for extended periods, and they never noticed any such thing. I knew the great and unforgettable A. S. Neill, the founder of Summerhill. Neill was the last man on earth to ridicule a child for saying strange things or behaving in an unusual way and yet, in the fifty-four years he headed the school, he did not once come across a Stevensonian case. I don't doubt that if Summerhill had been in a certain region of India or Thailand or Alaska a number of children with the appropriate reincarnation behavior would have been noticed. As far as I can tell, "the long night of suppression" Stevenson talks about exists only in his imagination.

Voltaire once observed that in England where there was a relatively high level of education (he is writing in the middle of the eighteenth century) miracles no longer happen, while in France, where the level of education was extremely low, miracles occurred with great frequency. We may be sure, he added, that if the level of instruction in England were to decline, miracles would again occur there in profusion.

In any event, Stevenson concedes that "suppression" does not tell the whole story and that "other factors may come into play." At this stage we are treated to one of his extravaganzas. Stevenson evidently lives in a cloud-cuckoo-land, and he regards the wildest and most fanciful assumptions, many of which are of questionable conceptual

---

46. See above, p. 136.

coherence, as being on an equal footing with straightforward empirical hypotheses. He resorts to such extravaganzas whenever the specter of cultural factors accounting for reincarnation beliefs raises its menacing head. If, he reasons, Westerners do in fact reincarnate they would almost certainly not have believed in reincarnation in their previous lives, which, Stevenson assumes, were also in the West. This lack of belief in reincarnation would have two effects on the reincarnated Westerner. In the first place, disbelief in reincarnation naturally includes a denial that anybody can remember an earlier life, and "this could act as a powerful suggestion inhibiting the carryover of actual memories from one life to another."[47] Nevertheless, memories of a previous life may "break through" the "negative suggestion" stemming from disbelief. This brings us to the second inhibiting factor. Because of his disbelief (and I suppose his ignorance), a Westerner is clearly at a grave disadvantage in such a situation compared with a Hindu, a Buddhist, or a Druse. All of them have "frameworks of belief" that make their memories intelligible. In the East this is true even of children. In India, for example, children are exposed to the teaching of reincarnation at a very early age. By the time, therefore, they have memories of previous lives, between the ages of three and five, Hindu and Buddhist children "can accept the memories for what they seem to be instead of rejecting them as alien and unlikely to be true."[48] It may nevertheless happen that even in the East parents have failed to tell a child about reincarnation. In the East this would not be fatal. For in his previous life the child was in all likelihood a believer in reincarnation, and hence he may remember not only events of the previous life but also enough of his previous belief-system to accept the memories as "natural."

It is ironic that Stevenson should object to psychoanalytic theories as unscientific on the ground that they are unfalsifiable or "irrefutable." This view is expressed in an exchange with S. E. Braude who is a professor of philosophy as well as a parapsychologist. Braude had reproached Stevenson for the superficiality of many of his interviews, a charge also leveled at him by Wilson and Chari, and one which I endorse. In the course of his reply, Stevenson asserts that "psychoanalysis has become discredited because of its irrefutability."[49] The answer to this is that most psychoanalytic theories are not at all unfalsifiable. Some of them, like the Freudian theories about the causation of paranoia and hysteria and the universality of the Oedipus complex are not only falsifiable but seem to be clearly false."[50] In any event, Stevenson is hardly the man to make this criticism. For he seems to have a special penchant for advancing to-

---

47. "Some Questions Related To Cases Of The Reincarnation Type," op. cit., p. 396.

48. Ibid., p. 397.

49. *Journal of Psychical Exploration*, 1992, p. 146. There is an excellent reply by Braude on p. 153.

50. Psychoanalysis has indeed fallen on evil days, but this is primarily due to the ineffectiveness of psychoanalytic therapy and to the recognition that several of Freud's theories are either false or based on insufficient evidence. I believe that there is much that is sound in Freud' s approach and that it would be a major misfortune if the whole of psychoanalysis were simply discarded. An explanation of what I find so valuable in Freud's approach is contained in my 1995 Prometheus Lectures—"Nietzsche, Freud, Reich" —given at the New School of Social Research in November 1995. A summary of this lecture appeared in the Spring 1996 issue of *Free Inquiry*.

tally unfalsifiable statements. How, for example, could one test his statement that disbelief in reincarnation in a previous life is liable to inhibit the reincarnation memories of Western children? How is one to verify or falsify any of Stevenson's statements about his "intermediate body" which is "nonphysical" but "composed of some kind of matter" and which invades the womb of the prospective mother, carrying with it memories and birthmarks? And what of the various theories he regards as possible explanations of the population increase—that "new human minds are created as needed and attached to human bodies," that "minds presently incarnated in human bodies have been promoted from previous incarnations in non-human bodies," and the conjecture that "many discarnate minds may be awaiting reincarnation"?[51]

Stevenson and "The Man of Miracles"

The October 1988 issue of the *Journal of the Society for Psychical Research* features a review by Stevenson of *Miracles are My Visiting Cards* by Erlandur Haraldsson, whom we already met as coauthor of *At the Hour of Death*. Haraldsson's book deals with the miracles performed by Sathya Sai Baba, the current superstar among Indian holy men, who is known in India as "the man of miracles." Sai Baba is especially noted for his production of what parapsychologists call "apports"—material objects out of the air or from unspecified locations.[52] Stevenson refers to the "instantaneous production of jewelry, sweets, and, above all, the fine-grained ash known as dibhut." The article in the Harper *Encyclopedia* also lists religious statues and objects made of gold, jewelry, photographs, business cards, and even stamps bearing Sai Baba's likeness which had not been officially issued by the government. He also reportedly "fills empty barrels with hot, steaming Indian food of most unusual flavors and produces enough to feed hundreds of people at a time." Apparently Sai Baba has a huge following. According to the Harper *Encyclopedia*, dozens of people regularly camp outside his ashram, hoping to get a glimpse of him, to receive an apport, touch him, or listen to a sermon. Sai has two luxurious homes and established an Educational Trust that runs five colleges. In addition to producing apports, Sai engages in levitations, bilocations, and other supernatural activities.

Haraldsson's investigations spanned over a ten-year period. He made a number of journeys to India, in some of them accompanied by Karlis Osis (the other co-author of *At the Hour of Death*) to interview Sai Baba as well as devotees and critics. Haraldsson does not offer any definite conclusion about the authenticity of Baba's miracles, but both he and Stevenson regard fraud as very unlikely. Haraldsson emphasizes that all the phenomena occur in full light and that Baba's clothes do not lend

---

51. See pp. 231–32.

52. The article "Apports" in the Harper *Encyclopedia of Mystical and Paranormal Experience* (San Francisco, 1991) gives the following definition: "an object, certain mediums and adepts come to materialize from thin air, or transport through solid matter." (p. 30)

themselves to concealment. A particularly important feature is the occasional pro-duction of an object which a person suddenly requested, and which was not easily available, such as a fruit out of season. Stevenson notes that some of Sai Baba's feats can be reproduced by magicians, but that, by their own admission, they cannot pro-duce objects that are unexpectedly requested.

All this sounds very impressive, but there is a catch. "From the beginning of Har-aldsson's enquiries," to quote Stevenson's review,

> Sai Baba made it clear that he would not agree to any experimental controls. He had some awareness of the importance of science to scientists and of the controls they desire, but science did not interest him. He saw and sees his life work as that of a re-ligious teacher, and the physical phenomena were for him only marginally signifi-cant indicators of his authority to teach and of his claim to have realized God.[53]

Stevenson does not regard this refusal as in any way suspicious. He talks, rather vaguely, about "descriptive science" which studies phenomena that do not lend them-selves to "experimental manipulation." We accept the legitimacy of descriptive science for the study of meteorites, volcanoes, and earthquakes—"why should we not also ac-cept it for the study in psychical research of spontaneous cases and physical phenom-ena?" Stevenson then comments on the value of the testimony of eyewitnesses:

> Eyewitness testimony is sometimes rated good enough to execute a criminal; why should we not believe it when less is at stake? Is the reason perhaps that, in cases like that of Sai Baba, more is at stake? If Sai Baba's phenomena are paranormal, as I my-self believe, the fact is of enormous importance for our understanding of the nature of ourselves and the universe we inhabit.[54]

The case of Sai Baba is of course interesting in its own right, but I have introduced it for only one reason. It shows Stevenson's excessive readiness to accept paranormal claims and his questionable judgment. He is rightly impressed by the fact that magi-cians, at least those he had consulted, cannot produce some of Sai Baba's feats. Against this, however, must be held Sai Baba's refusal to be subjected to experimental controls. The reason he gives for this refusal seems to be a transparent dodge. If he really possessed the paranormal gift of producing jewels, sweets, and other objects, "out of thin air," why does he not submit to controls? If he could really do all this, some very basic physical laws like the conservation principles would stand refuted and Sai Baba would become a world-famous figure in science. And of course, far from interfering with his work as a religious teacher, it would greatly enhance it. Something is fishy here. As the case of Uri Geller demonstrated, scientists are not the best people to examine Sai Baba's claims. We are not given details about the iden-

---

53. Op. cit., p. 225.
54. Ibid., p. 227.

tity of the magicians who were consulted, but my hunch is that somebody the caliber of Houdini would make short shrift of Sai Baba's miracles. I should mention here that according to Scott Rogo's *Miracles*, a book that is sympathetic to paranormal claims, "there is some indication that Sai Baba often fakes his purported miracles." When films taken of some of his performances are slowed down, Rogo continues, it becomes clear that "he is quite an expert at sleight-of-hand."[55] George Orwell, once remarked that a saint, i.e. a holy man, should be assumed guilty until proven innocent. As of now, this particular saint must be presumed guilty.

After writing the above remarks I came across *Looking for a Miracle*,[56] an excellent book by Joe Nickell, a former stage magician. Nickell located an Indian magician, B. Premamand, whose attitude toward the miracle-makers is similar to Houdini's contempt for mediums. According to Minnie Vaid-Fera in an article in *Imprint*,[57] Sai Baba does not perform in the presence of Premamand. Sai Baba only performs "within the hallowed and 'safe' precinct of his own ashram, helped by almost 5000 devotees." Sai Baba is one of a number of Indian "godmen" who regale multitudes of followers with the performance of assorted miracles. According to the article, all of them are clever fakers. The article contains a detailed description by Premamand of how miracles are manufactured. I cannot of course vouch for Premamand, but what he says fits in well with Sai Baba's refusal to be examined by scientists. I am reminded of Uri Geller who was quite prepared to produce his spoon-bending in the presence of physicists, but refused to appear on the same program as magicians.

It is amazing that Stevenson is prepared to scuttle basic laws of physics rather than conclude that this godman is a cheat like other godmen. As for the objects that Sai Baba produces without notice, perhaps the requests were after all not so unexpected.

Some Notes on Miracles and "Holy" Lying

I would like to add a few words in defense of Chari's thesis that the child reincarnation cases are charades, that they are "holy frauds" originating in lies by interested parties and propagated and played out by an "ignorant and superstitious multitude." This last phrase is quoted from David Hume who may be regarded as a Western counterpart to Chari. Hume was primarily concerned with the miracles of Christianity, but the objections to them are substantially identical with the objections to the reincarnation stories.

In Section X of Hume's *Enquiry Concerning Human Understanding* we are treated to a story related by Cardinal deRetz (1613–1679), the clerical politician and author of the famous *Mémoirs*:

---

55. *Miracles* (New York, 1982), p.90. Rogo also supplies details about one of Sai Baba's dubious bilocations.

56. Amherst, N.Y., 1993.

57. "On the Trail of Godmen," October 1987, pp. 59–64.

When that intriguing politician fled into Spain, to avoid the persecution of his enemies, he passed through Saragossa, the capital of Arragon, where he was shown, in
the cathedral, a man, who had served seven years as a doorkeeper, and was well
known to everybody in town, that had ever paid his devotions at that church. He had
been seen, for so long a time, wanting a leg; but recovered that limb by the rubbing
of holy oil upon the stump; and the cardinal assures us that he saw him with two legs.
This miracle was vouched by all the canons of the church; and the whole company
in town were appealed to for a confirmation of the fact; whom the cardinal found,
by their zealous devotion, to be thorough believers of the miracle. Here the relater
was also contemporary to the supposed prodigy, of an incredulous and libertine
character, as well as of great genius; the miracle of so *singular* a nature as could
scarcely admit of a counterfeit, and the witnesses very numerous, and all of them,
in a manner, spectators of the fact, to which they gave their testimony.

Hume adds that the cardinal himself "seems not to give any credit to it, and conse-
quently cannot be suspected of any concurrence in the holy fraud."[58]

I think that the vast majority of reasonable persons, not only unbelievers but also
Buddhists, Hindus, Moslems, Jews, as well as most contemporary Christians, would
agree with Hume and Cardinal deRetz that the story about the doorkeeper is false. But
if the story is false, how are we to explain that "all the canons of the Church" and "the
whole company in town" believed it, or at any rate said that they believed it? We shall
probably never know the precise answer, but it seems clear that somebody, probably
more than one person, was lying, and that when the story was spread to the credulous
townspeople, a large number of witnesses were prepared to vouch for it. The Cardinal,
in Hume's words, "considered justly that it was not requisite . . . to be able accurately
to disprove the testimony and to trace its falsehood, through all the circumstances of
knavery and credulity which produced it."[59] Hume quotes Francis Bacon's remark that
"writers on natural magic or alchemy . . . seem to have an unconquerable appetite for
falsehood and fable," adding that the same applies to the fabrication of miracles.

Lying is of course common in most departments of life, but it is not usually something that is admired or of which the lying individual is particularly proud. There are
notable exceptions to this rule. A person who is lying in order to protect a friend from
vicious criminals and who may be risking his own life is rightly admired, but such
cases are exceptional. People much more often lie for purely or largely selfish reasons. When it comes to lying on behalf of a religious tenet, including of course an alleged miracle, the liar can feel that he is lying in a noble cause and, so far from being
despised for his act, he will be greatly admired by most of those sharing his belief.
To quote Hume once again:

A religionist may be an enthusiast, and imagine he sees what has no reality; he may
know his narrative to be false, and yet persevere in it, with the best intentions in the

---

58. *An Enquiry Concerning Human Understanding* (Ed. L. A. Selby-Bigge), 2nd ed., pp. 123–24.
59. Ibid.

world, for the sake of promoting so holy a cause; or even where this delusion has not place, vanity, excited by so strong a temptation, operates on him more powerfully than on the rest of mankind in any other circumstances.[60]

Hume's remarks probably don't have as wide an application today as in past centuries, but they are still true of large numbers throughout the world, especially believers in the more dogmatic and primitive religions. It will be remembered that Dr. Ritchie[61] in the first public account of his grand tour of the astral world, provided a "corroboration" which was impressive but it was not true. He wrote, anonymously at that time, that he accurately predicted the location of an all-night cafe in Vicksburg, which he had visited during his astral trip. The prediction was conveyed to a fellow student, who was amazed. When he published the account under his own name many years later, it became a silent prediction, while there were three other students in the car. The anonymous article in *Fate* concludes as follows: "I like to add this postscript to my story because I think it helps some of you to believe."[62] As for K. K. N. Sahay, the father of Jagdish Chandra, the lawyer who conducted a publicity campaign on behalf of the reincarnation memories of his son and who was probably the source of the boy's memories, he was surely proud of his role in strengthening the faith of the people around him by his acts, even if this involved some lies. As the case developed, he probably no longer remembered that it had been set off by a couple of lies. I have observed that fanatics, not only in religion but also in politics and even in areas like philosophy, do not regard their lies as "real" instances of lying: they are told in the service of a higher truth and thereby become "true." The case of killing for a cause is quite similar. If they think about what they are doing at all, religious and political fanatics who murder perfectly innocent people will find some label other than "murder" such as "ethnic cleansing."

There is no need to labor this point any further, but I would like to quote a particularly perceptive passage on a related topic by the late C. S. Lewis, the well-known literary critic and Christian apologist:

> Theocracy is the worst of all governments. If we must have a tyrant, a robber baron is better than an inquisitor. The baron's cruelty may sometimes sleep, his cupidity at sometime be sated; and since he dimly knows he is doing wrong he may possibly repent. But the inquisitor who mistakes his own cruelty and lust for power for the voice of Heaven, will torment us infinitely because he torments us with the approval of his own conscience and his better impulses appear to him as temptations. And since theocracy is the worst, the nearer any government approaches to theocracy, the worse it will be.[63]

---

60. Op. cit., pp. 117–18.
61. See pp. 123–26 above.
62. *Fate*, December 1970, p. 50.
63. Quoted in *Church and State*, July-August 1990–91. My attention to this passage was drawn in a recent issue of *Pique*, the Newsletter of the Secular Humanist Society.

I am sure that Lewis is right about the evils of theocracy, but he is too kind to secular tyrants. Many of them are totally devoid of any moral scruples and will commit the most hideous atrocities without the slightest pangs of conscience. It seems true, however, that religious fanatics all over the world—in Muslim countries, in Israel, and in the United States—are power-hungry and will do almost anything to promote their holy causes.

Before leaving the subject of miracles, I would like to draw attention to some of Voltaire's observations. Like Hume, Voltaire was primarily concerned with the miracles of Christianity, but his remarks equally apply to all supposed miracles, East and West. "In order to believe in a miracle," Voltaire opens one of his discussions, "it is not enough merely to have seen it." The reason for this is that even careful observers can be deceived. Many "excellent persons" who are in general quite trustworthy "think that they have seen what they have not seen and heard what was never said to them." They thus become witnesses to miracles that did not take place. Before paying the slightest attention to such a claim, it is necessary that "the miracle should have been seen by a great number of very sensible people, in sound health, and preferably *disinterested in the affair.*" When "interest mixes with the transaction," as it almost invariably does in the case of religious believers, "you may consider the whole affair worth nothing.[64] The application to the reincarnation cases discussed earlier in this chapter and elsewhere in this book is obvious. In several of them people had lost somebody close to them and were desperately eager to get them back, and in the great majority of them, one or more strategic figures were believers in reincarnation. In practically all these cases, "interest" mixed with the "transaction." They are surely suspect; and further examination usually does show them to be "worth nothing."

The Ransom Report

In the same book (*The Search for Yesterday*) in which Rogo told the story of Barker's experiences, he mentioned the "Ransom Report." In the early 1970s Stevenson hired a lawyer by the name of Champe Ransom to assist him in the analysis of his data. According to Rogo, Ransom soon became highly critical of Stevenson's research methods and composed a report detailing his objections to Stevenson's methods. Rogo admitted that he had not been able to obtain a copy of Ransom's report but offered a description of its contents, which he conceded was based on hearsay. Rogo also asserted that Stevenson had asked Ransom not to circulate or publish his report. I mentioned Rogo's account in Part 4 of my series on reincarnation, published in *Free Inquiry* in 1986–1987. To my surprise and pleasure, Ransom turned out to be a reader of *Free Inquiry*. In a letter published in *Free Inquiry* (Fall 1987), Ransom first cate-

---

64. "Miracles," Section II, *The Philosophical Dictionary* (London, 1824), Volume 5, pp. 53–54, my italics.

gorically denied that Stevenson had ever asked him not to circulate or publish his critique. He then wrote:

> My experience as a research assistant at the Division of Parapsychology at the University of Virginia from 1970 to 1973 was an interesting but painful one. Eventually, I became disillusioned, mostly because of the zealous attitude of the researchers (as opposed to a more balanced one), the defensive attitude toward outside skepticism, and the weakness of the evidence. The more thoroughly I studied an alleged paranormal event, the less likely a paranormal explanation seemed right.[65]

I was relieved to hear that Stevenson had not tried to exercise any kind of censorship, but in fairness to Rogo, I should point out that the world at large would be entirely ignorant of the existence of the Ransom study if it were not for Rogo's discussion in his book. Ransom's work as Stevenson's assistant was done in the early 1970s, but it was not mentioned once in any of Stevenson's writings until January 1986 when he was, in effect, forced to respond to Rogo's book.

The following is a summary of Ransom's report, supplied by him at my request:

> My critique lists and discusses a number of methodological flaws in Stevenson's research. Three notable ones are that leading questions were asked, that the questioning period for each case was quite brief (one wonders what depth of research can be carried out in cases where a stranger from another culture drops in for 1-1$\frac{1}{2}$ to 4 days, which was a typical visit), and that the time that elapsed between the alleged occurrence of an event and the investigation of it was quite long, frequently years. Stevenson's cases seldom, if ever, contain any study or discussion of the child's story-telling inclinations in order to get attention. Similarly, there is no investigation of the playmates of the subject and the extent of *their* knowledge of the events in question. Still another set of factors Stevenson neglects concerns human fallibility. There are subtle distortions of memory; there is the tendency to unintentionally "fill in" a story in order to make it complete; there is a general lack of caution of many people in reporting what they have observed; there is the general unreliability in detail of personal observation; there is witness bias; and there is witness suggestibility. All of these are very real barriers to the gathering of accurate testimony. Little or no mention of these problems is made in the individual case reports. In addition, my critique details problems with Stevenson's reporting of the cases. Such problems include his presenting the conclusions of witnesses rather than the observational data that led them to their conclusions. This is important because different people can reasonably draw different conclusions from the same data. What one person reports as "anger" another may interpret as "embarrassment." Moreover, Stevenson failed to discuss any weaknesses in a witness's report except in a separate part of the book.

---

65. In his huge summary, "Past Life Memory Case Studies" (1990), from which I quoted previously, James G. Matlock, who writes like an out-and-out Stevensonian, quotes Ransom's denial that Stevenson had tried to suppress his report, but he omits any reference to Ransom's negative verdict on Stevenson's research.

(And even there weaknesses are discussed in a general way that does not clearly refer back to the individual cases.) Stevenson's cases then do not amount to even halfway decent evidence. In only 11 of the approximately 1,111 rebirth cases had there been no contact between the two families before investigation was begun. Of those 11, seven were seriously flawed in some respect. What this means is that in the great majority of cases, the two families had met years before a scientific investigation began, and that the likelihood of independent testimony was quite small. The rebirth cases are anecdotal evidence of the weakest sort.

Stevenson will no doubt claim that he and some of his associates have much better cases now than when Ransom was working with him. Better, perhaps; but not good enough. They do not even begin to overthrow what I called the formidable initial presumption against reincarnation.

Ian Wilson ends his highly critical chapter of Stevenson with the remark that in spite of all the objections he has raised, "Stevenson may yet prove himself the Galileo of reincarnation."[66] I do not see any danger of that. What is unfortunately very likely is that for a long time to come ignorant and superstitious people all over the world will continue to refer to Stevenson as the man who has provided strong scientific evidence, if not indeed conclusive proof, of reincarnation.

A Note Concerning Eyewitnesses

"I wish to add a few words in support of Voltaire's remark that many "excellent persons think they have seen what they have not seen and heard what was never said to them." For a number of years I was teaching a course in which the topic of capital punishment was discussed. In this connection, I had occasion to read what criminologists had discovered about the unreliability of eyewitnesses. The following is quoted form the fifth edition of E. Roy Calvert's *Capital Punishment in the Twentieth Century*.[67]

Adolf Beck was sentenced in 1896 to seven years' penal servitude for a series of robberies from women, and in 1904 was again convicted for similar offenses. On the first occasion he was identified by no less than ten women, and the second trial by five women, each of whom swore to his identity as the man who had swindled her; a handwriting expert testified on oath that the letters written by the real culprit were in Beck's handwriting; two prison officials wrongly identified Beck as a previously convicted man—Smith—who was afterwards proved to be the real perpetrator of the crimes for which Beck was found guilty. Rarely has evidence been so overwhelming as it was in this case, yet Beck was subsequently discovered to be absolutely in-

---

66. Op. cit., p. 63.
67. London, 1926. For early work on the subject see Hugo Münsterberg, *Psychology and Crime* (London, 1909). More recent studies are summarized in Robert Buckhout, "Eyewitness Testimony," *Scientific American*, Dec. 1974.

nocent. "There is no shadow of foundation," stated the official report, "for any of the charges made against Beck," and the Home Office awarded him £5,000 compensation. Yet it took Adolf Beck nine years to establish his innocence.

The Beck case is an extreme illustration of the fallibility of eyewitnesses, but it is by no means unique. In 1979, Father Bernard Pagano, a Catholic priest, was tried in Wilmington, Delaware, for holding up a number of stores. He was identified as the "gentleman robber" by a string of eyewitnesses and he was certain to be found guilty when the real culprit came forward and confessed. The culprit was a Catholic and could not bear to see the innocent priest punished.

It should be emphasized that in the Beck and Pagano cases and in those reported by Münsterberg and later criminologists, the eyewitnesses had no motive for lying. They were not out to get an enemy and they were not attempting to back up a religious or political cause. In the reincarnation cases based on the memories of young children, in the great majority of cases, the eyewitnesses did not write down immediately what they had heard and even in the few cases in which they did, the *were* trying to back up a cherished religious belief. Their reports, to use Voltaire's phrase, are "worth nothing."

17

The Dependence of Consciousness
on the Brain

The weightiest argument against reincarnation which, if valid, would also undermine most other forms of belief in survival, is based on the dependence of consciousness on the body and more particularly on the brain. I have mentioned it on several previous occasions, and in this chapter I will offer a full statement and defend the
argument against all major objections with which I am acquainted. To simplify the
discussion I will assume that some form of dualism is true. Some critics of the argument believe that it depends on the acceptance of materialism, but our discussion will
show that this is not so.

The Scope of the Argument

In a rudimentary form the argument can already be found in Lucretius and Pompon-
azzi (1462–1525) and, since Bishop Butler expressly argued against it in the first
chapter of his *Analogy of Religion,* we may infer that it was current among English
freethinkers in the early years of the eighteenth century. However, the first full statement with which I am familiar occurs in Hume's posthumously published essay on
immortality:

> Where any two objects are so closely connected that all alterations in which we have
> ever seen in the one are attended with proportionable alterations in the other; we
> ought to conclude, by all rules of analogy, that, when there are still greater alterations
> produced in the former, and it is totally dissolved, there follows a total dissolution
> of the latter. . . . The weakness of the body and that of the mind in infancy are ex-
> actly proportioned; their vigour in manhood, their sympathetic disorder in sickness;

279

their common gradual decay in old age. The step further seems unavoidable; their common dissolution in death. The last symptoms which the mind discovers, are disorder, weakness, insensibility, and stupidity; the forerunners of its annihilation. The further progress of the same causes increasing, the same effects totally extinguish it.[1]

Some of Hume's detailed observations are of course quite indefensible. There is surely no "exact" proportionality between physical and mental development or between bodily and mental "decay." Nor is it true that all human beings are "insensible" and "stupid" immediately before their death. Hume was also handicapped by the underdeveloped state of brain physiology in the eighteenth century. Nevertheless his statement conveys very vividly the basic idea of the argument.

More recent defenders have placed heavy emphasis on information about the relation between the brain and our mental states and processes. Unlike Hume, Professor J. J. C. Smart rejects dualism. As a materialist he maintains that mental states are identical with brain states, but he nevertheless endorses the body-mind dependence argument as valid within a dualistic framework.

Even if some form of philosophical dualism is accepted and the mind is thought of as something over and above the body, the empirical evidence in favor of an invariable correlation between mental states and brain states is extremely strong: that is, the mind may be thought of as in some sense distinct from the body but also as fundamentally dependent upon physical states. Without oxygen or under the influence of anesthetics or soporific drugs, we rapidly lose consciousness. Moreover, the quality of our consciousness can be influenced in spectacular ways by appropriate drugs or by mechanical stimulation of different areas of the brain. In the face of all the evidence that is being accumulated by modern research in neurology, it is hard to believe that after the dissolution of the brain there could be any thought or conscious experience whatever.[2]

I will add one other recent formulation which states the argument simply and forcefully and is based on the most recent evidence from neurology. "What we call 'the mind' ," writes Colin McGinn,

is in fact made up of a great number of subcapacities, and each of these depends upon the functioning of the brain.

Now, the facts of neurology

compellingly demonstrate . . . that everything about the mind, from the sensory-motor periphery to the inner sense of self, is minutely controlled by the brain: if your

---

1 "On the Immortality of the Soul," in P. Edwards (Ed.), *Immortality,* op. cit., p. 138

2. "Religion and Science," *The Encyclopedia of Philosophy* (New York and London, 1967), Volume 7, p. 161.

brain lacks certain chemicals or gets locally damaged, your mind is apt to fall apart at the seams. . . . If parts of the mind depend for their existence upon parts of the brain, then the whole of the mind must so depend, too. Hence the soul dies with the brain, which is to say, it is mortal.[3]

It should be emphasized that the argument does not start from the premise that after a person is dead he never again acts in the world. A correspondent in the *London Review* replied to McGinn by observing that we do not need his or the neuropathologist's "assistance to learn that all behavior stops at death." Similarly, John Stuart Mill in his chapter on "Immortality" in *Three Essays an Religion* thought the argument inconclusive on the ground that the absence of any acts by an individual after his death is as consistent with the view that he will "recommence" his existence "elsewhere" as it is with the assumption that he has been extinguished forever. Such remarks are due to a misunderstanding. The absence of any actions by the dead is certainly not irrelevant, but the argument is primarily based on the observed dependence of our mental states and processes on what goes on in the brain.

At first sight it may seem that, if valid, the argument merely rules out the survival of the disembodied mind and leaves other forms of survival untouched. In fact, however, it equally rules out reincarnation and the more sophisticated or replica-version of resurrectionism. This is so because the conclusion of the argument is that my mind depends on *my* brain. It does not merely support the less specific conclusion that my mind needs *some* brain as its foundation. If my mind is finished when my brain dies, then it cannot transmigrate to any other body. Similarly, if God created a duplicate of my body containing a duplicate of my brain, *my* mind would not be able to make use of it since it stopped existing with the death of my original body. The argument does not refute belief in the literal resurrection of the body. For on this view God will reconstitute our *original* bodies and hence also our original brains on the Day of Judgment.

Alzheimer's Disease and Comas

The literature on survival contains a number of standard rejoinders to the body-mind dependence argument. Before turning to them, I will consider two concrete instances of body-mind dependence which will help to bring out the full force of the argument. The first is Alzheimer's disease, a dreadful affliction that ruins the last years of a sizable percentage of the world's population. Almost everybody above the age of thirty has known some elderly relative or friend afflicted with this illness. I can therefore be

---

3. Fuller accounts of the dependence of consciousness on brain states may be found in Barry L. Beyerstein, "The Brain and Consciousness: Implications for Psi Phenomena," *Skeptical Inquirer,* Winter 1987–88; Antonio R. Damasio, *Descartes' Error* (New York, 1994); and S. L. Yudofsky and R. E. Hales (Eds.), *Textbook of Neuropsychiatry* (Westminster, 1992). I am indebted to Adolf Grünbaum for calling my attention to the last mentioned book.

brief in my description of what happens to Alzheimer patients. In the early stages the person misses appointments, he constantly loses and mislays objects, and he frequently cannot recall events in the recent past. As the illness progresses he can no longer read or write and his speech tends to be incoherent. In nursing homes Alzheimer patients commonly watch television, but there is no evidence that they understand what is happening on the screen. The decline in intellectual function is generally accompanied by severe emotional symptoms, such as extreme irritability and violent reactions to persons in the environment, as well as hallucinations and paranoid fears. In the final stages the patient is totally confused, frequently incontinent, and quite unable to recognize anybody, including the closest relatives and friends. At present Alzheimer's is incurable and, unlike in the case of Parkinson's disease, there are no known means of slowing down the deterioration. It is also as yet a mystery why Alzheimer's strikes certain individuals while sparing the majority of old people. However, a great deal is known about what goes on in the brains of Alzheimer patients. Alois Alzheimer, the neurologist after whom the disease is named, found in 1906 that the cerebral cortex and the hippocampus of his patients contained twisted tangles and filaments as well as abnormal neurites known as "neuritic" or "senile plaques." It has since been determined that the density of these abnormal components is directly proportional to the severity of the disorder. Autopsies have shown that Alzheimer victims have a vastly reduced level of an enzyme called "choline acetyltransferase," which is needed for producing the neurotransmitter acetylcholine. Although the reduced level of the enzyme and the neurotransmitter appear in the cortex, the origin of the trouble lies in another region of the brain, the nucleus basalis, which is situated just above the place where the optic nerves meet and cross. Autopsies have revealed a dramatic loss of neurons from the nucleus basalis in Alzheimer victims, and this explains why so little of the enzyme is manufactured in their brains.

The information just summarized has been culled from articles about Alzheimer's that have appeared in magazines and popular science monthlies in recent years. The authors of these articles are evidently not concerned with the question of survival after death, but they invariably use such phrases as "destruction of the mind" in describing what happens to the victims. In an article in *Science 84* entitled "The Clouded Mind," the author, Michael Shodell, speaks of Alzheimer's as "an illness that destroys the mind, leaving the body behind as a grim reminder of the person who once was there." Similarly, the cover story in *Newsweek* of December 3, 1984, which contained many heart-rending illustrations and listed some of the famous men and women who were suffering from Alzheimer's, was entitled "A Slow Death of the Mind." I think that these descriptions are entirely appropriate: a person who can no longer read or write, whose memory has largely disappeared, whose speech is incoherent, and who is totally indifferent to his environment has in effect lost all or most of what we normally call his mind. The relevance of this to our discussion is obvious. While still alive, an Alzheimer patient's brain is severely damaged and most of his mind has disappeared. After his death his brain is not merely damaged but completely destroyed. It is surely logical to conclude that now his mind is also gone. It seems preposterous to assert that, when the brain is completely destroyed, the mind suddenly returns intact, with its emotional and intellectual capacities, including its memory, restored. How does the *complete* destruction of the brain bring about a cure that has so far totally eluded medical science?

The same applies to people in irreversible comas. Karen Ann Quinlan lay in a coma for over ten years before she finally died. The damage to her brain had made her, in the phrase used by the newspapers, nothing more than a "vegetable." Her E.E.G. was flat; she was unable to speak or write; visits by her foster parents did not register the slightest response. A more recent widely publicized case was that of the great American tenor Jan Peerce. Peerce had amazed the musical public by singing right into his seventies with only a slight decline in his vocal powers. In the end, however, he was felled by two severe strokes, and he spent the last year of his life in an irreversible coma. Relatives and friends could get no response of any kind. Peerce died in December 1984, Karen Ann Quinlan in June 1985. Did the total destruction of the bodies of these individuals suddenly bring back their emotional and intellectual capacities? If so, where were these during the intervening periods?

The Body as the Instrument of the Mind

The first of the rejoinders I will consider does not dispute the manifold dependence of mental functions on brain processes. It is claimed, however, that these facts are not inconsistent with survival. They are indeed compatible with the view that the mind is annihilated at death, but they are also compatible with the very different position that the mind continues to exist but has lost its "instrument" for acting in the world, and more specifically, for communicating with people who are still alive. An excellent illustration of what the supporters of this rejoinder have in mind is supplied by Father John A. O'Brien in his pamphlet: *The Soul—What Is It?*[4] In order to carve a statue, Father O'Brien writes, a sculptor needs his tools, his hammer and chisel. If the tools are seriously damaged, the quality of his work will be correspondingly impaired, but this does not mean that the sculptor cannot exist if the tools are completely destroyed.

Variants of this argument are found in numerous Protestant theologians, in Catholic philosophers who have frequently relied on the distinction between what they call "extrinsic" and "intrinsic" dependence, and in several secular philosophers, including Descartes, Kant, James, Schiller, and McTaggart. "I do not agree with you," writes Descartes to Gassendi in his "Reply to the Fifth Objection" to his *Meditations,*

> that the mind waxes and wanes with the body; for from the fact that it does not work
> equally well in the body of a child and in that of a grown man, and that its actions

---

4. New York: The Paulist Press, 1946.

are often impeded by wine and other bodily things, it follows merely that while it is united to the body it uses the body as an instrument in its normal operations.[5]

Have we any reason, asks McTaggart, to suppose that "a body is essential to a self"? Not at all. The facts support the very different proposition that "while a self has a body, that body is essentially connected with the self's mental life." A self needs "sufficient data" for its mental activity. In this life the material is given in the form of sensations, and these can only be obtained by means of a body. It does not follow, however, that "it would be impossible for a self without a body to get data in some other way." McTaggart then offers an analogy which has frequently been quoted by believers in survival:

 If a man is shut up in a house, the transparency of the windows is an essential condition of his seeing the sky. But it would not be prudent to infer that, if he walked out of the house, he could not see the sky because there was no longer any glass through which he might see it.[6]

McTaggart is totally unimpressed by the evidence from brain physiology which, it is safe to say, he did not study in detail and which was very extensive even in 1906 when his book was published. He does not dispute that "diseases or mutilations of the brain affect the course of thought," but "the fact that an abnormal state of the brain may affect our thought does not prove that the normal states of the brain are necessary for thought."[7]

It may be instructive at this stage to consider some of the exchanges between Ian Stevenson and two of his skeptical interrogators, John Taylor, professor of mathematics at London University, and John Cohen, professor of psychology at Manchester, during the course of a BBC program that took place in the spring of 1976. The program dealt with the claims of Edward Ryall to have lived in the seventeenth century as John Fletcher that were discussed in Chapter 7.

Cohen: . . . memories are tied to a particular brain tissue. If you take away the brain, there is no memory.

Stevenson: I think that's an assumption. Memories may exist in the brain and exist elsewhere also.

Cohen: But we have not the slightest evidence, even a single case, of a memory existing without a brain. We have plenty of slight damage to a brain which destroys memory, but not the other way around.

5. My attention to this passage was called by Jonathan Bennett who quotes it on p. 132 of *A Study of Spinoza's Ethics* (Indianapolis: Hackett, 1984).

6. *Some Dogmas of Religion* (London, 1906), p. 105.

7. Ibid.

Stevenson: I feel that's one of the issues here—whether memories can, in fact, survive the destruction of the brain.

Taylor: Professor Stevenson, do you have any evidence, other than these reincarnation cases, that memories can survive the destruction of physical tissue?

Stevenson: No. I think the best evidence comes from the reincarnation cases.[8]

Taylor then brought up the well-known case of people who lose all or most of their memories as a result of brain injuries. Stevenson was not fazed.

Stevenson: Well, it's possible that what is affected is his ability to express memories that he may still have.

Taylor: But are you suggesting, in fact, that memories themselves are in some way nonphysically bound up, and can be stored in a nonphysical manner?

Stevenson: Yes, I'm suggesting that there might be a nonphysical process of storage.

Taylor: What does that mean? Nonphysical storage of what?

Stevenson: The potentiality for the reproduction of an image memory.

Taylor: But information itself involves energy. Is there such a thing as nonphysical energy?

Stevenson: I think there may be, yes.

Taylor: How can you define it? Nonphysical energy, to me, is a complete contradiction in terms. I can't conceive how on earth you could ever conceive of such a quantity. . . .

Stevenson: Well, it might be in some dimension of which we are just beginning to form crude ideas, through the study of what we parapsychologists call paranormal phenomena. We are making an assumption of some kind of process that is not, and maybe cannot be, understood in terms of current physical concepts. That is a jump, a gap, I freely admit.[9]

These exchanges bring out very clearly what is at issue between those who accept the body-mind dependence argument and the supporters of the instrument theory.

It has on occasion been suggested that we have no way of deciding between these two rival explanations of the relevant facts. I see no reason to accept such an agnostic conclusion. It seems to me that by retrodictive extrapolation to cases like Alzheimer patients or people in comas we can see that the alternative to annihilation proposed by the instrument theory is absurd. Let us consider the behavior of Alzheimer patients in the later stages of their affliction. The more specific the case, the clearer the implications of the rival views will appear. The mother of a close friend of mine, Mrs. D., re-

---

8. *The Listener,* June 3, 1976, p. 698.
9. Ibid.

cently died from Alzheimer's after suffering from the disease for about eight years. Mrs. D. was a prosperous lady from Virginia, the widow of a banker. In her pre-Alzheimer days she was a courteous and well-behaved person, and she had of course no difficulty recognizing her daughter or any of her other relatives or friends. I do not know what her feelings were about paralyzed people, but my guess is that she pitied them and certainly had no wish to beat them up. As her illness progressed she was put into a nursing home run by nuns who were renowned for their gentle and compassionate ways. She shared a room with an older lady who was paralyzed. For the first year or so Mrs. D. did not become violent. Then she started hitting the nurses. At about the time when she could no longer recognize her daughter, she beat up the paralyzed lady on two or three occasions. From then on she had to be confined to the "seventh floor," which was reserved for violent and exceptionally difficult patients.

Let us now see what the survival theorists would have to say about Mrs. D.'s behavior. It should be remembered that on this view Mrs. D., after her death, will exist with her mind intact and will only lack the means of communicating with people on earth. This view implies that throughout her affliction with Alzheimer's Mrs. D.'s mind *was* intact. She recognized her daughter but had lost her ability to express this recognition. She had no wish to beat up an inoffensive paralyzed old woman. On the contrary, "inside" she was the same considerate person as before the onset of the illness. It is simply that her brain disease prevented her from acting in accordance with her true emotions. I must insist that these *are* the implications of the theory that the mind survives the death of the brain and that the brain is only an instrument for communication. Surely these consequences are absurd: The facts are that Mrs. D. no longer recognized her daughter and that she no longer had any compassionate feelings about paralyzed old women. At any rate, we have the same grounds for saying this as we do in any number of undisputed cases in which people do not suffer from Alzheimer's and fail to recognize other human beings or fail to feel compassion.

The guards in Argentine dungeons who tortured and killed liberals had no compassion for their victims, and neither of course did the Nazis who rounded up and then shot Jews in Poland and elsewhere. We have exactly the same kind of evidence for concluding that Mrs. D., who probably did feel compassion for paralyzed people before she suffered from Alzheimer's, no longer felt compassion when beating up her paralyzed roommate. As for memories, all of us sometimes cannot place a familiar tune or remember the name of a person we know well; and in such cases it makes good sense to say that the memories are still there. Even when the name never comes back there is a suspicion that the memory may not have been lost: it is entirely possible that one could bring it back under hypnosis. However, the memory loss in Alzheimer's is totally different, and the same of course applies to people in irreversible comas. It is surely fantastic to maintain that during his last months Jan Peerce did recognize his wife and children and simply could not express his recognition. If anybody makes such a claim it can only be for ulterior metaphysical reasons and not because it is supported by the slightest evidence.

In his generous review of *Immortality*,[10] Ian Stevenson observes that I have "too readily accepted the promissory notes printed by the neuroscientists." He then addresses himself to my remarks about Alzheimer's Disease:

> First, amnesia may seem to be total, as in a severely inebriated person, and yet memories may return during sobriety; absence of accessible memory does not necessarily entail its destruction, and neuroscientists may yet devise a remedy that restores the memories of patients with Alzheimer's Disease. Second, even if the loss of memory is total and irreversible in Alzheimer's Disease (or other diseases) this does not compel us to believe that the memories have been destroyed. They may exist, but be inaccessible under prevailing conditions.

This does not answer my argument. If and when a cure for Alzheimer's is found, it will surely involve a modification in the brains of the patients. More basically, Stevenson has misconceived the point at issue: what are we to say about the mind or consciousness of an individual with irreversible brain damage? Are we to conclude that the patient's mind is gone, or that the mind is *fully* intact (just as it would be if the brain had not been damaged), but is unable to use the brain as its instrument? My point is that only the former makes sense in such a situation, but the believer is committed to the latter.

It might be added that quite aside from such disastrous brain disturbances as Alzheimer's, it is well known that many, perhaps most, people deteriorate with age, both intellectually and emotionally. Their memory declines, they are less capable of absorbing new ideas, they get less interested in the world around them, they constantly look for compliments and they also become crankier, more impatient, and more dogmatic in their views. This is far from universal and it is an interesting question why so many people deteriorate while a few do not. However, regardless of how this last question is answered, it is very generally agreed that the intellectual and emotional deterioration, where it does occur, is due to changes in the brain, although undoubtedly other factors are also at work. It is perfectly natural to say in such situations—and all of us speak and think like this, even believers in survival—that the person's mind has deteriorated with age. The annihilation theory is completely consistent with such a statement but the instrument theory is not. An advocate of the latter would have to say that the mind itself has not deteriorated and that the changes we note are due to the fact that the mind does not have an undamaged instrument at its disposal.

This is perhaps the place to comment on McTaggart's remark quoted earlier that "the fact that an abnormal state of the brain may affect our thought does not prove that the normal states of the brain are necessary for thought." This is fatuous nonsense. If we are investigating the necessary conditions of our physiological or our mental states, a study of disturbances in the relevant function can teach us a great deal. This is true of digestion, respiration, and circulation; and it is equally true of consciousness. By discovering the brain cause of Alzheimer's we automatically discovered one

---

10. *Journal of Scientific Exploration*, 1994, pp. 422–23.

of the necessary conditions for an undisturbed memory. Illness is not indeed identical with health, but a study of illness can disclose the necessary conditions for health.

The Absence of Direct Negative Evidence: Mill, Butler, Ewing

Mill's posthumously published essay on "Theism" contains a chapter on immortality in which he surveys and evaluates all the major arguments on both sides that were known to him. Mill finds all of them defective and concludes on a note of complete agnosticism. We have here, he writes, "one of those very rare cases in which there is really a total absence of evidence on either side" and "in which the absence of evidence for the affirmative does not, as in so many other cases, create a strong presumption in favor of the negative."[11]

Mill discusses in some detail the evidence from brain physiology. It supplies us with "sufficient evidence that cerebral action is, if not the cause, at least, in our present state of existence, a condition *sine qua non* of mental operations." We are entitled to conclude that the death of the brain would put a stop to all mental function and "remand it [the mind] to unconsciousness unless and until some other set of conditions supervenes, capable of recalling it into activity." The facts of brain physiology most emphatically do not prove that the mind cannot exist after death. "The same thoughts, emotions, volitions, and even sensations which we have here" may, for all we can tell, "persist or recommence somewhere else under other conditions." This is no less possible than that "other thoughts and sensations may exist under other conditions in other parts of the universe."[12] What Mill evidently seems to require in order to establish the negative case is that we observe the nonexistence of the thoughts, volitions, and sensations of the dead person; and this the body-mind dependence argument does not give us.

Independently of this argument, Bishop Butler insists on the same requirement and regards its nonfulfillment as a fatal flaw in the unbeliever's position. Not only do we never directly observe the nonexistence of human minds, but the same is also true of animals. We never "find anything throughout the whole analogy of nature" that could afford us "even the slightest presumption, that animals ever lose their living powers." This is so because we have "no faculties wherewith to trace any beyond or through death to see what becomes of them."[13] In the case of human beings and animals alike death only destroys "the sensible proof which we had before their death of their being possessed of living powers," but it does not "afford the least reason" for supposing that death causes the extinction of their minds.

A much more recent philosopher, the late A. C. Ewing, used the same kind of reasoning to rebut the unbeliever's argument. Ewing first observes that there is no logi-

---

11. *Three Essays on Religion* (London, 1876), p. 203.
12. Op. cit., p. 200.
13. *The Analogy of Nature,* Chapter 1.

cally necessary connection between bodily and mental events, something that all dualists would endorse. This means that no deductive argument is available to the unbeliever. At the same time he is also unable to mount an inductive argument. He cannot
do this because "we have never observed a mind being annihilated at death."[14] The only
one who could do this is the person himself. "No one could observe this," Ewing
writes, "but the mind in question itself, and even that could not, because it was annihilated, so, if a phenomenon, it is certainly an unobservable one."[15] Ewing is happy to
note that once we have disposed of the argument from the connection between body
and mind the field is left open "for any empirical evidence drawn from psychical research and any arguments for survival there may be based on ethics and religion."[16]

Butler deserves credit for realizing that his reasoning applies to animals and not
only to human beings. It is not clear that either Mill or Ewing saw this. However, not
even Butler carried the argument far enough. What reason do we have for denying that
purely inanimate objects have an "inner" psychic life? What evidence do I have that
the chocolate cream puff I am about to eat does not bitterly resent this murderous activity on my part and how do I know that a tennis ball I am about to serve does not
acutely suffer as a result of being hit? For that matter how do I know that the tennis
ball does not enjoy the experience of being hit? Since we have no access to the inner
life of tennis balls, if they have any, we cannot know either that the tennis ball does
or that it does not like being hit. Not only cannot we know that tennis balls do not have
an inner life. We also cannot know that they, or any other inanimate objects, do not
continue to have an inner, psychical life after the death of their bodies, whether as disembodied minds or in conjunction with replicas that will be produced in a resurrection world. It is true that we have no evidence that such an inner life will continue after
the death of their bodies, but we equally have none that it will not. A complete sus-
pense of judgment is the only defensible attitude.

All who regard panpsychism as either false or meaningless will surely regard the
fact that the rejoinder here under discussion can be extended to inanimate objects as
its *reductio ad absurdum*. Others will go further and treat the entire rejoinder as a *reductio ad absurdum* of dualism. For clearly we do know that tennis balls and cream
puffs do not have an inner life and we can and do know that human beings and animals have certain feelings and sensations. However, we have agreed to accept dualism throughout this discussion, and it can be shown that the rejoinder is invalid even
within a dualistic framework. After all, dualists allow that although we cannot inspect
the minds of others we can frequently know that they have certain experiences. We
can know that another person is in pain or that he is angry, and we can at least have
strong evidence that he has certain thoughts. Now, the same *kind* of evidence is
available to us that other people do not have these experiences. We can know that
somebody has ceased to be in pain, that his anger is gone, or that he no longer thinks

---

14. *Non-Linguistic Philosophy* (London, 1968), p. 173.
15. Ibid.
16. Ibid.

about a certain subject. I do not have to *be* the other person to know that he is no longer in pain or angry. By the same token I do not have to be Mrs. D., the Alzheimer patient, to know that her memory is gone and I equally do not have to be Jan Peerce in his coma to know that he no longer recognizes his family. In such cases we surely have the right to assert more than that the memories and thoughts have been "remanded to unconsciousness." This description fits a person under general anesthesia or during dreamless sleep who may very well return to full consciousness, but it is highly misleading about people in a coma or with advanced Alzheimer's. The only description that is fitting in such cases is that the thoughts and memories have been destroyed; and if they have been destroyed then they cannot be "recalled into activity" when a "different set of conditions supervenes."

A Note on Panpsychism

My dismissal of panpsychism as either false or meaningless may seem to be unduly dogmatic. Many famous philosophers and scientists have been panpsychists and the theory has been treated sympathetically by Thomas Nagel, one of the ablest philosophers on the current scene.[17] I will therefore add a few words on the subject. That panpsychism is either absurdly false, or else an empty statement, is not immediately obvious only if the theory is stated in very general terms. The moment we bring it down to something specific it will be seen that my verdict is just. We occasionally say about something that it is as dead as a doornail. According to panpsychists a doornail is not dead, at least not if "dead" means absence of consciousness. Now, we normally believe that doornails *are* dead in this sense, that they are not conscious entities. Our evidence for this is that they are not composed of the kind of organic or biological material of which plants and animals are composed, that they do not have brains and nervous systems or analogical structures and also, of course, that they do not behave like beings whom we regard as having emotions and thoughts. If the evidence just mentioned is sufficient to prove the commonsense view that doornails are dead then panpsychism is false. If it is not sufficient, what else is needed to prove that doornails are not conscious? Panpsychists presumably admit that it is at least conceivable that something might lack an inner psychic life. How could we recognize such an object? What features would the doornail have to possess in order to justify the conclusion that it does not have an inner life? What, in short, would falsify panpsychism? Somebody might object that panpsychism is not empty—that we can be reasonably but not entirely certain that the doornail is not conscious: we could know this only if we were doornails and found that we then had no consciousness. This is great stuff, reminding me of the Heideggerian attempts to find out what deadness is like to the dead.[18]

---

17. *Mortal Questions* (Cambridge, 1979), Chapter 13.
18. For the details of this Heideggerian quest, see my *Heidegger and Death* (La Salle, Ill., 1979).

I am afraid that I cannot attach any meaning to the conditional "if I were a doornail" and I doubt that anybody else can.

The Brain-Mind Dependence Thesis and What It Is Not— The Confusions of Penfield, Thouless, and Ducasse

Several writers have opposed the brain dependence argument on the ground that it presupposes questionable doctrines about the mind-body problem. To clarify the situation, I will distinguish between the following three theories:

(1) mental states are identical with brain states (materialism);
(2) mental states are distinct from brain states, but they are causally ineffective—they are mere by-products of brain states (epiphenomenalism);
(3) a living brain is a *necessary* condition for all mental states (I will call this the "brain-dependence thesis").

It should be clear that a defender of (3) may but need not support either (1) or (2). He can quite consistently favor dualistic interactionism. He can admit, for example, that my decision to leave the room can (together with certain other conditions) resulted in my leaving the room. However, he will add, that the decision to leave the room could not have existed and could not have been causally operative unless my brain was alive and certain of its areas were intact.

In light of these remarks, I will briefly consider the views of Wilder Penfield (1891–1976), the distinguished Canadian neurosurgeon, and R. H. Thouless (1894–1984), a well-known British psychologist of an earlier generation who, among other things, wrote *Straight and Crooked Thinking* (1936), a delightful book about everyday fallacies. Both of them were eager to maintain that the mind is an "independent entity" (i.e., that materialism is false) and that conscious states can influence the body (i.e., that epiphenomenalism is false). It is not clear that either of them actually believed in survival, but they argued that there is nothing in the known facts about the relation between consciousness and the brain which rules out life after death.

Thouless was the clearer of the two, and I will quote some strategic passages from his *Do We Survive Bodily Death?* which was published by the Society for Psychical Research in 1984. On his view and on Penfield's view, the brain is a "source of energy" and supplies "sensory information and memories" which are needed by the mind for the direction of its activities. There are some mental activities, notably believing and deciding, which cannot be performed by "the material brain itself." They can only be performed by the "immaterial mind." It should be mentioned that during some of his operations on epileptic patients, Penfield had succeeded in arousing memories by electrical stimulation of certain areas of the brain. However, there was no point on the brain at which electrical stimulation could cause a patient to believe or to decide. Thouless and Penfield concluded that *qua* deciding and believing being, the mind is an "independent entity," that in regard to these activities it does not depend on the brain. Thouless modestly adds that this is not an argument *for* survival since "the idea of the mind as an 'independent entity' is quite consistent with the idea that this entity ceases to exist when bodily death takes place."[19]

There is a simple reply to the Thouless-Penfield argument. The fact that Penfield could not produce beliefs or decisions by electrical stimulation of the brain in no way shows that they do not need what we may call a brain-base any less than memories and sensations. Suppose we grant, what Penfield has not shown that brain states cannot be the sufficient condition of beliefs or decisions, it does not follow that they are not necessary conditions for their existence. And we have the same kind of evidence that they *are* necessary conditions as we have in the case of memories and sensations. His strokes have made it impossible for Jan Peerce to recognize his family and they equally made it impossible for him to make decisions or entertain beliefs.

A similar reply can be offered to the argument presented by C. J. Ducasse in several places that the brain-dependent thesis presupposes epiphenomenalism and that epiphenomenalism is plainly false.[20] I disagree that epiphenomenalism is plainly false, but my main objection is that the brain-dependence thesis does not presuppose it. The supporter of the brain-dependence thesis maintains that the brain is a *necessary* condition for the existence of all conscious states and processes, but this does not imply that conscious states and processes are incapable of influencing behavior. Ducasse mentions the standard example supporting mind-body interaction, namely, "the fact that merely willing to raise one's arm normally suffices to cause it to rise." This is a very incomplete account of the facts of the case even if one accepts interactionism. If at the moment when the individual decided to raise his arm he had suffered a stroke, or if the brain had been damaged in certain other ways, the arm would not have gone up. This is all that the defender of the indispensability of an intact brain is committed to. He need not in the least deny that willing to raise the arm is causally relevant, i.e., that it is part of what in the context is the sufficient condition of the arm's movement. The scholastic philosophers distinguished between what they called a *causa in fieri* which literally means "cause in becoming" but is more accurately rendered as "productive cause" and *causa in esse* or "sustaining cause." My parents are my *causa in fieri* or at least a major part of it. The air I breathe and the food I eat are a part of my *causa in esse*: they keep me alive but they did not produce me. Using this terminology we may express Ducasse's confusion by saying that his opponent is committed to the assertion that an intact brain is a *causa in esse* of all conscious states and not to the much stronger claim that it is their *causa in fieri*.

---

19. *Do We Survive Bodily Death?* p. 38.

20. *A Critical Examination of Belief in Life After Death* (Springfield, Ill., 1961), pp. 75 ff.; *Nature, Mind and Death* (La Salle, Ill., 1951), p. 455; and "Life After Death Conceived As Reincarnation," in *In Search of God and Immortality* (Boston, 1961), p. 148.

Can The Brain Produce Thought?

It is a widely held belief that the brain, being a material thing, could never "in principle" produce something as different as mental states or processes. It is not clear whether those subscribing to this view maintain merely that brain states cannot be *sufficient* conditions of mental states. If this is all they claim, they would not be contradicting the brain-dependence thesis since the latter maintains no more than that a living brain is a *necessary* condition for mental states. However, most of them seem to mean that brain states are so different from mental states that they cannot even be necessary conditions for their existence, i.e., that consciousness does *not* depend on the brain for its existence.

I have over the years collected a large number of statements to the effect that the brain cannot possibly be the cause of consciousness. I will here offer a sample taken from the most diverse sources. Basing himself on a lecture by Sir Cyril Burt (1883–1971) entitled "Psychology and Psychical Research," published in 1968 in the *Proceedings of the Society for Psychical Research,* Arthur Koestler observes that

> there is no hope for life after death as long as we remain captives of that materialist philosophy which proclaimed—as Burt ironically phrased it—that the chemistry of the brain "generates consciousness much as the liver generates bile."

This "naive materialism," however, must be rejected because it cannot explain "how the motions of particles could possibly generate this 'insubstantial pageant of images and ideas.' "[21] In the same vein, the distinguished English theologian F. R. Tennant (1866–1957) asserted that "materialism cannot explain even the simplest type of conscious process." According to Tennant, there is an insuperable difficulty in conceiving "how a sensation or a feeling could be the necessary consequence or effect of . . . matter or mass-points."[22] Using almost the same language the eminent German philosopher and psychologist Oswald Külpe (1862–1915) concurred that materialism "is incapable of explaining psychological facts," it does not allow us "to make even the simplest and most easily apprehended psychical processes intelligible." The sensation of red or a tone of a certain pitch are "in no way more intelligible from the fact that we may trace them back to some particular activity of the brain."[23] Writing from a very different standpoint, the existential psychoanalyst Medard Boss, a disciple and close friend of Martin Heidegger, insists that "not a single human perception or thought . . . could ever be intelligibly derived from the physiological processes of the bodily metabolism, from any nerve functions, or from the so-called higher nervous activities which take place concomitantly." These words are put by Boss into the

---

21. Arnold Toynbee et al., *Life After Death* (London, 1976), p. 254.

22. "Materialism," in *Hastings Encyclopedia of Religion and Ethics,* Volume 8, p. 491.

23. *The Philosophy of the Present in Germany* (Leipzig, 1902: English trans., 1913).

mouth of a patient whose reasoning he greatly admired. "How did the doctor," the patient went on, "picture such a transformation of physical processes into mental, immaterial phenomena? Perhaps as some kind of magic evaporation?" "It is inconceivable," Boss writes a little later, now speaking in the first person, "how blind particles and quanta of energy of a body can suddenly see and perceive things as the things they are with all their meaningful connotations."[24] Here is Ian Stevenson:

> Our present knowledge of brains cannot explain the features of our mental images. No arrangement of neurons in the brain is circular like our experience of seeing a circle. The experience of seeing a circle, or a square, or almost any other shape, does not correspond to the spatial arrangement of neurons. In technical terms, the data of our perceptions and the arrangement of neurons in the brain are not isomorphic.[25]

My most recent sample comes from a review of R. Tallis's *The Explicit Animal* (1992), by the contemporary theologian Stephen R. Clark. Clark's target is the causal theory of perception which teaches that

> we get to know the world because the world affects our bodies, and there is an exchange of energy between them such that, for example, rapid molecular motion is transformed into a feeling of heat.

The trouble with the causal theory of perception is that

> there is no account of how such causal influence can even be conceived, let alone incorporated into a larger theory. As Glanvill said three centuries ago, "the freezing of the words in the air in northern climes is as conceivable as this strange union," whereby quantifiable energies are transformed into subjective qualia.[26]

What agitates all these writers is shown very clearly in a passage from *Death and Consciousness* (1985), by the contemporary American philosopher David H. Lund:

> How can the brain, a material substance, produce something as radically different from it as consciousness is? How can the brain create out of its own material substance a reality that has no mass, no shape, no size, and is not even in space?[27]

The answer to these questions is "Why not?" As Hume noted, only experience can tell us what causes what, and we possess no *a priori* evidence that the cause and effect cannot be "radically different." We have just as strong evidence for concluding that certain brain states bring about certain conscious states as we have for any num-

---

24. *Psychoanalysis and Daseins Analysis* (New York, 1963), pp. 9 and 33.
25. *Children Who Remember Previous Lives*, op. cit., p. 227.
26. *Times Literary Supplement*, August 6, 1993.
27. *Death and Consciousness* (Jefferson, N.C., 1985), p. 33.

ber of causal relations between purely physical phenomena which are not questioned by any of the above-mentioned writers. If the production of mental states by the brain does not fit in with the *a priori* preconceptions of a given philosopher, this is simply too bad. It is certainly true that not *any* particles in *any* arrangement can bring about consciousness. The particles arranged as billiard balls or as cream puffs cannot do this, but apparently the particles of living brain tissues do bring it about.

In a famous discussion of this issue, which is apparently unknown to any of the writers quoted in the preceding paragraphs, C. D. Broad raised the question of "just how unlike two events may be before it becomes impossible to admit the existence of a causal relation between them," adding that "no one hesitates to hold that draughts and colds in the head are causally connected, although the two are extremely unlike each other."[28] There are plainly vast numbers of cases in which everybody agrees that there is a causal relation in spite of the unlikeness of cause and effect: smoking produces cancerous lesions in the lungs, anti-depressants and shock therapy produce major emotional changes and, as mentioned in the previous section, electrical stimulation of the brain produces memories and mental images.[29] If we find that a certain brain state or more generally a certain physical condition is dependably followed by a certain mental state we have thereby "explained" or "accounted" for the mental state. We have made it "intelligible."[30] It might be noted that most of the writers I have quoted believe that the mind can influence the body, but if their reason for rejecting brain-mind causation were valid it would also undermine their own view about mind-brain causation.

The upshot of this discussion is that the unlikeness of mind and brain does not in any way invalidate the brain-dependence thesis. Brain states may be, for all that has been shown to the contrary, sufficient conditions, and they quite certainly *are* necessary conditions of mental states. In reaching this conclusion, one is not "captive" of a "naive materialism": to say that the brain produces thoughts in no way implies that the thoughts themselves are material.

---

28. *The Mind and Its Place in Nature* (London, 1925), p. 98.

29. See Wilder Penfield's contribution to P. Lasslett, *The Physical Basis of Mind* (Oxford, 1951), pp. 61–62.

30. There is an excellent discussion of this topic in C. J. Ducasse, *Nature, Mind and Death,* op. cit., pp. 430–31. "There is neither more nor less mystery," Ducasse writes, "in physico-psychical or in psycho-physical causation than there is in physico-physical causation. The causal relation, itself, is exactly the same." Ducasse concludes that "the question as to *how* an event causes what it does cause is meaningless if *proximate* causation is in view. It is meaningful only as regards *remote* causation since what the question 'how?' asks for is an account of the causal steps intermediary between the two events concerned" (Ducasse's italics).

Epistemological Versus Ontological Priority

In *Children Who Remember Previous Lives,* Stevenson presents an argument, derived from Sir Arthur Eddington's *Science and the Unseen World,* which would have delighted idealist philosophers like F. H. Bradley and Josiah Royce. "What we know of brains," Stevenson begins, "cannot explain consciousness." If anything, the opposite is true: "It would be more fitting to acknowledge the primacy of consciousness itself. We all experience it, and all our knowledge occurs in it." He then quotes Eddington to the effect that, "mind is the first and most direct thing in our experience: all else is remote inference." Without consciousness, Stevenson proceeds, "we could not observe brains or imagine anything about them, including the probably false idea that their workings and nothing else produce consciousness." He then concludes with a triumphant flourish that "an understanding of consciousness may ultimately explain brains, but brains will never explain consciousness; and I do not think anything else ever will."[31]

There are two objections to this argument. In the first place it presupposes the subjectivistic epistemology of Descartes and the British tradition—Locke, Hume, Russell, and Ayer. This epistemology has been severely criticized during the last half-century by philosophers of very different backgrounds. I do not wish to press this objection both because it would require discussion of a large and difficult question and also because I am not sure that the critics of the subjectivist epistemology are in the right. However, I have no such misgivings about the second objection. Stevenson confuses what may be called epistemological with ontological priority. Let us grant, for the sake of argument, that we could not know anything about the brain or the relations between it and consciousness unless we had visual and tactile sensations. This shows nothing at all about the "status" of either the brain or of consciousness. If experience shows that consciousness cannot exist without the brain, that is that. How we come to know it is quite irrelevant. It is presumably by sensations that we come to know that there was a time when minds did not exist and that probably there will again be such a time: the fact that we obtained this knowledge by means of sensations in no way invalidates it.

"Extra-Cerebral" Memories

It will be recalled that in the exchanges in the BBC discussion of the Ryall case the question came up whether memories can exist without the brain. Professors Cohen and Taylor regarded the notion of extra-cerebral memories as totally absurd. Professor Stevenson vehemently disagreed. "Memories may exist in the brain," he said, and

---

31. *Children Who Remember Previous Lives,* op. cit., p. 226.

exist elsewhere also." The best evidence that they may exist elsewhere, Stevenson continued, comes from his own reincarnation research. On the question of the "storage" of memories he remarked that there"might be a nonphysical process of storage." The memories "might be in some dimension . . . which cannot be understood in terms of current physical concepts."[32]

Unlike Stevenson, the late Professor H. H. Price did not believe in reincarnation, but he took communications from or through mediums very seriously. As far as I know he remained an agnostic on the subject of survival, but he insisted that if brain physiology supplies us with evidence against the existence of extra-cerebral memories, certain of the data assembled by parapsychologists provide evidence in its favor."It will, of course, be objected," Price wrote, "that memories cannot exist in the absence of a physical brain, nor yet desires, nor images either." Against this it must be emphasized that "any evidence which directly supports the Survival Hypothesis (and there is quite a lot of evidence which does) . . . is *pro tanto* evidence against the Materialistic conception of human personality,"[33] by which Price here simply means the view that consciousness depends on the brain for its existence.

I will confine myself to two brief comments. First, Price is quite right in maintaining that the issue is one of weighing the evidence from brain physiology against that from parapsychology. For my own part I do not see how any rational person can hesitate in regarding the former evidence as *vastly* more impressive. Stevenson's evidence, which deserves to be taken more seriously than that of any other reincarnationist was examined in Chapter 16. It is full of holes and really cannot be regarded as on the same level as that of the brain physiologists. I hesitate to speak about mediumistic communications, but most of these, by the almost common consent of the more respectable students of the subject, have a tendency to break down on close examination. Some impressive cases remain but even they do not compare in solidity with the careful, controlled studies of brain physiologists. Next, it should be pointed out that many parapsychologists are not supporters of belief in any kind of survival and, what is perhaps more to the point, rejection of extra-cerebral memories has no logical bearing on the "this-worldly" phenomena studied in parapsychology. Telepathic communications, to take one example, are between persons who have brains; and if these communications really occur, they do not have the slightest tendency to support the existence of any extra-cerebral mental processes. As for Stevenson's nonphysical storage depot of extra-cerebral memories—"the dimension which cannot be understood in terms of current physical concepts"—it must surely be dismissed as nothing but a vague picture which is of no scientific value whatsoever.

---

32. *The Listener,* op. cit., p. 686.
33. "Survival and the Idea of 'Another World,' " in J. R. Smythies (Ed.), *Brain and Mind* (London, 1965), p. 18.

The Mind and the Soul

The last rejoinder to be considered involves a distinction between the mind, which is identical with the phenomenal or empirical self whose existence is not disputed by Hume and other empiricists, and another nonphysical entity to which various labels have been applied. It is the immaterial or spiritual substance of Clarke, Butler, and Reid and numerous other philosophers, past and present, it is the Atman of the Hindu version of reincarnation, the noumenal self of Kant, and the soul (in one of its senses) of the Christian and Jewish traditions. It is argued that, although the mind may indeed so closely depend on the body that it must cease with the body's death, the same is not true of the soul. The soul is the "I" that "owns" both the body and the mind. I am five feet seven inches tall, I weigh one hundred and fifty pounds, I have blue eyes and brown hair; but I also have certain sensations and feelings and thoughts. I have various physical skills and I also possess certain emotional and intellectual dispositions. It is this underlying "I"—the subject of both the body and the mind—that has not been shown to require a body for its existence.

There are two objections to this rejoinder, each of them fatal. In the first place, although the way we speak in certain contexts suggests an underlying subject of both body and mind, there is no reason to suppose that it exists. Hume's theory that human beings are nothing but "bundles of impressions and ideas" is seriously inadequate. Each of us, at least while he is sane, has a sense of himself, more specifically, a sense of himself as continuing the same person from moment to moment. However, what this consists in is not the totally unchanging metaphysical entity that Hume rightly rebelled against. It is a sense of continuity in certain bodily sensations (especially of our limbs and certain muscle groups) and of our various tastes, opinions, and habits—more generally of our emotional and intellectual dispositions. These, together with our bodies, make us the kinds of persons we are. Although our emotional and intellectual dispositions are subject to change, unlike our moods and sensations, they are relatively stable. If this is what is meant by "soul," there is no reason to deny that we have a soul; but the soul in this sense is just as dependent on the body and the brain as any particular sensations, feelings, and thoughts.

The second objection to this rejoinder is that if there were such a thing as the spiritual substance or the metaphysical soul, it would not be what anybody means by "I." Human beings who are afraid of death dread the annihilation of the *empirical* selves and it is these empirical selves which they would like to survive. This is true of Western and Eastern believers alike. Several believers in the metaphysical soul have admitted as much. Joseph Priestley quotes the following passage from Richard Baxter (1615–1691), the seventeenth-century English Nonconformist theologian:

> The soul cannot have a disorder lodged in itself, nor be subject to any disease. . . .
> It can suffer no alteration in its own substance, if that substance be not annihilated.
> We would have the soul to grow up, to decay, to sleep, to be mad, to be drunk. Who

does not see all these are ridiculous fancies, too gross to be entertained concerning a simple uncompounded substance?[34]

Pierre Gassendi, who was both a Catholic priest and an atomistic materialist, also professed belief in the metaphysical soul. At the same time he believed that insanity was a brain disease. Since the soul or reason (Gassendi preferred the latter word) did not depend on the body, he concluded quite consistently that the soul or reason remained sane even when the individual had become insane. Gassendi's consistency led to a *reductio ad absurdum* of his position. If I go mad and if at the same time my soul remains sane then I and my soul are not the same thing.

---

34. *Disquisitions on Matter and Spirit*, Section 4, p. 40.

Irreverent Postscript
God and the *Modus Operandi* Problem

W hen I was eight years old my family moved from the first district in Vienna ("die innere Stadt") to the third district in which "fancier" people resided. In my first school about half the children were Jewish and there was very little overt anti-Semitism. In the school in the third district there were few Jewish children and the teacher of my class ("Herr Lehrer Wagner") constantly indulged in anti-Semitic remarks. He never beat children in class—Vienna still had a Social Democratic city administration and corporal punishment of any kind was strictly forbidden. However, he frequently took a misbehaving boy into the corridor and the boy would come back crying and bleeding in the head. He extended this treatment only to children from working-class homes where he could be sure that the parents would not complain. He did not subject me to it, because he knew that my father was a lawyer.

In Vienna we had school six days a week. When I came home on Saturdays I would pray to God to kill Herr Lehrer Wagner. To my disappointment my prayers were never answered and on Monday mornings I had to face him once again. I envisaged God as a man, much larger in size than ordinary human beings, living on a cloud in the sky. When, during the recent Gulf War, pictures of General Schwarzkopf appeared in the newspapers I recognized the God of my childhood. He had been a magnified version of the General. I am not sure now how I thought that God was going to kill my teacher if he was going to answer the prayer, but I think it was by means of some immensely powerful "death rays" that were going to penetrate the skin and destroy his heart.

Whatever its defects, this childish theology was entirely coherent. I could describe what God was like and I could at least in outline suggest the *modus operandi* of God's annihilation of my teacher. My theology was not really very different from

301

that of the tabloids or from the belief of the ancient Greeks in Zeus, his wife Hera and the other gods living on Mount Olympus. *The Sun,* a journal with peccable reputation, featured, in its issue of December 8, 1992, a page with a picture of huge eyes interspersed and surrounded by white specks. "This sensational photograph," the caption read, "shows two giant eyes floating through space and some people claim the pictures are a clear sign that God is watching us." One of the people holding this view was no less an authority than Dr. Igor Vaskarevich, Professor of Theology at the University of Warsaw. (Whether such a person actually exists is anybody's guess.) He told *The Sun* that the eyes in space "offer concrete evidence of a higher being watching over his creation," adding that "these photos will sway millions of people who until now have been doubtful and unwilling to worship God." As for the Greek gods, they were of course *embodied* beings. To Hera's extreme dismay Zeus repeatedly visited the earth, transforming himself into a human being, and attempting to seduce beautiful young women. It may be of interest to add that both Zeus and Hera usually traveled to the earth on a cloud.

Sophisticated theologians have very different ideas about God. God does not live on a cloud or on Mount Olympus. In fact He is strictly nowhere because He is a pure mind. Now, the question I want to raise is how such a God could possibly interfere in the world. How, for example, could he answer my prayer to kill Herr Lehrer Wagner? And how could he hear my prayer in the first place? How could a disembodied mind hear anything? However, suppose that he could hear my prayer. How could he, not being physical, apply the force that would send the rays into my teacher's heart? More basically, how could a pure mind create the physical universe or for that matter how could he create anything at all?

As an afterthought I would like to offer a comment about the statement by a bigoted Christian preacher not long after Ronald Reagan's first inauguration that God does not hear the prayer of a Jew. No doubt thinking about the Jewish vote and some of the more enlightened people in his own camp, the President speedily issued a denial, assuring the world that God does hear the prayers of Jews no less than those of Christians. I hate to side with bigots, but for reasons explained in the preceding paragraph, I agree with the Christian preacher that God does not hear the prayer of Jews. I would only add that he cannot hear the prayer of Christians or anybody else either.

The *modus operandi* considerations show that God conceived as a pure mind cannot interfere in the world. They do not show that such a being does not exist. (I may say in passing I cannot attach any sense to the notion of a pure mind, but this is a different issue.) The *modus operandi* considerations do help to undermine all the most familiar forms of the design argument in a way that has not been appreciated by the critics as well as the champions of the argument. In its most familiar form the design argument maintains that organs like the eye or the ear are teleological systems like watches or more generally machines made by men and that we are entitled to infer a superhuman designer as their cause. Now, it has to be emphasized that the human designer of the watch is not a pure mind: he needs his hands and, more basically, his body including of course the brain, to design and to produce the watch. It has often been pointed out that since the human designer works on preexisting materials, the argument does not yield a Creator as distinct from a Demiurge or arranger. What has not been noted is that the argument does not give us a pure mind. If it is otherwise valid, it would give us a host of *embodied* arrangers. In a much-quoted eighteenth-century hymn Charles Addison declared that "the hand that made us is divine." Addison presumably did not intend to be taken literally, but if we follow out the terms of the design argument, what he said *should* be taken literally. The analogy does not indeed require us to say that the super-human arranger has hands, but he must have some bodily instruments to arrange the pre-existing materials into systems like the eye or ear. Supporters of the design argument try to avoid this consequence not only because of its "vulgarity" and its "demotion" of God into a physical craftsman, but also because observation evidently falsifies any such claim. We do observe human architects, engineers and their helpers, assembling such teleological systems as airplanes, motorcars, computers, and of course simple objects like watches, but no craftsman of any kind has ever been observed to arrange eyes, ears or any of the other parts of animals and plants.

It would be quite accurate to describe the theology of children, the tabloids, and the ancient Greeks (among others) as "physicalistic." Sophisticated theologians usually dismiss it as crude and primitive. They imply that their own nonphysicalistic theology is vastly superior. It seems to me that the reverse is true. The only drawback of physicalistic theology is that it is false, but it is at least intelligible and it is also not beset by *modus operandi* problems.

Index